THE EVOLUTION
of
ECONOMIC SYSTEMS

THE EVOLUTION
of
ECONOMIC SYSTEMS

*Varieties of Capitalism in the
Global Economy*

BARRY CLARK
University of Colorado at Boulder

New York   Oxford
OXFORD UNIVERSITY PRESS

Oxford University Press is a department of the University of Oxford.
It furthers the University's objective of excellence in research,
scholarship, and education by publishing worldwide.

Oxford   New York
Auckland   Cape Town   Dar es Salaam   Hong Kong   Karachi
Kuala Lumpur   Madrid   Melbourne   Mexico City   Nairobi
New Delhi   Shanghai   Taipei   Toronto

With offices in
Argentina   Austria   Brazil   Chile   Czech Republic   France   Greece
Guatemala   Hungary   Italy   Japan   Poland   Portugal   Singapore
South Korea   Switzerland   Thailand   Turkey   Ukraine   Vietnam

Copyright © 2016 by Oxford University Press

For titles covered by Section 112 of the US Higher Education
Opportunity Act, please visit www.oup.com/us/he for the
latest information about pricing and alternate formats.

Published by Oxford University Press
198 Madison Avenue, New York, New York 10016
http://www.oup.com

Oxford is a registered trademark of Oxford University Press

Library of Congress Cataloging-in-Publication Data
Names: Clark, Barry Stewart, 1948- author.
Title: The evolution of economic systems : varieties of capitalism in the
    global economy / Barry Clark.
Description: 1st edition. | New York : Oxford University Press, 2016. |
    Includes index.
Identifiers: LCCN 2015039302 | ISBN 9780190260590
Subjects: LCSH: Comparative economics. | Capitalism.
Classification: LCC HB90 .C5197 2016 | DDC 330.12/2--dc23 LC record
    available at http://lccn.loc.gov/2015039302

Printing number: 9 8 7 6 5 4 3 2 1

Printed in Canada
on acid-free paper

TABLE OF CONTENTS

Chapter 14 **NEWLY INDUSTRIALIZING ECONOMIC SYSTEMS:**
BRAZIL, INDIA, IRAN, AND SOUTH KOREA   283

PREFACE

E conomic systems are like air and water—essential to our existence yet barely noticed until they become unsuitable to meet our needs. When the Soviet Union disintegrated in 1991, mankind breathed a collective sigh of relief. An oppressive and dysfunctional economic system had collapsed, seemingly ending the only alternative to democratic capitalism. All nations would at last be able to enjoy freedom and prosperity.

Nearly twenty-five years later, that optimism has faded. Russia has failed to thrive since its adoption of capitalism, whereas China, still ruled by a nondemocratic Communist Party, has emerged as a global superpower. The Japanese economic system, once the envy of the world, is now in its third decade of stagnation. Growth has ground to a halt in Europe, with unemployment rates in double digits in some countries. The United States has still not fully recovered from the Great Recession of 2008. Developing nations in Africa, Latin America, Asia, and the Middle East are struggling as demand for their exports remains weak. Around the world, an entire generation is coming to maturity with diminished opportunities and growing insecurity. Clearly, we have yet to develop the recipe or recipes for economic success in the twenty-first century. The study of economic systems is once again relevant, and social scientists are responding to the crisis with renewed efforts.

Economists once claimed sole province over the study of economic systems, but in recent years, sociologists, anthropologists, political scientists, historians, geographers, and psychologists have breached the once-rigid barriers separating the social sciences. A new multidisciplinary approach is leading to an understanding of economic systems as encompassing much more than markets. Market activity occurs within a web of economic, political, social, and cultural institutions (e.g., labor unions, government regulations, social norms, and religions), so the actions of market participants are guided by prevailing rules and conventions governing competition. An economic system is an ensemble of institutions created at various points in history to serve different purposes. Even when nearly all nations are basically capitalist in the sense of relying on private property and markets, their markets are embedded in and fundamentally shaped by other non-economic institutions.

By comparing the economic systems of different nations, social scientists hope to reveal the institutional constellations contributing to or thwarting economic success. A multidisciplinary approach to understanding economic systems is materializing within a wide variety of subdisciplines and research agendas, including comparative political economy, social economics, game theory, behavioral economics, economic anthropology, new and old institutional economics, social structures of accumulation, economic history, regulation theory, new economic sociology, social systems of production, economic geography, and varieties of capitalism. Although social scientists often rely on sophisticated statistical analysis and mathematical modeling in their efforts to reveal patterns of causation and complementarity in the interactions of different institutions, this book has the more modest objective of introducing readers to some of the insights gained through this research and applying an interdisciplinary approach to understanding the historical evolution of national economic systems.

In evaluating the relative performance of different economic systems, value judgments are unavoidable. Economists have traditionally attempted to minimize value judgments by focusing on quantifiable measures of performance such as levels of income, unemployment rates, and growth rates, but the choice of standards for evaluation is itself a value judgment. By avoiding value-laden performance criteria such as justice, human development, and the quality of democracy, economists neglect aspects of economic performance that are vitally important to citizens' own assessments of their economic system. I attempt an objective coverage of all aspects of economic systems by presenting the strongest arguments for and against different institutional configurations, but to quote British economist Joan Robinson (1903–1983), "Every human being has ideological, moral, and political views. To pretend to have none and to be purely objective must necessarily be either self-deception or a device to deceive others."

To avoid deception, I will clarify my own value commitments. I believe that markets are central to any successful economic system for the foreseeable future. I also believe that markets perform best when constrained and supported by appropriate political and social institutions. More specifically, I believe that markets require government regulation, particularly of labor markets, financial markets, and actions affecting the natural environment; that wealth and power should be sufficiently dispersed to provide genuine opportunity for all citizens to lead fulfilling lives and make positive contributions to society; and that vibrant communities are essential to successful economic systems. Based on these values, I reach conclusions about the effectiveness of various policies and institutions. Although I provide the reasoning behind my conclusions, they should not be accepted uncritically. I encourage readers to assess the opposing arguments, consider the validity of my reasoning and conclusions, and then form their own ideological, moral, and political views. Undertaking this intellectual challenge is essential not only to personal growth but to democratic efforts to improve the quality of economic systems.

Much of the material presented in this book is distilled from previous efforts by social scientists who have laid the foundations for a new multidisciplinary approach to understanding economic systems. I am particularly indebted to the following individuals for their pioneering efforts: Michel Aglietta, George Akerloff, Gar Alperovitz, Masahiko Aoki, Philip Arestis, Pierre Bourdieu, Samuel Bowles, Robert Boyer, John Campbell, David Coates, Joshua Cohen, Colin Crouch, Richard Edwards, Herbert Gintis, David Gordon, Peter Hall, Robert Heilbroner, David Held, J. Rogers Hollingsworth, David Kotz, Paul Krugman, Douglass North, Mancur Olson, Elinor Ostrom, Michael Reich, Robert Reich, Dani Rodrik, Joel Rogers, Vivian Schmidt, David Soskice, Joseph Stiglitz, Susan Strange, Wolfgang Streeck, Richard Swedberg, Kathleen Thelen, Thomas Weisskopf, and Oliver Williamson.

Boulder, Colorado
September 2015

ABOUT THE AUTHOR

Barry Clark (PhD, University of Massachusetts–Amherst) is Professor Emeritus and former Chair of the Economics Department at the University of Wisconsin–La Crosse. He currently teaches at the University of Colorado–Boulder and has also taught at Ripon College; the University of Massachusetts–Amherst; Tufts University; the Pennsylvania State University; and the University of Wisconsin–La Crosse. Clark has written a text on political economy for Praeger and has published numerous articles on political economy. His career focus, however, has been on teaching and making difficult ideas accessible to a broader group of students.

INTRODUCTION

Twenty years ago, the field of comparative economic systems seemed destined for the proverbial "dustbin of history." Russia and China had acknowledged the failure of communism. Attempts to move toward socialism in Sweden and France during the 1980s had proven disastrous. Capitalism prevailed; an increasingly influential "Washington consensus" called on all nations to reduce the size and scope of government involvement in the economy in order to allow markets to guide the process of economic development.

At the same time, innovations in transportation and communications technology, combined with lower barriers to trade and fewer restrictions on the movement of capital across national borders, created a unified global economy in which each nation faced strong competitive pressures to remove political and social constraints on the operation of markets. Given these historic changes, it seemed just a matter of time until all nations would have nearly identical economic systems. One prominent social scientist proclaimed the "end of history," predicting that countries around the world would move toward a homogeneous democratic capitalism (Fukuyama 1992).

However, such predictions proved to be premature as citizens and their elected representatives have stubbornly refused to abandon traditional national institutions. Sweden elected a social democratic administration in 1995, Britain and France did the same in 1997, and Germany followed suit in 1998. After abandoning communism, Russia and China have, with varying degrees of success, fashioned unique forms of capitalism defying conventional economic wisdom in the West. Japan clings to many of its traditional economic institutions despite more than two decades of stagnation, and the United States is currently enduring political gridlock as Republicans and Democrats engage in an epic struggle to determine the future course of the economy. Newly industrializing countries such as India, South Korea, and Iran, have fashioned unique economic systems. In Latin America, leftist governments prevail in Cuba, Brazil, Bolivia, Uruguay, Venezuela, Ecuador, Nicaragua, and El Salvador. The lack of convergence toward a single system attests not only to the inertia of national institutions but also to the continuing viability of different forms of capitalism.

The field of comparative economic systems arose during the 1920s and 1930s, as rapid growth in the Soviet Union coupled with the Great Depression in capitalist nations spurred growing interest in the relative strengths and weaknesses of communism and capitalism. Communism is no longer considered a viable option, but capitalism exists in a variety of different forms. Comparing the merits of different types of capitalism has become increasingly important as governments seek to fashion the most suitable institutions for meeting the expressed goals of their citizens.

After two centuries of experience with capitalism, we might expect that competition between nations would have revealed the superior economic system. However, economic systems are composed of numerous institutions, so definitive conclusions concerning the efficacy of any single institution are difficult. Comparisons between countries are also complicated by the fact that economic performance varies over time. For example, Britain was the dominant economic power in the world during most of the nineteenth century but became the "sick man of Europe" in the twentieth century. The United States surpassed Britain to become the world leader by the early twentieth century, only to sink into the Great Depression. At the same time, the Soviet Union was growing at an annual rate of 10 percent and achieved industrialization more rapidly than any nation in previous history. Impressive French economic performance during the 1950s led John Kennedy to suggest that America should learn from the French. Sweden attracted worldwide attention during the 1960s with its ability to combine a high standard of living with social equality promoted by a generous welfare state. Although most capitalist nations suffered through inflation and unemployment in the 1970s, the German economy maintained relatively stable wages and prices along with peaceful labor relations and a strong export sector. The success of the Japanese economy during the 1980s inspired companies around the world to emulate many of its business practices. China, with its hybrid of capitalism and socialism, is today the fastest-growing economy in the world.

The fact that different economic systems have succeeded at various points in history demonstrates the fallacy of relying solely on current success as a measure of the universal efficacy of any economic system. That success may be grounded on institutions that are not sustainable over time, or it may be attributable to noneconomic institutions unique to a single nation. Comparisons of economic systems require an appreciation of the role of politics, culture, and history in shaping the performance of markets.

As an introduction to the study of economic systems, a brief economic history of the twentieth century will be helpful. At the beginning of the century, capitalism prevailed in all industrialized nations. Socialist, anarchist, monarchist, and communist political parties existed, but they remained marginal and posed no immediate threat to the dominance of capitalism. However, in 1917, a relatively small group led by Lenin gained control of the Russian government for the avowed purpose of establishing the first communist economic system. A second challenge to capitalism emerged in Italy eight years later when Benito Mussolini and his followers established the first fascist economic system. Fascism spread to Germany when the devastation wrought by the Great Depression ushered in the rule of Adolf Hitler in 1933. A few years later, Japan also turned to fascism. When Hitler launched a full-scale attempt to conquer all of Europe, capitalist and communist nations united to defeat the fascist coalition of Germany, Italy, and Japan.

In the postwar era, both capitalism and communism generated respectable rates of economic growth, and nuclear arsenals on each side ensured the uneasy coexistence of the two systems. During the four-decade-long Cold War, the United States contained communism by preventing expansion of the Soviet Union and China's spheres of influence. Both communist and capitalist nations offered aid and technical assistance to developing nations in efforts to create satellite states supportive of the benefactor's economic system.

Although capitalism and communism stood in sharp contrast, each system gradually incorporated elements of the other. Governments of capitalist nations established a variety of social benefits designed to provide a degree of economic security to all citizens, assumed responsibility for stabilizing the economy, and enacted regulations to ensure that business decisions coincided with the public interest. At the same time, communist nations experimented with markets, financial incentives, decentralized decision-making, and some private ownership of property. This trend raised hopes for a peaceful convergence toward a "mixed economy" in which government and the market would each compensate for the shortcomings of the other.

That optimism evaporated as the performance of both capitalism and communism began to deteriorate during the 1970s. Capitalist nations suffered from slowing rates of growth combined with high rates of inflation and unemployment. As a result, public confidence in both government and large corporations plummeted. The economic performance of communist nations was even worse. Growth rates slowed and goods were shoddy and in short supply. Daily life grew increasingly grim as citizens endured low standards of living, surveillance by the government, and the ever-present threat of being labeled a dissident. Bribery and other forms of corruption prevailed, serving to undermine respect for the law and government authority.

As recently as 1989, approximately one-third of the global population lived in communist nations. When the Soviet Union allowed its Eastern European satellite states to abandon communism and then did so itself in 1991, citizens in both capitalist and communist nations expressed jubilation that freedom had finally prevailed over tyranny and oppression. However, the victory celebration was short-lived. The new Russian capitalist economy collapsed, leaving most citizens with lower standards of living than they had endured under communism. Even today, after twenty-five years of capitalism, the economies of eastern European countries, Russia, and the former republics of the Soviet Union continue to underperform.

Capitalism also experienced daunting problems. After a recession in 2001, an unusually weak recovery created few additional jobs. Then, beginning in 2007, the capitalist nations experienced the worst recession since the Great Depression of the 1930s. Had governments not acted quickly to bail out failing banks and corporations, the Great Recession of 2008 might have been cataclysmic. Despite government efforts to revive capitalist economies, economic growth has been anemic, with the unemployment rate remaining more than 5 percent in the United States and even higher in Europe. Southern Europe has been hit the hardest, with unemployment rates of 25 to 30 percent among adults and more than 50 percent among youth. The persistent weakness of capitalist economic systems raises the specter of "secular stagnation" in which high unemployment and sluggish growth become the new norm with no end in sight.

With the exception of China and a few smaller Asian countries, including Taiwan, Singapore, and South Korea, citizens of industrialized nations are experiencing deep uncertainty about the future of their economic systems. To win elections, political parties within each nation have created diametrically opposed solutions to economic problems. On one side stand the proponents of "austerity," who call for minimizing the role of government through deep cuts in taxes, regulations, and social services as well as restricted growth of the money supply. One the other side are the proponents of "stimulation," who argue that nations cannot fully rebound from the Great Recession without significant spending by government and growth of the money supply.

The English philosopher/economist John Stuart Mill (1806–1873) had relevant advice for today's protagonists: "In all intellectual debates, both sides tend to be correct in what they affirm, and wrong in what they deny." Advocates of austerity affirm the strengths of markets while denying the shortcomings of markets and the essential role of government in a successful economic system. In contrast, advocates of stimulation affirm the strengths of government but often deny government's inherent weaknesses. The two sides refuse to openly acknowledge that both markets and governments are fundamentally flawed institutions. To an extent, markets and governments can offset each other's shortcomings and therefore be mutually supportive. However, each institution also possesses the capacity to undermine the effectiveness of the other.

The struggle to find the optimal balance between government and markets is the central theme of political conflict within nations. At times, the problem appears to be solved as demonstrated by decades of prosperity, but changing conditions undermine the existing system and debates over reform begin anew. The debate has currently reached a stalemate; neither side has a popular mandate to fully implement its agenda. When voters remain uncertain about how to improve their economic system, political leaders hesitate to initiate any bold departures from the status quo.

This book introduces the reader to the field of comparative economic systems and raises awareness of the difficult choices facing nations as they attempt to cope with the economic challenges of the twenty-first century. Two introductory chapters lay the groundwork for the book, Chapters Three and Four examine both the historical evolution and the strengths and weaknesses of markets and government as institutions for coordinating economic activity. Chapter Five introduces community, an often-neglected component of any economic system, and suggests that greater efforts to strengthen communities may improve the functioning of both governments and markets. Chapters Six through Thirteen examine the historical evolution of economic systems in the United States, Britain, France, Germany, Sweden, Russia, China, and Japan. In Chapter Fourteen, the economic systems in four newly industrializing countries—Brazil, India, Iran, and South Korea—are analyzed. Chapter Fifteen, the concluding chapter, considers the effects of contemporary globalization on national economic systems and proposes reforms for improving the performance of the global economy.

REFERENCE

Fukuyama, Francis. 1992. *The End of History and the Last Man*. New York: Avon Books.

Chapter 1

UNDERSTANDING ECONOMIC SYSTEMS

"No valid solution to economic problems can be found solely using economic theory and quantitative aspects of social life. Analysis of societies obviously requires a synthesis of all the social sciences"

MAURICE ALLAIS (1911–2010),
1988 Nobel Laureate in Economic Science

"For the world is not to be narrowed till it will go into the understanding, but the understanding is to be expanded and opened till it can take in the image of the world."

FRANCIS BACON (1561–1626),
English philosopher and scientist

On a sultry day in the summer of 1997, I visited the ancient Buddhist temple of Angkor Wat in northern Cambodia. Returning to the capital city of Phnom Penh required a four-hour boat trip down a narrow waterway leading to the Mekong River. Coming around a bend, men on another boat motioned for us to stop. As the two boats pulled alongside each other, I could see AK-47 machine guns slung over the shoulders of crew members on the other boat. After several minutes of heated debate between the two captains, the captain of my boat handed over some money and we were allowed to proceed.

For the remainder of the journey, the social scientist in me tried to make sense of what had just occurred. I could imagine several scenarios. The men on the other boat might have been local pirates extorting money from a boat filled with tourists. Or perhaps they were employees of the local village government collecting a tax from boats passing through their jurisdiction. They might have been soldiers from the national army with authorization to collect fees along the river. At that time, Cambodia was ruled by a coalition of two bitterly opposed political parties, so a fourth possibility was that soldiers loyal to one party were confiscating money from anyone entering the region they controlled. Indeed, as I arrived in Phnom Penh, a full-blown coup d'etat was in progress, with truckloads of armed soldiers racing through the city and the sound of distant gunfire.

The point of sharing this experience is to illustrate that without knowing the political and social context, I was unable to determine the meaning of the exchange of money for use of the river. Who had authority to grant access to the river? If the local village customarily collected fees from passing boats, then the men on the boat were tax collectors rather than pirates. But what if the national government did not recognize the right of local villages to impose fees on the use of rivers? In that case, the men on the boat were rebels refusing to acknowledge the authority of the national government. Or what if the government itself consisted of competing factions with neither side able to exert sovereign authority over the nation? Then the men on the boat might be pirates, tax collectors, and rebels simultaneously, depending on one's point of view.

In the past, economists traditionally ignored such questions. They treated the determination of property rights, political authority, and social norms as "exogenous factors" to be dealt with by political scientists, sociologists, or anthropologists. Economists could then focus their attention exclusively on the process by which supply and demand interact within **markets** to determine prices and ultimately the **allocation** of **resources**. (Note: The initial use of potentially unfamiliar terms in each chapter is highlighted in bold font to indicate that a definition appears in the glossary.) Although an exclusive focus on markets offers considerable insight into the functioning of economic systems, that insight comes at a cost. When markets are portrayed as operating in isolation from history, politics, and **culture**, the unique features of different economic systems are easily overlooked and markets themselves are misunderstood.

In recent years, however, economists and other social scientists have developed a more holistic and interdisciplinary approach to understanding economic systems (Hall and Soskice 2001; Boyer and Saillard 2002; Bowles 2004; North 2005; Ostrom 2005; Rodrik 2008; Hodgson 2015). From this perspective, an **economic system** is the framework of economic, political, social, and cultural **institutions** organizing and coordinating production, exchange, and consumption of goods and services in a particular **society**. An economic system determines prices and quantities for all goods and services, the methods of production used, who performs which tasks, and the distribution of goods among individuals. Social scientists have been motivated to develop a more encompassing method of analysis because no economic system can be adequately described or understood without investigating the nature and historical evolution of its broad institutional matrix.

An institution may be an organization such as a labor union, a university, or a stock exchange. However, social scientists more often define an institution as a cluster of rules coordinating a particular type of human interaction. By establishing rights and obligations, institutions organize social, political, and economic behavior into predictable patterns. For example, labor unions are based on rules specifying the payment of dues by members and the right to bargain collectively with employers. Universities operate with rules concerning academic conduct, grading, and student rights. A stock market could not function without rules about disclosure of information and prohibitions against deceptive trading practices.

The prevalence of institutions indicates that economic systems are based on more than calculations of self-interest by individuals engaged in market activity. Although the market is often touted as an arena in which individuals are free to choose, the market could not function without a supportive array of institutions coordinating human behavior. The pursuit of self-interest may be essential to economic prosperity, but it can also be destructive. In the words of British economist Lionel Robbins (1898–1984), "the pursuit of self-interest, unrestrained by suitable institutions, carries no guarantee of anything except chaos" (Robbins 1965, 56).

Institutions may be either formal or informal. Formal institutions such as laws, regulations, and contracts arise when the negative consequences of the pursuit of self-interest are sufficiently harmful that the benefits of restraint outweigh the costs of monitoring and enforcement. For example, drivers are required by law to stay on one side of the road because the freedom to randomly choose a lane would be deadly. The benefit of saved lives is greater than the cost of police enforcement.

However, no such law applies to pedestrians' use of sidewalks because collisions can be easily avoided and pose only a minor inconvenience when they do occur. But an unspoken understanding (at least in countries that drive on the right side of the road) that people will usually stay to the right on a sidewalk facilitates the flow of pedestrian traffic. This custom is an example of an informal institution. Other examples include standing in line, shaking hands, and tipping in restaurants. Informal institutions arise spontaneously over time and include social conventions, values, norms, and traditions that facilitate human interaction by reducing conflict, risk, and uncertainty. Violations of informal institutions are not punishable by law but may elicit negative responses from other people.

Although institutions may constrain behavior, they also can empower individuals by expanding the range of feasible outcomes. For example, a labor union gives workers greater bargaining power than they would have as individuals. Taxation allows citizens to gain national defense, highways, and public education. Environmental regulations conserve resources and protect the quality of air and water. So institutions not only prevent harmful behavior but also enable humans to achieve goals that would otherwise be unattainable. In the words of American economist John R. Commons (1862–1945), institutions are "collective action in control, liberation, and expansion of individual action" (Commons 1934, 73).

Institutions arise due to **collective action problems**, which occur when the pursuit of self-interest leads to worse results than could be achieved by following formal or informal rules designed to promote "the common good" or "the public interest." Stated differently, collective action problems occur when individuals face incentives to make choices that are detrimental to the groups in which they participate. Even if individuals want to promote the public interest, collective action problems may deter them because their sacrifice of short-term gain is futile unless others make similar sacrifices. For example, any corporation voluntarily incurring additional costs to dispose of its waste in an ecologically sound manner will have little discernible effect on pollution unless other firms do the same. To compound the problem, the socially responsible corporation may lose its **competitive advantage** due to additional costs of waste disposal. As a result, no single corporation has an incentive to reduce pollution unless a law requires all firms in its industry to do the same.

Two classic examples of collective action problems are "the tragedy of the commons" (Hardin 1968) and "the prisoner's dilemma." In the former, the commons refers to land near villages in medieval England and Scotland set aside for use by anyone. Each farmer had a self-interested motive to graze sheep on the commons since the grass was free. However, if all farmers took advantage of the free grass, the commons would be overgrazed and incapable of supporting vegetation. By pursuing their short-term self-interest, the farmers ruined the commons and created a situation that none of them wanted.

The prisoner's dilemma refers to a hypothetical situation in which two people suspected of jointly committing a crime are brought into a police station for interrogation. The police separate the two prisoners and offer each the following options and potential sentences (Table 1.1).

Each prisoner has a self-interested motive to confess in hopes that the other will not confess and the first prisoner will go free. If both prisoners pursue their self-interest by confessing, they both receive a five-year sentence. However, if each trusted that the other would adhere to an informal rule to never confess to a crime, they would achieve the best possible outcome of a one-year sentence for each.

The prisoner's dilemma sheds light on real-world institutions such as the law prohibiting advertising for cigarettes on television and radio. When originally proposed, the law had the support of the tobacco industry because firms realized that the effectiveness of advertising for their particular brands was largely canceled by other firms' advertising for alternative brands. Yet no company could voluntarily stop advertising without losing market share to competitors. By supporting the ban on advertising, tobacco companies resolved the collective action problem, resulting in lower advertising costs for each firm with no loss of market share.

Institutions formed to resolve collective action problems are vulnerable to **opportunism** and **defection**. Opportunistic behavior occurs when individuals

Table 1.1 A Prisoner's Dilemma

		PRISONER B	
		CONFESS	DON'T CONFESS
PRISONER A	CONFESS	Both get 5 years	B gets 10 years A goes free
	DON'T CONFESS	A gets 10 years B goes free	Both get 1 year on a lesser charge

or businesses violate laws or informal rules with the expectation that their behavior will go unnoticed and therefore have no negative consequences. For example, insider trading on the stock market and shoplifting are opportunistic violations of the law, whereas telling a lie violates only an informal rule. Defection from an institutional constraint is advantageous only when most other people continue to abide by the rule. If large numbers defect, the resolution of the collective action problem unravels and everyone is harmed.

Philosophers have long recognized the danger to society posed by the opportunistic pursuit of narrow self-interest. The German philosopher Immanuel Kant (1724–1804) proposed a "categorical imperative" to discourage opportunism by demonstrating its immorality. For Kant, morality required acting in a manner that would be acceptable if everyone else did the same. Because widespread opportunism would destroy the institutions designed to solve collective action problems and thereby harm everyone, Kant concluded that opportunism is immoral (Kant [1785] 2013). The Scottish philosopher David Hume (1711–1776) relied not on morality but on political institutions to curb opportunism. He advised: "In contriving any system of government . . . every man must be supposed a knave, and to have no other end, in all his actions, than private interest" (Hume [1740] 1963, 40). By acknowledging the problem posed by opportunism, Hume demonstrated the need for laws and regulations to prevent self-interest from undermining the common good. The Scottish philosopher and economist Adam Smith (1723–1790) recognized opportunism in the behavior of business people "who have generally an interest to deceive and even oppress the public, and who accordingly have, upon many occasions, both deceived and oppressed it" (Smith [1776] 1937, 250). Smith proposed that competition in the market provided a restraint on opportunism.

Collective action problems are pervasive, and they increase as economic systems mature through industrialization and growth. Global climate change is emerging as the ultimate collective action problem. Each household and business seeks to minimize the private cost of energy, which, given current technology, means burning fossil fuels such as oil and coal. However, this individual pursuit of short-term self-interest may make the planet uninhabitable in the future. When collective action problems occur, markets need to be supplemented by additional institutions to yield optimal results.

THREE DIMENSIONS OF ECONOMIC SYSTEMS

Social science appeared only recently in human history. Although ancient and medieval philosophers wrote about the societies in which they lived, these inquiries became scientific only after the cumulative effects of the Renaissance, the scientific revolution, and the Enlightenment. By the late eighteenth century, Adam Smith developed an insightful description and analysis of the newly emerging capitalist economic system. His 1776 book *The Wealth of Nations* firmly established a new social science called "political economy." In its formative years, the scope of political economy was quite broad; Smith was simultaneously an economist, a political theorist, a moral philosopher, a sociologist, and an historian.

By the late nineteenth century, social science was incorporating mathematical techniques and methods of data analysis borrowed from the physical sciences. At that time, most social scientists concluded that the advancement of knowledge required specialization of intellectual labor. They divided human affairs into three realms—**economy**, **polity**, and **civil society**. Economists analyzed the economic realm where resources and goods are exchanged for money in the market; political scientists focused on the governing process; and sociologists, anthropologists, and social psychologists dealt with the rest of human activity, including culture, values, and norms.

The recent efforts to develop an interdisciplinary approach to understanding economic systems do not ignore the distinctions between economy, polity, and civil society. The separate analyses of these three dimensions of human activity yield valuable insights. However, the three realms interact with each other, and therefore an exclusive focus on any one dimension provides only a partial and potentially misleading depiction of the functioning of economic systems.

To develop this interdisciplinary method requires an understanding of the three dimensions—economy, polity, and civil society. Each dimension has a primary **governance structure** coordinating the actions of individuals through both constraint and facilitation, prohibiting some choices and enabling others (Williamson 1996). Each dimension also relies on different incentives to guide individual choices in a manner promoting the common good.

The Economy

The economy is the activities and institutions directly involved in producing, exchanging, and consuming goods and services. In the modern economy, the primary governance structure is the market in which buyers and sellers interact to determine prices of resources, goods, and services. Markets enable individuals and businesses to pursue their self-interest by engaging in transactions with other individuals and businesses. Many different markets exist, including labor markets, financial markets, and markets for each product or resource. However, all these distinct markets are interrelated as any change in one market affects many other markets. The aggregation of all markets is often referred to as *the market*.

The market allocates resources by establishing prices that guide the choices of individuals and businesses in deciding which goods to consume or produce. Markets establish prices for each good through the interaction of supply and demand, and competition keeps the price of any good near an equilibrium level at which the quantity desired by buyers is equal to the quantity provided by sellers. When **perfect competition** and **complete markets** exist, markets maximize the value of output measured in monetary terms by allocating resources to their most highly valued use. In other words, resources are directed toward the production of those goods and services desired by individuals and businesses willing and able to pay for them.

Individuals may be motivated to engage in economic activity for a variety of reasons, but we shall define **economic behavior** as the calculated pursuit of self-interest by maximizing gain and/or minimizing sacrifice. Gain may take the form of monetary benefits or simply satisfaction and happiness. Similarly, sacrifice may involve monetary costs, but it also includes time and effort. The individual behaving economically, sometimes referred to as *homo economicus*, calculates potential costs and benefits of alternative courses of action and chooses the route with the greatest net benefit.

The Polity

The primary governance structure of the polity or political sphere is the **state**, which possesses authority to establish laws governing a specified territory and to exercise coercion in enforcing those laws. A state is a sovereign political entity subject to no higher authority, but to be precise, states may agree to concede a degree of **sovereignty** by establishing multistate organizations such as the United Nations, the European Union, and the World Trade Organization. For our purposes, the terms *state* and *government* may be used interchangeably. However, a distinction is usually made between the two terms; states are more long-lasting entities, whereas governments may change with each election.

The state coordinates human activity by enacting and enforcing laws and by commandeering resources, usually through taxation and fees, to provide essential goods and services that cannot be produced profitably by private businesses (e.g., national defense and highways). Only the state can legitimately use coercion and even violence to enforce its rules. Yet most citizens accept the authority of the state because they value the security gained by having their property and personal rights clearly defined and protected from violations by other citizens or by the state itself. The English philosopher Thomas Hobbes (1588–1679) noted that without the state, life would be "solitary, poor, nasty, brutish and short" (Hobbes [1651] 2014, 62).

The state provides citizens with an arena in which they can resolve collective action problems. With its powers to tax and to enact laws, the state enables individuals and businesses to act collectively to meet goals that would not be attainable through the pursuit of self-interest in the market. Furthermore, a well-administered state gives citizens a sense of belonging to a national community. The symbols of national unity such as flags, monuments, and anthems instill pride and allegiance. Patriotism motivates individuals to look beyond their self-interest and to engage in efforts to promote the common good.

Political behavior has mixed motivations. On one hand, political behavior may be identical to economic behavior as citizens and corporations pursue their self-interest through the political process by seeking maximum benefits from government at minimum cost to themselves in the form of taxes and regulations. Yet the motives of self-interest and monetary gain cannot fully explain political behavior. Voters sometimes support programs that offer no direct material benefits to themselves or that increase their taxes. For example, some wealthy citizens favor higher taxes on affluent households, and some households without children favor higher taxes to fund education. These sentiments can be explained by a second motivation underlying political behavior—the desire to live in a society conforming to one's personal values, including concern for the well-being of others, for the quality of public institutions, and for the protection of the natural environment. The state enables citizens to act collectively to reform the society in which they live.

Civil Society

The borders of civil society, although imprecise, encompass the activities of people when they are not working, shopping, or engaged in formal political activity. The primary governance structure of civil society is community. Although a community often refers to a neighborhood or town, in a broader sense, a community is a group of people with shared interests who attempt to advance those interests through interaction and cooperation. Communities may be based on categories such as ethnicity, race, religion, occupation, kinship, nationality, or institutional affiliation. Examples of communities include churches, clubs, cooperatives, professional associations, and universities. Even corporations and labor unions may function as communities to the extent that individuals socialize, form values, and learn patterns of behavior within them.

Members of a community share a sense of collective identity even if they have never met one another. Individuals engage in communities primarily through social behavior—conversing, playing, and cooperating in joint activities. Unlike the market, where *homo economicus* engages in the pursuit of self-interest, communities depend on **reciprocity** in which kindness is returned with kindness and retaliation is directed toward antisocial behavior, even when retaliation entails sacrifices and therefore conflicts with self-interest. In contrast to *homo economicus*, members of a community are expected to behave as *homo reciprocans* (reciprocal man), exhibiting empathy, hospitality, generosity, compassion, and fairness because they expect those same behaviors from their fellow members. Reciprocity is motivated by human needs for friendship, learning, personal identity, respect, social status, and a sense of belonging.

Communities coordinate the activities of their members primarily through social sanctions and support. Social sanctions include expressions of disapproval such as frowns, scowls, shaking the head, scolding, and simply the threat of gossip, shaming, ridicule, shunning, and the withdrawal of reciprocity. Social support takes the form of smiling, nodding, congratulations, praise, applause, affirmation, popularity, recognition, and increased social status.

Markets and communities are based on two quite distinct sets of social norms. The self-interested economic behavior condoned in the market is frowned on in communities, where individuals are expected to place concerns for fairness, reciprocity, and morality above the pursuit of self-interest. Much of contemporary political conflict revolves around the tension between the two sets of social norms governing behavior in markets and communities. Greed and selfishness are widely condemned within communities yet taken for granted in market behavior. The admiration for people such as Bill Gates and Warren Buffet stems from their ability to accumulate wealth through the pursuit of self-interest in the market while also "giving back" to the community.

Despite the contrasting governance structures, behaviors, and incentive systems of the economy and civil society, the two depend on each other as the values and behaviors formed in civil society have a significant impact on the nature of an economic system. Markets could not function without the disposition to trust and to cooperate that is nourished by communities. Market transactions are usually anonymous and impersonal, but the reciprocity learned in communities creates the expectation that strangers can be trusted (Seabright 2010). Without reciprocity, collective action problems would multiply as individuals availed themselves of every opportunity to advance their self-interest at the expense of others.

The self-interested behavior of the market can also play a positive role within communities. The willingness of members to take on leadership and service roles in the community may be motivated by a sense of duty but also by prospects of gaining higher social status and personal advancement. Reciprocity is strengthened by expectations that treating others well will pay off in the future when they return the favor. In the absence of self-interest, the capacity for trust and generosity would leave individuals vulnerable to opportunism by others. To protect themselves, individuals engage in a vigilant assessment of the give-and-take of social interaction. Beyond a certain threshold, a perception of imbalance or injustice may cause them to either withdraw from relationships or retaliate. In summary, both markets and communities function best when self-interest and reciprocity are balanced.

DETERMINANTS OF ECONOMIC SYSTEMS

Why are economic systems not the same in all nations? If one system works best, we might expect that it would be universally adopted. Yet a survey of the globe reveals a variety of forms of **capitalism** as well as examples of **fascism**, **socialism**, **communism**, and even remnants of **feudalism**, **mercantilism**, empires, and primitive tribes. This array suggests that any nation's system results from a unique combination of different factors. Assigning priority to some factors over others is difficult because of the continual interaction between them. However, the following factors stand out as most important in determining the contours of any economic system.

Geography

A nation's economic system is shaped by its endowment of natural resources, including deposits of minerals and ores, hardwood forests, fertile soil, sources of energy, navigable rivers, natural harbors, and a hospitable climate. The significance of global location is illustrated by the fact that the most economically developed nations are located in the temperate zone midway between the equator and the poles. However, geography does not necessarily determine a nation's economic destiny. Advancing technology permits nations to compensate for geographical disadvantages through, for example, trade with other nations, heating and air conditioning, irrigation, fertilizing, and flood control.

History

Historical events such as war, plague, economic **depression**, **hyperinflation**, colonialism, immigration, and political revolution have initiated fundamental changes in economic systems. When the event is so catastrophic that existing institutions are ill-equipped to cope with the situation, a new economic system emerges and endures long after the disaster has passed. For example, the Great Depression during the 1930s led to fundamental changes in the economic systems of industrialized nations, and many of the new institutions created during that era (e.g., minimum wage laws, social security, and collective bargaining) still exist today.

Technology

Technology is both a cause and result of change in economic systems. As economic systems evolve, new opportunities for technological innovation appear, and innovation, in turn, fosters further evolution of the system. An innovation as simple as the horse collar allowed farmers to till more acres, thereby raising agricultural productivity, expanding trade and commerce, and eventually contributing to the emergence of capitalism. Today, however, technology can be transferred from one nation to another with relative ease, so the role of technology in explaining the variety of economic systems has diminished. Yet technological innovation continues to render some institutions obsolete and therefore exerts pressures for change on all economic systems.

Economic Institutions

Examples of economic institutions include corporate governance, labor relations, financial markets, international trade policy, antitrust policy, contract law, macroeconomic policy, antidiscrimination laws, and minimum wage laws. The state creates most economic institutions because collective action problems prevent market participants from establishing their own laws and regulations. When economic systems malfunction, as evidenced by high unemployment, slow growth, inflation, increasing inequality, or trade imbalances, changes in economic institutions become more likely.

Political Institutions

Political institutions determine the manner in which the state formulates laws, regulations, and public policy, which in turn shape the economic system. Examples of political institutions include national constitutions, voting procedures, the composition of legislative bodies, the processes by which political decisions are made, the delegated powers of different branches of government, the legal system, and rules applying to political parties, political action committees, and financial contributions to the political process.

Cultural Institutions

The nature of an economic system depends on a nation's culture, including political and economic ideology, religion, morality, gender roles, and attitudes about individual responsibility, social obligations, and the importance of work. Culture largely determines a nation's priorities, its acceptance of moral and political restraint on individual choice, and the importance attached to community. Successful political and economic ideologies provide justification for institutions by making them appear natural. In the words of French sociologist Pierre Bourdieu (1930–2002), "the most successful ideological effects are those which have no need of words, and ask no more than complicitous silence" (Bourdieu 1977, 188).

The Distribution of Power

Power is the ability to make one's will effective. Some individuals and groups possess more power than others because they control more resources, exert more political influence, or (as is often the case) do both. The balance of power between conflicting interests shapes the institutions and outcomes of an economic system.

Collective Action

The institutions comprising an economic system exhibit substantial inertia. When systems function smoothly, change is unlikely, but when an economic system encounters difficulty in meeting the wants and needs of citizens, its legitimacy is called into question. At that point, the collective action of individuals and businesses, expressed either through the formal political system or through direct action such as labor strikes, demonstrations, protest movements, or the formation of interest groups may hasten the transition to a new economic system. Collective action usually requires ideological foundations to provide direction and purpose to demands for social change.

INSTITUTIONAL CHANGE AND ECONOMIC SYSTEMS

Humans form institutions, but once formed, institutions constitute the structure of society that shapes human behavior. Institutions exhibit stability and inertia for several reasons. First, highly functional institutions foster values and behaviors compatible with their own sustainability. As individuals learn the formal and informal rules of their society, they tend to conform to those rules. In addition, institutions typically benefit certain groups more than others, and the beneficiaries have a strong incentive to preserve the status quo. However, institutions arise in response to specific historical situations, and when the situation changes, old institutions may become obsolete, resulting in social and political conflict as well as poor economic performance.

The impetus for institutional change comes primarily from two related motives—efficiency and power. The former is based on improvements in productivity gained by redesigning the rules governing human interaction. For example, prior to the introduction of the factory system in eighteenth-century England, artisans and craftsmen enjoyed considerable autonomy and possessed a variety of skills. As the Industrial Revolution progressed, these workers were brought together under one roof where they were required to specialize in a narrow task and their work effort was monitored by supervisors. The factory system prevailed in part because it was a more efficient organization of production, but also because it enhanced the power of business owners to increase profitability.

The twin motives of efficiency and power are not necessarily compatible, particularly in forming political and social institutions. For example, the practice of gerrymandering, whereby politicians get to select their voters by redrawing congressional districts, is an exercise in power that arguably reduces efficiency by creating gridlock in legislatures. Racial and ethnic discrimination are inefficient and yet maintain the power of dominant groups. As for economic institutions, the competitive pressures of the market should, in theory, support only those institutional changes that improve efficiency. However, some groups in the market have more power than others and use that power to suppress competition by creating new institutions to preserve and increase their power. Examples include **tariffs**, subsidies, and lobbying.

When institutions become obsolete, new institutions may evolve spontaneously from the cumulative effect of individuals discovering ways to reduce conflict and increase efficiency. However, institutional change often encounters a collective action problem. Individuals may lack the incentive or the ability to form new institutions even if the change would benefit everyone. As a result, major transformations in economic systems usually require government action to revise laws and regulations to change patterns of behavior.

Institutions tend to endure as long as they are efficient and serve useful purposes for those with power. Even when institutions begin to fail, they usually continue to benefit some groups, so political conflict arises over whether to preserve the institution, make mild reforms, or abandon the institution. Mild reforms are usually sufficient to maintain the current economic system, but at certain junctures in history, the prevailing institutions cause the economy to perform so poorly that a popular consensus develops in favor of major reforms.

The turning points in the institutional framework of capitalism cluster around three decades—the 1890s, the 1930s, and the 1970s. Notice that the transition periods are separated by four decades. This may be a coincidence, but significant change often becomes possible only after the groups who most benefited from and were ideologically wedded to the old institutions are no longer alive. If the forty-year pattern continues to prevail, then current economic systems face another transformation in the near future.

The scope of change may be constrained by two factors. First, changes in economic systems exhibit a phenomenon called **path dependence**. A nation's current and past institutions partially determine the direction of future changes. A case in point is Russia's abandonment of communism in favor of capitalism. This transition appears to represent a total rejection of one economic system in favor of another, but capitalism in Russia exhibits the continuing influence of institutions from both its communist past and its feudal roots prior to the twentieth century. Similarly, the current economic systems of many European nations continue to reflect the timing and manner in which they made the transition from feudalism to capitalism. Like individuals, economic systems cannot escape their pasts.

A second constraint on institutional change is posed by the need for **institutional coherence**. Economic systems thrive when their many different institutions reinforce one another (Hall and Soskice 2001). Attempts to introduce a new institution may fail if it lacks compatibility with the rest of the system. For example, Sweden has an extensive array of government benefits established when the country was ethnically homogeneous and exhibited a high degree of social solidarity. The same level of government benefits in the United States might arouse intense opposition due to cultural values stressing individual responsibility and self-reliance.

As the global economy struggles to recover from the Great Recession of 2008, traditional institutions are under increasing strain. If current economic systems can once again perform well, they are likely to endure. But a long-term stagnation or decline will undermine faith in existing institutions as citizens react to growing insecurity, environmental degradation, and perceptions of injustice. In the future, public dissatisfaction may override institutional inertia, and a new economic system will be forged. Charting the optimal course for that change requires a thorough understanding of the functioning and historical evolution of economic systems.

REFERENCES

Bourdieu, Pierre. 1977. *Outline of a Theory of Practice*. New York: Cambridge University Press.

Bowles, Samuel. 2004. *Microeconomics: Behavior, Institutions, and Evolution*. Princeton, NJ: Princeton University Press.

Boyer, Robert, and Yves Saillard. 2002. *Regulation Theory: The State of the Art*. New York: Routledge.

Commons, John R. 1934. *Institutional Economics*. New York: Macmillan.

Hall, Peter, and David Soskice, eds. 2001. *Varieties of Capitalism: The Institutional Foundations of Competitive Advantage*. New York: Oxford University Press.

Hardin, Garrett. 1968. "The Tragedy of the Commons," *Science* 162: 1243–1248.

Hobbes, Thomas. (1651) 2014. *Leviathan*. New York: Oxford University Press.

Hodgson, Geoffrey M. 2015. *Conceptualizing Capitalism: Institutions, Evolution, Future*. Chicago: University of Chicago Press, 2015.

Hume, David. (1740) 1963. *Essays Moral, Political and Literary*. Oxford: Oxford University Press.

Kant, Immanuel. (1785) 2013. *Groundwork for the Metaphysics of Morals.* New York: Cambridge University Press.

North, Douglass C. 2005. *Understanding the Process of Economic Change.* Princeton, NJ: Princeton University Press.

Ostrom, Elinor. 2005. *Understanding Institutional Diversity.* Princeton, NJ: Princeton University Press.

Robbins, Lionel. 1965. *The Theory of Economic Policy in English Classical Political Economy.* London: Macmillan.

Rodrik, Dani. 2008. *One Economics, Many Recipes: Institutions and Economic Growth.* Princeton, NJ: Princeton University Press.

Seabright, Paul. 2010. *The Company of Strangers: A Natural History of Economic Life.* Princeton, NJ: Princeton University Press.

Smith, Adam. (1776) 1937. *An Inquiry into the Nature and Causes of the Wealth of Nations.* New York: Modern Library.

Williamson, Oliver. 1996. *The Mechanisms of Governance.* New York: Oxford University Press.

ADDITIONAL READING

Aligica, Paul Dragos. *Institutional Diversity and Political Economy: The Ostroms and Beyond.* New York: Oxford University Press, 2013.

Amable, Bruno. *The Diversity of Modern Capitalism.* New York: Oxford University Press, 2003.

Aoki, Masahiko, Timur Kuran, and Gerard Roland, eds. *Institutions and Comparative Economic Development.* New York: Palgrave Macmillan, 2012.

Barma, Naazneen H., and Steven K. Vogel, eds. *The Political Economy Reader: Markets as Institutions.* New York: Routledge, 2008.

Basu, Kaushik. *Prelude to Political Economy: A Study of the Social and Political Foundations of Economics.* New York: Oxford University Press, 2003.

Bourdieu, Pierre. *The Social Structures of the Economy.* London: Polity, 2005.

Carruthers, Bruce G., and Sarah L. Babb. *Economy/Society: Markets, Meanings, and Social Structures,* 2nd ed. Los Angeles: Sage, 2013.

Crouch, Colin. *Making Capitalism Fit for Society.* Cambridge: Polity, 2013.

Clift, Ben. *States, Markets and Global Capitalism.* New York: Palgrave Macmillan, 2014.

Ebner, Alexander, and Nikolaus Beck, eds. *The Institutions of the Market: Organizations, Social System, and Governance.* New York: Oxford University Press, 2008.

Fligstein, Neil. *The Architecture of Markets: The Economic Sociology of Twenty-First Century Capitalist Societies.* Princeton, NJ: Princeton University Press, 2001.

Kotz, David M., Terrence McDonough, and Michael Reich, eds. *Social Structures of Accumulation: The Political Economy of Growth and Crisis.* New York: Cambridge University Press, 1994.

Morgan, Glenn, Richard Whitley, and Eli Moen, eds. *Changing Capitalisms? Internationalization, Institutional Change, and Systems of Economic Organization.* New York: Oxford University Press, 2005.

North, Douglass C. *Institutions, Institutional Change and Economic Performance.* New York: Cambridge University Press, 1990.

Ostrom, Elinor. *Governing the Commons: the Evolution of Institutions for Collective Action*. New York: Cambridge University Press, 1990.

Przeworski, Adam. *States and Markets: A Primer in Political Economy*. New York: Cambridge University Press, 2003.

Rose, David C. *The Moral Foundations of Economic Behavior*. New York: Oxford University Press, 2014.

Storr, Virgil. *Understanding the Culture of Markets*. New York: Routledge, 2012.

Streeck, Wolfgang, and Kathleen Thelen, eds. *Beyond Continuity: Institutional Change in Advanced Political Economies*. New York: Oxford University Press, 2005.

Swedberg, Richard. *Principles of Economic Sociology*. Princeton, NJ: Princeton University Press, 2003.

Westra, Richard, Dennis Badeen, and Robert Albritton, eds. *The Future of Capitalism after the Financial Crisis: The Varieties of Capitalism Debate in the Age of Austerity*. New York: Routledge, 2015.

Chapter 2

ASSESSING ECONOMIC SYSTEMS

"The political problem of mankind is to combine three things:
economic efficiency, social justice and individual liberty."

JOHN MAYNARD KEYNES (1883–1946),
British economist

"Such terms as 'values' and 'culture' are not popular with
economists, who prefer to deal with quantifiable factors. Still,
life being what it is, one must talk about these things."

DAVID LANDES (1924–2013),
American economist

Evaluating the performance of different economic systems requires the selection of appropriate standards. In an effort to avoid value judgments, economists have traditionally focused on those criteria suitable to measurement and quantification (e.g., growth rate, unemployment rate, and the level and distribution of income). However, citizens expect their economic system to meet additional criteria which, despite being nonquantifiable, are no less important.

CRITERIA FOR ASSESSING ECONOMIC SYSTEMS

The criteria for assessing economic systems are not always consistent with each other. Any attempts to conceptualize the ideal economic system should be made with full awareness of inevitable trade-offs among them. For example, a highly prosperous economic system may ultimately fail to be sustainable. The variations in economic systems around the world today reflect, in part, differences in the importance attached to each criterion by citizens and political leaders in different nations. There is no single objective standard by which to assess the performance of an economic system, but the following criteria are particularly relevant.

Prosperity

Broadly defined, the concept of **prosperity** could include goals such as longer average life expectancy, reduced infant mortality rates, environmental quality, a low crime rate, and excellent education and healthcare systems. However, we shall view prosperity as simply rising levels of income and wealth. Prosperity is desirable because it expands the range of opportunities for individuals to develop their capacities and to fulfill their wants and needs.

Freedom

Most people have a strong desire to be self-directing in the sense of having choices about the ways they work, consume, socialize, express themselves, and are governed. **Freedom** is linked to prosperity insofar as higher levels of income broaden people's range of choices. However, other conditions for freedom include a democratic political system, well-defined and protected rights, a civil society that is tolerant and supportive of diversity, and a state committed to ensuring equal opportunity for all citizens.

Justice

Justice is fulfilled when individuals receive that to which they have a right or deserve. In a legal sense, justice requires that people be treated fairly in the judicial system, with criminals receiving punishment proportionate to the seriousness of their crimes. In an economic sense, justice requires that opportunities, responsibilities, and rewards be distributed in accordance with individual rights. The meaning of justice varies over time and among nations because individual rights are socially and politically defined. Even within a single nation at a point in time, different conceptions of justice may vie for supremacy as citizens disagree about the specific nature of human rights. For example, Americans are currently struggling with the question of whether access to affordable healthcare is a human right. Widespread perceptions of injustice can cripple an economic system by undermining the legitimacy of major institutions and thereby making citizens resistant to authority emanating from both the public and private sectors. The government of the former Soviet Union lost legitimacy in part because it routinely violated human rights.

Stability

A stable economic system maintains a relatively constant rate of growth, stable prices, and low rates of unemployment. Stability is consistent with changes in consumer preferences, **technology**, and availability of resources as long as these changes are processed quickly without causing periods of **recession** or **inflation**. Examples of instability include the Great Depression of the 1930s, which led to fundamental changes in the economic systems of Western nations. The traumatic experience of **hyperinflation** in Germany during the 1920s, followed by the Depression, caused many citizens to welcome the rise of Adolf Hitler and **fascism**. More recently, the Great Recession of 2008 brought the global economy to the brink of collapse. Stability is desirable not just for the economy but also for the **polity** and **civil society** as citizens seek security against major disruptions in their lives.

Peace

Citizens desire peace not only to avoid the death and misery caused by war but so that resources can be devoted to creating prosperity rather than destruction. As the technology of armed conflict has advanced, the danger posed by war now includes the total annihilation of the human race. Peace also refers to harmonious relations within nations and communities. Peace and prosperity complement each other because hatred, bigotry, and conflict divert human energy and resources from productive activity.

Sustainability

Sustainable growth requires that current generations conserve natural resources and protect the environment so that future generations are able to enjoy a quality of life at least comparable to our own. The concept of **sustainability** is imprecise given the uncertainty surrounding future sources of energy, discoveries of new resources, and technological advances. Yet in light of pressing environmental issues such as climate change, the destruction of the ozone layer, deforestation, depletion of aquifers, and air and water pollution, sustainability has become an increasingly important criterion for assessing economic performance.

Human Development

The ultimate purpose of an economic system is not to produce commodities but to improve the quality of human life. Although human development requires basic necessities such as a healthful diet, education, healthcare, and housing, people need much more to achieve their full potential, including a stimulating culture, programs and facilities for developing talents, meaningful work, fulfilling leisure activities, and supportive communities.

Democracy

Democracy can take many forms, but its underlying principle is that citizens should have an effective voice in determining the laws and policies by which they are governed. Democracy serves not just to curb abuses of state power but also to promote human development. By empowering citizens, democracy releases the creative energy and ambition that fuel prosperity.

HOW ECONOMIC SYSTEMS SUCCEED

Why are some nations so much more successful than others? Successful economic systems have achieved a constellation of economic, political, and social institutions serving to advance a particular nation's goals. In modern societies, the primary goal has typically been prosperity, but in the past and perhaps in the future, prosperity may be secondary to any of the other criteria of economic performance. For example, if environmental degradation ultimately threatens human survival, sustainability may become the top priority in evaluating economic systems.

The Successful Economy

To develop and grow, an economy must yield a surplus and make productive use of that surplus. A surplus arises when more goods are produced than are required to maintain the current level of resources. Maintaining the labor force requires that workers be provided with sufficient goods to enable them to continue working and to rear the next generation of workers. Maintaining **physical capital** requires replacing obsolete and depreciated machinery, equipment, and buildings. The maintenance of land may require planting trees and applying fertilizer. The size of the surplus depends not only on the quantity and quality of resources and the current state of technology but also on the effectiveness of the economic, political, and social institutions supporting the production process.

The surplus is used productively when it is directed toward increasing capital in all its various forms. The accumulation of capital over time leaves the current generation with a vast array of factories, buildings, machinery, transportation systems, communication systems, energy grids, knowledge, and skills. Capital exists in five different forms.

Physical Capital

A simple definition of physical capital is man-made goods used in the production of other goods. Physical capital used by businesses includes buildings, machinery, tools and equipment, and inventories. Such capital created by governments takes the form of **infrastructure** such as highways, dams, and bridges.

Financial Capital

This form of capital consists of money used to purchase assets that are expected to yield a financial return (e.g., profit, interest, rent, or capital gains). Examples of such assets include economic resources to be used for producing goods and services, financial assets such as stocks and bonds, or other assets such as gold and land.

Human Capital

Economists use the term **human capital** to describe the knowledge, skills, and aptitudes that increase human **productivity**. Education and job training represent investments in human capital.

Social Capital

Social scientists have not yet reached consensus on the precise meaning of **social capital**. For our purposes, social capital consists of networks and organizations that facilitate individual or collective action by generating a sense of community. The human capacities for sympathy and cooperation are the primary source of social capital, but the presence of social capital serves to foster and reinforce community spirit in the form of trust, shared information, goodwill, fellowship, solidarity, and reciprocity. Social capital could also be called "organizational capital" insofar as it promotes the productivity of any organization ranging from clubs and teams to firms and business associations. Even the political process relies on social capital (e.g., political parties and caucuses) to build consensus and cooperation. Governments can create social capital by enacting laws and regulations to facilitate the formation of groups and communities.

Cultural Capital

Like social capital, cultural capital remains a source of controversy among social scientists. We shall define cultural capital as the values, attitudes, norms, customs, and beliefs contributing to increased productivity. Examples of cultural capital are a strong work ethic, honesty, punctuality, respect for the rights of others, and respect for the rule of law. Notice the considerable overlap between cultural capital and human capital. Sociologists use the term *cultural capital* to refer to personal attributes leading to higher social status (e.g., knowledge of culture, etiquette, manner of speech), whereas economists use the term *human capital* to include those abilities directly contributing to individual productivity (e.g., programming skills, knowledge of mathematics). However, the two concepts are linked insofar as higher social status often accompanies more productive work and vice versa.

Economists have traditionally focused on physical capital, financial capital, and, more recently, human capital, but sociologists and anthropologists recognize the importance of social and cultural capital in contributing to economic success. These latter forms of capital have been formed and transmitted by previous generations and are just as much a part of their legacy as are factories, machines, and highways. When developing nations fail to thrive despite infusions of financial and physical capital, one reason may be a lack of social capital and cultural capital, which serve as the glue holding economic systems together.

The process by which capital expands over time is called **capital accumulation**. A successful economy accumulates capital by producing more than is consumed and then devoting that surplus to the creation of additional capital. Capital accumulation is accomplished not just by businesses investing in physical capital. It also involves government investments in infrastructure and investments by communities and families in social organizations and childrearing. When the process of capital accumulation functions smoothly, a growing stock of capital raises the productivity of labor, leading to a larger surplus and the financial means to create still more capital. Capital accumulation increases prosperity by raising the productivity of labor. The more a society produces, the more is available for consumption.

The manner in which a surplus is generated and controlled varies with different economic systems. In primitive societies, a surplus served no purpose because production was aimed primarily at survival. Without money as a means to facilitate trade or store wealth, primitive people had little desire for food, clothing, or shelter beyond meeting their basic needs. Yet, without a surplus, these early societies remained economically stagnant for millennia, with each succeeding generation simply reliving the past.

Primitive tribes were often displaced or conquered by large empires, which emerged and thrived because they were able to create a surplus by suppressing the cost of productive resources and by improving technology. Empires often kept the cost of labor low by using slaves or by coercing labor from the indigenous population. The cost of other productive resources was minimized by invading, looting, and conquering areas outside the empire. Technology improved as empires devoted resources to early forms of scientific research in metallurgy, agronomy, hydraulics, and transportation.

The foremost goal of the rulers of empires was to maintain, if not increase, the power of the empire. Toward that end, many of them wisely used part of the surplus to invest in infrastructure such as roads, aqueducts, and irrigation systems. However, empires ultimately failed as economic systems for two reasons. First, the rulers typically controlled production from the top down and therefore discouraged independent commercial activity. Second, rulers used a large portion of the surplus for unproductive purposes. They maintained their own power and legitimacy by supporting large armies, religious institutions to impart divine status to themselves, and massive monuments for their glorification.

Capitalism triumphed over all previous economic systems because it fostered the production of a larger surplus and generated competitive pressures to use that surplus productively. Capitalism's success is based on three factors. First, the competitive pressures created by markets compel producers to use the least-cost method of production and to strive continually to improve productivity by developing better technology. This drive to reduce costs of production leads to a growing surplus in the form of profit, which is controlled by business owners or capitalists. Second, once a surplus is created, market competition compels capitalists to reinvest in further improvements in technology and expansion of productive capacity. Capitalists who fail to do so become less efficient than their rivals and are potentially driven out of business. Third, by establishing private property rights, capitalism ensures that rewards for productive activity accrue to individuals. These incentives unleash more human energy and creativity than was ever forthcoming in previous economic systems organized by communities or states.

To understand the process by which capitalism fosters the accumulation of capital, a diagram may be helpful (Figure 2.1). Note that this diagram is not a complete depiction of a capitalist economy but simply a heuristic device to illustrate the expansion of capital.

The following discussion offers a detailed analysis of Figure 2.1.

Step A. Capitalists seek to increase their wealth by using financial capital to purchase resources (i.e., land, labor, and physical capital) for producing goods that can be sold at a profit.

Step B. Payments for resources become income for the households selling those resources. Most households have only labor to sell, but land, capital, and entrepreneurship are also owned by households, even if indirectly through the ownership of shares of corporate stock.

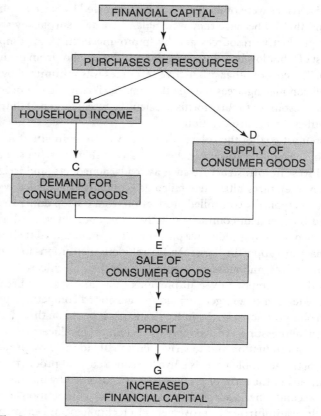

Figure 2.1 The Process of Capital Accumulation.

Step C. Households use their income to purchase goods and services. Any saving should flow into the financial system (i.e., banks, the stock market, the bond market), where it will be borrowed by other households or businesses desiring to spend more than their current income. **Interest rates** should move up or down until the amount of money saved is equal to the amount borrowed, so that any money not spent by one household or business is borrowed and spent by someone else.

Step D. By compelling firms to minimize their cost of production, competition ensures that producers will use the fewest resources and the best available technology.

Step E. The interaction of supply and demand leads to the sale of consumer goods at prices that clear the market.

Step F. Although there is no guarantee that every good produced will be sold at a profit, market competition quickly drives nonprofitable firms out of business and only profitable production survives.

Step G. Competition creates pressures on capitalists to reinvest their profits. Any business not reinvesting its profits in expansion, technological innovation, and product improvement will fall behind its competitors and eventually fail.

In summary, the combination of competitive pressures and flexible prices should eliminate any imbalances or impediments to the accumulation of capital.

The drive to maximize profit and the presence of competitive markets compel businesses to minimize costs of production by conserving resources and utilizing the most efficient technology. Profit maximization also requires that businesses produce goods that consumers want to buy. Finally, survival in a competitive market requires that profits be reinvested in expanding and improving production.

Several additional concepts are useful in understanding the historical process of economic growth. As a surplus develops, resources become available to fund exploration and to improve transportation and communication systems. As a result, the distance over which trade is feasible grows larger as increasing numbers of consumers and producers are brought together in a unified market. This widening of the market means that individuals and regions no longer need to be self-sufficient. They can specialize in particular types of production and then trade with other individuals or regions. The types of production chosen will be determined by an economic principle called **comparative advantage**.

Comparative advantage arises when some goods can be produced relatively more efficiently in a particular location or by a particular person due to unique natural resources, infrastructure, skills, or knowledge. For example, France, Italy, and Spain have traditionally held comparative advantage in producing wine because of their soil and climate. Athletes such as LeBron James have a comparative advantage in playing basketball.

Comparative advantage may increase over time as regions or individuals gain greater proficiency by specializing in the production of one good. Adam Smith described a pin factory where discrete tasks had been assigned to ten different workers who then became adept at their particular skills. He estimated that without specialization of labor, each worker could have produced no more than twenty pins per day. In fact, however, each worker's average daily output was 4,800 pins (Smith [1776] 1937). By increasing productivity, specialization of labor reduces per-unit production costs, increases output, and contributes to a growing surplus. Thus a positive feedback loop develops in which the creation of an economic surplus provides resources for widening markets. This allows for greater specialization of labor and increased productivity, which in turn contribute to a growing economic surplus.

The Successful Polity

The state is the primary **governance structure** of the **polity**. States may be differentiated along two dimensions: (1) the degree to which the state is involved in the economy through, for example, regulation, taxation, antitrust laws, macro policy, and income redistribution, and (2) the degree to which economic interests influence the state and undermine its autonomy through lobbying, campaign contributions, and bribes. The diagram in Figure 2.2 illustrates the resulting four types of state.

In a failed state, private interest groups vie with each other to control the political process, and the government lacks sufficient power and authority to carry out its responsibilities to provide law and order, well-defined property rights, national defense, public health, a stable currency, and economic stability. Failed

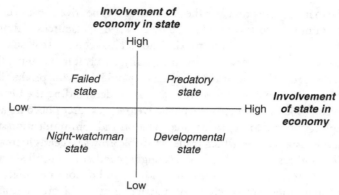

Figure 2.2 Classification of States.

states are often characterized by ethnic violence, religious conflict, and civil war (Rotberg 2003; Chomsky 2007).

A **predatory state** emerges when one private interest group or social class succeeds in gaining control of the state. The controlling group includes not only individuals in government, but also their allies in the private sector. The state becomes a tool by which the dominant group uses the coercive power of government to extract wealth from the rest of the population.

The night-watchman state does little more than protect private property rights by providing national defense and a legal system of police, courts, and prisons. Private interest groups have little incentive to influence the night-watchman state because it has no authority to redistribute income or enact favorable regulations. The night-watchman state is a theoretical ideal favored by libertarians but does not exist anywhere in the world.

The **developmental state** actively promotes the well-being of its citizens by providing infrastructure to support economic development. It also encourages participation in the political process while remaining independent of particular factions or interest groups. Because the developmental state is engaged in regulating the economy, private interest groups may attempt to manipulate government for their own benefit. However, a successful developmental state is sufficiently autonomous to resist the pressures of private interests that conflict with the public interest.

The foregoing analysis suggests that a successful polity requires that the state be relatively insulated from the influence of money and impartial toward the different interest groups within society. So, the night-watchman state and the developmental state are the only candidates for a successful polity. Although the night-watchman state, otherwise known as the laissez-faire state, appeals to libertarians and other advocates of free markets, even Adam Smith acknowledged a legitimate role for the state in providing national defense, roads, harbors, a legal system, and taxation. Today, all successful economic systems have varying degrees of a developmental state. Developmental states meet the following criteria:

- They are strong enough to restrain those private interests conflicting with the common good.
- They have sufficient power to prevent private groups from using the state to advance their own interests. Without this power, the state is vulnerable to "capture," whereby the strongest private interest groups effectively become the government.
- They are able to enforce laws and to offer protection against violations of citizens' rights by other citizens or nations.
- Their exercise of power is sufficiently restrained so that government itself does not violate citizens' rights.
- They make "credible commitments" that are trusted by private citizens and businesses. For example, when owners of capital engage their assets in risky ventures, they need confidence that government will not arbitrarily confiscate their property.
- They encourage democratic participation by citizens but enact laws and procedures to prevent special interest groups from exerting undue influence on the political process.
- They use the power of taxation to extract part of the surplus from the private sector, but that surplus is used to create infrastructure and to pursue other democratically determined goals.

A successful polity also requires legitimacy in the eyes of citizens. The rise and expansion of democracy in the nineteenth century emerged from the growing belief among aristocrats and powerful business interests that a stable and prosperous economy needs a government perceived as legitimate by most citizens. Without legitimacy, the coercive power of the state is likely to be viewed as tyrannical and oppressive rather than promoting the public interest.

The Successful Civil Society

Civil society consists of the networks of communities standing between the individual and the larger, more impersonal operations of states and markets. Examples of communities include neighborhoods, labor unions, civic organizations, business associations, recreational sports teams, and churches. In a vibrant civil society, communities are effective in fulfilling the following functions.

Creating and Sustaining Capital

Communities serve to create and transmit human, social, and cultural capital from one generation to the next. This process is accomplished through positive role models, peer pressure, and effective childrearing. Certain values and behaviors such as punctuality, reliability, creativity, productivity, honesty, and fairness are reinforced through positive social feedback, and nonproductive behaviors such as dishonesty and irresponsibility are met with social sanctions.

Solving Collective Action Problems

Successful communities widen the range of choices facing their members by solving collective action problems. Whereas states rely on laws and regulations to solve these problems, communities have the advantage of developing informal rules based on implicit agreements among members to abide by certain practices (Ostrom 1990). For example, respect for the rights of others is probably more effective than formal laws in deterring crime within a neighborhood.

Providing Identity, Meaning, and Purpose

Mainstream economic theory takes individual preferences as given, but values and tastes form within communities as people develop personal identities and find meaning and purpose in their lives. Without healthy communities to nurture the moral, intellectual, and social development of individuals, the performance of economic systems will suffer.

Facilitating Political Governance

Communities promote good citizenship by instilling virtues such as civic pride, a willingness to become informed about and vote on public issues, respect for law, and a sense of solidarity and trust among citizens. Communities also relieve the state of some responsibilities by establishing rules and standards of conduct. For example, professional organizations such as the American Medical Association and the American Bar Association penalize practitioners who violate professional ethics. A neighborhood may establish a crime watch program that reduces the burden on police.

*   *   *

Creating a successful civil society would be easier if clear guidelines existed concerning the forms of social organization most conducive to community development. However, different communities exist for different purposes, and their success may require differences in size, diversity, exclusivity, and the degree of hierarchy.

Size

Larger communities usually have more resources and greater ability to achieve their goals. However, smaller communities provide members with more opportunities for engagement and face-to-face interaction, both of which foster human development.

Diversity

By definition, members of a community share some characteristics, but in other respects, members may be highly diverse. Diversity brings together the wisdom and practices of different cultures and interests. Diversity exposes community members to alternative values and lifestyles and thereby broadens the range of choice. At its best, diversity gradually leads to the elimination of oppressive cultural traits such as racism, xenophobia, misogyny, and homophobia. However, homogeneity also offers advantages. A homogeneous community is likely to have a strong sense of solidarity and cohesion that fosters cooperation, trust, loyalty, mutual aid, and sensitivity to the well-being of others.

Exclusivity

Some communities welcome anyone wishing to join, whereas others are selective. Exclusive communities tend to be more cohesive and unified because they base membership on criteria deemed essential to the functioning of the community. On the other hand, open communities gain the benefits of diversity as a wide range of interests and perspectives provides fertile ground for innovation and growth.

Hierarchy

A hierarchical community concentrates authority in the hands of relatively few members. Hierarchy may be conducive to accomplishing specific, well-defined goals such as maximizing profit or winning a war. The advantage of hierarchy is the ability to make decisions quickly without extensive consultation involving large numbers of people. Hierarchy may also facilitate decision-making by placing authority in the hands of individuals with the most knowledge or expertise. Yet, egalitarian structures of authority may also prove valuable in some communities by creating opportunities for participation and a sense of belonging for its members.

HOW ECONOMIC SYSTEMS FAIL

Precapitalist economic systems eventually failed either because they did not produce a surplus, because the surplus was used for nonproductive purposes, or because they were vanquished by contact with a more technologically-advanced economic system. However, capitalist economic systems are also subject to periodic failures despite their capacity to generate large surpluses. These failures may be caused by problems in any or all of the three dimensions of the system—economy, polity, and civil society.

Failure of the Economy

The same diagram previously used to analyze a successful economy (Figure 2.1) can also be used to understand problems that may destabilize the economy by disrupting the flow of money, resources, and goods. (see Figure 2.3).

The following discussion provides detailed analysis of Figure 2.3.

Step A. A large portion of financial capital is owned by investors who, with no allegiance to any particular business or nation, are guided solely by profit maximization. Financial capital may not be used to purchase resources if the expected **rate of return** on speculative assets such as stocks, houses, gold, or collectibles exceeds the profitability of investments in the production of goods and services. Just as water flows to its lowest point, financial capital flows to the highest risk-adjusted rate of return.

Step B. One of the resources purchased from households is labor. Unlike other resources, labor is not delivered at the time of sale. The employer typically purchases a

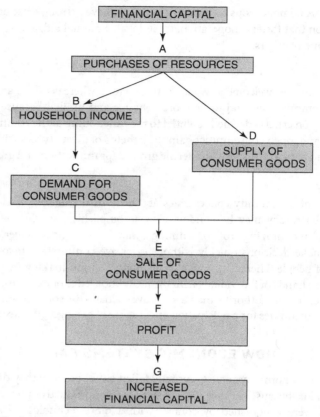

Figure 2.3 The Process of Capital Accumulation.

specified amount of time on the job without any guarantee of how much labor will actually be forthcoming. Employers may receive less labor than they expected due to strikes, work stoppages, or a decline in work effort.

Step C. Even if financial capital is used to purchase resources and that money becomes household income, households do not spend all their income on consumer goods. Households save part of their income, and when the economy functions smoothly, interest rates rise or fall until saving is matched by an equal amount of borrowing by households and businesses choosing to spend more than their current income. However, high-income households save a larger portion of their income than do low-income households. If the distribution of income shifts in favor of wealthy households, (1) saving as a percentage of total income will increase, and (2) demand for consumer goods may fail to keep pace with rising output. This inadequate level of consumer spending is called **underconsumption**, which may also occur when fear of recession or political unrest causes consumers to feel insecure about the future. The increased saving associated with underconsumption should theoretically drive down interest rates and stimulate borrowing, but the desire to borrow may also drop due to pessimism about the future of the economy. Businesses have little interest in borrowing to expand production when demand for consumer goods is weak.

Step D. Businesses purchase resources based on the expectation that the resulting production of goods can be sold at a profit. However, their expectations may be excessively optimistic, leading to **overinvestment** in productive capacity. This overinvestment becomes apparent when unsold inventories begin to accumulate. At that point, businesses recognize their **excess capacity**, scale back the volume of production, and lay off workers. Reducing employment may solve the problem for an individual business, but if many businesses simultaneously dismiss workers, the problem of underconsumption arises because unemployed workers have no income with which to purchase goods.

Step E. In theory, the prices of consumer goods should rise or fall until the quantity demanded equals the quantity supplied. However, expectations and lack of competition may prevent prices from adjusting. For example, large corporations are often reluctant to lower prices when demand for their product weakens because they expect a recovery in the future. Instead of lowering prices, they reduce output and lay off workers. Again, when many businesses simultaneously lay off workers, underconsumption may occur because those unemployed workers lack purchasing power.

Step F. Profit may fail to materialize because of either higher-than-expected costs of production or lower-than-expected revenue. Insufficient profit results in business failures, cancellation of planned investments, layoffs, reduced household income, and declining demand.

Step G. To the extent that corporations are able to suppress competition, they weaken the pressure to reinvest profits. Profits may instead be used to buy back existing shares of stock, to acquire competing firms, to increase dividends, or to raise salaries and bonuses for top-level management.

The preceding analysis illustrates the importance of both supply and demand in sustaining economic growth. Supplies of resources, including financial capital, are a necessary, but not sufficient, condition for growth. In addition, demand for products is needed to provide the incentives for owners of resources to engage their assets in productive activity. An understanding of the role of demand sheds light on the question of how much profit is healthy for a capitalist economic system. In the nineteenth century, many economists assumed that more profit meant more growth because profit provides the funds for investment in expanding productive capacity. To increase profits, they favored policies to minimize production costs (including wages). However, low wages can potentially restrict consumer demand and therefore slow economic growth. So, although high profits provide ample financial capital for investment, without strong demand for business products, there is no incentive to invest. Profits are necessary for growth in a capitalist economy, but they can become so high that demand is suppressed and the economy stagnates. In the words of Adam Smith, "the rate of profit . . . is always highest in the countries which are going fastest to ruin" (Smith [1776] 1937, 250).

To summarize, the economy may fail due to imbalances between supply and demand that create obstacles to the flow of money, resources, and goods through the market. Although the theory of perfect competition purports to demonstrate that flexible wages, prices, and interest rates will always resolve such imbalances, that theory overlooks real-world phenomena such as concentrated corporate power, labor unions, lack of information, uncertainty, and the role of emotions and expectations in determining human behavior.

Failure of the Polity

Each of the four types of state introduced earlier in this chapter has the potential to block economic development. A failed state will almost certainly be accompanied by a stagnant, if not declining, economy because government lacks the power to conduct the most basic public functions of providing infrastructure, maintaining law and order, protecting property rights, and collecting taxes. Failed states are usually scenes of pervasive violence as private groups struggle for dominance. Current examples of failed states include Iraq, Syria, Somalia, the Democratic Republic of the Congo, Sudan, Chad, Yemen, Libya, and Afghanistan.

A predatory state provides the infrastructure needed to enable the economy to produce a surplus because the primary purpose of the state is to extract that surplus for the benefit of those connected to government. However, the economy in a predatory state typically stagnates because too much of the surplus is used for nonproductive purposes (e.g., lavish lifestyles for insiders, a large army and police force to suppress dissent, and monuments to glorify the state). Predatory states eventually become dysfunctional as citizens realize that their government has been captured by special interests. Growing cynicism and anger make it difficult for politicians to secure sufficient revenue through taxation to fund essential public goods. Any willingness on the part of citizens to accept sacrifices for the common good dissipates with the perception that government is serving the interests of only a small segment of the population. Predatory states are often associated with violent power struggles between groups because control of the state secures access to the nation's wealth through confiscation, taxation, and bribes. With manpower and resources devoted to political conflict, the economy steadily deteriorates.

The potential failure of a night-watchman state is more controversial. Libertarians claim that a state providing little more than protection of property rights is the key to a successful economic system as individuals are free to pursue their self-interest without government interference (Friedman 1962; Nozick 1974). This argument assumes that the only institutions needed to organize and coordinate an economic system are a legal system to enforce private property rights and markets. The market, however, contains numerous limitations that yield undesirable results requiring the support of appropriate political, social, and cultural institutions.

Even a developmental state, however well-intentioned, may derail the economy with misguided policies. Problems often develop when a legitimate function of the state is taken to an extreme. If regulations become too burdensome, taxes too high, public debt too large, or individual security too assured, the economy will inevitably suffer.

Failure of Civil Society

The quality of a nation's civil society may impede economic development. Communities fail to support a healthy civil society when they exhibit the following three characteristics:

Oppression

Some communities place such high value on cohesion and conformity that they oppress both their own members and outsiders. Members of oppressive communities tend to lack creativity, willingness to take risks, and entrepreneurial energy. They often remain mired in traditional values and lifestyles that are antithetical to economic growth. Communities based on ethnicity or religion may be particularly susceptible to intolerance and mistrust of outsiders. The Taliban in Afghanistan and the Puritans in seventeenth-century America are examples of oppressive communities. The Puritans forbade Christmas celebrations and Saturday night festivities.

Aggression

Communities also pose threats to the economic system when their members seek to impose particular interests and values on the rest of society. This aggression may take the form of fomenting racial, ethnic, or religious intolerance or using political and economic power to promote community interests at the expense of the public interest. The Ku Klux Klan is an example of the former, whereas certain political action committees and industry associations illustrate the latter.

Fragmentation

An excessively fragmented community, like a failed state, lacks sufficient solidarity to create and transmit norms and values. The members of a fragmented community view other members as simply a means to achieve their own individual goals. With little sense of belonging to a cohesive group, individuals may take advantage of every opportunity to advance their interests by any means possible without regard for the well-being of others. As the pursuit of self-interest becomes the dominant type of behavior, cynicism and mistrust abound, both of which dampen the energy and confidence essential to a thriving economy.

Fragmentation poses a potentially more serious problem. Nineteenth-century sociologists such as Ferdinand Tönnies (1855–1936) and Emile Durkheim (1858–1917) expressed concern that industrialization was destroying traditional communities and creating a rootless, amoral, and anxious citizenry (Durkheim [1897] 1951; Tönnies [1887] 1957). Twentieth-century philosophers such as Hannah Arendt (1906–1975) and Jose Ortega y Gasset (1883–1955) amplified this concern by attributing the rise of fascism to the decline of traditional communities (Arendt 1968; Ortega y Gasset [1932] 1994). Without supportive communities, isolated individuals have difficulty in forming personal identities. Lacking meaning and purpose in their lives, they are susceptible to the rhetoric of demagogues promising to revitalize communities and restore a nation's glory.

REFERENCES

Arendt, Hannah. 1968. *The Origins of Totalitarianism.* New York: Harcourt, Inc.

Chomsky, Noam. 2007. *Failed States: The Abuse of Power and the Assault on Democracy.* New York: Holt.

Durkheim, Emile. (1897) 1951. *Suicide: A Study in Sociology*. Glencoe, IL: Free Press of Glencoe.

Friedman, Milton. 1962. *Capitalism and Freedom*. Chicago: University of Chicago Press.

Nozick, Robert. 1974. *Anarchy, State, and Utopia*. New York: Basic Books.

Ortega y Gasset, Jose. (1932) 1994. *The Revolt of the Masses*. New York: W. W. Norton.

Ostrom, Elinor. 1990. *Governing the Commons: The Evolution of Institutions for Collective Action*. New York: Cambridge University Press.

Rotberg, Robert I., ed. 2003. *When States Fail: Causes and Consequences*. Princeton, NJ: Princeton University Press.

Smith, Adam. (1776) 1937. *An Inquiry into the Nature and Causes of the Wealth of Nations*. New York: Modern Library.

Tönnies, Ferdinand. (1887) 1957. *Community and Society*. East Lansing: Michigan State University Press.

ADDITIONAL READING

Acemoglu, Daron, and James A. Robinson. *Why Nations Fail: The Origins of Power, Prosperity, and Poverty*. New York: Crown Business, 2012.

Blyth, Mark. *Great Transformations: Economic Ideas and Institutional Change in the Twentieth Century*. New York: Cambridge University Press, 2002.

Chandler, Alfred D., Jr., Franco Amatori, and Takashi Hikino, eds. *Big Business and the Wealth of Nations*. New York: Cambridge University Press, 1999.

Clark, Gregory. *A Farewell to Alms: A Brief Economic History of the World*. Princeton, NJ: Princeton University Press, 2009.

Ferguson, Niall. *The Great Degeneration: How Institutions Decay and Economies Die*. New York: Penguin Press, 2013.

Fukuyama, Francis. *Trust: Social Virtues and the Creation of Prosperity*. New York: Free Press, 1996.

Galbraith, James K. *The End of Normal: The Great Crisis and the Future of Growth*. New York: Simon & Schuster, 2014.

Ghani, Ashraf, and Clare Lockhart. *Fixing Failed States: A Framework for Rebuilding a Fractured World*. New York: Oxford University Press, 2009.

Harrison, Lawrence E., and Samuel P. Huntington. *Culture Matters: How Values Shape Human Progress*. New York: Basic Books, 2000.

Kay, John. *Culture and Prosperity*. New York: HarperCollins, 2004.

Landes, David S. *The Wealth and Poverty of Nations: Why Some Nations Are So Rich and Some So Poor*. New York: W. W. Norton, 1998.

Maddison, Angus. *Explaining the Economic Performance of Nations*. Aldershot, UK: Edward Elgar, 1995.

Olson, Mancur. *Power and Prosperity: Outgrowing Communist and Capitalist Dictatorships*. New York: Basic Books, 2000.

Ridley, Matt. *The Rational Optimist: How Prosperity Evolves*. New York: HarperCollins, 2010.

Warsh, David. *Knowledge and the Wealth of Nations: A Story of Economic Discovery*. New York: W. W. Norton, 2006.

Wilensky, Harold L. *Rich Democracies: Political Economy, Public Policy, and Performance*. Berkeley: University of California Press, 2002.

Chapter 3

MARKET-CENTERED ECONOMIC SYSTEMS

> "The market is a very good servant, but a very bad master."
> SUKHAMOY CHAKRAVARTY (1934–1990),
> Indian economist

> "To allow the market mechanism to be the sole director of the
> fate of human beings and their natural environment . . . would
> result in the demolition of society."
> KARL POLANYI (1886–1964),
> Hungarian economic anthropologist

Markets coordinate economic activity by aggregating the choices of individual consumers and producers to form prices. Choices about what to produce and sell constitute supply, whereas choices about what to buy determine demand. Supply and demand interact to establish a price for each product and resource, and these prices serve as signals or incentives steering the choices of both consumers and producers toward the production of the most highly valued goods and services. In theory, the aggregation of individual choices about what to buy and sell results in an equilibrium in each market at which the quantity of a good demanded by consumers is equal to the quantity supplied by producers. This ability of markets to coordinate economic activity while leaving individuals free to make choices is one of the primary arguments in favor of market-centered economic systems. However, markets also have serious limitations that require supportive and corrective political, social, and cultural institutions.

MARKET-CENTERED ECONOMIC
SYSTEMS IN HISTORY

Markets Before Capitalism

Market-centered economic systems are usually called **capitalism**. They developed gradually over time but did not become dominant until the early nineteenth century. However, markets have existed since members of neighboring primitive tribes first met to engage in trade. Tribes tended to trade only for goods unavailable within their territories. Typically, trade was conducted by specific members of the tribe, so only a small segment of the population actually participated in market exchanges. Most goods produced by tribes remained within the community and were distributed to members in accordance with custom and tradition.

Markets remained peripheral to the lives of most people for tens of thousands of years. Individuals and tribes had little need to trade until improvements in agriculture and animal husbandry enabled the production of a surplus. When that happened, tribes no longer needed all members to be engaged in securing basic necessities. With a surplus of food, some members could devote their energies to producing goods such as jewelry, clothing, and weapons. Some of these products could then be traded for different goods fashioned by other tribes. However, markets remained primitive as traders usually relied on barter as a means of exchange.

To develop more fully, markets required two new institutions. The first was money. Barter was a highly inefficient method for making exchanges because it required that each tribe possess goods desired by the other tribe. Long before the minting of metallic coins, humans adopted the practice of using designated objects as money. For example, if several tribes agreed to use sea shells as money, then a tribe could trade its goods for sea shells, knowing that the shells could be used to exchange for goods with other tribes.

The second institutional innovation essential to a flourishing market was the rise of the **state**. States evolved as one group gained dominance, usually through violence, over an extended territory. States used their power to reduce the uncertainty and mistrust between individuals and groups that posed obstacles to trade. To trade with confidence, individuals needed to know precisely what goods they were exchanging, whether their trading partner was trustworthy, and whether they would have an enforceable right to the good after the exchange. States promoted trade by defining and enforcing property rights, by enacting laws and imposing sanctions against offenders, and sometimes by issuing a common metallic currency. States also increased trust by creating a unified **polity** within which citizens shared a common culture.

Because manufacturing in early societies was typically small-scale and often confined to a single household, producers had little need to purchase land, hire workers, or borrow money. As a result, markets for land, labor, and **financial capital** were virtually nonexistent. Any large-scale production requiring significant numbers of people (e.g., building pyramids, canals, and roads) was coordinated by the state, and the work was often done by slaves. Markets were primarily confined to the exchange of consumer goods.

As human civilization progressed, markets were often kept apart from the rest of society because **economic behavior** was viewed as detrimental to the virtues underlying a good society. Participants in markets were assumed to be self-interested and therefore vulnerable to temptations to gain personal advantage by cheating and deceiving their trading partners. In ancient Athens, market exchanges were confined to a space called the *agora* and kept separate from the *pnyx* where political deliberations took place. The Greeks believed that market activity potentially undermined good citizenship because need and greed tended to overwhelm the human capacity for ethical behavior and a commitment to justice.

Religions throughout the world have expressed concerns over the effects of engaging in market activity. Biblical writers prohibited interest on loans (Exodus 22:25), told the story of Jesus expelling merchants and moneylenders from the temple (Matthew 21:12), and offered the famous adage that "the love of money is the root of all evil" (1 Timothy 6:10). The Bible warns individuals seeking wealth that "it is easier for a camel to go through the eye of a needle than for a rich man to enter the kingdom of God" (Matthew 19:24). The Koran also bans interest on loans and the Prophet Muhammad claimed that "two hungry wolves, if let loose amongst a flock of sheep, cause less harm than a man's eagerness to amass wealth and status." Buddha described two alternative paths of life: "One is the path that leads to material wealth. The other is the path that leads to Nirvana."

The Catholic Church continued to discourage Christians from engaging in moneylending for interest until the beginning of the seventeenth century. Before that time, Jews in many parts of Europe were prohibited from owning land, so the Christian ban on interest created opportunities for Jews in banking and finance. The Church also stipulated that merchants could charge no more than a "just price" to cover their costs and permit them to maintain their current standard of living. This doctrine was designed to suppress the temptation toward greed, but it also served to discourage accumulations of wealth that might pose a challenge to the authority of the Church.

To summarize, although markets existed prior to capitalism, they did not fundamentally shape society. They were kept spatially separate because the self-interest underlying market behavior was deemed dangerous to politics and community life. Markets were deeply embedded in political and social institutions designed to constrain self-interest and the accumulation of wealth.

The Rise of Capitalism

The first nation to develop a capitalist economic system was Britain, in the early nineteenth century. The new system emerged out of institutional changes that had been in progress for centuries. The primary political prerequisite for capitalism was a state that met two criteria. First, it had to be powerful enough to provide essential **infrastructure** such as well-defined and enforced property rights, law and order, a common currency, and roads and bridges. Second, the power of the state had to be sufficiently limited so that citizens felt secure against arbitrary confiscation of their property and violations of their civil rights by the state. This second condition was usually fulfilled only after successful and often violent challenges by citizens to the authority of the state.

The British government met both these criteria as early as the seventeenth century. The Roman Empire had been less dominant in England than in the rest of Europe, leaving local tribes to manage their own affairs. This experience with sovereign rule bred a strong resistance to centralized political authority. In 1215, English noblemen forced King John to sign the Magna Carta, limiting the power of the monarchy and establishing Parliament as an independent legislative body. Continuing dissatisfaction with the monarchy resulted in a civil war and the beheading of King Charles I in 1649. After eleven years without a king, the monarchy was restored, but conflict between Parliament and the king continued. In the Glorious Revolution of 1688, King James II was forced to leave the country and was replaced by William of Orange. Determined to limit the power of the monarchy, Parliament enacted a Bill of Rights in 1689. With this document, a political institution essential for the rise of capitalism had been secured—a stable government sufficiently strong to protect property rights and enforce contracts but not so powerful that it could undermine manufacturing and commerce through excessive taxation, regulation, and arbitrary confiscation of property.

Certain cultural institutions also influenced the rise of capitalism. The Protestant Reformation, initiated by Martin Luther (1483–1546) in 1517, legitimized the pursuit of wealth by proposing that worldly success increased a person's chances of salvation. In addition to condoning interest on loans, Protestantism promoted individual responsibility and free thinking. It encouraged hard work and thrift, which combined to increase saving and investment. The emerging capitalists who reinvested their profits rather than squandering them on lavish lifestyles represented the epitome of Protestant virtue (Weber [1905] 2001; Tawney [1926] 2015). When King Henry VIII broke away from the Catholic Church and formed the Church of England in 1534, he effectively made England a Protestant nation.

During the seventeenth and eighteenth centuries, writers such as John Locke (1632–1704), David Hume (1711–1776), and Adam Smith (1723–1790) offered compelling defenses of private property and individual freedom. English scientists, including Francis Bacon (1561–1626) and Isaac Newton (1643–1727), contributed to an intellectual environment conducive to the later development of innovations such as the steam engine and the spinning jenny that would spur the Industrial Revolution.

Another cultural advantage supporting the development of capitalism in England was the presence of informal codes of conduct (Mokyr 2012). English business people were generally honest and trustworthy. They realized that a good reputation increased the likelihood of success in business, and therefore they eschewed opportunistic behavior such as fraud and deceit that might have increased profit in the short run but would eventually damage their reputations. In addition, many of the early entrepreneurs belonged to nonconformist religious groups such as Quakers, Unitarians, Methodists, Puritans, and Congregationalists, so their strong religious beliefs reinforced their commitment to ethical behavior. Others may have been seeking social status by emulating the gentlemanly manners of the aristocracy.

Major institutional changes are usually accompanied by theoretical demonstrations of their advantages. The justification for capitalism came most importantly from the Scottish philosopher and economist Adam Smith. His 1776 book *The Wealth of Nations* provided a moral and intellectual defense of capitalism that remains influential even today. The pursuit of self-interest, which had long troubled philosophers and religious thinkers, was touted by Smith as the source of economic prosperity. The competitive market would guide self-interested behavior into socially useful channels by providing monetary incentives for individuals to produce goods desired by others.

Even with the essential political and social institutions in place, capitalism could not fully develop without markets for resources. Although markets in consumer goods existed for centuries prior to the rise of capitalism, markets in labor, land, and money required conscious intervention and even coercion by the state and by powerful private groups. Prior to the advent of capitalism, rural England consisted of large estates owned by the aristocracy and populated by peasant farmers who were required to turn over part of their produce to the landlord. However, as technological improvements in the production of textiles caused an increase in the demand for wool, landlords evicted tenant farmers and built fences and stone walls to graze sheep. This "enclosure movement" created a market for labor as homeless farmers migrated to the cities and sought work in the emerging factories.

A market for land was advanced by three developments in England. When King Henry VIII rejected Catholicism, the land owned by the Catholic Church was confiscated and sold. Also, in the early seventeenth century, much of the land owned by the monarchy was sold to private parties. Finally, most villages and towns had a commons open to anyone for grazing animals, gathering firewood, or foraging for food. The sale of the commons to private owners contributed not only to the supply of marketable land but also to the growth of labor markets because many peasants who relied on access to the commons had no choice but to migrate to cities in search of employment.

A market for money required concentrations of wealth in the hands of individuals who were willing to undertake the risk of lending and investing. A considerable mass of wealth already existed in the hands of the English aristocracy, who, unlike their counterparts in continental Europe, were quite adaptable in switching from land ownership to capital investments as the surest means to expand wealth. New accumulations of wealth also arose among merchants, who devised what historians call the "putting-out system." They delivered raw materials such as wool to rural households where family members would spin and weave the wool into cloth. The merchants subsequently retrieved the finished product and delivered it to market.

Another source of wealth was external to England. Although Spain led the way in plundering and looting gold and silver from the New World, English pirates sometimes intercepted Spanish galleons as they returned home and commandeered their treasure. In fact, the British monarchy actually commissioned pirates to do just that and turn over the captured gold and silver to the government.

In summary, the necessary economic, political, and social institutions for capitalism existed in Britain by the end of the eighteenth century. Some of the institutions resulted from external factors (e.g., the development of new technology for weaving cloth in Flanders and the plunder of New World resources) and some evolved spontaneously as individuals pursued their self-interest. However, to a significant extent, capitalism was created by the exercise of power. A powerful coalition of merchants and aristocrats successfully challenged state authority, and landowners forcibly evicted peasants from the countryside. The state privatized land formerly owned by the Church or the Crown brought gold and silver into the nation to create pools of wealth for borrowing and lending, protected property rights, enforced contracts, and provided the extensive physical infrastructure essential to market operations. As the market became the dominant institution for coordinating the economic system, the unleashing of self-interest from previous political and social constraints resulted in an explosion of innovation that would lead to the creation of more wealth during the next two centuries than had been produced in all previous history combined.

Varieties of Capitalism

The essential institutions of capitalism include private property, wage labor, and the dominance of the market as the primary **governance structure**, but each nation has unique institutions that shape the scope and functioning of markets. Several distinct varieties of capitalism have appeared during the past two hundred years with considerable overlap between the different systems. For example, all nations have welfare systems, but the term *welfare capitalism* describes those countries in which the welfare system is so extensive that it becomes a major component of the nation's institutional makeup. Similarly, all nations have government regulations, but the term *regulated capitalism* refers to a system in which regulations are the primary method by which government seeks to modify the operation of markets. Although social scientists have not reached consensus on labeling the varieties of capitalism, we shall refer to the following distinct systems:

Competitive Capitalism

In its initial form, capitalism consisted of competitive markets for both resources and products. Markets were competitive because both businesses and suppliers of land, labor, and capital were small and numerous. The role of government was largely confined to providing basic infrastructure such as national defense, a legal system, and roads. Competitive capitalism prevailed in the United States between 1815 and 1896 and in Britain from 1800 to 1932.

Organized Capitalism

As changing technology required large-scale production, corporations replaced the small businesses found in competitive capitalism. With so much capital tied up in single companies, the financial risks of failure were enormous. Corporations first sought to insulate themselves from competition by driving their rivals out of business, but that strategy was ruinous for all involved. Instead, businesses formed organizations such as trusts, cartels, networks, and associations to enable them to cooperate with one another. Similarly, workers formed labor unions to increase their bargaining power with employers. This new form of organized capitalism prevailed in the United States from 1897 to 1932, in Sweden from 1870 to 1931, in Japan between 1868 and 1934, and in Germany from 1946 to 1998.

State Capitalism

France and Germany did not begin major industrialization until the mid-nineteenth century, by which time large-scale technology was required in order for businesses to compete effectively. Because Britain and the United States had at least a half-century head start on economic development, France and Germany opted to skip competitive capitalism. Instead, they relied on government to promote economic development by encouraging business associations, funding extensive infrastructure, supervising labor relations, and operating some state-owned enterprises. State capitalism prevailed in France from 1815 to 1944 and in Germany from 1871 to 1932. State capitalism reappeared toward the end of the twentieth century as Russia and China abandoned communism. Neither country was willing to fully embrace competitive capitalism, so they fashioned a form of state capitalism in which government continues to play a major role.

Regulated Capitalism

Emerging from the Great Depression of the 1930s, Americans demanded assurance from their government that such a calamity would never be repeated. The preferred solution involved enlarging the scope of governmental authority to regulate the economy. Antitrust policy would maintain competition, macroeconomic policy would ensure stability, and regulation of labor markets would promote justice. This regulated capitalism appeared only in the United States between 1933 and 1979. After the Depression, other developed nations concluded that more than regulation was needed to improve the performance of their economic systems.

Welfare Capitalism

Some nations place such high priority on stability and justice that governments provide a wide array of social welfare programs aimed at assuring economic security for all citizens. This form of capitalism existed in Britain between 1933 and 1978, in Sweden from 1933 to 1991, and in France from 1983 to 1995.

Planned Capitalism

At the end of World War II, two capitalist countries took state involvement in the market economy to unprecedented levels. France and Japan engaged in government planning to establish goals for their economies and to improve the coordination of business decisions. Unlike planning in **communism** or **fascism**, these plans merely created broad guidelines designed to provide businesses with information about future resource availability and likely demand for products. Both France and Japan eventually scaled back their use of planning after encountering severe economic difficulties later in the twentieth century.

Neoliberal Capitalism

During the 1970s, high rates of unemployment and inflation afflicted most Western nations. In Britain and the United States, the elections of Margaret Thatcher (1925–2013) and Ronald Reagan (1911–2004) reflected a growing disenchantment with both regulated and welfare capitalism. Neoliberal capitalism was designed to revitalize market economies by substantially reducing the role of government. The term *neoliberal* is potentially confusing because the effort to minimize government is usually associated with free-market conservatism. However, **neoliberalism** represents a revival of the laissez-faire policies associated with **classical liberalism**. Beginning around 1980, both Britain and the United States attempted to reinvigorate economic growth by reducing the role of government and increasing the reliance on markets to coordinate economic activity. Britain moved away from neoliberal capitalism in the mid-1990s, but neoliberal policies continued in the United States until the Great Recession of 2008.

POTENTIAL STRENGTHS OF THE MARKET

The market has potential to make positive contributions to each of the criteria for assessing economic performance outlined in Chapter Two.

Prosperity

Markets achieve prosperity by promoting both static and dynamic efficiency. **Static efficiency** (also called **economic efficiency** or allocative efficiency) requires efficiency in both production and consumption. Efficiency in production requires either maximizing output from the economy's available resources or minimizing the cost of producing that output. Markets promote efficiency in production because competition compels firms to utilize the technology and combination of resources that minimize the cost of production. In theory, any firm that does not minimize costs will be unable to match the product price of its competitors and will be driven out of business.

Efficiency in production is necessary for economic efficiency but not sufficient. An economy might be efficient in production by devoting all resources to a single good, but clearly that would not be desirable from the viewpoint of consumers. Efficiency in consumption requires that consumers devote their spending to those goods and services giving them maximum satisfaction. In the pursuit of profit, firms will produce those goods and services which consumers are willing and able to buy.

When efficiency in both production and consumption has been met, the economy achieves economic efficiency. Resources are allocated toward the production of those goods and services most highly valued in monetary terms by consumers. Resources are fully utilized, the most efficient technology is used, and the value of output is maximized. Economists say that **Pareto optimality** has been reached, meaning that no alternative allocation of resources could improve the well-being of one person without detracting from the well-being of another. No real-world market ever achieves economic efficiency, but competitive markets create strong pressures to push economies in that direction.

Whereas static efficiency occurs at a single point in time, **dynamic efficiency** measures the increase in output over time from a given amount of resources due to innovations in technology and product quality. Economic growth depends on both dynamic efficiency (**intensive growth**) and the development of additional productive resources (**extensive growth**). The market performs well in promoting both forms of growth. Firms in a competitive market have strong incentives to innovate because the first firm to develop a new technology to reduce production costs or improve product quality gains a **competitive advantage** and enjoys increased profit until rivals are able to adopt the same innovation. Markets also offer strong incentives for the development of new resources. Additional supplies of resources drive down resource prices, thereby enabling firms to reduce production costs and increase profits. For example, firms develop synthetic substitutes to replace more expensive materials or engage in drilling, mining, and exploration to discover new sources of natural resources.

Innovation is not without its downside. Every new product or technology renders some existing products or technologies obsolete. This process of simultaneous innovation and obsolescence was termed *creative destruction* by the economist Joseph Schumpeter (1883–1950). Prosperity depends on innovation, but innovation often renders the skills of some workers obsolete and results in factory closures. However, markets also provide incentives for retraining, relocating, and upgrading idle resources.

Markets provide strong incentives for prudent and industrious behavior by placing both negative and positive consequences of decisions directly on the individual person or business. When individuals know they will personally reap the rewards or suffer the consequences of their action, they are motivated to consider their choices carefully. As a result of the market's incentives, additional resources are made available, the quality of resources is upgraded, and innovation and risk-taking are encouraged.

The market accomplishes one more task that is essential to growth and prosperity. In real-world markets, each individual has only limited information and knowledge. However, the market overcomes this shortcoming by establishing prices on the basis of which individuals and businesses can make rational choices about employing resources and purchasing products. The price of each commodity reflects vast amounts of information about factors affecting the supply and demand for that good, but no person needs to possess all that information. In other words, the market compensates for our limited capacity for knowledge (Hayek 1945).

Freedom

Markets have always been associated with individual freedom, and defenders of capitalism often dismiss any of its shortcomings as inconsequential compared to the protection of freedom. In a market economy, households enjoy freedom to choose what products to buy, where to work and live, how much money to save, and what resources to develop and offer for sale. Freedom for businesses includes choice over which goods to produce, the prices of those products, and the resources and technology used in production.

However, the market itself imposes a form of discipline by directing individuals and firms to make choices contributing to efficiency and growth. A primary virtue of the market is that this discipline is exerted not through coercive state power or social sanctions but with monetary incentives in the form of prices. This ability of the market to steer self-interested individual choices toward socially beneficial outcomes without visible coercion was discerned by Adam Smith; every individual "intends only his own gain, and he is . . . led by an invisible hand to promote an end which was no part of his intention" (Smith [1776] 1937, 98). Smith's "invisible hand" is the competitive market, and the "end" to which he refers is the prosperity of the nation.

The discipline imposed by the market reflects the aggregated choices of millions of consumers who either approve or disapprove of other people's resources, products, and activities by the manner in which they spend their money. The market rewards individuals and businesses whose choices and actions respond to consumer demand and penalizes those who fail to meet that criterion.

Finally, the market promotes freedom by dispersing power. Whereas policies enacted by the state are collective and binding on all citizens, decisions in the market are made by individual consumers and businesses. Each household and each business is a small nexus of power with the sovereign authority to make choices affecting its well-being. Although this power is limited precisely because the decision-making unit is only one among millions and therefore must conform to the dictates of the market in order to be rewarded, individual sovereignty in a free market is not constrained by any identifiable person, group, or political authority.

Justice

A generic definition of justice requires that individuals receive what they have a right to or deserve. However, this definition raises the question of how rights are determined. Two methods for determining rights support the justice of markets and capitalism. The first was developed by American economist John Bates Clark (1847–1938). His "marginal productivity theory of income distribution" demonstrates that under conditions of perfect competition, both labor and capital are rewarded in accordance with their productive contribution to output. This theory has served as a cornerstone for the moral defense of capitalism. If the productivity of resources determines their owner's income, then capitalism fairly rewards individuals regardless of traits such as race, ethnicity, religion, or social status. Indeed, the market has historically eroded privileges based on any criterion other than productivity.

A second approach to defending the justice of markets was developed later in the twentieth century by the libertarian philosopher Robert Nozick (1938–2002). He argued that because the distribution of income and wealth results from inheritance and exchanges of goods, services, and resources among individuals, as long as all bequeathals and exchanges are voluntary, the resulting distribution of income is fair (Nozick 1974).

More broadly, the market promotes justice by providing opportunities for social mobility. Citizens are less likely to perceive inequality as unjust when a dynamic economy opens new avenues for advancement. By placing much of the responsibility for personal income in the hands of individuals, the market offers every participant a chance to succeed. With no political authority determining the value of each person's productive efforts, there is no one to blame for any disappointment since success or failure is attributable to impersonal market forces.

Stability

The market promotes stability by quickly responding to changes such as the development of new technology, discovery of new resources, depletion of existing resources, or changes in consumer tastes. Through the price mechanism, these changes elicit appropriate reactions as businesses and consumers adjust their production and consumption decisions before any serious imbalances arise. Competitive market pressures reward those who promptly and effectively respond to changing conditions. For example, discovery of new oil reserves will increase the supply of oil. Although a surplus of oil may temporarily occur, producers will lower the price in order to eliminate the surplus. Conversely, the depletion of oil reserves may temporarily cause a shortage, but producers respond to the shortage by raising the price. In either case, the market causes the price to move toward an equilibrium level at which the amount of oil offered by producers is equal to the amount buyers choose to purchase.

Peace

The French philosopher Charles de Montesquieu (1689–1755) coined the term *doux commerce* (gentle commerce) to describe the process by which markets promote peace among both individuals and nations. He claimed that engaging in commerce causes participants to treat others with civility and respect. Success in the market depends on the choices of other people to buy a particular good; therefore, individuals and businesses have a strong incentive to develop good reputations. This goal is accomplished by being cordial, honest, trustworthy, and respectful of others. These behaviors, in turn, create a stable society with minimal conflict. Although the human passions for money and power could potentially lead to violence, the market converts these powerful emotions into rational calculations aimed at making money by engaging in activities valued by other people (Hirschman 1977).

The same harmonizing process that makes individual interests compatible also operates among nations. Those nations engaged in extensive trade with each other rarely go to war. Each nation benefits from trade and has no desire to destroy its partner. International trade makes nations supportive of each other's prosperity in order to expand the market for exports.

Finally, the market promotes peace by creating prosperity. When the size of the "economic pie" is growing, a "win-win" situation develops, allowing all groups to gain without detracting from the well-being of anyone else. In contrast, a stagnant economy leads to "zero-sum game" in which one group's gains come at the expense of other groups, leading to increasing conflict over the distribution of income and wealth.

Sustainability

The issue of sustainability becomes more relevant with each passing decade as global temperatures rise, ice caps melt, ocean levels rise, and storms become more severe. The market contains several mechanisms that serve to protect the environment. Competitive markets compel businesses to minimize costs and therefore to minimize the use of resources. Any waste of resources causes inefficiency, and inefficient firms will be driven out of the market. In addition, through a process called **scarcity pricing**, the market provides strong incentives to conserve resources in danger of depletion. As the supply of a particular resource dwindles, its price rises. Businesses respond to higher resource prices by using less of the resource and by developing either alternative natural resources or synthetic resources. Finally, to the extent that markets create prosperity, they provide a large surplus of financial capital available for developing new technologies to reduce pollution and conserve resources.

Human Development

Economic systems produce people as well as goods and services by providing the institutional environment in which humans develop their identities, preferences, and behaviors. People in market-centered economic systems are generally law-abiding, considerate, and respectful of others. These attitudes may be due to innate moral instincts or cultural traditions. However, markets reinforce those instincts and traditions by making individual success dependent on developing a good reputation, which, in turn, requires making a favorable impression on the other people with whom individuals interact.

Markets also promote human development by creating competition for rewards based on productivity. Financial incentives and opportunities to gain social status motivate individuals to shoulder responsibilities, innovate, take risks, and increase their **human capital** by acquiring knowledge and skills. Markets encourage self-reliance and experiments with diverse lifestyles and forms of expression. In this process of self-discovery, formerly dormant talents and desires are awakened. The productivity and innovation flowing from energized individuals is a major source of the dynamism of market economies.

Democracy

A clear historical connection exists between capitalism and democracy. Expansion of the market gave rise to centers of wealth and power beyond the reach of monarchs and emperors. Prior to capitalism, violent clashes between private groups and the state spanned centuries as revolutions, civil wars, and social unrest challenged the authority of oppressive governments. Only with the rise of capitalism did the private sector gain sufficient power to force governments to grant citizens the right to select their political representatives through regular elections. Democracy developed gradually, with only male property owners allowed to vote initially; popular pressure eventually extended the franchise to include nearly all adult citizens.

Markets restrain abuses of political power by enabling individuals or businesses dissatisfied with public policy to relocate to another jurisdiction (Hirschman

1970). Also, the importance of individual property rights in a market-centered economic system has typically led to the recognition of civil rights such as freedom of the press and freedom of speech, both of which serve as bulwarks against political tyranny.

POTENTIAL WEAKNESSES OF THE MARKET

When the market is securely embedded in appropriate political and social institutions, it does a superb job of coordinating economic activity and preserving individual freedom. But in the absence of institutional constraints and supports, the market can penetrate and dominate states and communities, thereby undermining the very institutions necessary for its own success.

Reduced Prosperity

The ultimate purpose of any economic system is not to produce commodities but to improve the well-being of citizens. Even if the market achieves economic (static) efficiency, this simply means that resources are devoted to the production of those goods most highly valued in monetary terms by consumers. The actual composition of that output will depend on the distribution of income and wealth that provides some people with more purchasing power than others. For example, the efficient market might devote resources to manicures for pet dogs while some children lack adequate nutrition and healthcare. Efficiency does not imply the maximization of material well-being but rather the production of goods for consumers who are willing and able to pay for them.

The market potentially achieves economic efficiency only when **perfect competition** and **complete markets** exist, but neither of these conditions is ever met in real-world economies. Perfect competition requires that the following conditions are met: (1) each market consists of many small buyers and sellers with no control over price; (2) resources are perfectly mobile, meaning they can be shifted from one use to another at no cost; (3) the product of each industry is homogeneous, meaning that all sellers in a specific market produce exactly the same good; and (4) all participants in the market possess full information. In addition to being perfectly competitive, the market must be complete to achieve efficiency. Completeness requires the existence of markets for all goods, both present and future, so that individuals are able to engage in all mutually beneficial transactions.

The market fails to be efficient when any of these conditions are violated. Economic efficiency is diminished when businesses are large rather than small, when resources are immobile, when products are differentiated, when information is lacking, and when markets are incomplete or even missing altogether.

Large Businesses

For many businesses, doubling all resource inputs causes output to more than double. As a result, per-unit production costs decline as firms become larger. This phenomenon, known as **economies of scale** or increasing returns to scale, is explained by factors such as the ability of large firms to improve productivity through a greater division of labor, to utilize large-scale technology, to buy inputs in bulk at discounted prices, and to borrow money at lower interest rates. Lower per-unit costs enable large firms to gain a competitive advantage and drive smaller firms out of the market. The few remaining firms, called **oligopolies**, possess considerable **market power** to raise prices and increase profits. In some cases, economies of scale may be so extensive that competition is eliminated entirely and only one firm survives. This situation, called a **natural monopoly**, is found most often in utilities such as electrical power and cable television providers. The potential for abuse of market power by natural monopolies is so obvious that they are usually regulated, if not owned, by government.

Economies of scale potentially jeopardize both static and dynamic efficiency because firms with substantial market power are partially insulated from competitive pressure to minimize cost and innovate. Paradoxically, however, economies of scale may also stimulate innovation. Large firms facing less competition are able to earn more profit, and that money can be devoted to research and the development of new products and technologies. However, in the absence of effective competition, additional profit may simply be used for higher dividends or increased compensation for owners and management. In other words, large firms have the financial means to innovate but may lack the incentive to do so. The choice between reinvestment and increased dividends is determined by management's commitment to long-term growth versus short-term gain.

Other factors may lead to larger businesses as well. The same quest for profit that compels firms to increase efficiency also leads to strategies to suppress competition and gain control over markets. One anticompetitive strategy is **collusion**, in which businesses agree to cooperate with each other either explicitly or tacitly. The former occurs when firms formally agree to limit competition in order to raise prices. A **cartel**, such as the Organization of Petroleum Exporting Countries (OPEC), is an example of explicit collusion. In most countries, explicit collusion violates antitrust laws and therefore rarely occurs. However, tacit collusion can often accomplish the same purpose with minimal legal obstacles. Tacit collusion might take the form of a verbal agreement between two chief executive officers or even an unspoken understanding that firms will not undercut each other in price or aggressively seek to increase their market share. One form of tacit collusion is **price leadership**, in which one firm, usually the largest in an industry, sets the price and all other firms in the industry match that price. Tacit collusion is facilitated by economies of scale because cooperation is more easily achieved among a smaller number of large firms.

Collusion can also occur in labor markets as workers form unions to bargain collectively with employers. Because of their large numbers, workers historically had great difficulty in effectively colluding until governments protected them from intimidation by employers, gave them the right to bargain collectively, and exempted them from antitrust laws. The rationale for allowing workers to collude is that the market power of employers should be balanced by the market power of workers.

Although explicit collusion is illegal, businesses can accomplish the same goal of increasing market power by merging with or acquiring other firms. These **mergers** and acquisitions can be horizontal, vertical, or conglomerate. A horizontal merger occurs between two firms operating at the same stage of production of the same product. A vertical merger entails the joining of two firms operating at different stages in the production of the same product. A **conglomerate merger** involves the combining of two unrelated firms. Antitrust laws are intended to permit only those mergers and acquisitions that maintain sufficient competition, but the enforcement of these laws has varied over time.

Resource Immobility

Efficiency requires that entrepreneurs and investors be able to quickly move resources into or out of an industry in response to changing opportunities for profit. However, resources are typically less than fully mobile. Labor resources are human beings with attachments to particular communities who may be unwilling or financially unable to relocate. Both labor and capital resources may be asset-specific, meaning that they are suitable for a particular type of production but not easily transferable to another. Furthermore, the market is rife with **barriers to entry** that block new businesses or workers from entering a specific industry.

Economies of scale pose barriers to entry because new firms are typically small and therefore have higher average costs of production than large, well-established firms. Other barriers result from conscious strategies by businesses to discourage new firms from entering their industries. Examples of firm-created barriers to entry abound. A business may sell its product through only one retailer in a particular region. Or a firm may devote extensive resources to constant innovation and thereby gain such daunting technological superiority that potential rivals concede defeat. In the past, some businesses resorted to **predatory pricing** by temporarily slashing their prices to drive competitors out of business and then raising prices once they gained dominance over an industry. Another strategy for creating barriers to entry is to gain control of an essential resource. In the 1940s, the Aluminum Company of America (ALCOA) tried to buy all the known reserves of bauxite (aluminum ore) so that no other firm could produce aluminum. Only an antitrust lawsuit by the US government prevented this scheme from succeeding. Finally, firms in an industry may form an association to regulate entrance. In 1903, for example, the Association of Licensed Automobile Manufacturers denied Henry Ford a license to produce automobiles. When Ford began production without a license, he was sued, and the case was not resolved in Ford's favor until eight years later.

If businesses cannot create barriers to entry through their own power, they often turn to government for assistance. The term *rent seeking* refers to efforts by businesses and other private groups to raise their income by suppressing competition or by securing benefits directly from government. One form of rent seeking is to enlist the power of government to restructure or regulate a market. Rent seeking is pursued through lobbying, campaign contributions, gifts such as paid vacations, and promises of future employment for politicians and government bureaucrats. Businesses seek not only subsidies and government contracts for their products but also programs and regulations to alter the market in ways that increase their income. For example, patents allow businesses to maintain a monopoly on innovations for approximately twenty years. Required licenses for businesses such as taxis and service professionals have the effect of reducing supply and keeping prices high. Zoning laws restrict the areas where business can locate. Tariffs and other import restrictions protect domestic businesses from foreign competition. More generally, nearly all government regulations tend to discourage new competition due to compliance costs. Corporations and professional associations often lobby in favor of additional regulations not only to discourage new entrants to their industry but to reduce opportunistic behaviors such as false advertising by their competitors and to protect themselves from lawsuits.

Product Differentiation

Sellers make every effort to reduce direct competition by distinguishing their product from that of rivals. These differences may be real or simply created in the minds of consumers through advertising and clever marketing. Although product differentiation gives consumers a wider range of choices, it also reduces economic efficiency by giving firms market power. Brand loyalty permits sellers to raise prices without losing many customers, which leads to excess profit.

Lack of Information

Efficiency requires that consumers and businesses possess full knowledge of all aspects of the market, including the prices and qualities of products and resources, available technology, and the profitability of different business opportunities. In the real world, however, market participants typically struggle to make decisions in the face of ignorance and uncertainty. When information is lacking or asymmetric (i.e., a person on one side of a transaction has information not known by the other party), the market becomes inefficient because not all mutually beneficial transactions occur. In extreme cases, a market may not form at all. For example, no market exists for insurance against divorce because newlyweds have much more information about the potential longevity of their marriages than do insurance companies. The newlyweds most likely to purchase insurance against divorce would be those with the gravest doubts about their marriage. Insurance companies, anticipating a high number of claims, would set rates so high that few people would purchase the insurance, and therefore a market would fail to materialize. The same logic explains why there is no market for private insurance against unemployment.

In other cases, markets may exist but are inefficient because they do not ensure the completion of all mutually beneficial transactions. Before the development of the Internet, the market for used cars was plagued by lack of information. Sellers knew much more about the quality of their cars than did buyers, so buyers offered a low price, fearing undisclosed mechanical problems. As a result, the sellers of good used cars often refused low offers. As fewer good cars were sold through the used car market, the probability of purchasing a bad used car increased, and buyers offered even lower prices. This downward "death spiral" is caused by what economists call **adverse selection**. The individuals most likely to sell a car through the used car market were the owners of deficient cars hoping to unload their vehicle on an unsuspecting buyer. Adverse selection also afflicts the insurance industry. Health insurance is most appealing to people in poor health, and homeowner's insurance is more likely to be purchased by people living in unsafe neighborhoods. As a result of adverse selection, insurance rates rise and many people who would like to be insured decide to go without.

A second problem caused by lack of information is called **moral hazard**. Whereas adverse selection occurs prior to the purchase of a good or the signing of a contract, moral hazard arises after the transaction is completed. Moral hazard appears when one party to a transaction behaves in ways hidden from and harmful to the other party. For example, a person with homeowner's insurance may stop locking doors and windows. A financial advisor may deposit a client's money in a mutual fund that provides a kickback to the advisor. An agent for a professional athlete may negotiate a contract with hidden benefits for the agent. The potential for moral hazard contributes to mistrust among buyers and sellers and may prevent some transactions from occurring.

Missing and Incomplete Markets

A market for a particular good may fail to form for a variety of reasons.

- The **transaction costs** of gathering information, drawing up a contract, and monitoring and enforcing compliance with the terms of the contract may be sufficiently high to deter buyers and sellers from completing a transaction.
- The property rights attached to a good may be so unspecified or unenforceable that buyers are reluctant to purchase it.
- The terms of a future transaction may be so complex or unknown that a contract cannot fully specify all possible outcomes.
- Potential producers of a good may not be able to exclude nonpayers from enjoying its benefits and therefore cannot sell it.
- Buyers and sellers may not trust each other sufficiently to engage in transactions.
- If two goods are complementary, a market for one good may fail to materialize without the presence of the other good. For example, the market for electric cars is impeded by a lack of charging stations, and entrepreneurs are reluctant to provide charging stations until more people own electric cars.
- Potential buyers may not have access to credit that would enable them to complete a purchase.

The two major problems resulting from missing and incomplete markets are **externalities** and **public goods**. An externality is a cost or benefit affecting people other than the producer or consumer of a good. External costs, also called negative externalities, arise when the cost of an action or good to society as a whole (social cost) exceeds the private cost to an individual or business. For example, the private cost of producing steel includes wages for steel workers and the cost of iron ore, but the social cost also includes the damage to the environment caused by industrial pollution. External benefits, also called positive externalities, arise when the benefit of an action or good to society as a whole (social benefit) exceeds the private benefit to an individual or business. The private benefit of obtaining a flu shot is that the recipient will not become infected, but the social benefit includes the reduced likelihood that other people will contract the disease.

The presence of externalities causes inefficiency because individuals and businesses make decisions by assessing only private benefits and costs. Economic efficiency requires consideration of all social costs and benefits. By failing to recognize external costs and benefits, the market leads to the production of too many goods with negative externalities and too few goods with positive externalities.

Externalities occur because of missing markets. For example, if there were a market for clean air, then people harmed by pollution could buy cleaner air by paying polluters to reduce emissions (Coase 1960). Imagine a polluting factory with only three families living in the vicinity. The families might meet and agree to collectively pay a certain amount of money to the owner of the factory in exchange for reduced pollution. Now a market for clean air has arisen. Notice, however, that this market is realistic only when the number of participants is quite small. The three families know and trust one another, and little time or effort is required to formulate their offer to the factory owner. In the real world, however, such transactions would require agreement among large numbers of people who do not know each other and have different interests. The transaction costs of coordinating negotiations involving large groups of people would impede efforts to reduce externalities through the market.

When the market for a good is missing entirely, all the potential benefits of that good are external to the market. Such goods are called public goods and meet two criteria. First, they are nonexclusive or indivisible, meaning that the benefits apply to everyone regardless of willingness to pay. Second, public goods are nonrival, meaning that one person's use of the good does not diminish its availability for others. Examples of public goods include national defense and highways. The market fails to provide public goods due to the **free-rider problem**. Consumers have no incentive to pay for a good whose benefits they can enjoy without paying, and businesses cannot profitably produce a good that consumers will not buy. Public goods pose a **collective action problem**. If individuals pursue their narrow self-interest by taking a free ride, the resulting absence of public goods is detrimental to everyone. Public goods are produced when individuals act collectively through the state to provide funding with taxes.

Even though the market cannot provide public goods, they are essential to its functioning. Without public goods such as well-defined property rights, a legal system, a regulatory system, stabilization policies, standardized weights and measures, and a stable currency, markets would wither. Government itself is a public good. Every citizen benefits from effective government and no citizen can be excluded from enjoying those benefits. As a public good, government requires a collective effort by citizens through their participation and taxes.

Other public goods such as physical and social infrastructure are also essential to the performance of the market. Physical infrastructure is publicly funded **physical capital** that provides a supportive framework within which economic activity can flourish. Examples of physical infrastructure include roads, bridges, tunnels, communication systems, and the equipment involved in police protection, fire protection, and national defense. Social infrastructure consists of institutions providing services with widespread positive externalities such as publicly funded education, healthcare, and job training.

Only a few goods such as national defense and well-defined property rights are pure public goods. Most examples of public goods are actually quasi-public. Nonpayers could be excluded, but doing so would be impractical or socially undesirable. All highways could be toll roads, all education could require students to pay admission to enter the classroom, and individuals could be charged each time they visit a library or rely on police or fire protection. However, because these services provide substantial positive externalities, they are typically treated as public goods financed through taxation.

* * *

A final constraint on the market's ability to foster prosperity is the potential conflict between static efficiency and dynamic efficiency. Static efficiency, or efficiency at a particular point in time, requires perfect competition. Yet perfect competition drives prices down to the point where profits are just sufficient to enable firms to continue in operation. Profits are a major source of funding for research and development of new technologies and products; thus, the low profits associated with static efficiency may ultimately undermine innovation and reduce dynamic efficiency.

Static efficiency and dynamic efficiency may also conflict because entrepreneurs engage their talents and funds when they believe that they have unique information or resources that cannot be quickly acquired by competitors. Perfect competition, in which resources are perfectly mobile and all participants possess full information, may therefore discourage entrepreneurship and the development of new technologies and products. In that case, the market cannot achieve efficiency in both the static and dynamic senses.

Economies of scale create another potential trade-off between static and dynamic efficiency. Static efficiency requires competition among many small firms, but dynamic efficiency is fostered by the economies of scale associated with large firms. So economies of scale are simultaneously a major source of dynamic efficiency and yet destructive of perfect competition and static efficiency. The loss of static efficiency is acceptable because dynamic efficiency is far more important than static efficiency in promoting prosperity. In other words, dynamic efficiency resulting from imperfect competition between large firms yields more rapid growth than static efficiency resulting from perfect competition between small firms. Governments acknowledge the priority of dynamic efficiency over static efficiency when they grant patents that reduce static efficiency by restricting competition but promote dynamic efficiency by encouraging innovation. However, to the extent that perfect competition among small firms is sacrificed in the quest for economic growth, the market can no longer be trusted to channel the pursuit of self-interest into socially beneficial behavior. The actions of Wall Street banks leading up to the 2008 financial crisis provide a vivid illustration of this point. The very size of these banks encouraged them to take on excessive risk, secure in the knowledge that government would not allow them to fail because the repercussions might destroy the entire economy.

Limited Freedom

The concept of freedom combines two different meanings—**negative freedom** and **positive freedom** (Berlin 1969). Negative freedom exists when humans make choices without interference or coercion by other individuals or by government. The market offers a wide range of negative freedom, but the limitations of that concept can be seen by imagining a group of people stranded in a lifeboat without food or water. Nobody is coercing them, so they are free in a negative sense despite being powerless to change the situation and probably facing death. However, a fuller account of freedom includes not just freedom from coercion but also freedom to effectively pursue one's goals and aspirations. This positive freedom requires that individuals have access to the material requisites for human development (e.g., adequate nutrition and housing), to public infrastructure provided by government such as educational and legal systems, and to supportive social relations based on shared values and trust. The freedom of the people in the lifeboat would be enlarged by having not only food and water but also infrastructure such as search and rescue teams and satellites providing the global positioning system (GPS) and cell phone service.

The market restricts positive freedom by providing inadequate income to some individuals, by failing to provide public goods, and by undermining the social cohesion generated by communities. In the market, individuals who own few productive resources receive correspondingly limited incomes and therefore may lack the financial means to make effective choices. For example, children of low-income families may be free to attend college in the sense that there is no personal or governmental interference but not if they cannot afford the cost of tuition. The market also limits freedom by constraining consumer choice to those commodities capable of being produced at a profit. In other words, the market fails to respond to citizen's desires for public goods. As an example, entrepreneurs would not be free to start businesses without well-defined and protected property rights, which are provided by the state. Similarly, freedom could be constrained by lack of highways or police protection.

Injustice

Although a perfectly competitive market may reward individuals in accordance with the productivity of their resources, every developed nation in the world grants citizens certain rights extending beyond claims based on the ownership of resources. Civil rights such as free speech, freedom of the press, and freedom to worship are compatible with the market because even individuals with few resources can exercise those rights. But other rights such as the right of alleged criminals to an attorney, the right to education, or the right to basic necessities of life require resources for their protection, and the market will not provide these resources to people who are unable to afford them. Public support for nonmarket economic rights is based in part on fears that widespread poverty might lead to violence and revolution. However, support for economic rights also arises from the perception that capitalism creates an unfair degree of inequality. Several arguments support this proposition.

Lack of Competition

Real-world markets are never perfectly competitive, so incomes are not determined solely by the productivity of resources. For example, economies of scale create market power, enabling some individuals to gain income in excess of productivity. Similarly, a person possessing information not known by others (e.g., information about a corporation that might affect the price of its stock) may be able to use that knowledge to gain income unrelated to productivity. More generally, successful efforts to suppress competition create a distribution of wealth and income based on power as well as productivity.

Surplus Labor

If productivity determines an individual's income, then an increase in the productivity of labor should result in higher wages. However, rapid growth of the labor force may result in surplus labor that suppresses wages despite rising productivity.

Illegitimate Property Rights

Many of today's property rights have their origins in past injustices such as slavery, expropriation of Native American and Mexican lands, theft of gold from the Incas, fraud, coercion, extortion, and, more generally, the use of wealth to dominate and control both the market and the political process. The libertarian philosopher Robert Nozick acknowledged that if the pattern of ownership of productive resources is unfair, so then is the distribution of income resulting from engaging those resources in production (Nozick 1974). The injustice is largely invisible because once property rights are established, their origins are often forgotten.

Productivity of Public Goods

The array of public goods serving as infrastructure for all economic activity makes a significant contribution to a nation's productivity. For example, Bill Gates' entrepreneurial skills would be less productive without a well-educated populace able to quickly master computer skills. Lawyers would be less productive without a legal system, courtrooms, and police to apprehend criminals. Because public goods belong to all citizens through their government, rewards based on productivity require that a portion of a nation's total income accrue to government. This goal is accomplished through taxation, but the market itself fails to reward the productivity of public goods and therefore violates justice.

Nonmarket Economic Rights

The market responds only to those human needs and desires backed by money, and money is typically earned through engaging one's resources in productive activity. However, productivity is not the only basis for determining rights deserving of income. If it were, seriously handicapped people would have no means of survival other than the compassion and generosity of others. Rights might also be based on need or on nonmarket contributions to society. For example, married homemakers have a right to financial support from their working spouses. Every child has a right to public education. Every alleged criminal has a right to legal counsel. In some countries, access to healthcare is treated as a right of every citizen.

The philosopher John Rawls (1921–2002) rejected the claim that productive contribution should be the basis for justice because productive abilities are partially determined by genetic endowments over which people have no control. He claimed that inequality is fair only to the extent that it creates incentives for productive activity leading to greater efficiency and growth that benefits all citizens (Rawls 1971).

In 1944, Franklin Roosevelt devoted his State of the Union address to outlining a proposed economic bill of rights for all Americans. Each citizen would have a right to employment yielding a living wage, freedom from unfair competition, a modest home, adequate medical care, education, and social insurance against sickness, accident, unemployment, disability, and old age. Congress refused to enact Roosevelt's proposal, but the United States and most other developed nations have instituted a variety of social benefits to advance his vision of a just society.

Justice as a Public Good

Justice fits the definition of a public good insofar as it provides widespread benefits and is both nonrival (i.e., one person's enjoyment does not diminish its availability for others) and nonexclusive (i.e., nobody can be excluded from enjoying its benefits). All citizens desire justice, yet justice cannot be sold in the market because its benefits are nonexclusive. Individual contributions to charity are insufficient to achieve justice because many people will be free riders, choosing to enjoy the benefits (e.g., less visible suffering, less crime, more equal opportunity) of other people's charitable contributions without bearing part of the cost.

Instability

Markets have historically exhibited cycles of boom and bust. Economists do not agree on the reasons for these cycles because cycles at different times in history have had different causes. However, the common denominator underlying all recessions in a capitalist economy is fear by lenders and investors that profits will decline and that their assets will lose value. Pessimism causes investors to withdraw funds from productive engagement, businesses to lay off workers and cancel plans for expansion, and consumers to purchase fewer goods and services. If recessions are caused by pessimism, and pessimism is caused by expectations of falling profits, what causes profits to fall? The instability of a capitalist economy results from market failures that create imbalances in and impediments to the flow of money, resources, and goods.

Lack of Information

All participants in the market face uncertainty about the future. As a result, their decisions are affected by instincts, emotions, and what Keynes called "animal spirits." During periods of rapid growth, optimism prevails, and market participants act on the basis of what former Federal Reserve chairman Alan Greenspan called "irrational exuberance." For example, banks may become so optimistic that they begin lending money to individuals and businesses with poor credit histories or inadequate collateral. Investors bid up the prices of stocks in anticipation of future increases in corporate earnings. Corporations may engage in **overinvestment** as they expand so rapidly that productive capacity exceeds demand. Consumers may take on more debt than they are able to repay. This excessive investment, lending, and debt fuel speculative bubbles in which asset values (e.g., prices of stocks, housing, and land) rise to unsustainable levels. Eventually, lenders and investors anticipate the end of the economic boom, and the mood changes from optimism to pessimism. As investors rush to retrieve their money, panic sets in, financial markets sink, and a recession begins.

Negative Externalities

When investors, banks, brokerage firms, and hedge fund managers calculate the risk of their financial decisions, they consider only the consequences for themselves or their firms. Their calculations do not include the potential damage to the entire economy if their excessive optimism leads to speculative bubbles that eventually cause a financial collapse (Posner 2009). By failing to consider the negative externalities associated with their decisions, investors assume too much risk.

Lack of Competition

The industries supplying resources to other businesses (e.g., mining, oil, steel, timber, farm equipment, and electricity) tend to be very capital-intensive. As a result, they experience significant economies of scale, which result in a few oligopolies dominating each industry. Lack of competition gives these firms market power to raise prices, thereby reducing the profitability of firms purchasing those resources. For example, OPEC triggered a global recession by quadrupling the price of oil in 1973.

Lack of competition among resource suppliers becomes increasingly problematic during periods of strong economic growth. As a general rule, about three dollars of additional capital equipment (e.g., machinery, buildings, and tools) are required to produce an additional dollar of output. As a result, demand for capital equipment tends to increase approximately three times faster than demand for consumer goods, causing prices of capital goods (which are costs for businesses) to rise faster than prices of consumer goods. The net effect is reduced profitability for firms producing consumer goods and services and increased likelihood of recession.

Excessive Inequality

Economists have long acknowledged that the initial stages of economic growth in any country may be accompanied by increasing inequality, but they presumed that growth in a modern capitalist economy would raise both wages and property income at roughly the same rate (Kuznets 1955). However, according to Keynes and more recent empirical research, growth may lead to such extreme inequality that the stability of the entire economic system is jeopardized (Rajan 2010; Stiglitz 2013; Piketty 2014). The connection between inequality and instability stems from the fact that high-income households tend to spend a smaller percentage of their income than do low-income households. Low-income households typically spend all of their income to meet basic needs, whereas high-income households easily save substantial portions of their income. Growing inequality means that a larger share of national income is going to households with high rates of saving, so consumption spending may fail to keep pace with rising income. This **underconsumption** threatens profitability and therefore increases the likelihood of recession.

Underconsumption can be exacerbated when businesses respond to falling profits by cutting wages. Lower wages may improve the profits of a single business, but if all businesses cut wages, workers have less purchasing power, the demand for goods drops, and businesses are likely to experience declining revenue and profits. Wages are unique in the economy because they represent both the largest portion of costs for most businesses and the largest source of revenue. Within the domestic economy, a widespread policy of wage cuts to reduce costs is self-defeating because lower wages also reduce business revenue.

Free-market economists often dismiss the foregoing analysis of instability, claiming that any imbalances will be quickly resolved by adjustments in prices, wages, and interest rates. They argue that the forces of supply and demand in any given market push prices to an equilibrium level, and because the macroeconomy is simply the aggregation of all individual markets, the economy should quickly adjust to a new equilibrium. However, these arguments are based on the unrealistic assumptions of perfect competition. Lack of information opens the door for human emotions such as fear and greed to destabilize markets. Lack of competition prevents prices from moving quickly to an equilibrium level. Excessive inequality creates an imbalance between savings and investment. Finally, as Keynes argued, even if the economy does eventually stabilize, that equilibrium may be accompanied by recession and high levels of unemployment.

Social Conflict

The market may promote peace by creating mutual benefits from trade among individuals, regions, and nations, but since the advent of capitalism in the early nineteenth century, the world has experienced two world wars and uncountable regional conflicts. Capitalism may bear some responsibility for this record of violence. Like the great empires of antiquity, capitalism has exhibited a close association with **imperialism**, the attempt to dominate and control other nations. Until the mid-twentieth century, nations practiced imperialism primarily through the establishment of colonial empires, with industrialized countries battling one another for control over additional territory. However, modern imperialism typically entails efforts by industrialized nations to control governments in developing countries. At least three factors potentially link capitalism and imperialism.

Access to Resources

Competition compels firms to minimize costs of production, and consequently, they search the globe for less expensive resources. In many instances, the resources are located in developing countries, so firms must make substantial investments in the physical capital required for extraction, processing, and transportation. To protect their assets from indigenous uprisings or expropriation by foreign governments, firms often turn to their own governments for support in the form of financial aid and military assistance to countries experiencing political turmoil. This intervention in foreign countries often increases international tensions and conflict.

Markets for Exports

Capitalist economies are prone to developing excess capacity, resulting in a level of output exceeding consumer demand. This problem can be resolved by opening new markets overseas, thereby reaching millions of new potential customers. Historically, governments of industrialized nations have sought to open foreign markets by applying both economic and political pressure. For example, in the mid-nineteenth century, the British invaded China after that nation resisted British exports of opium grown in India.

Outlets for Surplus Capital

Financial capital periodically accumulates faster than it can be profitably invested in the domestic economy. Seeking higher rates of return, businesses and individuals may turn to foreign investment opportunities. Again, once capital is engaged overseas, investors in industrialized nations turn to their governments for assistance in minimizing the risk of confiscation and political instability by installing and supporting friendly regimes in developing nations. This intervention in the domestic politics of other nations often triggers violence and even revolution as illustrated by the Islamic revolution that overthrew the Shah of Iran in 1979 or the Sandinista revolution that ousted the Somoza regime in Nicaragua the same year.

In addition to the conflict fostered by imperialism, competition in markets pits individuals and groups against each other in the struggle for jobs and business success. Although competition has many virtues, it potentially contributes to racism, sexism, homophobia, and ethnic hostility as groups seek to elevate themselves by demeaning others.

Lack of Sustainability

A sustainable economic system is able to exhibit strong performance well into the future. For several reasons, capitalism may be incapable of sustaining not only the natural environment but also itself.

Externalities

Markets do not recognize external costs such as the damage done by pollution. In fact, markets create pressures on firms to pollute. In the absence of regulations, the least costly way to dispose of waste is usually to dump it into the air or water. Any firm incurring the added expense of reducing pollution will have higher production costs and therefore suffer a competitive disadvantage. Externalities pose a collective action problem. Polluting serves the short-term interest of each firm in maximizing profit, but a polluted environment threatens human existence.

Short-sightedness

Owners of capital tend to be impatient; they seek the highest rate of return in the shortest time possible. As a result, the market favors short-term investments yielding immediate profit. However, the benefits of efforts to reduce pollution extend over many generations. The choices businesses make concerning energy sources, production techniques, and levels of output typically fail to take into account the costs and benefits for future generations.

Growth Imperative

Capitalism has been compared to a bicycle—it either moves forward or topples over. In other words, the viability of capitalism depends on growth. Without the expectation of new profitable investment opportunities, the surplus generated by producing and selling commodities would sit idle and the economy would stagnate. Stagnation implies high unemployment and political unrest; therefore, governments attempt to maintain the conditions for growth even at the expense of the environment, as exemplified by the reluctance to confront the issue of global climate change. If capitalism must grow in order to sustain itself, then a future ecological catastrophe can be avoided only by expanding resources through space exploration, by developing new technologies that dramatically conserve resources or rely on synthetic/renewable resources, or by making the transition to an economic system that does not require growth (Klein 2014).

Institutional Crowding Out

Capitalism may undermine the institutional prerequisites for its own long-term viability. The economist Joseph Schumpeter (1883–1950) noted that capitalism relies on the survival of precapitalist institutions such as cohesive families and communities, respect for authority, and a commitment to virtues such as honesty, loyalty, reciprocity, and quality workmanship. By rewarding the pursuit of self-interest, capitalism gradually erodes the nonmarket institutions providing the supportive framework within which markets function.

Restricted Human Development

Capitalism undoubtedly offers individuals a wider range of choices than has existed in any previous economic system. At the same time, however, the market channels human development in directions most compatible with profitability and capital accumulation. This process takes three forms.

Adaptive Preferences

Individual desires are shaped by past experiences and expectations about the future. If individuals learn from an early age that marketable commodities provide the most accessible sources of satisfaction, their preferences adapt to focus on commodities instead of nonmarketable pleasures such as artistic expression, friendship, learning, enjoyment of nature, or community involvement (Elster 1983). Advertising and other forms of marketing add to the pressure to focus on consumption as the most reliable route to happiness.

The capacity to think about and plan for the future is usually considered a hallmark of maturity. However, the market impedes long-term thinking as sellers push commodities with the promise of immediate gratification. As a result, individuals devote less time to the more difficult tasks of broadening their skills, knowledge, and capacities. From the perspective of sellers, the ideal consumer is childlike—impulsive, easily manipulated, and unwilling to delay gratification.

Restricted Development of Skills and Knowledge

Competitive markets create pressures on firms to minimize costs through specialization of labor. Specialization may promote human development for those engaged in technically and intellectually challenging occupations. However, for many workers, specialization leads to monotony, boredom, and a limited set of skills. Adam Smith expressed concern that the repetitive nature of specialized labor would make workers "as stupid and ignorant as it is possible for a human creature to become" (Smith [1776] 1937, 734).

Decline of Virtue

A virtuous person behaves in accordance with moral principles. Philosophers and theologians have long struggled to define the principles of morality, but they are unanimous in concluding that moral behavior sometimes conflicts with the pursuit of self-interest. Yet the market creates strong pressures on participants to engage in acquisitive, selfish behavior. In an attempt to reconcile the conflict between morality and self-interest, modern societies have implicitly developed two different ethical systems—one for the market and one for the community. In the market, the pursuit of self-interest is lauded as the wellspring of prosperity, and individuals are rewarded for this behavior with high incomes. In contrast, communities often view the same behavior as antisocial and potentially destructive.

Because self-interest is such a powerful motivation, economic behavior has gradually spread from the market to the polity and civil society. As a result, virtues such as kindness, honesty, trustworthiness, loyalty, and generosity are threatened as humans bend the rules and cut corners to gain a competitive advantage. The decline of virtue degrades not only community life but the functioning of the market itself, which relies on the moral integrity of participants. Intense competition may weaken social bonds, causing alienation, apathy, and self-destructive behavior. These psychological conditions often manifest themselves in lower productivity, crime, and substance abuse, all of which detract from the efficiency of markets as well as undermining communities and states.

Erosion of Democracy

Although both capitalism and democracy give consumers and citizens a voice in shaping their lives, an irresolvable tension exists between the two. In capitalism, individuals' influence over the market is proportional to their wealth, whereas in democracy, each person has one vote of equal weight. The conflict between capitalism and democracy explains the resistance among capitalists and aristocrats in the nineteenth century to extending the right to vote. The upper classes feared that majority rule would result in public policies designed to redistribute wealth. To prevent this outcome, powerful individuals and groups intervene in the democratic political process to protect and advance their private interests. This penetration of economic interests into government threatens democracy in the following ways:

Rent Seeking

In economic theory, rent is any income in excess of what a resource could earn in a perfectly competitive market. Businesses, labor unions, and other interest groups engage in continual efforts to gain rent by suppressing competition either through their own market power or by enlisting the support of government through lobbying, campaign contributions, and promises of future jobs to politicians and bureaucrats. In some cases, rent seeking is so successful that a government agency is effectively "captured" by the very groups it is supposed to regulate. At that point, lobbyists may actually write the legislation submitted for approval by politicians.

Political Entrepreneurs

As money becomes increasingly important in politics, economic behavior extends into the political arena. Like business owners, many politicians now behave as entrepreneurs, favoring policies they believe will maximize votes and campaign contributions to ensure their reelection. Political entrepreneurs tend to ignore the concerns of groups with low income or low voter turnout in the same way that businesses are not interested in consumers who cannot afford their product. Moreover, just as businesses tend to focus on short-term profitability, political entrepreneurs exhibit **rational myopia**. To win reelection, they favor policies delivering immediate results and requiring few sacrifices. Rational myopia explains the growth of national debt as politicians authorize spending for more government benefits without corresponding increases in taxes.

Rational Ignorance

A healthy democracy requires that citizens actively engage in the political process. However, *homo economicus* may not vote because the costs of becoming well-informed about public affairs and going to the voting booth outweigh the negligible possible benefit that a single vote will affect the outcome of an election. This **rational ignorance** is a symptom of economic behavior spreading into the polity. Participation in politics declines, and democracy is weakened.

CONCLUSION

The market is an admirable yet flawed institution. Its strengths are sufficiently appealing that it will most certainly remain a primary governance structure of modern economic systems. However, the market's shortcomings require an array of noneconomic institutions to support, supplement, and constrain its operation. From the Great Depression in the 1930s until about 1980, conventional wisdom among economists, political leaders, and the general public favored a "mixed economy" in which government played an active role in improving the performance of the market. Yet the elections of Ronald Reagan in the United States and Margaret Thatcher in Britain marked the rise of a new "market fundamentalism" that defended markets as fully capable of organizing and coordinating economic activity with little reliance on government other than the provision of national defense and a legal system to protect property rights and enforce contracts.

The intellectual roots of market fundamentalism (also called neoliberalism, **libertarianism**, or free-market conservatism) date back to the classical economics of the early nineteenth century, but recent versions rely most prominently on the works of Friedrich Hayek (1899–1992) and Milton Friedman (1912–2006) (Friedman [1962] 2002; Hayek [1944] 2007). These economists vehemently defended free markets as essential to promoting prosperity and protecting individual freedom. They viewed efforts by government to pursue other goals such as justice, stability, peace, sustainability, human development, and democracy as potential threats to both prosperity and freedom.

The proponents of market fundamentalism imagine that the free market is a natural, self-regulating state of affairs that would spontaneously emerge if government ended its interference. However, the market cannot provide the basis for its own existence. A market-centered economic system appeared only after states made conscious efforts to create institutions that would foster production, trade, innovation, and the accumulation of capital. Far from being a natural outgrowth of the individual pursuit of self-interest, the market is a politically, socially, and culturally constructed phenomenon consisting of myriad formal and informal institutions determining rights and obligations, barriers and opportunities, and the distribution of power.

Even if a free market could form, it would fail to sustain itself. Competition creates pressures on firms to reduce production costs by developing more capital-intensive technology. But the large-scale operations associated with capital-intensive technology result in economies of scale, which in turn create barriers to entry and diminish competition. With weak competition, the market loses its ability to coordinate production and guide the pursuit of self-interest into socially beneficial channels.

The pursuit of self-interest in the absence of political and social constraints would lead to chaos. *Homo economicus* is an opportunistic creature who will take advantage of others whenever the benefits outweigh the costs. Cheating, deception, dishonesty, and other forms of sociopathic behavior would become widespread as individuals with more wealth, power, information, and guile routinely take advantage of less fortunate members of society. The resulting loss of social cohesion would undermine the trust essential to market transactions.

Finally, a free market would fail because human behavior is not entirely individualistic. Humans are also social creatures with the capacity to form organizations based on shared interests. This ability to cooperate can be channeled through the political system to create institutions that constrain the market to promote the public interest, but it can also magnify the weaknesses of the market. When individuals form private groups in order to gain increased power to more effectively pursue their self-interest, they often engage in self-aggrandizing, antisocial behavior designed to suppress competition and take advantage of weaker groups. Only laws and regulations prevent these interest groups from manipulating the market for their own purposes. Participants in a free market would resemble the groups who currently operate outside the law such as mafias, gangs, drug cartels, and Russian-type oligarchs.

Ironically, market fundamentalism poses a threat to markets and capitalism. By attempting to eliminate most of the political institutions that support and constrain the market, fundamentalism would reveal the shortcomings of markets and thereby undermine their legitimacy. In this respect, market fundamentalism bears some resemblance to the crude Marxism adopted by the former Soviet Union. Both seek to impose a pure ideological vision on real-world economic systems. Just as the Soviet Union destroyed the legitimacy of communism, free markets could easily turn public opinion against capitalism. Both the unregulated market and the nondemocratic state are forms of totalitarianism subjecting society to a single governance structure.

Market fundamentalism appeals to the simplistic belief that all problems in modern economic systems are caused by government and that nations could return to an earlier era of traditional values, good jobs, and secure incomes by minimizing the role of government. But market fundamentalism represents more than just a harmless exercise in nostalgia. By denying the flaws of the market, proponents of market fundamentalism impede the development of institutions for coping with those shortcomings. Acknowledging the market's limitations is a prerequisite to improving its performance.

REFERENCES

Berlin, Isaiah. 1969. *Four Essays on Liberty.* Oxford: Oxford University Press.

Coase, Ronald. 1960. "The Problem of Social Cost." *The Journal of Law and Economics* 3:1–44.

Elster, Jon. 1983. *Sour Grapes: Studies in the Subversion of Rationality.* New York: Cambridge University Press.

Friedman, Milton. (1962) 2002. *Capitalism and Freedom.* Chicago: University of Chicago Press.

Hayek, Friedrich. (1944) 2007. *The Road to Serfdom.* Chicago: University of Chicago Press.

_____. 1945. "The Use of Knowledge in Society." *American Economic Review* 35(4): 519–530.

Hirschman, Albert O. 1970. *Exit, Voice, and Loyalty.* Cambridge, MA: Harvard University Press.

_____. 1977. *The Passions and the Interests.* Princeton, NJ: Princeton University Press.

Klein, Naomi. 2014. *This Changes Everything: Capitalism and the Climate.* New York: Simon & Schuster.

Kuznets, Simon. 1955. "Economic Growth and Income Inequality." *American Economic Review* 45 (March): 1–28.

Mokyr, Joel. 2012. *The Enlightened Economy: An Economic History of Britain 1700–1850.* New Haven, CT: Yale University Press.

Nozick, Robert. 1974. *Anarchy, State, and Utopia.* New York: Basic Books.

Piketty, Thomas. 2014. *Capital in the Twenty-First Century.* Cambridge, MA: Harvard University Press.

Posner, Richard A. 2009. *A Failure of Capitalism.* Cambridge, MA: Harvard University Press.

Rajan, Raghuram G. 2010. *Fault Lines: How Hidden Fractures Still Threaten the World Economy.* Princeton, NJ: Princeton University Press.

Rawls, John. 1971. *A Theory of Justice.* Cambridge, MA: Harvard University Press.

Smith, Adam. (1776) 1937. *An Inquiry into the Nature and Causes of the Wealth of Nations.* New York: Modern Library.

Stiglitz, Joseph. 2013. *The Price of Inequality: How Today's Divided Society Endangers Our Future.* New York: W. W. Norton.

Tawney, R. H. (1926) 2015. *Religion and the Rise of Capitalism.* London: Verso.

Weber, Max. (1905) 2001. *The Protestant Ethic and the Spirit of Capitalism*, 2nd ed. London: Routledge.

ADDITIONAL READING

Appleby, Joyce. *The Relentless Revolution: A History of Capitalism.* New York: W. W. Norton, 2010.

Blyth, Mark. *Austerity: The History of a Dangerous Idea.* New York: Oxford University Press, 2013.

Brennen, Jason. *Why Not Capitalism?* New York: Routledge, 2014.

Cassidy, John. *How Markets Fail: The Logic of Economic Calamities.* New York: Farrar, Straus and Giroux, 2012.

Coates, David. *Models of Capitalism: Growth and Stagnation in the Modern Era.* London: Polity, 2000.

Crouch, Colin. *Capitalist Diversity and Change: Recombinant Governance and Institutional Entrepreneurs.* New York: Oxford University Press, 2005.

Herzog, Lisa. *Inventing the Market: Smith, Hegel, and Political Theory.* New York: Oxford University Press, 2013.

Kuttner, Robert. *Everything for Sale: The Virtues and Limitations of Markets.* New York: Alfred A. Knopf, 1997.

Leeson, Peter T. *Anarchy Unbound: Why Self-Governance Works Better Than You Think.* New York: Cambridge University Press, 2014.

Lindblom, Charles E. *The Market System: What It Is, How It Works, and What to Make of It.* New Haven, CT: Yale University Press, 2001.

MacMillan, John. *Reinventing the Bazaar: A Natural History of Markets.* New York: W. W. Norton, 2002.

McCraw, Thomas K. *Creating Modern Capitalism.* Cambridge, MA: Harvard University Press, 1998.

Nooteboom, Bart. *How Markets Work and Fail, and What to Make of Them.* Northampton, MA: Edward Elgar, 2014.

Pryor, Frederic L. *Capitalism Reassessed.* New York: Cambridge University Press, 2010.

Scott, Bruce R. *Capitalism: Its Origins and Evolution as a System of Governance.* New York: Springer, 2011.

Sandel, Michael J. *What Money Can't Buy: The Moral Limits of Markets.* New York: Farrar, Straus and Giroux, 2012.

Satz, Debra. *Why Some Things Should Not Be for Sale: The Moral Limits of Markets.* New York: Oxford University Press, 2010.

Schmookler, Andrew B. *The Illusion of Choice: How the Market Economy Shapes Our Destiny.* Ithaca: State University of New York Press, 1993.

Schwartz, Barry. *The Costs of Living: How Market Freedom Erodes the Best Things in Life.* New York: W. W. Norton, 1994.

Slater, Don, and Fran Tonkiss. *Market Society: Markets and Modern Social Theory.* Malden, MA: Polity, 2001.

Spies-Butcher, Benjamin, Joy Paton, and Damien Cahill. *Market Society: History, Theory, Practice.* New York: Cambridge University Press, 2012.

Swanson, Paul. *An Introduction to Capitalism.* New York: Routledge, 2012.

Vogel, Steven K. *Free Markets, More Rules: Regulatory Reform in Advanced Industrial Countries.* Ithaca, NY: Cornell University Press, 1996.

Chapter 4

STATE-CENTERED ECONOMIC SYSTEMS

"Government should do for people only what they cannot do better by themselves, and no more."

ABRAHAM LINCOLN (1809–1865),
President of the United States

Of the four types of states described in Chapter Two, **predatory states** and **developmental states** are most relevant in understanding the functioning of economic systems. Failed states are found only in developing nations lacking successful economic systems, and night-watchman states do not exist. Predatory states function as legalized mafias, using the coercive power of government to extract surplus from citizens. This extortion may be perfectly legal because the state makes the laws, and any dissent may trigger even greater oppression as the state redoubles efforts to secure its power. The extracted surplus accrues to state officials and their allies in the private sector who may use part of it for productive investments in **infrastructure**—but only to the extent that a viable economy is necessary to continue the extraction of surplus in the future.

STATES AND ECONOMIC SYSTEMS

Developmental states and predatory states share several common features. Both function through the exercise of power by a relatively small group of rulers. Although democratic states have elected rulers, the power of a democratic state rests on its ability to defeat groups challenging its authority outside the electoral process. Both predatory and developmental states also rely on mandatory taxation to commandeer part of the surplus created by economic activity. Both possess a monopoly on the legitimate use of coercion and violence. These shared characteristics arise because a fundamental purpose of states is to prevent self-interested individuals from making choices that harm others (e.g., robbing banks, polluting the environment, or ignoring stop signs). States also exist to enable citizens to achieve goals that cannot be pursued through the market due to **collective action problems**. Mandatory taxation, laws, and regulations secure compliance with institutions designed to promote the public interest as determined through the democratic political process.

Despite similarities in the structure and functioning of predatory and developmental states, the differences between them are significant. Predatory states are open to manipulation by private groups seeking to use the power of government to advance their own narrow interests. Bribery and other forms of corruption proliferate as state officials enrich themselves by granting favors to special interest groups. In contrast, developmental states are ideally staffed by competent politicians and bureaucrats whose primary motivation is promoting the public interest (Evans 1995).

A developmental state is a strong state in two senses. First, it has the power and financial means to carry out its positive role in promoting economic development. Second, it has sufficient autonomy to resist efforts by interest groups to gain benefits through the political process that do not serve the public interest. A failed state violates the first condition, and a predatory state does not meet the second one. A developmental state may be smaller in size and scope than a predatory state because the latter is pulled in many directions by conflicting interest groups, and as a result, it has difficulty in establishing priorities and setting goals.

What determines whether a state will be predatory or developmental? The following factors are relevant in explaining the performance of governments in different nations.

Culture
A nation's **culture** plays a significant role in determining the quality of its political governance. For example, both Germany and the United States endured the Great Depression, but Germany turned to total government control and planning of the economy whereas the United States simply expanded government regulation of business activity. These different responses reflected the fact that US culture is highly individualistic, making Americans resistant to excessive government authority.

Constitution
A constitution establishes the rules by which all other laws and political procedures are formed. A constitution determines the division of authority between various branches and levels of government, and thereby places limits on the exercise of power. A predatory government may attempt to change the constitution for its own advantage, but most constitutions are written in a manner that makes revisions difficult.

Distribution of Power
Nations with greater inequality in the distribution of power are more likely to have predatory states. Power arises from either wealth or political influence, each of which supports the other. Wealth buys political influence, and political influence attracts wealth. Predatory states thrive on economic inequality and restricted democracy.

Quality of Leadership
Predatory states can be self-perpetuating because the opportunities for personal power and enrichment attract corrupt politicians. Once in power, politicians are

able to appoint judges, control the media, and use the military and police to secure their privileges. In contrast, most politicians in developmental states simply fill a role in the vast machinery of government. However, an economic crisis may create an opportunity for a visionary leader to change the role of the state in a manner that improves the economic system.

Quality of Democracy

Democracy comes in many forms. Predatory states are more likely to arise when citizens are apathetic, voting is restricted, politicians are underpaid, election campaigns are very expensive, private campaign contributions are unrestricted, and the political process lacks transparency and accountability.

STATE-CENTERED ECONOMIC SYSTEMS IN HISTORY

Early Empires

The origins of states can be traced back to the transition from nomadic hunting/gathering tribes to stationary communities. Technological improvements in agriculture and animal husbandry resulted in longer life spans, growing populations, and the ability of farmers to produce more food than they consumed. This surplus food encouraged a division of labor in which some individuals became specialized artisans and craftsmen.

The development of a surplus was a mixed blessing. On one hand, survival became less tenuous, and humans could settle in one location, build homes, cultivate land, and breed domestic animals. On the other hand, the existence of a surplus created conflict both within and between communities. Once communities could produce more than they consumed, they needed rules about who would control the surplus. As reliance on communal sharing was gradually replaced by family ownership of property, disputes inevitably arose over conflicting claims to property. Who would get to use the most fertile land, fish in the best spots, or gather fruit and berries from trees and bushes? Communities needed political institutions to settle disputes and maintain social order.

The first informal states were established by tribal elders to provide guidelines for reducing conflict over property rights. Conflicts within communities were relatively minor because members were bound together by shared traditions and values that facilitated the resolution of disputes. However, these social bonds were less reliable between communities, causing disputes to often escalate into violence. Communities were vulnerable to aggression by other communities for whom plunder was easier than producing for themselves. Out of this continuing violence emerged the earliest formal states (Finer 1999).

The circumstances differed in various parts of the world, but by 6000 BCE, states existed in the Middle East. States formed when one community gained the upper hand in conflict with other communities and used the threat of further violence to consolidate its rule over an extended area. The conquered communities often acquiesced to the state to gain security from violence, and if states were well-governed, the lives of their subjects actually improved. By uniting many smaller communities into a single political entity, states widened markets by creating opportunities for trade across regions. The widening of the market raised productivity by fostering **economies of scale** and increased specialization of labor.

These Middle Eastern states slowly evolved into empires (e.g., Egyptian, Akkadian, Assyrian, and Babylonian) beginning around 3000 BCE. Other empires arose throughout the world, and a major factor in determining their longevity was the quality of governance. The Egyptian empire lasted until 30 BCE when it fell to the Roman Empire. The Chinese empire lasted from 221 BCE to 1912 CE. The Mayan empire endured for eleven centuries before collapsing from environmental degradation around 900 CE. In contrast, the Aztec and Inca empires lasted only a hundred years before being vanquished by Spanish conquistadors in the early sixteenth century.

Those empires functioning as developmental states used their power to coordinate production and enlarge the economic surplus. They kept the cost of sustaining the labor force low by relying on either slave labor or coercion of indigenous people. Developmental empires raised labor productivity by devoting resources to **public goods** such as roads, canals, bridges, irrigation systems, common currencies, codified legal systems, scientific research, exploration, and artistic creations that served to unify the populace with a common cultural heritage. Rising productivity led to larger surpluses with which to promote further economic development. The more successful an empire became in increasing standards of living for its subjects, the fewer resources were needed for nonproductive functions such as suppressing dissent and legitimizing power.

In contrast, the leaders of predatory empires focused less on promoting economic development and more on using the surplus to maintain power through political, military, and religious control of the populace. Large standing armies protected against invasions and engaged in domestic policing. Rulers enjoyed lavish lifestyles and legitimized state power through religious rituals and the construction of pyramids, temples, palaces, and other monuments to glorify the state and its rulers. Over the span of many centuries, those empires failing to use the surplus for productivity-enhancing infrastructure tended to decay and disappear. Slow growth meant a smaller surplus for the state to extract, which, in turn, reduced its ability to suppress internal conflict and to protect its members from attacks by rival empires.

Mercantilism

The collapse of the Western Roman Empire in 476 CE left a political vacuum in Europe. The next three centuries, referred to as the Dark Ages, were characterized by a virtual absence of a functioning economic system as roving tribes (e.g., Goths, Vandals, Saxons, Angles, Franks, Huns, and Slavs) violently struggled to claim **sovereignty** over territories. With little significant trade, technological innovation, or division of labor, looting and conquest of other tribes was often the only alternative to subsistence living.

Efforts to reestablish a state-centered economic system led to the founding of the Holy Roman Empire in 800 CE, but the combination of a stagnant economy and the rulers' lack of power meant that a centralized state was unable to extract sufficient surplus to govern effectively. Instead, a community-centered economic system called feudalism prevailed in Europe for the next seven centuries. Beginning in the twelfth and thirteenth centuries, rudimentary states formed within feudalism as rulers gained dominance over particular territories, but these states were small and weak, leading to constant violence among them. Any state not actively expanding its territory was likely to be invaded by a more aggressive neighboring state.

This conflict proved to be beneficial for economic development because success in warfare required states to gain control over resources by extracting a large surplus from the economic activity within its territory. In other words, military competition between states forced rulers to create favorable conditions for production, trade, and innovation. Those states capable of fostering production of the largest surplus and using it to successfully wage war survived while less productive states were vanquished (Tilly 1990).

By the seventeenth century, the need for funds to sustain military conquests grew so intense that some states engaged in arbitrary taxation and outright confiscation of the surplus. Monarchs relied on the aristocracy as their base of political support; therefore, they preferred to extract wealth from the rising class of merchants. Resistance to arbitrary taxation and other abuses by government led to the 1649 beheading of King Charles I in England. Gradually, monarchs realized that they needed to form an alliance with merchants in order to gain political and financial support. A new economic system called **mercantilism** served this purpose.

The leading practitioners of mercantilism were Britain, France, the Netherlands, Spain, and Portugal. The system was based on creating a harmony of interests between the state and merchants. Merchants paid taxes to fund the state, and the state used its military and political power to promote business interests both at home and abroad. Domestically, mercantilist states protected merchants and manufacturers with extensive regulations designed to suppress competition. This supervision by government ensured higher profits for businesses, thereby enlarging the surplus available to the state through taxation.

To increase foreign trade, mercantilist states used their military power to establish colonial empires serving as both sources of raw materials and markets for manufactured goods. States also enacted policies to restrict imports and promote exports. For example, British colonies were not permitted to produce manufactured goods that would compete with domestic British products. To keep prices of British imports low, colonies were barred from selling goods to any country except Britain. To keep the prices of British exports as high as possible, colonies were required to buy manufactured goods only from Britain. Colonies were also subject to arbitrary taxation since they had no representation in the British parliament. The American Revolution of 1776 was, in large part, a reaction to British mercantilism.

The British state also regulated international competition by issuing Crown Charters. The monarch would grant a single company the exclusive right to trade in a particular part of the world. The East India Company, for example, had a virtual monopoly on trade between Britain and India, and the Hudson Bay Company dominated trade between Britain and Canada. The British resorted to extreme measures to maintain the **competitive advantage** of their merchants and manufacturers. To eliminate competition with domestic textile manufacturers, the British severed the thumbs of hand weavers in India and smashed their looms. Exporting a highly valued breed of sheep from Britain was punishable by death.

Proponents of mercantilism believed that maximizing the value of exports and minimizing the value of imports were essential to increasing a nation's wealth. At that time, **trade deficits** were settled by shipping gold from one country to another, so a nation with a consistent **trade surplus** gained a steady inflow of gold. The attraction of gold lay in its function as a universal means of exchange. If a state needed to maintain military bases abroad or to engage in war, gold quickly secured the needed resources anywhere in the world.

In his 1776 book, *The Wealth of Nations*, Adam Smith presented a strong critique of mercantilism. He argued that government intervention in the economy benefited merchants and manufacturers at the expense of the general public. Nations would prosper if government simply allowed markets to operate freely. His message found a receptive audience. Britain was just entering the Industrial Revolution, and new entrepreneurs tended to oppose mercantilism for a variety of reasons. First, many of them belonged to nonconformist religious groups such as Quakers and Unitarians who opposed government authority in principle. Second, because many of the new technologies associated with the Industrial Revolution existed only in Britain, entrepreneurs were confident in their ability to succeed without state protection. Third, the prosperity accompanying the Industrial Revolution attracted many foreign merchants, manufacturers, and bankers to Britain, and they resisted mercantilist restrictions on the flow of goods and money across borders. Finally, mercantilist **tariffs** on imported grain were unpopular with business owners because higher food prices necessitated higher wages.

Despite extensive interference with markets, mercantilism served as an essential phase in setting the stage for the emergence of **capitalism**. Without regulation of manufacturing and commerce, the risks facing early investors and entrepreneurs would have been sufficiently daunting to prevent or at least delay the full development of markets. In addition to defining and protecting property rights, mercantilist states unified fragmented markets by abolishing local barriers to trade, subsidizing shipbuilding, financing exploration, maintaining armies and navies, enforcing laws and contracts, promoting standardization of weights and measures, and generally creating a sheltered environment of reduced risk to encourage business investment. Even the obsession with accumulating gold served the purpose of expanding the money supply, keeping interest rates low, and generating mild **inflation** that benefited businesses by enabling them to sell their products at higher prices. Mercantilist states also fostered a sense of national unity, which promoted commerce by creating trust and a shared culture among citizens.

In Britain, the mercantilist state went even further by intentionally promoting the development of national markets for labor, land, and money. These markets were essential for entrepreneurs needing access to resources. Britain was the nation in which mercantilism was practiced most extensively, and it was the first nation to develop a capitalist economy. The mercantilist state, far from being an impediment to commerce, was instrumental in creating capitalism (Polanyi 1944; Epstein 2000).

Fascism and Communism

Fascism and **communism** share so many characteristics that some observers view them as two versions of the same economic system. However, they are fundamentally different, and their advocates have always been bitter enemies. The two systems share the following characteristics:

- Both arose in reaction to the social disruption wrought by capitalism during the nineteenth and early twentieth centuries.
- Both oppose capitalism and markets for breeding class conflict, exploitation, and alienation.
- Both oppose democratic states as weak and incapable of forging powerful, unified nations.
- Both replace markets with government planning of the economy.
- Both are totalitarian, meaning that a single political party uses coercion and violence to eliminate opposition parties and any other private organizations that might challenge the dominance of the state.
- Both attempt to mobilize all citizens to work under the direction of the state toward a common goal of national power and economic growth.
- Both suppress individualism and self-interest by demanding ideological purity and devotion to the state.
- Both motivate citizens through emotional appeals to patriotism, loyalty, and duty.
- Both blame "enemies of the people" for domestic problems and target those groups for violent suppression.

The fundamental difference between the two systems is that fascism defends private property, whereas communism seeks to abolish it. Government planning of the economy under fascism is accomplished through consultation between government bureaucrats and leading private industrialists. In communism, by contrast, a state planning agency, using input from the managers of state-owned enterprises, formulates a blueprint for the economy and transmits directives to the managers who receive bonuses for meeting or exceeding production quotas.

Fascism and communism also differ on social and cultural issues. Fascists often defend the genetic superiority of certain racial or ethnic groups and therefore oppose egalitarian social policies. Members of inferior groups may face extermination. Fascists have experimented with eugenics, the practice of controlling human reproduction by encouraging members of superior groups to have children while members of inferior groups may be sterilized or forced to abort pregnancies. In contrast, communists defend "international working class solidarity" and the "brotherhood of mankind." Social benefits in communist countries are, in principle at least, universally available without regard to race or ethnicity.

Both fascist and communist nations have demonstrated a proclivity for war, **imperialism**, and genocide. This fact raises an interesting question—could a peaceful, nonexpansionist fascist or communist nation exist? The historical record would indicate a negative answer for the following reason. Every nation depends on resources from outside its borders. Because both fascist and communist nations reject markets, they seek to secure access to foreign resources through domination and control rather than trade. This quest for new territory often leads to war.

Fascism first appeared in Italy after World War I under the leadership of Benito Mussolini (1883–1945). Subsequently, both Germany and Japan embraced fascism (called Nazism in Germany) and joined with Italy to form the Axis alliance in an attempt to conquer the Eurasian land mass during World War II. The term *fascism* derives from a weapon called a *fasces* carried at the front of the Roman army as it marched to war. Consisting of a tightly-bound bundle of rods with an attached axe blade, the *fasces* was purely symbolic. Each rod was fragile and easily broken, but the rods bound together became a powerful weapon. Extending the symbolism to society, each citizen, acting alone, is relatively powerless, but when all citizens unite to pursue collective goals, a nation becomes strong.

Milder versions of fascism appeared in Portugal under Antonio Salazar between 1933 and 1968, in Spain under Francisco Franco between 1936 and 1975, in Brazil under Getúlio Vargas between 1937 and 1945, and in Argentina under Juan Perón between 1946 and 1955. More recently, fascist ideology has reappeared in the Ba'ath Party in the Middle East, as exemplified by the rule of Saddam Hussein in Iraq from 1979 to 2003 and Hafez al-Assad and his son Bashar al-Assad in Syria from 1971 to the present. Fascism has experienced a mild resurgence in Western nations as groups representing the extreme right of the political spectrum (often called "neo-Nazis") blame their country's problems on immigration, Jews, and other minorities. Most prominent among these groups are the National Front in France, the Ku Klux Klan in the United States, and Golden Dawn in Greece.

Communism materialized for the first time with the Bolshevik revolution in Russia in 1917. At the end of World War II, the Soviet Union occupied much of Eastern Europe and created satellite states in Poland, Hungary, East Germany, Czechoslovakia, Romania, Bulgaria, Albania, and Yugoslavia. Some of these states closely resembled the Soviet Union, but others, such as Hungary, Czechoslovakia, and Yugoslavia managed to maintain a degree of independence and developed economic systems in which markets played a significant role. China became communist in 1949 and sought to promote communism in Korea, Vietnam, Laos, and Cambodia. Cuba had a communist revolution in 1959 under the leadership of Fidel Castro. Today, communism has virtually disappeared, with North Korea being the primary surviving example.

Socialism

Socialism lacks a clear definition. Karl Marx (1818–1883) envisioned socialism as the transitional stage between capitalism and communism in which the state owns and controls the means of production. Marx believed that socialism would necessarily exist for decades if not longer before achieving the industrial base and human development required for communism. In communism, the state would "wither away" and the economy would be coordinated by the "associated producers." Accepting Marx's taxonomy would imply that communism has never existed and that China, the Soviet Union, and its Eastern European satellite states were actually socialist.

The term *socialism* is also used to describe any nation with an extensive welfare system and government intervention in the economy. By this definition, most of Europe is socialist, and, if conservative critics are to be believed, the United States is well on its way to becoming socialist. However, neither of these definitions is very useful in distinguishing socialism from either communism or capitalism.

Socialism is difficult to conceptualize because many different models of socialism have been developed. These idealized models typically include full democracy, civil rights, a degree of economic security for all citizens, and extensive government efforts to correct the shortcomings of the market. However, beyond those commonalities, differences emerge concerning the extent of private versus public ownership of the means of production, the extent to which planning supersedes markets, and the degree to which economic equality is pursued.

No existing capitalist system is pure in the sense of relying exclusively on private property and markets, so every capitalist system contains elements of socialism. In the United States, for example, a large portion of the land as well as most of the transportation infrastructure is owned by federal and state governments. But at what point in moving toward public property and government control of the economy does capitalism become socialism, and what distinguishes socialism from communism? Consider the diagram in Figure 4.1, Classification of Economic Systems.

Capitalism is located in the upper right quadrant, indicating that private property is prevalent and the market functions as the primary mechanism for coordinating production. Communism appears in the lower left quadrant, where planning replaces markets to coordinate production and private ownership of

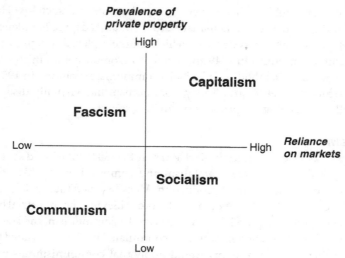

*Prevalence of
private property*

High

Capitalism

Fascism

Low ——————————————————————— High   *Reliance
on markets*

Socialism

Communism

Low

Figure 4.1 Classification of Economic Systems.

property is minimal. Fascism, in the upper-left quadrant and situated above and slightly to the right of communism, is based on a high prevalence of private property and greater reliance on markets than communism. Socialism, in the lower-right quadrant, appears below and slightly to the left of capitalism, indicating less reliance on markets and lower prevalence of private property than capitalism.

Socialism occupies a middle ground between capitalism and communism in which private property and markets coexist with public property and planning. This conception of socialism implies that Western European nations are not socialist. Nearly all businesses in those nations remain privately owned, and governments are ultimately subordinate to market forces as they struggle to comply with the competitive pressures imposed by international trade and capital flows.

Unlike communism, socialism taps into the human energies associated with the individual pursuit of self-interest and democratic political rights. Markets and private property are encouraged to the extent that they promote social goals such as prosperity, democracy, and justice. Democratic socialists seek a viable balance between market and plan, private and public property rights, and economic equality and material incentives.

Attempts at socialism have failed, most notably in the Eastern European nations of Yugoslavia, Hungary, and Czechoslovakia prior to the breakup of the Soviet Union. Other European nations such as France and Sweden made significant movements in the direction of socialism, only to retreat in response to the displeasure of international investors and currency speculators. Indeed, globalization has created seemingly insurmountable obstacles to socialism. A state may succeed in gaining dominance over its domestic markets, but without controlling international flows of capital and commodities, the state's power remains subordinate to market forces.

POTENTIAL STRENGTHS OF THE STATE

Prosperity

States perform a variety of functions contributing to the efficiency and growth of the economy.

Providing Infrastructure

Infrastructure is the array of public goods forming a supportive framework for all economic activity. Some infrastructure takes the form of **physical capital**, including transportation systems (e.g., highways, harbors, bridges, tunnels, seaports, airports, and mass transit systems), water management systems (e.g., dams, canals, irrigation systems, water treatment plants, and sewage systems), energy and communication systems, and the buildings and equipment devoted to public services such as education, law enforcement, and fire protection. Infrastructure also includes public institutions that increase overall productivity such as education, job training programs, the legal system, well-defined property rights, a stable currency, agricultural extension programs, and publicly funded healthcare and research. Without public investments in developing physical capital, **human capital**, **social capital**, and **cultural capital**, private businesses and investors would be unable to effectively accumulate **financial capital**.

Correcting Externalities

The market is inefficient whenever the actions of one person or business generate either costs or benefits for others that are not reflected in market prices. States can correct **externalities** by taxing activities generating negative externalities and subsidizing activities with positive externalities. Externalities can also be corrected through regulations that prohibit or mandate certain activities such as polluting or getting vaccinated. Finally, because externalities arise due to missing markets, the state can correct externalities by creating a market. For example, pollution can be controlled through a "cap-and-trade" system whereby the government sells licenses to emit a limited amount of pollution.

Providing Information

The state can improve the efficiency of markets by providing participants with more information than they might gather as individuals. Truth-in-advertising laws limit the dissemination of false information. Product-labeling laws compel manufacturers to reveal information about ingredients and potential risks. Financial disclosure laws require corporations to publicize their financial statements so that potential investors can make informed decisions.

Maintaining Competition

States use antitrust policy (also called competition policy) to prohibit business strategies such as **interlocking directorates**, **predatory pricing**, explicit collusion, and **mergers** and acquisitions that significantly reduce competition in an industry. Competition can also be improved by lowering **barriers to entry** to increase the mobility of resources. For example, a state might exempt small businesses from certain regulations or provide loans and counseling services to new entrepreneurs.

Reducing Transaction Costs

Transaction costs are the costs of making transactions in addition to the direct cost of producing a good or service. Examples of transaction costs include the cost of gathering information prior to a purchase, the costs of negotiating the terms of the exchange, and the costs of drawing up and enforcing contracts. States reduce transaction costs and therefore facilitate exchanges by providing information about products, enacting consumer protection laws, and providing a legal system to enforce contracts and settle disputes over the terms of contracts. Finally, states lower transaction costs by creating a sense of national unity and identity that fosters trust in fellow citizens.

Creating Comparative Advantage

Comparative advantage is the ability of one person, region, or nation to produce a good relatively more efficiently than elsewhere. A nation with comparative advantage in a particular industry will tend to specialize in and gain dominance over that industry. Comparative advantage depends partly on resource endowments (e.g., deposits of minerals and ores, climate, and quality of soil), but the state can create comparative advantage by, for example, funding education and training programs, research and development, and transportation and communication systems.

Redirecting the Surplus

To promote growth, businesses should reinvest their profits in expanding productive capacity and improving technology. However, businesses may also overinvest, resulting in excess capacity that sits idle. Alternatively, profits can be used for consumption, for speculative purchases of assets such as land, houses, art, gold and collectibles, or simply hoarded. Through taxation of profits and high incomes or through borrowing by selling bonds, the state may divert part of the surplus for more productive uses such as public investment in infrastructure.

Freedom and Justice

The state promotes **negative freedom** by protecting citizens from violations of their property, civil, and human rights. However, the state is even better suited to promoting **positive freedom** by opening opportunities through provision of infrastructure such as education, roads, energy grids, and clean water. The state's efforts to expand freedom, which usually promote justice as well, include the following:

Solving Collective Action Problems

Some goods desired by citizens cannot be provided by the market due to collective action problems. These problems arise when individuals pursuing their self-interest create results that none of them wanted. A better outcome could be achieved by cooperating to act collectively, and the state provides an arena in which collective action is possible. Public goods and externalities exemplify collective action problems, and many other situations fit the definition. Consider the length of the workday. In the early years of capitalism, prior to government regulations, the typical workday lasted fourteen hours or longer. Employers had an obvious interest in a longer workday, and workers, given the choice between a long workday or unemployment, willingly worked for fourteen hours. However, the results of this individual pursuit of self-interest were undesirable for all concerned. Workers became so exhausted that their health suffered, their productivity declined, and their families were neglected. By shortening the legal workday, the state restricted the freedom of employers and workers to negotiate labor contracts, but this restriction actually enlarged the scope of freedom by allowing workers to pursue meaningful activities beyond the workplace and by shielding employers from the competitive pressure to minimize production costs by maximizing the number of hours worked regardless of the long-term consequences for workers.

The idea that narrowing the range of individual choice can expand freedom may seem contradictory, but think of the state as the conductor of a symphony orchestra. The conductor establishes rules governing the actions of the musicians, yet, by doing so, the musicians are able to create an experience for the audience that would be impossible without this discipline. The restrictions imposed by the conductor actually enhance the ability of the musicians to pursue their goal of musical excellence.

Protecting Civil Rights

The state expands freedom and justice by enforcing civil rights, including freedom of speech, freedom of the press, freedom of religion, and freedom from discrimination. Freedom from discrimination restricts the freedom of citizens to discriminate, but any civil right limits the freedom of others to violate that right.

Providing Merit Goods

Merit goods are those goods deemed to be so essential to human well-being that governments provide them to citizens regardless of ability to pay. Examples might include food, shelter, education, and healthcare. Merit goods may be justified either by calling them human rights or by appealing to the positive externalities created by reducing suffering and enlarging opportunity. The provision of merit goods by the state expands the freedom of recipients and achieves greater social justice. **Demerit goods**, on the other hand, are deemed to be so harmful that individual freedom and well-being are increased by banning them. Examples of demerit goods include harmful drugs, human trafficking, and child pornography. Individuals using these goods are often suffering from addiction or subject to coercion, so prohibition may actually increase freedom.

Promoting Equal Opportunity

If citizens are to be free to realize their full potential and to achieve success proportionate to their efforts and abilities, they need equal opportunity. Although equality of opportunity is often contrasted with equality of result, the two terms are inextricably linked. When the distribution of income and wealth becomes highly unequal, the resulting differences in children's schooling, home environment, or neighborhood violate equality of opportunity. The state can promote greater equality of opportunity by protecting civil rights and by providing merit goods. Another strategy for increasing equality of opportunity is to require preferential treatment (e.g., affirmative action policies) for previously disadvantaged groups. However, this approach raises concerns about the potential injustice of treating people unequally based on race, gender, or ethnicity.

Redistributing Income

To the extent that a market-determined distribution of income is so unequal as to be unjust, states promote justice by relying on progressive taxation that requires affluent households to pay higher tax rates. Income may also be redistributed in more subtle ways such as farm price supports, minimum wage laws, and rent control.

Restructuring the Market

Efforts by the state to expand freedom and justice through provision of merit goods, protection of civil rights, or redistribution of income sometimes encounter resistance from nonbeneficiaries who claim that their freedom is being violated. For example, as a result of civil rights laws, owners of restaurants and hotels are no longer free to discriminate in serving customers. Mandatory taxation causes some citizens to resent the use of government funds for purposes they find objectionable. This perception of diminished freedom can be reduced by restructuring markets rather than redistributing income. As an example, applying antitrust laws to maintain competition increases the chances for smaller firms to survive. Legalizing unions and collective bargaining expands the ability of workers to gain higher wages.

Stability

Before the Great Depression, states took little responsibility for maintaining stability in the economy. Most economists attributed **recession** and inflation to external factors such as gold discoveries or technological innovations over which the state had no control. However, the severity of the Great Depression, coupled with a new macroeconomic theory developed by British economist John Maynard Keynes (1883–1946), persuaded governments around the world to actively engage in efforts to maintain stable economic growth. A variety of policies have been used for this purpose.

Fiscal Policy

Fiscal policy is the use of government spending and taxation to change the level of economic activity. Keynes recommended more government spending and/or tax cuts during recessions to stimulate demand. On the other hand, if excess demand causes inflation, the appropriate fiscal policy consists of reduced government spending and/or increased taxes. A progressive income tax may also serve to minimize recessions by leaving more money in the hands of low-income households who will spend most or all of it.

Monetary Policy

Monetary policy, which is conducted by the central bank of a nation (e.g., the Federal Reserve System in the United States), entails reducing the money supply during inflation and increasing the money supply to prevent or recover from a recession. As the money supply changes, interest rates and borrowing usually change, and the level of economic activity rises or falls accordingly. Central banks change the money supply primarily by buying or selling previously-issued government bonds.

Financial Regulation

The financial sector of the economy, including banks and markets for financial assets such as stocks and bonds, experiences instability due to the powerful role of human expectations and emotions. For example, individuals do not buy additional vehicles because they expect General Motors to sell more cars, but they do buy more shares of General Motors stock based on that expectation. Waves of optimism and pessimism cause financial markets to swing wildly at times, and unstable financial markets may cause the entire economy to suffer. Governments attempt to stabilize financial markets by placing limits on bank lending, by requiring full disclosure of information about financial assets, and by creating agencies to monitor financial markets and punish lawbreakers.

Industrial Policy

Industrial policy is broadly defined as any effort by government to steer the economy toward specific goals. A comprehensive set of policies is designed to promote the development of certain targeted industries and thereby to promote more rapid growth for the economy as a whole. Japan and France are most often cited as practitioners of industrial policy. Their governments have engaged in economic planning and favored certain industries with subsidies, loans, and other incentives to expand.

Trade Policy

Government can affect the level of economic activity by changing the volume of exports and imports. **Trade policy** includes changing tariffs and quotas on imports, changing subsidies for exports, negotiating trade agreements with other countries (e.g., the North American Free Trade Agreement), and devaluing or revaluing the currency.

Peace

States promote peace between nations through diplomatic negotiations. Most nations have embassies throughout the world where diplomats communicate with their foreign counterparts to resolve conflicts before violence occurs. In addition, various international organizations such as the United Nations and the World Trade Organization function to maintain peaceful international relations. States also contribute to domestic tranquility by fostering a sense of shared identity which contributes to greater trust, unity, and social solidarity. Finally, by providing a legal system, states facilitate the resolution of conflict without resort to violence.

Sustainability

The state has an advantage over private firms in protecting the environment. Whereas any single business faces competitive pressures to minimize costs and therefore dispose of waste as inexpensively as possible, government has the capacity to consider the long-term effects of global climate change, acid rain, deforestation, destruction of the ozone layer, resource depletion, and pollution of air and water. States attempt to determine acceptable levels of pollution and then establish various incentives and disincentives to alter the private decisions of businesses and citizens. Three broad strategies enable the state to foster a more sustainable economic system.

Environmental Regulations

When concerns about the environment became a major public issue in the 1970s, governments initially responded by formulating standards for tolerable levels of air and water pollution. However, these regulations were criticized for being insensitive to differences in the cost of controlling pollution in various industries and for providing no incentive to reduce pollution beyond mandated levels.

Taxes and Subsidies

Instead of relying on environmental standards to control pollution, government can improve the quality of the environment by taxing polluting activity and subsidizing the development of "green" products and technologies. The use of taxes and subsidies simply changes incentives while leaving individuals and firms free to pursue their self-interest. Taxes can take the form of charges on emissions or effluent fees levied on the amount of pollution discharged into the air and water. Subsidies may include grants to fund research and development of alternative energy sources.

Creating Markets

Externalities arise due to missing markets. If a market for clean air existed, citizens could negotiate with polluting businesses to pay for the reduction of pollution. Such a market does not exist because large numbers of people would have to cooperate in agreeing on the size of the payment and monitoring compliance with a contract. However, states can create markets for clean air by issuing permits or licenses giving the holder the right to emit a specified amount of pollutant. These licenses are auctioned to the highest bidder, so those firms for whom reducing pollution is extremely costly submit the highest bid and obtain a license. This "cap-and-trade" system reduces pollution in the least costly manner and provides incentives for firms to reduce pollution in order to avoid licensing fees. As changing technology causes firms to need more or fewer licenses, businesses may buy and sell licenses among themselves.

Human Development
Markets cater to only those aspects of human development sustained through marketable commodities. States supplement markets by promoting the non-commercial aspects of human development such as education, healthcare, disease control, libraries, and museums. States also provide merit goods such as school lunches for low-income students, early childhood development programs, and food stamps. States subsidize the arts, making events such as performances by symphony orchestras or dance companies accessible to a wider audience and broadening capacities for appreciation. Finally, states protect citizens from harm by funding research on products and issuing warnings or bans to protect public health and safety. Examples include occupational health and safety laws and warnings about potential harmful effects of prescription drugs, alcohol, and cigarettes.

Democracy
Ideally, democratic states develop public institutions reflecting the will of the majority of citizens while simultaneously protecting the civil rights of all citizens. Although these dual goals may sometimes conflict with each other, there are several ways to achieve them. The following discussion describes four methods.

Election Laws
Governments have the power to determine the rules by which elections are held. Governments can abolish any restrictions on the rights of adult citizens to vote and make illegal any attempts to coerce or entice voters through threats or financial payments. Governments can also secure fair elections by limiting the size of campaign contributions so that wealth does not enable some citizens to exert greater influence over the political process.

Protecting Civil Rights
If citizens are to make their voices heard in a democracy, they need government protection of their rights to speak and publish without fear of reprisal. In addition, equal opportunity to participate in the political process requires that other civil rights such as freedom from discrimination be protected.

Transparency

The functioning of a healthy democracy needs to be open and visible to the public. State secrets should be confined to those areas in which the government's ability to serve the public interest would be compromised by transparency. Examples of transparency include filming legislative sessions, publishing the proceedings of those sessions, and giving citizens the right to access government records.

Federalism

Political authority in most developed nations is divided between national, state, and local governments. This system of federalism captures the best of both centralized and decentralized power. Decentralized government is appealing because it operates closer to citizens and is therefore more sensitive to their concerns. However, centralized government is more effective in resolving collective action problems because it can establish and enforce uniform rights and laws for all citizens within its jurisdiction.

POTENTIAL WEAKNESSES OF THE STATE

Throughout history, states have committed innumerable atrocities. Although the worst modern offenses are associated with communist and fascist states, even democratic states sometimes behave reprehensibly. Examples include the incarceration of American citizens of Japanese descent during World War II and the US government's tolerance of racial discrimination in the American South prior to the civil rights movement of the 1960s. States can inflict substantial harm on economic systems. In the case of predatory states, this damage is the result of powerful groups pursing their self-interest at the expense of society, but even developmental states, however well-intentioned, have the capacity to undermine economic performance.

Reduced Prosperity

Government policies may impede the efficiency and growth of the economy both by wasting resources and by interfering with the market's ability to efficiently allocate resources.

Government Inefficiency

For years, US Senator William Proxmire (1915–2006) issued an annual Golden Fleece Award to draw attention to the most egregious examples of government waste. Governments are inefficient for several reasons. First, government is shielded from market pressures to minimize costs. If costs rise, government can increase taxes or borrow money by selling bonds. Second, government employees do not face the same incentives for productivity as do workers in the private sector. The salaries and job security of bureaucrats are typically unrelated to the performance of their agencies. Third, whereas private businesses can measure success by profitability, government agencies have no clear criteria by which to assess performance. Fourth, the political process provides an imprecise means for citizens to register their preferences since elections are infrequent and voters must select among candidates offering entire packages of programs. Finally, politicians must periodically run for reelection and therefore have an incentive to favor spending on programs providing immediate benefits to voters rather than public investments in infrastructure yielding benefits far into the future.

Reduced Efficiency of the Market

Government may inadvertently reduce market efficiency by creating barriers to entry in the form of regulations, licenses, and permits. In addition, any regulation of prices interferes with the market's ability to achieve an equilibrium price at which the market clears. For example, minimum wage laws prevent some individuals from obtaining jobs by preventing wages from falling to their equilibrium level.

The uniformity of government laws and regulations can also be a source of inefficiency. Because governments are typically responsible for a wide jurisdiction, they lack detailed local information and therefore may prescribe policies inappropriate for specific industries or regions. Finally, the power of government to alter market forces creates an incentive for businesses and other interest groups to gain influence over the political process. This **rent-seeking** activity (e.g., lobbying, campaign contributions, and promises of future jobs for politicians and bureaucrats) diverts resources from more productive uses in the private sector. Successful rent seeking creates inefficiency by causing government to alter the allocation of resources for the benefit of powerful interest groups.

Redirecting the Surplus

Government taxation extracts part of the economic surplus that might otherwise have been used for private investment in expanding productive capacity. This extraction does not pose a problem if government uses the tax **revenue** for public investments in productivity-enhancing infrastructure such as education, transportation systems, or research and development. However, if the money is spent on programs that do nothing to raise productivity, then economic growth may be slowed.

Unintended Consequences

Well-intentioned government programs sometimes create undesirable results. For example, welfare programs may discourage contributions to private charities because some citizens feel that they have fulfilled any moral obligations to fellow citizens by paying taxes. Social security programs may reduce private saving because individuals believe they will need less of their own money to live comfortably after retirement. In India, government aid to disabled citizens causes some desperate individuals to cut off an arm in order to receive financial assistance. In the Philippines, the worldwide ban on the sale of human organs has created a thriving black market, causing some indigent citizens to sell one of their kidneys to a broker.

Limited Freedom

Laws and regulations limit negative freedom by coercing individuals to make choices they would otherwise not make. People in the United States are not free to drive on the left side of the road or to refuse to pay taxes without risk of punishment. They are forced to buy car insurance and emission control systems if they want to operate automobiles. These restrictions on negative freedom usually apply only to activities that potentially harm others. In other words, government restricts the freedom of some citizens to protect the rights of all.

States also restrict freedom to solve collective action problems. For example, if commercial fishermen were free to catch as many fish as they wanted, fish populations would be rapidly depleted, and both fishermen and consumers would be harmed. To solve this collective action problem, governments set legal limits on when and how many fish may be caught.

Finally, states may diminish the range of choices by imposing uniform rules and regulations insensitive to differences in local cultures and circumstances. In some cases, special exemptions are granted in recognition of religious or cultural values. For example, although the hallucinogen peyote cactus is classified as an illegal drug in the United States, some Native Americans may legally consume it as part of their spiritual ceremonies.

Injustice

If justice is defined as reward in accordance with productivity in the market, then any government program that redistributes earned income would appear to be unjust. Both social welfare programs such as food stamps and corporate welfare programs such as subsidies and tax breaks represent payments unrelated to past productivity. The prospect of gaining rewards without productive contributions to society fuels rent seeking as various groups seek to influence government for their own benefit. Alternatively, if justice is defined more broadly as reward in accordance with individual rights, states contribute to injustice by failing to secure equal opportunity for all citizens. Examples include public schools that provide unequal quality of education in different neighborhoods and the government's failure to prevent discrimination.

Instability

Market-centered economic systems are inherently unstable, but government policies may exacerbate that instability.

Political Business Cycle

Keynesian economics calls for government to adjust its levels of spending and taxation to offset any deficiency or excess of spending in the private sector. In fact, however, government budgets reflect politicians' desires to satisfy various interest groups by spending more on popular programs and keeping taxes low. Moreover, this effort to "buy votes" with government benefits may intensify prior to an election. A **political business cycle** occurs when politicians seeking reelection overstimulate the economy prior to the election and then intentionally slow the economy after the election in order to dampen inflationary pressures created by the stimulus.

Time Lags
Even if states could adjust their spending and taxation without political considerations, these changes may still destabilize the economy due to the existence of three time lags. A recognition lag occurs between the beginning of a recession or inflation and government's recognition of the problem. An implementation lag denotes the time required to formulate and implement the appropriate policy response. Finally, an impact lag consists of the time it takes for a policy to actually affect the economy. Taken together, these three time lags may take a year or longer, so that by the time the policy takes effect, the condition of the economy may have changed and the policy becomes destabilizing instead of stabilizing.

Crowding Out
When government spending exceeds tax revenue, the resulting deficit is usually financed by selling government bonds to borrow money. This borrowing, in turn, may cause interest rates to rise as government competes with private borrowers for available funds. Higher interest rates may discourage private borrowing, thereby reducing or **crowding out** private investment. This phenomenon does not necessarily occur, but it poses a potential problem created by **deficit spending** during periods of strong economic growth when the demand for credit is high.

Rational Expectations
When rates of both inflation and unemployment rose during the late 1970s, conservative economists developed the concept of **rational expectations** to demonstrate that government efforts to reduce unemployment may make matters worse. They claimed that individuals make choices based on all available information including their past experiences. If previous efforts to reduce unemployment by stimulating the economy with expansionary fiscal and monetary policy resulted in more inflation, then citizens might expect more inflation each time the government increases spending or the money supply. To protect themselves from the effects of expected inflation, businesses raise prices and workers demand wage increases. Higher wages discourage hiring, so the end result is more inflation, with no reduction in unemployment.

Social Conflict
States may cause resentment and hostility within a nation by favoring some groups over others. In fact, states sometimes intentionally foment ethnic,

religious, or racial antagonisms to prevent the populace from uniting in opposition to the state. States also declare war against rival states, but is the state itself the cause of war and other lesser conflicts between nations? Several arguments suggest a potentially positive answer to this question.

Stimulating the Economy

Citizens are more likely to approve of their government when the economy is prosperous, and war, or even the threat of war, typically provides a short-term stimulus to the economy. Government spending on weaponry and other equipment creates demand for additional production and a resultant increase in jobs. Businesses and workers in the defense industry obviously benefit from war, but the short-term stimulus creates profitable opportunities outside the defense industry as well. As rent seeking creates increasingly close ties between corporations and the state, governments are more likely to resort to war to boost the economy, gain popular support, and create demand for the products of defense contractors who contribute to political campaigns.

Unifying the Nation

War often causes citizens to unite against a common enemy. Patriotism temporarily overrides internal divisions based on class, race, or ethnicity. When political leaders are concerned about social conflict and low approval ratings, they may view war as a potential means to bring the nation together.

Increasing Political Power

In a democracy, political power is intentionally restrained by a constitution and by the ability of voters to replace any politician with whom they are dissatisfied. However, during wartime, citizens often concede enlarged powers to the government due to the threat of destruction by an enemy. For politicians and bureaucrats, war may be a viable strategy to expand their authority.

Lack of Sustainability

State-centered economic systems have been replaced by market-centered systems; therefore, they obviously lack sustainability. The reasons for the decline of state-centered system have varied over time and place. Early empires fell because of lack of competitive pressures to innovate, diversion of the surplus to unproductive activities, imperial overreach, and oppression. Mercantilism declined when merchants and manufacturers gained sufficient economic and political power to resist the authority of the state. Communism, fascism, and socialism proved incapable of matching the efficiency and freedom of market-centered economic systems.

Restricted Human Development

A state that takes substantial responsibility for ensuring the well-being of every citizen may undermine individual responsibility and self-reliance, thereby creating dependency among citizens. The English economist John Stuart Mill (1806–1873) wrote: "A state that dwarfs its men . . . will find that with small men no great thing can really be accomplished." Social benefits provided by the state may also weaken the civic virtue of all citizens by reducing concern for others. Welfare programs are impersonal and may displace community responsibilities to aid others in times of need. More generally, when the state takes responsibility for functions such as protecting the environment or preventing crime, citizens may become disengaged and passive, failing to develop knowledge, skills, and behaviors that might broaden their capacities and improve society.

Erosion of Democracy

Democracy gives citizens a voice in shaping their political institutions. A general principle of democratic governance is that the majority rules as long as the rights of the minority are not violated. States can erode democratic principles in several ways.

Suppression of Civil Rights

States have the power to determine rights; therefore, they can oppress minorities by refusing to recognize or enforce certain rights. Examples include the refusal to allow women in most countries to vote prior to the twentieth century and Jim Crow laws in the American South upholding racial segregation.

Barriers to Entry in Politics

Businesses are not alone in attempting to reduce competition by restricting entry into their industries. Politicians also enact rules that prevent citizens not aligned with a major political party from gaining representation in the legislature. In the United States, some states have restricted voter eligibility by enacting voter identification laws and reducing voting hours, both of which pose obstacles to voting, particularly for low-income citizens. In addition, recent US Supreme Court decisions have removed virtually all limits on financial contributions to political campaigns, thereby creating a barrier to entry for candidates unable to raise large sums of money.

Bundled Legislation

Many bills proposed in legislatures would fail to gain majority support if voted on separately. In a process called **logrolling**, legislators agree to support one another's individual bills to gain passage of an entire slate of bills. This process results in **bundled legislation**, in which a single piece of legislation may contain hundreds of different bills. Individual legislators may object to dozens of the bills, but to secure passage of the bills important to them, they must vote in favor of the entire package. Bundled legislation effectively removes many bills from the democratic process of majority rule.

Political Entrepreneurship

As money becomes increasingly essential to conduct successful political campaigns, many politicians feel compelled to act as **political entrepreneurs**. This term once referred to politicians who favored policies that they believed would maximize the number of votes they received in the next election. However, as the role of money in politics has increased, political entrepreneurs are now selling public policy in exchange for campaign contributions to ensure reelection. They frequently ignore the needs of low-income voters in the same way that businesses ignore consumers who cannot afford a product. Their receptivity to rent seeking by corporations and other interest groups is reflected in the Washington slogan, "pay to play." As a result of political entrepreneurship, the democratic ideal that each citizen possesses an equal voice in the governing process is violated, and governments no longer focus on promoting the public interest.

Collective Action Problems

To the extent that democracy relies on decentralized government, collective action problems arise in the **public sector** as well as the private sector. For example, although most citizens support government aid in response to natural disasters, a local government in an area not subject to earthquakes may act as a free rider by refusing to contribute to relief from that disaster. Similarly, local governments in noncoastal areas may be reluctant to assist in recovery from tsunamis and hurricanes. Only a centralized government is capable of resolving the problem by requiring all citizens to share in the burden of disaster relief through taxation.

Another problem with decentralized government arises when local governments establish policies favored by local residents but contrary to the national interest. For example, prior to the rise of nation states in Europe, many towns charged tariffs on goods moving through their jurisdiction. These barriers to trade resulted in less regional specialization and retarded economic development. National governments solved this collective action problem with laws prohibiting local tariffs. Today, the European Union has gone even further by banning tariffs on trade among member nations.

Other examples of collective action problems arising from decentralized government include tax concessions and welfare benefits. Local and state governments often grant tax concessions and other incentives to attract new businesses. This strategy works as long as other jurisdictions do not offer the same incentives, but if all governments grant concessions, then these incentives no longer attract businesses from other jurisdictions and simply result in less revenue for governments to provide essential public goods. Similarly, local and state governments may reduce welfare benefits, hoping that needy families will move elsewhere. But if welfare benefits are uniformly reduced in all jurisdictions, the desired effect on relocation is lost and poverty increases.

CONCLUSION

Successful economic systems require a developmental state, yet without institutional safeguards, developmental states can deteriorate into predatory states. The problem arises because developmental states provide public goods and, in so doing, alter the market's allocation of resources. This power to redirect market outcomes makes the developmental state an appealing target for individuals, groups, and corporations seeking to gain benefits beyond what they could earn in an unregulated market. As this rent seeking proliferates, the developmental state increasingly takes on the characteristics of a predatory state, with government becoming the means by which interest groups enrich themselves at the expense of the rest of the population (Galbraith 2008). Much of the current public anger directed toward government is based on a growing recognition of the predatory aspects of modern states.

Predatory states can be curbed in two ways. For libertarians, the solution is to minimize the size and functions of the state so that rent seekers have nothing to gain through politics. However, this strategy overlooks government's developmental role as an integral part of any successful economic system. A more viable solution is to strengthen the state so that it is sufficiently powerful and autonomous to withstand efforts by rent seekers to control it. However, this autonomy raises a problem. How can the state be sufficiently insulated from rent seeking and yet be accessible, accountable, and responsive to the legitimate concerns of citizens? In other words, can a developmental state distinguish between "the will of the people" and the efforts of interest groups to gain benefits through political means?

In the past, the drafting authors of constitutions sought to structure governments in ways that would balance autonomy and accessibility. They often established bicameral legislatures consisting of a lower chamber whose members were more accessible due to smaller districts and more frequent elections, and an upper chamber whose members retained greater autonomy because they represented large regions and held longer terms in office. In Britain, the autonomy of the upper chamber, the House of Lords, was originally protected by making many of the seats hereditary. Even today, members of the House of Lords are not elected but are either senior bishops in the Church of England or appointed by the Queen.

Despite constitutional safeguards against rent seeking, the increasing penetration of states by market pressures (i.e., money in politics) has forced all politicians to become more responsive to interest groups in order to secure the financial contributions required for reelection. In the United States, this process has been accelerated by two Supreme Court decisions (*Citizens United v. Federal Election Commission* in 2010 and *McCutcheon v. Federal Election Commission* in 2014) removing nearly all restrictions on financial contributions in politics. These rulings seem likely to increase the predatory nature of the US government because the groups willing to make the largest contributions are those who expect the most valuable benefits from government in return. Several institutional changes could potentially protect the autonomy of the state by restricting the influence of money in politics.

- *Public funding of political campaigns.* When politicians are dependent on large private contributions to finance effective campaigns, the state is unlikely to remain entirely neutral with respect to the different interest groups in society. Various solutions to this problem have been proposed. Governments could provide matching funds for private contributions from small donors only. Alternatively, an income tax credit could be given in the form of a voucher to be donated to the candidate of one's choice. Financing political campaigns with government funds would reduce the pressure to exchange political favors for campaign contributions.

- *Increased transparency.* The political process could be made more transparent by, for example, requiring disclosure of the source of all campaign contributions and public notice of the connections between the sources of funding and each politician's votes on key issues. Greater transparency would aid voters in determining which politicians are beholden to which interest groups.

- *Increased accountability.* Gerrymandering is the process by which politicians in most states of the United States are able to select their voters by redrawing the borders of congressional districts every ten years. The result is that many politicians face no viable challengers from other political parties and therefore are not held accountable for their votes in the legislature. In 2011, the state of California solved this problem by forming a bipartisan Citizens Redistricting Commission to determine congressional districts. With the party composition of districts more balanced, politicians who favor special interests are more likely to be removed in the next election.

- *Redefining corporations and speech.* The *Citizens United* and *McCutcheon* decisions by the US Supreme Court were based on two highly controversial assumptions—that corporations are persons and that financial contributions are a form of speech and therefore protected by the First Amendment to the Constitution. Congress could effectively overrule the Supreme Court by legislatively reversing these two assumptions.

- *Reforming media regulations.* An independent media is essential to unveiling corruption and rent seeking. Yet recent waves of mergers and acquisitions by media giants, as well as increasing dependence of the media on corporate advertising, is undermining the investigative journalism that uncovers influence peddling in high places. Stricter enforcement of antitrust laws in the media industry and changes in government policies regarding access to airwaves and the Internet would mitigate this problem.

Even with these reforms, government would not be immune to rent seeking. Money and political power are inseparable—those with money gain power and those with power gain money. However, institutional reforms can weaken that connection, enabling states to remain sufficiently autonomous to perform their developmental functions and contribute to the improved performance of economic systems.

REFERENCES

Epstein, S. R. 2000. *Freedom and Growth: the Rise of States and Markets in Europe 1300–1750*. New York: Routledge.

Evans, Peter B. 1995. *Embedded Autonomy: States and Industrial Transformation*. Princeton, NJ: Princeton University Press.

Finer, S. E. 1999. *The History of Government from the Earliest Times, Vol. 1 Ancient Monarchies and Empires*. New York: Oxford University Press.

Galbraith, James K. 2008. *The Predator State*. New York: Free Press.

Polanyi, Karl. (1944) 2001. *The Great Transformation: The Political and Economic Origins of Our Times,* 2nd ed. Boston: Beacon Press.

Tilly, Charles. 1990. *Coercion, Capital and European States: 990–1990*. Oxford: Basil Blackwell.

ADDITIONAL READING

Besley, Timothy. *Principled Agents?: The Political Economy of Good Government*. New York: Oxford University Press, 2007.

Dieterle, David A., and Kathleen C. Simmons. *Government and the Economy: An Encyclopedia*. Santa Barbara, CA: Greenwood Press, 2014.

Fukuyama, Francis. *Political Order and Political Decay: From the Industrial Revolution to the Globalization of Democracy*. New York: Farrar, Straus, and Giroux, 2014.

Glazer, Amihai, and Lawrence S. Rothenberg. *Why Government Succeeds and Why It Fails*. Cambridge, MA: Harvard University Press, 2005.

Jessop, Bob. *The Future of the Capitalist State*. Cambridge: Polity, 2002.

Lange, Matthew, and Dietrich Rueschemeyer, eds. *States and Development: Historical Antecedents of Stagnation and Advance*. New York: Palgrave Macmillan, 2005.

Levy, Jonah D., ed. *The State after Statism*. Cambridge, MA: Harvard University Press, 2006.

Madrick, Jeff, and Ruth O'Brien. *The Case for Big Government*. Princeton, NJ: Princeton University Press, 2010.

Maier, Charles S. *Leviathan 2.0: Inventing Modern Statehood*. Cambridge, MA: Harvard University Press, 2014.

Micklethwait, John, and Adrian Woolridge. *The Fourth Revolution: The Global Race to Reinvent the State*. New York: Penguin Press, 2014.

Persson, Torsten. *Political Economics: Explaining Economic Policy*. Cambridge, MA: MIT Press, 2002.

Przewoski, Adam. *Democracy and the Limits of Self-Government*. New York: Cambridge University Press, 2010.

Rubin, Edward L. *Soul, Self and Society: The New Morality and the Modern State*. New York: Oxford University Press, 2015.

Schuck, Peter H. *Why Government Fails So Often*. Princeton, NJ: Princeton University Press, 2014.

Stiglitz, Joseph. *The Role of the State*. Oxford: Basil Blackwell, 1989.

Sunstein, Cass. *Simpler: The Future of Government*. New York: Simon & Schuster, 2013.

Tanzi, Vito. *Government versus Markets: The Changing Economic Role of the State*. New York: Cambridge University Press, 2011.

Woo-Cumings, Meredith, ed. *The Developmental State*. Ithaca, NY: Cornell University Press, 1999.

Woshinsky, Oliver H. *Explaining Politics: Culture, Institutions, and Political Behavior*. New York: Routledge, 2008.

Chapter 5

COMMUNITY-CENTERED ECONOMIC SYSTEMS

"The community stagnates without the impulse of the
individual. The impulse dies away without the sympathy
of the community."

WILLIAM JAMES (1842–1910),
American philosopher

Community-centered economic systems prevailed for thousands of centuries
before empires arose to organize human affairs through centralized state control. The eclipse of community lasted in the West until the fall of the Roman
Empire in 476 CE left Europe in the Dark Ages with neither a state nor a functioning **market**. In the near-absence of both trade and effective political authority, roving tribes battled each other for control of territory. By the ninth century,
a new community-centered economic system called feudalism began to form.
Feudalism lasted roughly seven centuries in western Europe and even longer in
eastern Europe. By the sixteenth century, feudalism was gradually being
replaced by **mercantilism**, which then gave rise to **capitalism**, so any vestiges of
community-centered systems in modern times occur only among primitive
tribes isolated from the rest of the world or in the form of local experiments in
social anarchism.

Communities function within **civil society**, which is the primary focus of
sociologists and anthropologists. In fact, the academic field of sociology arose in
the late nineteenth century, largely in reaction to economists' portrayal of society
as a market in which **economic behavior** is the dominant form of human
interaction. Early sociologists such as Emile Durkheim (1858–1917), Max Weber
(1864–1920), and Ferdinand Tönnies (1855–1936) expressed deep concern about
the deleterious effects of the market on communities. Durkheim believed that
without cohesive communities, humans were susceptible to alienation and even
suicide. He feared that the market, where calculated self-interest prevails, threatened the trust, morality, and emotional bonds that hold communities together.
As capitalism increasingly pushed masses of displaced individuals from rural
villages into large industrial cities, Durkheim hoped that workers would form
new communities based on their occupations.

The distinction between economics and sociology was succinctly summarized by American economist James Duesenberry (1918–2009): "Economics is all about how people make choices; sociology is all about why they don't have any choices to make" (Duesenberry 1960, 233). In other words, economists view society as a market in which individual choices determine social outcomes, whereas sociologists focus on the process by which the institutions of society shape human behavior. Both approaches are essential to understanding the functioning of economic systems.

Advocates of communities are found on both ends of the political spectrum. On the political left, communitarians claim that strong communities are essential to nurture virtuous behavior that is undermined by the impersonal forces of both market and state (Etzioni 1998; Tam 1998). On the political right, proponents of **social conservatism** seek to reinvigorate **intermediate institutions** to serve as buffers between the individual and the state (Berger and Neuhaus 1996). These institutions include families, neighborhoods, churches, clubs, civic associations, recreational organizations, and charitable enterprises. Social conservatives claim that a nation lacking strong communities will inevitably give rise to an overpowering state (Nisbet 1953). In the absence of community, individuals are reluctant to make charitable contributions, care for neighbors in crisis, or participate in civic activities. As a result, the state must assume increasing responsibility for protecting vulnerable citizens and maintaining social order.

COMMUNITY-CENTERED ECONOMIC SYSTEMS IN HISTORY

Primitive Tribes

The earliest economic systems were formed by tribes living communally and relying on hunting and gathering for their subsistence. As social creatures, humans naturally clustered together in groups, but tribes also served an economic function. Belonging to a tribe increased the chances of survival by raising productivity through a division of labor. The assignment of social roles and distribution of goods were based on traditions that evolved to ensure the survival of the tribe. For example, hunters might get the largest portion of a carcass because their caloric needs were higher. However, hunters were obliged to share their prey with others so that the basic needs of all productive members were met. In tribes whose survival was precarious, unproductive members such as the sick and the elderly might be left to die if supporting them jeopardized the group.

Behavior and activities in primitive tribes were coordinated primarily through informal codes of conduct establishing the rights and responsibilities attached to each social role. These unwritten rules were transmitted from one generation to the next as children grew up learning what to expect from others and what was expected of them. When individuals violated community norms, peer pressure was exerted through scolding, reprimanding, shunning, or ostracizing.

Members of these early tribes had an interest in improving productivity only insofar as their survival was at stake. They developed bows and arrows, hatchets, knives, and spears not only to kill animals but to defend themselves against members of hostile tribes. They became increasingly adept at building shelters and preparing food, but once their basic needs were met, they had little interest in performing additional work or innovating (Sahlins 1974). This apparent lack of ambition was due to the fact that there was no use for a surplus. Wealth could not be accumulated and stored in the form of money, and only a few exotic items could be obtained through trade with other tribes, so there was little reason to produce beyond current needs. Once survival was assured, tribal members devoted their time to strengthening and enjoying community bonds through ceremonies, storytelling, chanting, dancing, art, and sports. Life continued virtually unchanged from one generation to the next.

Primitive tribes were highly functional, as evidenced by the fact that they were the sole **governance structure** for the first several hundred thousand years of human existence. Indeed, they still remain in parts of the world today such as the Amazon rain forest and New Guinea. They managed to survive virtually without markets, because goods produced by the tribe were shared rather than traded, and also without a state, because collective decisions were made through group discussion and consensus. However, as a result of their lack of economic development, most primitive tribes were eventually vanquished by more powerful states and empires.

Feudalism

Following the collapse of the western Roman Empire, Europe lacked any centralized political authority and reverted back to a community-centered economic system. After three centuries of the Dark Ages, Charlemagne (748–814) founded the Holy Roman Empire in 800 CE. However, this empire lacked the financial means to carry out basic functions such as providing military defense and other **public goods**. To gain financial solvency and military power, Charlemagne and his successors allotted large parcels of land called *manors* or *fiefs* to warriors in exchange for financial support and pledges of military service.

The warriors became lords of the manors, living in castles surrounded by villages and farmland populated by serfs or villeins. The lords wielded sovereign authority over their manors, but they remained enmeshed in a hierarchical power structure with obligations to pay tribute to overlords, who, in turn, supported the emperor. Despite the formal existence of an empire, Europe during the early Middle Ages was not a state-centered economic system. The primary governance structure was the local manor, where the lord and serfs lived together in a community based on traditional social roles. This system, called feudalism, prevailed throughout much of Europe from the ninth to the fifteenth centuries and in Russia until the mid-nineteenth century.

Each manor was largely self-sufficient, with custom and tradition determining the rights and duties of each individual in a system of mutual obligation. Serfs either turned over part of their produce to the lord or worked part-time on his land. In return, the lord was obligated to provide defense against the marauding tribes of Vandals, Huns, and Goths that occasionally swept through Europe. The lord also allowed serfs to use his workshops and tools, served as a judge in settling disputes between serfs, and shared his grain reserves in times of famine. Both the lord and the serfs understood the informal rules of life on the manor and neither had authority to change the traditional system. The lord did not own the serfs or the land in the sense that he could sell the land, evict the serfs, or arbitrarily increase his claim to the serfs' produce. Most serfs were also constrained by tradition. They could not sell the land on which they worked nor leave the manor in search of better opportunities.

Like primitive tribes, the feudal manor was economically stagnant. Human desires were quite simple because most people were preoccupied with mere survival against the threats of invasion, famines, and plagues. The manors typically lacked **economies of scale**; each family tilled its own small strip of land. With virtually no currency or external trade, the only reason to produce an economic surplus was to pay the tributes owed by each lord to his overlord and to support the church. The absence of competition between manors resulted in little pressure or incentive to use the surplus for **capital accumulation** and innovation to increase productivity. Instead, the surplus was used to reinforce the existing hierarchical class structure by supporting the lords, their armies, the clergy, and the construction of castles and cathedrals.

Feudalism gradually disintegrated for several reasons. Beginning in the ninth century, caravans of traveling merchants entered Europe carrying goods shipped into Venice from the Middle East and Asia. Their regular encampments and fairs gradually developed into towns and cities such as Paris and Frankfurt. Initially, the rise of commerce had little effect on feudalism because the Catholic Church was committed to maintaining the status quo and used its considerable authority to limit the effects of commercial activity. For example, the Church declared that charging interest on loans was a mortal sin punishable by excommunication. The Church also formulated the "doctrine of the just price," which required merchants to sell goods for no more than the cost of acquiring and transporting them to the point of sale. In other words, merchants were prohibited from making profit. The Church's intent was twofold—to save souls from the sin of avarice and to prevent a new social class of merchants from accumulating wealth that might upset the stable feudal order and challenge the authority of the Church.

Another obstacle to commercial growth was the lack of effective central political authority. The Holy Roman Empire was too weak to provide the **infrastructure** essential to support trade. Roads were treacherous, no uniform currency or weights and measures existed, laws were few and lacked reliable enforcement, and property rights were only vaguely defined. In the absence of a strong central state, feudal lords were free to impose **tariffs** on goods transported through their jurisdictions. In 1400, merchants transporting goods the length of the Rhine River were required to pay sixty different tolls along the way. These trade barriers effectively retarded economic development.

Gradually, however, the cumulative effects of commerce undermined feudal institutions. The availability of silk, spices, and other exotic goods caused lords who previously had no use for a surplus to demand a larger share of the serfs' produce to buy these goods. Many serfs responded to this increased oppression by fleeing the manors to become artisans and craftsmen in the emerging towns where traveling merchants were establishing permanent settlements. Although this exodus violated feudal tradition, many towns granted a former serf the status of "freeman" after a year of residence.

A second factor contributing to the decline of feudalism was the Crusades, an effort by feudal lords to restore Christian control over the Holy Lands in the Middle East. Large armies of lords and their conscripted serfs fought against Muslims in battles from the eleventh to the thirteenth centuries. In the end, the Crusades not only failed but hastened the decline of feudalism by disrupting production. With many of the lords and serfs absent from the manors, the burden on remaining serfs intensified, which encouraged an even greater exodus to the towns. The Crusades also bankrupted many lords who had committed all their assets to the holy war. However, other lords returned from the Crusades with considerable treasure and were now interested in **investment** and profit-making rather than returning to the unrewarding routine of the feudal manor.

Finally, feudalism was dealt natural blows by the Great Famine (1315–1317) and the Black Death (bubonic plague; 1348–1350). Twenty-five million people (a third of Europe's population) died from the plague. The resulting labor shortage gave serfs increased bargaining power and led to peasant revolts against oppressive lords. To keep serfs from leaving the manor, many lords changed the status of peasants from serf to renter. If a lord were particularly desperate, he might entice serfs to remain on the manor with a promise of ownership of land after a number of years.

As the feudal manor disintegrated, a different form of community arose in towns and cities. Craftsmen in the same trade formed cooperative communities called guilds to protect and promote their interests. Members paid dues, swore oaths of allegiance, and agreed to abide by the guild's rules. In some cases, guilds were so powerful that they became the governing bodies of cities.

Guilds monopolized a particular trade or craft within a city or region. They suppressed competition by collectively setting prices, determining levels of output, establishing standards of quality, and discouraging innovations that might render their skills obsolete. They banned advertising and created barriers to entry by requiring aspiring new members to serve apprenticeships of three to twelve years followed by a period of working for daily wages in another city (hence the name *journeyman*). Only then could a person become a master craftsman with full privileges of guild membership. Guilds provided financial benefits to members in the form of support for the elderly, widows, and orphans as well as covering funeral expenses. In some cities, guilds even prescribed appropriate dress and conduct for their members. By the fourteenth century, there were 350 guilds in Paris alone.

Feudalism ended sooner in England than in France—and sooner in France than in Germany. As wealth began to accumulate in the hands of urban merchants and business people (the bourgeoisie), monarchs discovered that greater surplus could be extracted from the bourgeoisie than could ever be taken from the feudal lords. Moreover, the bourgeoisie supported the state because they needed improved infrastructure and because they believed that the state was more likely to serve their interests if it depended on them financially. As central governments consolidated power in each nation, Europeans gradually made the transition from a community-centered economic system to a state-centered economic system called mercantilism.

Social Anarchism

Theories of anarchism take two different forms. Individualist anarchism (also called **libertarianism**) proposes a society based on private property and markets with virtually no governmental authority and few social constraints or obligations. In contrast, social anarchism (also called communal anarchism, anarcho-syndicalism, or utopian socialism) envisions a society composed of small, cooperative communities with shared ownership of property and minimal reliance on either market or state.

By the early 1800s, industrialization in Europe was creating considerable distress. Rampant poverty, horrendous working conditions in many factories, squalid cities, and the virtual absence of publicly funded amenities such as education, parks, and healthcare made life difficult. Reacting to these conditions, utopian visionaries sought to recreate a community-centered economic system by formulating detailed plans for small, relatively self-sufficient villages with communal ownership of property.

In France, Charles Fourier (1772–1837) proposed communities called *phalanxes* of 1,620 people living and working together. He envisioned a future in which there would be phalanxes around the world, all loosely confederated under the auspices of a World Congress of Phalanxes. Fourier believed that cooperation, sociability, and a strong work ethic were natural human attributes perverted by the rise of industrial capitalism and the consequent destruction of traditional communities. Hundreds of phalanxes were established throughout Europe and the United States, but none endured.

Another social anarchist was Robert Owen (1771–1858), a wealthy industrialist whose factory in New Lanark, Scotland, served as a showcase for his vision of a new economic system. He paid high wages and provided his employees with good housing, education, healthcare, recreational facilities, and a community store. Visitors came from around the world to witness this experiment, but Owen had even bigger ambitions. He imagined communities of 1,200 people on at least 1,000 acres of land. Everyone would live in one large building constructed around a community square. Food preparation would be done in a community kitchen and meals would be taken in a common dining hall. In 1825, Owen and a group of followers emigrated to the United States and established a community called New Harmony in southern Indiana. It lasted less than two years before disintegrating in the face of internal dissension and economic hardship.

Numerous other intentional communities sprang up throughout the United States. Many of the first colonists such as the Puritans were highly communal, enforcing rigid rules of behavior and intolerant of dissent or outsiders. The Shakers, a religious sect begun in England, established communities throughout the northeast in the late eighteenth and early nineteenth centuries. By the mid-nineteenth century, a wave of largely self-sufficient communities appeared, including the Oneida community in New York, Brook Farm in Massachusetts, and the Amana colonies in Iowa (Kanter 1972). All of these experiments failed to thrive economically and eventually disbanded. Their small size precluded the **economies of scale** gained through division of labor and large-scale technology.

Social anarchists believe that any form of government beyond the local community is inherently oppressive and will serve the interests of the rulers rather than citizens. Social anarchists advocate local autonomy for communities in which citizens are actively engaged in self-governance and productive assets are collectively owned. Two Russian social anarchists, Mikhail Bakunin (1814–1876) and Peter Kropotkin (1842–1921), urged workers and peasants to take control of factories and land in order to form independent communities. Social anarchism materialized in 1871 when the workers of Paris took over the city and established the Paris Commune. They built barricades to prevent the army from interceding and governed the city themselves until the army finally suppressed the uprising after two months.

Twentieth-century examples of social anarchism include the International Workers of the World (IWW), a labor union founded in the United States in 1903. The IWW (nicknamed the Wobblies) advocated worker ownership and control of businesses and was most active in the mining and timber industries of the western United States. During the Spanish Civil War (1936–1939), workers in the Catalonia region of Spain took over and managed most of the factories in the region. That experiment ended when the supporters of Generalissimo Francisco Franco (1892–1975) won the war and restored private ownership. Perhaps the best current example of social anarchism is the Mondragon Corporation, a federation of 289 worker-owned firms in the Basque region of Spain. These firms face global competition, so the combination of the depressed European economy and imported goods from low-cost manufacturers in Asia has challenged Mondragon's survival. One of its largest firms declared bankruptcy in 2013.

POTENTIAL STRENGTHS OF COMMUNITY

Conventional wisdom holds that community-centered economic systems are a relic of the past. However, communities remain valuable in providing support for both market and state. Unlike the impersonal nature of markets and states, members of communities typically encounter each other repeatedly and establish personal relationships. These social bonds give communities certain advantages in improving the performance of economic systems.

Prosperity

Communities promote prosperity by compensating for some of the shortcomings of the market, including **transaction costs**, **externalities**, lack of **public goods**, and insufficient **social capital**.

Reducing Transaction Costs

In market transactions, buyers are often uncertain about the quality of products, the honesty of sellers, or the reliability of prices as accurate indicators of the value of products. This lack of information creates transaction costs as buyers seek information about products and the reputations of sellers; negotiate contracts stipulating future obligations; and, in the event of broken contracts, pursue enforcement remedies. Through repeated face-to-face interaction, people in communities are able to reduce transaction costs by sharing information and developing trust. Shared information and trust reduce the perceived risk of buying and investing. A handshake may serve as an unwritten contract and eliminate the costs of lawyers' fees.

Reducing Negative Externalities

The market creates negative externalities when the actions of individuals and businesses impose costs on other people. In a community where people are concerned about their reputations and have established social relationships, individuals and businesses are more likely to be sensitive to the effects of their actions on others and therefore refrain from creating negative externalities. For example, people who have good relationships with their neighbors are less likely to litter, let their house and yard deteriorate, or play loud music.

Providing Public Goods

The market is not well-suited to providing public goods due to the **free-rider problem**. Most individuals will not voluntarily pay for a good when they cannot be excluded from enjoying its benefits. However, communities may overcome the free-rider problem either by instilling a sense of social obligation and duty or through social sanctions. For example, in some neighborhoods, volunteer watch groups supplement police protection in preventing crime. Individuals may participate in these groups because they feel a civic duty or because they seek a reputation as an active participant in the neighborhood. People in communities provide volunteer services by performing tasks such as picking up litter, planting trees, and maintaining trails.

Creating Capital

The market is well-suited to the accumulation of financial and physical capital. However, communities are the primary incubators of social capital, **cultural**

capital, and **human capital**, and recent work in the field of economic growth suggests that these less tangible forms of capital play a larger role in promoting prosperity as economies mature. (Romer 1994; Acemoglu 2009). Social capital includes all institutions and organizations that improve economic performance by generating trust, shared information, social norms, goodwill, fellowship, solidarity, and cooperation. High levels of social capital reduce the number of lawsuits and contribute to security of property rights, thereby increasing commercial activity.

Examples of social capital include neighborhoods, clubs, strategic alliances between businesses, and nonprofit organizations. Businesses may create social capital by instilling a sense of community within the workplace (Cohen and Prusak 2001). Strategies for increasing social capital include fostering teamwork, sharing profits through employee stock-ownership programs (ESOPs), providing retreats and opportunities for recreation, and referring to employees as "associates" or "partners." To the extent that workplaces are communities, workers develop a sense of belonging and pride that increases productivity by reducing shirking, theft, and other opportunistic behaviors.

Cultural capital consists of the values, attitudes, norms, and beliefs that contribute to greater productivity. Communities create and transmit cultural capital through socialization including education, parenting, social activities, and sports. Cultural capital appears in the form of a strong work ethic, honesty, loyalty, a sense of fairness, personal responsibility, an ability to cooperate with others, respect for the rights of others, and respect for the rule of law. These character traits contribute to both personal success and economic development.

Human capital is the skills and knowledge that increase labor productivity. Families, neighborhoods, and community organizations are essential supplements to state-funded schools in rearing the next generation and creating human capital. In fact, studies suggest that family and neighborhood may be more influential than formal education in determining personal success.

Freedom

As Western political and economic theory emerged out of the Enlightenment of the eighteenth century, a primary focus was the defense of individual freedom and autonomy against the restrictions imposed by church and state. Humans were portrayed as rational, fully formed creatures able to live like Robinson Crusoe marooned on an island. They chose to participate in economic systems to attain a higher standard of living and to gain protection for themselves and their property. This view of humans as isolated, autonomous individuals who come together only to promote their economic self-interest led to a conception of freedom as the absence of external constraint by government or by other individuals.

Communities, with their social norms and monitoring of behavior, would seem to pose significant restrictions on individual freedom. However, a deeper understanding of the concept of freedom reveals a harmony between community and freedom (Taylor 1982). According to sociologists and developmental psychologists, personal identity is formed by social relations. In other words, people's values, beliefs, desires, and aversions are all shaped by the communities in which they live (Taylor 1999). Yet humans do not simply play a role created for them by their communities. They continually engage in critical evaluation of themselves and their communities to determine whether they approve of the person they are becoming. They can reject relationships and even leave communities, but those choices are made in the context of the social conditioning created by communities.

Acknowledging the role of social relations in forming personal identity implies a broader conception of freedom. To be free from overt constraint by government or other people so that individuals can pursue their desires may actually create an obstacle to freedom. The autonomous individual, if such a person could exist, would be devoid of purpose and meaning. The rules, norms, and relationships provided by communities, far from restricting freedom, enable individuals to form identities that provide the source of their goals and aspirations (Akerlof and Kranton 2010). In the words of sociologist Emile Durkheim, "the rule, because it teaches us to restrain and master ourselves, is a means of emancipation and of freedom" (Durkheim [1925] 1961, 49). For Durkheim, the absence of social constraint would leave individuals slaves to their unlimited desires and therefore doomed to frustration and what he called "anomie." Sociologist Robert Nisbet expressed the same idea, claiming that without social institutions, the individual is left "free in all his solitary misery" (Nisbet 1953, 213).

The freedom created by community is positive in the sense that it empowers individuals to develop and pursue meaningful life plans. Whereas the market pits individuals against each other and promotes the pursuit of self-interest, communities provide a context within which individuals can experience themselves as social beings capable of virtuous behavior and harmonious relations with others. Ironically, the pleasure-seeking *homo economicus* is doomed to frustration because unlimited desires are, by definition, insatiable. Quoting Durkheim once again, "To pursue a goal which by definition is unattainable is to condemn oneself to a state of perpetual unhappiness" (Durkheim [1897] 1951, 248).

Solving Collective Action Problems

Communities are sometimes able to expand freedom by solving **collective action problems** without government intervention (Ostrom 1990). Recall that collective action problems arise when the pursuit of individual self-interest produces a result that none of the participants wanted. Communities reduce the likelihood of collective action problems by fostering trust and cooperation, which serve to suppress **opportunism** and **defection**. Opportunistic behavior is also restrained in communities because members are aware that their actions are being monitored by others. Any opportunism is likely to elicit negative consequences such as shunning and loss of social status. As an example of a community solution to a collective action problem, consider the salary cap in professional sports. In the past, the wealthiest team owner could offer the highest salaries to outstanding athletes in an attempt to buy a championship. However, the quality of competition suffered because the teams of less wealthy owners had little chance of winning. If weak competition caused fans to lose interest in the game, all owners would be damaged. The solution to this collective action problem was an agreement among owners to cap athletes' salaries. This restriction created better competition, more support by fans, and increased profit for owners. By cooperating to establish a rule, the team owners achieved a better result than if each acted separately in pursuit of self-interest.

Expanding Choice

Many people belong to multiple communities and are surrounded by other communities to which they do not belong. This diversity provides a wider range of lifestyle choices as people experiment with different communities in the process of developing their identity. The presence of alternatives creates opportunities to leave communities failing to meet one's interests and needs and to join more supportive communities. In economics, this process is known as the **Tiebout effect**.

Peace and Justice

Justice requires the protection of rights. Violations of rights typically create social conflict, so without justice, there can be no peace. This adage applies to relations between individuals, communities, and nations. Communities promote peace and justice by taking initiative to define rights and to secure their protection.

Political Activism

Some communities form to focus public attention on certain injustices such as racism, sexism, homophobia, and discrimination against people with disabilities. Their success is evident in legislation establishing governmental protection of civil rights and prohibiting discrimination.

Community Service

Many professional associations require their members to engage in community service to broaden public access to, for example, legal counseling or healthcare. Many nonprofits and nongovernmental organizations (NGOs) are devoted to promoting human rights to heathcare, a clean environment, and education. Communities may support a human right to the basic necessities of life by establishing soup kitchens, food banks and homeless shelters or by rallying to raise funds for a member in need of expensive medical treatment.

Socialization

Healthy communities instill virtue in their members, and justice is a primary virtue. Through the socialization process, community members learn to respect the rights of others and to reach consensus without resorting to force or violence. Socialization makes laws against violence and discrimination more effective because citizens have already internalized a commitment to peace and justice. This capacity for peaceful interaction extends to international relations. For example, the organization Sister Cities International was established in 1956 to give communities rather than states the opportunity to forge peaceful bonds among citizens in different nations. More than five hundred US cities have partnered with nearly two thousand sister cities around the world.

Multiculturalism

Communities provide the context within which **culture** develops. Culture, in turn, creates shared values, traditions, behaviors, and art forms. Culture is a powerful force in reducing conflict within communities, but cultural differences between communities can threaten peace. In recognition of the importance of building bridges between cultures, many communities have intentionally sought to increase their members' awareness of other cultures. The resulting appreciation of and sensitivity to different cultures serves to reduce conflict between communities. For example, the success of the US civil rights movement during the 1960s was based in part on the popularity of black music among white youth. The music brought black and white communities together in shared appreciation. The growing popularity of various ethnic cuisines is also breaking down cultural barriers. Interfaith dialogues serve to reduce hostility between religious groups.

Reciprocity

Reciprocity is the tendency to treat others in the same way they treat us—to repay kindness with kindness and to retaliate against betrayal and injustice. Whereas economic behavior is based on calculations of self-interest, reciprocity may conflict with self-interest. For example, we may tip a waiter for good service even if we never intend to eat in that restaurant again. Individuals may seek revenge against a perceived injustice even if doing so requires a sacrifice on their part. Reciprocity promotes peace and justice by reducing opportunistic behavior that creates conflict. To the extent that humans internalize the social norm of reciprocity, their self-interest becomes largely consistent with meeting their social obligations within a community.

Sustainability

Communities contribute to the sustainability of not only the natural environment but also the other two governance structures—market and state.

Sustaining the Environment

The socialization process within communities instills values supportive of a sustainable natural environment. Members of cohesive communities tend to be more sensitive to the rights and needs of others and therefore less likely to degrade their surroundings. People who identify with their communities are more concerned about the future of the environment because most communities endure longer than any individual member. Finally, because reducing pollution poses a collective action problem, communities provide a forum or venue in which members can organize to gain political influence over environmental policies. For example, many communities throughout the United States are attempting to ban the practice of hydraulic fracturing ("fracking") to extract natural gas from the earth.

Sustaining the Market

Without the virtue and personal integrity fostered by communities, the market would be severely impaired if not destroyed. The unrestrained pursuit of self-interest would lead to deceit, cheating, and dishonesty, which in turn would erode the trust essential to market transactions. Without communities, markets would degenerate into a chaotic clash of self-interests.

Sustaining the State

States could not maintain law and order unless the vast majority of citizens were socialized by communities to obey laws and respect the rights of others. A state in which citizens lacked virtue would either disintegrate into violent factions or else become totalitarian as government would be forced to suppress individual freedom to preserve social order.

Human Development

Individuals and communities are not separate entities; they develop and nurture each other. Without supportive communities, individuals face difficulty in developing a clear conception of who they are, what they want, and how to go about achieving their goals. So community and individual autonomy coexist in a symbiotic relationship. Autonomy is based on self-determination, but to know what kind of person we wish to become, we need purposes and meanings that develop from engagement in communities. Fragmented and dysfunctional communities are often crime-ridden because members aggressively seek immediate gratification without regard for the well-being of others or for their own futures.

In addition to providing an arena in which individuals develop personal identities, communities enable their members to achieve a higher form of existence that may be called the virtuous life. Many philosophers and religious thinkers have distinguished between a lower level of existence, in which humans are not much different from other animals in pursuing their needs and desires, and a higher form in which humans have internalized ethical norms so that their desires are congruent with morality and social obligations. Only in the higher form of existence do people achieve freedom from selfish compulsions that create conflict and separate them from their communities.

The process by which communities breed virtue is based on both socialization and self-interest. Socialization occurs through the feedback individuals receive from others. Through words, facial expressions, and body language, humans continually mold the values and behaviors of those around them. In healthy communities, this socialization process creates a code of ethics that forms the basis for virtues such as compassion, empathy, social conscience, and a sense of justice.

The pursuit of self-interest within communities also contributes to virtuous behavior. When people encounter the same individuals repeatedly, opportunistic behavior may be punished with retaliation and will negatively affect future interactions. Knowing this, members have an incentive to suppress opportunism in order to develop good reputations. For example businesses operating within communities may voluntarily make financial contributions to charities and scholarships that, while seeming to conflict with short-term profit-maximization, actually increase profits by creating goodwill and enhancing the reputation of the business.

Democracy

Democracy emerged only after hard-fought battles throughout the world to gain the right to vote. Yet democracy today is facing a crisis. Apathy and cynicism are widespread, voter turnout is low, and the political process in many developed nations is increasingly dysfunctional as partisan bickering prevents governments from enacting needed legislation. A large part of this dysfunction is attributable to voters who are unwilling to accept the responsibilities entailed by citizenship in a democratic nation. Those responsibilities include not just voting regularly but also being well-informed about public issues and actively engaging in political discussions with each other and with elected representatives. Both voters and their political leaders need ongoing dialogue so that divergent viewpoints can be challenged and subjected to the collective wisdom of the community. Communities can potentially improve the quality of democracy in several ways.

Promoting Civic Virtue

By shaping personal identities, communities cause members to broaden the scope of their interests to include the well-being of the community as a whole. This social conscience gives rise to patriotism, loyalty, and a sense of duty, which in turn motivate participation in civic affairs. People who are actively engaged in their communities are more likely to vote because they are concerned about the quality of the community as well as their own self-interest. Civic virtue makes citizens less resistant to paying taxes, particularly for funding public goods such as education, whose benefits accrue unevenly across the population. Politicians who are firmly grounded in a community are more likely to promote the public interest instead of using their office to gain personal wealth and power. The quality of political discourse improves as citizens learn to see beyond their own narrow interests and to compromise in order to reach consensus.

Supplementing the State

Communities may perform various functions that would otherwise become the responsibility of government. To the extent that communities instill virtue in their members, fewer violations of the law occur, and fewer laws are needed to maintain social order. The scope of formal laws can be restricted to those behaviors deemed so harmful to society that the cost of enforcement is outweighed by the benefit of maintaining public safety and security.

Communities also reduce the burden of governing by providing public goods. Private charities cover some of the gaps in public welfare programs. Parents may supplement the efforts of public schools in educating their children. Neighbors keep an eye on each other's property. During natural disasters such as floods, communities are sometimes more important than government in providing immediate relief. Indeed, people often report that they have never felt a greater sense of community than during a natural disaster.

Decentralization

In a community, individuals can voice their concerns and participate in governance. This "grassroots democracy" provides a venue for public input into the political process and breeds good citizenship by developing knowledge, communication skills, and the ability to cooperate and compromise.

Virtual Communities

The Internet has revitalized democracy by enabling individuals to quickly create virtual communities to share information, formulate political strategies, and plan collective action. The Internet allows every citizen to have a voice, not just as an individual, but, more powerfully, as a member of a like-minded community.

POTENTIAL WEAKNESSES OF COMMUNITY

Like states and markets, communities have shortcomings. Although the positive aspects of good families, cohesive neighborhoods, and civic organizations are obvious, communities also include interest groups, trade associations, labor unions, political parties, gangs, mafias, and groups based on religion, ethnicity, or nationality. These communities can potentially impede the performance of an economic system.

Reduced Prosperity

According to microeconomic theory, **economic efficiency** is promoted by competition in which many small, independent businesses and consumers exchange goods and resources for money. Communities, as aggregations of individuals or businesses, potentially violate perfect competition and therefore may interfere with prosperity.

Immobility of Labor

Economic efficiency requires perfect mobility of resources, including labor. However, individuals have emotional and financial attachments to their communities and therefore may be reluctant to relocate to better opportunities elsewhere. The culture of some communities may stress loyalty and duty to such an extent that individuals will sacrifice opportunities for personal advancement in order to devote themselves to the community.

Inefficiency

People in communities are not subject to the intense competitive pressures of the market. As a result, they may be less efficient in making decisions and accomplishing goals. For example, a community's commitment to participation and consensus may result in lengthy debates and meetings that delay decisive action.

Institutional Sclerosis

Some communities take the form of interest groups such as trade associations, professional groups, and political action committees whose purpose is to lobby the government for legislation that will increase the income of their members. These rent-seeking efforts contribute nothing to the productive capacity of the economy and actually drain resources from more productive uses. Rather than creating wealth, resources are used to redistribute wealth, usually from less powerful communities to more powerful communities. The effect of widespread rent seeking is to restructure the market with various **barriers to entry**, subsidies, and regulations, which impede the free flow of resources to their most productive uses. This obstruction of the market has been termed *institutional sclerosis* because it is analogous to the clogging of arteries carrying blood through the circulatory system (Olson 1982). As interest groups proliferate, the market becomes less flexible in responding to change. The result may be a less efficient and dynamic economy.

Discrimination

Some communities discriminate against nonmembers. Economic theory suggests that discrimination reduces efficiency in several ways. First, cronyism and nepotism result in people being hired and promoted based on characteristics other than productivity. Second, discriminating communities may erect barriers to entry that exclude potentially productive members. Finally, discriminating communities may refuse to sell to nonmembers as exemplified by restaurants and hotels in the southern United States that would not serve African Americans prior to the 1964 Civil Rights Act. All these forms of discrimination interfere with prosperity by reducing economic efficiency.

Cultural Conflict

The cultures of two different communities may be so antagonistic that normal commerce is restricted or halted. When this happens, both sides suffer from the lost benefits of specialization and trade. For example, from 1959 until very recently, the United States refused to trade with Cuba in an effort to topple the Castro regime. The United States lost access to inexpensive sugar, and Cubans had to rely on automobiles manufactured in the 1950s. In extreme cases of conflict, valuable resources may be wasted attacking the enemy and retaliating for previous offenses. The former Yugoslavia was torn apart during the 1990s as Serbs, Croats, Muslims, and other ethnic groups sought revenge for atrocities that occurred hundreds of years ago. Iraq is currently disintegrating as Sunnis, Shiites, and Kurds struggle for sovereign control over different regions of the country.

Local Obstacles to Commerce

For centuries, local communities have tried to enrich themselves by enacting regulations, tariffs and other fees on commerce. Today, the constitutions of most countries give the national government exclusive authority to regulate commerce between regions in order to prevent local self-interest from interfering with the national economy. Another form of local resistance is associated with the acronym NIMBY (not in my backyard). NIMBY refers to local objections to decisions by government or businesses to locate an undesirable facility or project in a particular community. For example, no community wants a nuclear power plant or a toxic waste dump in the immediate vicinity.

Limited Freedom

Communities tend to be homogeneous because they are often formed by people with similar interests and values. Although this homogeneity reduces conflict, it also creates the potential for oppression. In the seventeenth century, Puritans in New England burned women at the stake for allegedly practicing witchcraft and executed Quakers for violating a ban on Quakers in that area. Three centuries later, the freedom of African Americans in the southern United States was restricted by Jim Crow laws enacted by white communities to maintain racial segregation. Antimiscegenation laws in the United States, Nazi Germany, and South Africa prevented marriages between people of different races. Although these laws were enacted by states, they were a response to prevailing sentiments in the dominant community.

In the community-centered system of medieval Europe, individuals had few opportunities for social mobility; people's fate was largely determined by their parents' social status. More recently, India in the nineteenth century had a rigid caste system that imposed similar restrictions on social mobility. Members of the lowest caste were deemed so despicable that they were called "untouchables." Although India has enacted numerous laws aimed at dissolving the caste system, its effects have not been entirely eradicated.

Even tolerant communities may inadvertently restrict positive freedom due to past injustices. After racial discrimination became illegal in the United States in 1964, the absence of African Americans in positions of prestige and authority meant that black children had few role models to emulate, and their aspirations were narrowed accordingly.

Social Conflict

Although communities undoubtedly transmit culture from one generation to the next, part of that culture may include prejudices, stereotypes, and hatred toward members of other communities. Conflict between communities has several sources.

Identity Politics

Many communities are nested within larger communities, and conflict may arise over the degree of **sovereignty** held by each level of community. Communities based on race, religion, or ethnicity are particularly vulnerable to oppression by a dominant culture, and conflict arises when they attempt to gain greater sovereignty. This struggle for self-determination is referred to as **identity politics**. These communities seek more than just integration and equal rights; members want recognition and acceptance of their differences from the dominant culture. This clash of cultures can easily generate conflict and even violence as exemplified by the use of dogs, billy clubs, and fire hoses to subdue protestors during the Civil Rights movement of the 1960s or the shooting of three people during a standoff between the American Indian Movement and US marshals at Wounded Knee, South Dakota, in 1973.

Nationalism

Patriotism is an important source of personal identity for many people. Armies could not be formed and wars fought if all citizens based their decisions solely on calculations of individual costs and benefits. A sense of national community motivates citizens to make sacrifices that *homo economicus* would most likely avoid. However admirable this self-sacrifice may be in defending the nation from external threat, the same loyalty to one's nation can also fuel aggression and war. Patriotism can degenerate into nationalistic fervor with cries of "my country, right or wrong."

Predatory States

A **predatory state** typically forms when one community gains control of government and uses that power to enrich itself at the expense of other communities. Nations with predatory states frequently experience conflict and violence. The state may intentionally foment dissension between communities in order to fragment society and discourage unified opposition to the state. Alternatively, the state may blame a particular community for causing the nation's problems. This "scapegoating" has the effect of unifying the dominant community against a common enemy, leading to oppression of the minority community. For example, Germany's government attempted to exterminate Jews during World War II and campaigns of genocide have sought to achieve "ethnic cleansing" in Bosnia and Rwanda. The struggle for political dominance in predatory states is often violent because the community that controls the state also secures substantial economic benefits.

Discrimination

Social scientists have long debated the causes of the human tendency to discriminate between "us" and "them" or to designate a particular group as "the other."

Discrimination may simply arise from psychological efforts to gain self-esteem by devaluing people who are different, but communities may also play a role. The earliest humans were members of tribes. Tribes fought with each other for control of scarce resources, so members of other tribes were assumed to be threats to one's safety. Over time, this prejudice was transmitted from one generation to the next. Even in modern times, discrimination may occur as one community seeks an advantage in competition for jobs and business success by denigrating members of another community. Communities may reinforce the prejudices of their members by offering validation and affirmation with derogatory jokes, slurs, and stereotypes.

Lack of Sustainability

The term *sustainability* refers not only to protecting the natural environment but also to preserving institutions. Communities may face difficulty in sustaining themselves due to institutional **crowding out** by both market and state. The market is driven by the powerful force of self-interest, and when that motive conflicts with the virtuous behavior on which communities rely, virtue is often the loser and communities begin to disintegrate. Moreover, the process by which the market displaces communities can be self-perpetuating. As economic behavior spills over into community life, individuals observe that others are gaining advantage by pushing the boundaries of ethics and the law in pursuit of self-interest. When opportunism in the form of cheating, deceit, and cutting corners becomes sufficiently widespread, individuals who remain virtuous are potentially disadvantaged and may feel compelled to reciprocate (Macpherson 1962).

In several respects, communities and markets conflict with each other. Markets encourage mobility of labor and capital, whereas communities are based on loyalty and attachment. Markets promote self-reliance and the pursuit of self-interest, whereas people in communities expect others to cooperate and promote the common good. Markets are amoral in the sense that any profitable good or service is produced, whereas communities function with a shared sense of morality that may prohibit certain goods or behaviors. As the market penetrates more deeply into all spheres of social life, increasing numbers of individuals may abandon communities, viewing them as constraints on the pursuit of self-interest.

The state also poses several potential threats to the sustainability of communities. First, the state has authority to make certain community practices illegal. For example, Mormons practiced polygamy in the nineteenth century until the US government banned multiple marriages. The Ku Klux Klan used violence and intimidation to promote its belief in white supremacy until the government eventually began prosecuting lynchings, bombings, and assassinations. Second, states undermine communities by taking responsibility for many of their functions. When the state provides a social safety net and an array of public goods, citizens become less dependent on communities for support. To the extent that an institution no longer serves a useful function, it tends to wither and die (Nisbet 1953).

As both market and state erode the role of communities, a vicious circle develops. The decline of community weakens virtue, which reduces participation in civic life and causes communities to disintegrate further. As communities perform fewer functions, the market and the state expand to fill the void, rendering communities even less relevant in people's lives. The only communities that may be immune to this downward spiral are those such as trade associations and lobbying groups that exist to advance the economic interests of their members.

Restricted Human Development

Although communities are essential to well-rounded human development, peer pressure to conform to social norms may stifle individual curiosity, creativity, and innovation. Japanese culture is commonly criticized for overemphasizing conformity to the extent that entrepreneurship and innovation are suppressed. World history is replete with examples of entrepreneurs who were separate from the mainstream culture in which they lived. Many of the leading entrepreneurs of the British Industrial Revolution were religious dissidents. A disproportionate number of entrepreneurs in Southeast Asia are Chinese emigrants. The same is true for Indian emigrants in East Africa, German emigrants in South America, and Jews throughout the world. The innovative energy that fueled the early development of the personal computer came primarily from individuals who were involved in the "counterculture" in the United States during the 1970s. As outsiders, these entrepreneurs were unburdened by pressures to conform to the dominant culture. They could question conventional wisdom and envision new products and technologies.

Communities based on race, ethnicity, or religion are particularly prone to suppress individuality. To preserve internal cohesion, they demand faith and loyalty to conventional norms. Dissent is often treated as a threat to the community and is actively resisted. Over time, members of the community tend to become parochial and narrow-minded. People who are committed to such communities often fail to explore the full range of choices open to them. They find meaning and purpose in their lives simply as members of the group while neglecting the more challenging project of forging their own sense of self. Stepping outside one's community may sometimes be necessary to fully develop personal capacities.

Erosion of Democracy

Communities such as political action committees and special interest groups seek to promote their interests by influencing the political process. Through lobbying, campaign contributions, and other forms of influence-buying, they can potentially subvert the will of the majority. For example, polls indicate that the majority of Americans favor tightening gun control laws, eliminating import quotas on sugar, and ending subsidies to tobacco farmers. Yet relatively small special interest groups are able to exert disproportionate pressure on Congress to block such reforms.

The economist Mancur Olson (1932–1998) offered an explanation for the power of small communities (Olson 1965). Members of small communities have strong incentives to engage in rent seeking to secure benefits from government because the benefits are concentrated on a small group of people, and therefore each person stands to gain substantially. With sufficiently strong incentives, small communities may overcome the free-rider problem as individuals voluntarily contribute money for lobbying, become politically active, and base their vote on a single issue. As a result, politicians are more responsive to the concerns of small but highly-organized communities.

The incentive for small communities to influence the political process is only half the explanation for their disproportionate powers. Because the costs of successful rent seeking at the federal level are borne by the national community (i.e., all taxpayers), the burden on any individual taxpayer is minimal. As a result, citizens have little incentive to actively oppose the favors granted to special interest groups. To summarize, the benefits of successful rent seeking are highly concentrated while the costs are dispersed. As a result, small communities have strong incentives to influence government, and the large national community has little incentive to oppose those efforts.

Successful rent seeking fuels more rent seeking. As some communities gain economic benefits through the political process, other communities are motivated to do the same. Just as communities may cause institutional sclerosis in the market, they also potentially clog the functioning of government, leading to **demosclerosis** (Rauch 1999). As a consequence of widespread rent seeking, politicians tend to develop **rational myopia** because interest groups want immediate benefits with no sacrifice. The **national debt** grows, and the political process becomes biased in favor of present consumption over investment in future development. Finally, as interest groups become more numerous, their conflicting pressures on government lead to political gridlock and dysfunction.

CONCLUSION

Of the three governance structures we have examined, communities are the most vulnerable to institutional crowding out. Markets threaten communities by promoting self-interested economic behavior at the expense of commitments to the norms and cultures constituting communities. States undermine communities by absorbing many of their functions and by replacing informal institutions with uniform laws and regulations. Yet healthy communities are essential to the success of modern economic systems because they instill civic virtue and serve as incubators for human capital, innovation, and knowledge. New institutions are needed to protect and revitalize communities against the corrosive effects of both markets and states.

Community Development Grants

Governments have the ability to improve communities through funding for cultural and recreational activities and organizations that bring people together by fostering cooperation, shared experiences, and common values. Examples include funding for the arts, festivals, cultural heritage centers, museums, recreational sports facilities, farmers markets, and libraries. Granting tax-exempt status to nonprofit organizations has the same effect as subsidies.

Social Benefits

To protect communities from the corrosive effects of markets, governments can offer social benefits to encourage activities such as childrearing, care for the elderly, and community service. For example, governments might offer stipends or tax deductions for dependent children, educational expenses, and charitable donations.

Laws and Regulations

Some government regulations and decisions are supportive of community development. Neighborhoods can be preserved through zoning laws, the location of new highways, and the availability of mass transit. Laws related to plant closings and layoffs cushion the shock to a community of losing a major employer. Environmental regulations reduce the likelihood that a community will be destroyed by excessive air and water pollution or by a toxic waste dump. Laws requiring employers to offer paid leaves of absence for births allow new parents to bond with their children.

Selective Stimulus

Not all communities are equally valuable in building a successful economic system. Communities whose primary purpose is to advance the economic interests of their members (e.g., professional associations and industry groups) may actually interfere with efficiency by devoting resources to rent seeking through efforts to reduce competition and gain benefits from government. On the other hand, communities whose primary function is to build social, cultural, and human capital (e.g., youth organizations, service clubs, and neighborhood associations) contribute positively to economic performance and therefore are deserving of public resources to increase their efficacy.

The Principle of Subsidiarity

Communities can be revitalized by regaining certain functions that have been taken over by state and federal governments. The principle of subsidiarity calls for decentralizing public responsibilities to the lowest level at which they can be effectively conducted. Examples of communities taking responsibility for public functions include neighborhood watch groups, volunteer fire departments, churches that sponsor food pantries, and clubs that pick up litter along highways.

REFERENCES

Acemoglu, Daron. 2009. *Introduction to Modern Economic Growth.* Princeton, NJ: Princeton University Press.

Akerlof, George A., and Rachel E. Kranton. 2010. *Identity Economics: How Our Identities Shape Our Work, Wages, and Well-Being.* Princeton, NJ: Princeton University Press.

Berger, Peter L., and Richard J. Neuhaus. 1996. *To Empower People: The Role of Mediating Structures in Public Policy*, 2nd ed. Washington, DC: American Enterprise Institute.

Cohen, Don, and Laurence Prusak, 2001. *In Good Company: How Social Capital Makes Organizations Work*. Cambridge, MA: Harvard Business Review Press.

Duesenberry, James. 1960. *Demographic and Economic Change in Developed Countries*. New York: National Bureau of Economic Research.

Durkheim, Emile. (1925) 1961. *Moral Education*. New York: Free Press of Glencoe.

———. (1897) 1951. *Suicide: A Study in Sociology*. Glencoe, IL: Free Press of Glencoe.

Etzioni, Amitai. 1998. *The Essential Communitarian Reader*. Lanham, MD: Rowman & Littlefield.

Kanter, Rosabeth Moss. 1972. *Commitment and Community: Communes and Utopias in Sociological Perspective*. Cambridge, MA: Harvard University Press.

Macpherson, C. B. 1962. *The Political Theory of Possessive Individualism*. New York: Oxford University Press.

Nisbet, Robert A. 1953. *The Quest for Community*. New York: Oxford University Press.

Olson, Mancur. 1965. *The Logic of Collective Action: Public Goods and the Theory of Groups*. Cambridge, MA: Harvard University Press.

———. 1982. *The Rise and Decline of Nations*. New Haven, CT: Yale University Press.

Ostrom, Elinor. 1990. *Governing the Commons: The Evolution of Institutions for Collective Action*. New York: Cambridge University Press.

Rauch, Jonathan. 1999. *Government's End: Why Washington Stopped Working*. New York: Public Affairs.

Romer, Paul M. 1994. "The Origins of Endogenous Growth," *The Journal of Economic Perspectives* 8(1): 3–22.

Sahlins, Marshall. 1974. *Stone Age Economics*. London: Tavistock.

Tam, Henry. 1998. *Communitarianism: A New Agenda for Politics and Citizenship*. Basingstoke, UK: Macmillan.

Taylor, Charles. 1999. *Sources of Self: The Making of the Modern Identity*. New York: Cambridge University Press.

Taylor, Michael. 1982. *Community, Anarchy, & Liberty*. New York: Cambridge University Press.

ADDITIONAL READING

Aioki, Masahiko, and Yujiro Hayami, eds. *Communities and Markets in Economic Development*. New York: Oxford University Press, 2001.

Albert, Michael, and Robin Hahnel. *Looking Forward: Participatory Economics for the 21st Century*. Boston: South End Press, 1999.

Alexander, Jeffrey. *The Civil Sphere*. Oxford: Oxford University Press, 2006.

Bell, Daniel. *The Cultural Contradictions of Capitalism*. New York: Basic Books, 1976.

Bellah, Robert N., Richard Madsen, William M. Sullivan, Ann Swidler, and Steven M. Tipton. *The Good Society*. New York: Alfred A. Knopf, 1991.

Block, Peter. *Community: The Structure of Belonging*. San Francisco: Berrett-Koehler, 2008.

Boswell, Jonathan. *Community and the Economy: The Theory of Public Co-operation*. New York: Routledge, 1990.

Bowles, Samuel, and Herbert Gintis. *A Cooperative Species: Human Reciprocity and Its Evolution*. Princeton, NJ: Princeton University Press, 2013.

Brooks, David. *The Social Animal: The Hidden Sources of Love, Character, and Achievement*. New York: Random House, 2012.

Bruyn, Severn. *A Civil Economy: Transforming the Market in the Twenty-First Century*. Ann Arbor: University of Michigan Press, 2000.

Chomsky, Noam. *On Anarchism*. New York: The New Press, 2013.

Daley, Herman E., and John B. Cobb, Jr. *For the Common Good: Redirecting the Economy Toward Community, the Environment, and a Sustainable Future*. Boston: Beacon Press, 1989.

Eberly, Don, and Ryan Streeter. *The Soul of Civil Society*. New York: Lexington Books, 2002.

Etzioni, Amitai, *The New Normal: Finding a Balance between Individual Rights and the Common Good*. Piscataway, NJ: Transaction Publishers, 2014.

Fukuyama, Francis. *Trust: The Social Virtues and the Creation of Prosperity*. New York: Free Press, 1995.

Garnett, Robert F. Jr., Paul Lewis, and Lenore T. Ealy, eds. *Commerce and Community: Ecologies of Social Cooperation*. New York: Routledge, 2015.

Hirst, Paul. *Associative Democracy: New Forms of Economic and Social Governance*. Cambridge: Polity, 1994.

Janssen, Marco, and Elinor Ostrom. *Working Together: Collective Action, the Commons, and Multiple Methods in Practice*. Princeton, NJ: Princeton University Press, 2010.

Knowles, Rob. *Political Economy from Below: Economic Thought in Communitarian Anarchism, 1840–1914*. New York: Routledge, 2004.

Marglin, Stephen. *The Dismal Science: How Thinking Like An Economist Undermines Community*. Cambridge, MA: Harvard University Press, 2010.

Mason, Andrew. *Community, Solidarity, and Belonging*. New York: Cambridge University Press, 2000.

McKnight, John, and Peter Block. *The Abundant Community: Awakening the Power of Family and Neighborhoods*. San Francisco: Berrett-Koehler, 2012.

Putnam, Robert D., and Lewis Feldstein. *Better Together: Restoring the American Community*. New York: Simon & Schuster, 2004.

Rothstein, Bo. *Social Traps and the Problem of Trust*. New York: Cambridge University Press, 2005.

Chapter 6

THE US ECONOMIC SYSTEM

"Let us not forget that government is ourselves and not an alien power over us."

FRANKLIN D. ROOSEVELT (1882–1945),
President of the United States

"Government is not the solution to our problem, government is the problem."

RONALD REAGAN (1911–2004),
President of the United States

The United States began its economic development with numerous advantages. Geographically, it enjoyed a relatively temperate climate, navigable rivers, limitless land, hardwood forests, and fertile soil. Culturally, the United States was unburdened by legacies from feudalism. In the northern part of the country, at least, there were no rulers oppressing landless peasants, no class hatreds, and no dutiful submission to one's superiors. In the southern part, the economy was based on slavery, which discouraged industrial development in that part of the country but promoted exports of cotton and sugar. Both the early colonists and the revolutionary founding fathers viewed themselves as starting with a clean slate on which to create a nation of self-governing citizens that would serve as a model for all mankind.

COMPETITIVE CAPITALISM 1815–1896

We shall use the year 1815 to mark the beginning of **capitalism** in the United States. That date is highly debatable; arguments can be made that the United States was capitalist at the time of its birth in 1776 or that it was not fully capitalist until after the Civil War. However, in 1776, the US economy was essentially preindustrial. Because Britain prohibited colonists from producing most manufactured goods, few American businesses were equipped with recent technology. **Markets** were primarily local due to inadequate transportation and communication **infrastructure**, and only about 6 percent of the population engaged in wage labor (Bowles et al. 2005). Most economic activity took place on family farms; in the shops of self-employed craftsmen such as blacksmiths, cobblers, and wheelwrights; on Southern plantations using slave labor; and within Native American tribes.

Constitutional Government

As recently emancipated colonists, Americans sought to place strict limits on the power of government. In 1781, the thirteen original states ratified the Articles of Confederation, which confined the functions of the Continental Congress to national defense and foreign diplomacy. With no authority to tax, the national government had to plead with state governments to finance its limited functions. Illustrating the **free-rider problem**, state governments routinely refused these requests in hopes that some other state would shoulder the burden.

The Continental Congress also lacked authority to regulate business activity, so states were free to impose various taxes, tolls, and **tariffs** to generate **revenue**. These barriers to trade slowed economic development by discouraging interstate commerce. In 1789, a convention of representatives from each state met in Philadelphia to draw up a constitution that would, among other things, establish the balance of power between national and state governments. At the convention, three distinct visions of the proper role of government emerged. James Madison (1751–1836) cautioned against relying on the virtue of citizens to promote the public interest. He assumed that both individuals and communities were self-interested and would attempt to gain control of any power vested in the government. Madison proposed a system of checks and balances both within the national government and between national and state governments. Just as competition in the economy constrains the pursuit of self-interest, a balance of power in government would prevent narrow factions from dominating the **polity**.

Alexander Hamilton (1757–1804) was more sympathetic to **mercantilism**, advocating a strong, centralized government to actively promote economic development and to resolve **collective action problems** posed by the pursuit of self-interest by states and communities. Hamilton proposed a national bank, high tariffs on imported goods to protect American businesses, and greater power for the national government to provide **public goods** such as highways and canals.

In sharp contrast to Hamilton, Thomas Jefferson (1743–1826) believed that a natural human capacity for virtue and cooperation would allow the nation to be governed largely by local governments. However, he acknowledged that virtue could be corrupted by concentrated political power and wealth that threatened the independence of citizens. Jefferson envisioned a nation of small communities consisting of farmers, craftsmen, and small business owners, each with sufficient property to protect against domination by either big government or big business.

Despite their differences, these three "founding fathers" managed to forge a set of compromises resulting in the US Constitution. The location of the new nation's capital was also part of that compromise; the New Yorker Hamilton agreed to situate the capital along the Potomac River, and the Virginian Jefferson accepted a stronger central government. Madison's concerns were reflected in the constitutional diffusion of government authority accomplished by establishing a balance of power between the executive, legislative, and judicial branches and by adopting a system of federalism in which power was divided among national, state, and local governments. These provisions were designed to protect Americans from both state power and "rule by the mob." In other words, the Constitution prevented either a minority or a majority from exercising its will at the expense of the individual rights of citizens. In 1791, ten amendments to the Constitution specified these rights in the form of the Bill of Rights.

The Constitution barred the federal government from interfering with private enterprise unless commerce crossed state borders. At the time, interstate commerce was minimal, so government had virtually no role in the economy other than providing national defense and maintaining a legal system to protect private property and individual rights. When France and Britain declared war on each other in 1807, they began seizing American cargo ships in the Atlantic. In response, the United States placed an **embargo** on imports from those countries. The protection from foreign competition allowed American manufacturers to thrive, leading Congress in 1816 to approve a 20 percent tariff on imports. That figure would rise to an average of 45 percent after 1866, providing the bulk of the federal government's revenue until World War I. Government also granted extensive subsidies to private businesses to encourage the construction of canals and roads. The state of New York sold bonds to finance the Erie Canal beginning in 1817. When rail transport became technologically feasible, government invested in mixed private-public enterprises and gave the railroad industry millions of acres of public land as well as the use of eminent domain to encourage the expansion of rail lines. The Civil War (1861–65) required an even larger role for government, but the fear of political power and the importance attached to private property kept the economic functions of government relatively limited. The immediate economic impact of the Civil War, besides devastating the Southern economy, was the integration of the eastern and midwestern economies and the effective end of opposition to industrialization by Southern representatives in Congress.

Private Enterprise

Most businesses were small and labor-intensive; therefore, **negative externalities** such as pollution were minimal, and the public felt little need for government regulation of business. As the population grew and pioneers moved westward, **barriers to entry** in most industries remained low, and competition served to discipline the behavior of firms. For example, if one firm charged exorbitant prices, consumers could buy from another business. The first corporations appeared shortly after independence, but they were formed primarily for the purpose of gathering money from multiple investors to construct public goods such as roads, tunnels, and canals. A corporation could not operate without a government-issued charter that subjected the company to various forms of public supervision and oversight to ensure that the public interest was being served and that corporations were not seeking to influence government. Corporate records could be inspected by the government, and corporate charters automatically expired unless renewed.

Beginning in the 1830s, corporations began producing consumer goods for sale to the public. However, they remained relatively small until the Civil War when government contracts for the production of military goods stimulated growth and profitability. As corporate profits soared, they were able to lobby and bribe legislators and judges in an effort to secure contracts and block proposed government regulations. Abraham Lincoln (1809–1865) recognized the potential danger posed by concentrated economic power, warning that "corporations have been enthroned . . . an era of corruption in high places will follow . . . until wealth is aggregated in a few hands . . . and the republic is destroyed" (Shaw 1950, 40). An 1886 court decision increased corporate power by ruling that a corporation is a person with all the rights and protections from government authority accorded to citizens by the Constitution.

Unorganized Labor

Recurring waves of immigration increased the supply of labor, but the availability of inexpensive land in the West led to steady migration away from Eastern cities and consequent depletion of the industrial labor force. Wages for skilled workers were higher than in Europe, but because many of the immigrants lacked training and/or did not speak English, wages for unskilled workers remained low. A famine caused by a potato blight in Ireland in 1845 and a failed revolution in Germany in 1848 led to massive immigration from both those countries. Some of the immigrants could afford transatlantic passage only by selling themselves into indentured servitude, which required them to work for a specific employer at low wages for a number of years. Slave traders forcibly brought millions of Africans to the United States to work on the cotton and sugar plantations of the South. The Civil War finally resolved the issue of slavery, freeing four million slaves at the cost of more than 600,000 deaths.

The eagerness of many Americans to undertake the arduous trek westward was an indication of the poor working conditions in early factories. Skilled workers gained some bargaining power by forming **craft unions** open only to those with a particular skill. The first craft union appeared among printers in Philadelphia in 1790. However, the mass of general laborers remained at the mercy of their employers. In small businesses, workers could develop a personal relationship with the owner and expect to be treated well. But as businesses grew larger and competition intensified, the drive to minimize costs overrode concerns for the well-being of workers. With virtually no legal protection, workers were vulnerable to physical abuse, arbitrary firings, and unsafe working conditions. Employers had little incentive to create safe working conditions because they were not liable for deaths or injuries suffered on the job and a worker could be easily replaced. One coal mine owner reputedly stated that he would rather lose a man to a mining accident than a mule because replacing the man cost nothing.

Craft unions held minimal bargaining power because only a small percentage of workers in any single business belonged to the same union. To remedy this problem, a nationwide labor union called the Knights of Labor formed in 1869; by the 1880s, it had 800,000 members. However, the strategy of organizing workers of all trades into a single union failed due to the conflicting interests between workers in different occupations. The Knights could never muster widespread support for any single negotiation with an employer.

Union organizers faced a dilemma. Workers hesitated to join a union and pay dues until they became convinced that the union could secure higher wages and improve working conditions. Yet unions could be effective only with the strength conferred by a large membership. When Samuel Gompers (1850–1924) founded the American Federation of Labor (AFL) in 1886, he sought to steer a middle course between the weaknesses of both independent craft unions and the national union formed by the Knights of Labor. As an umbrella organization encompassing many different craft unions, the AFL gained strength in numbers while maintaining distinct unions for each particular occupation.

After the Civil War, former slaves continued to be vulnerable to exploitation. African Americans were arrested for contrived petty crimes such as loitering or jaywalking and sentenced to work for a local plantation owner to repay their "debt to society." However, after subtracting the owner's costs of food, clothing, and shelter, the "debt" was barely reduced and the former slave might end up working for years on the plantation. This system of "debt peonage" perpetuated the conditions of slavery long after the Civil War ended. Only slightly less egregious was the institution of sharecropping, in which former slaves worked the land of a plantation owner under the agreement that a specified percentage of the crop belonged to the owner. The abundance of former slaves seeking work ensured that the portion left for the sharecropper was barely sufficient for subsistence.

Culture

Many immigrants arrived in America seeking relief from arbitrary political authority, religious persecution, or economic hardship. The decision to leave friends and communities behind required personal characteristics such as ambition, self-reliance, and a strong desire for independence. Most immigrants were motivated to succeed by the belief that in America, personal ability, hard work, and perseverance would determine their fate. This individualistic culture partly explains the impressive record of entrepreneurship and innovation in America. With few commitments to communities or traditions, entrepreneurs were typically self-reliant, free thinkers unconstrained by social norms. American culture provided fertile ground for entrepreneurship and a strong work ethic.

As a new nation, America's communities were less cohesive and tradition-bound than communities in Europe. Early Americans were highly mobile, often willing to relocate to take advantage of better opportunities. The belief that individuals had equal opportunity for success unleashed a torrent of human energy. Some individuals were fabulously successful while others remained mired in poverty. By the latter part of the nineteenth century, a new class system was emerging that would challenge the American ideal of equal opportunity for all.

Americans had mixed reactions to the rise of social and economic inequality. Among the successful, a new ideology called *social Darwinism* explained inequality as the inevitable and desirable outcome of competition between inherently unequal individuals. Just as Charles Darwin (1809–1882) had demonstrated that the evolution of species is based on the principle of survival of the fittest, the social Darwinists argued that economic inequality resulted from genetically superior individuals rising to the top of the social hierarchy. Inequality provided incentive for talented individuals to exercise their abilities and thereby benefit society as a whole. Social Darwinism also implied that little should be done to assist the poor because their poverty was evidence of genetic inferiority. If they died at a young age, their inferior genes would not be passed on to future generations.

In contrast to this rugged individualism, other Americans were troubled by growing class distinctions and exhibited a strong desire to work collectively for the common good. The French sociologist Alexis de Tocqueville (1805–1859) traveled throughout America in 1831–33 and observed an "art of association" that brought citizens together for community activities. Throughout the first century of the nation's history, periodic "Great Awakenings" occurred as religious revivals inspired rapid growth of religious groups. After the Civil War, these movements focused less on personal salvation and more on social reform, as manifested by the social gospel movement and the founding of the Young Men's Christian Association, or YMCA. Popular community activities included barn raisings, quilting bees, square dances, and parades.

The Demise of Competitive Capitalism

The Civil War fundamentally changed the American economy by requiring the mobilization of **resources** on an unprecedented scale. With support and direction from the federal government, railroads expanded to transport troops and supplies, and businesses modernized factories to produce the weapons of war. For the first time in its short history, the United States was on the verge of creating a national market, making it possible for goods produced in one location to be sold throughout the entire country. The widening of the market meant that businesses could expand their scale of operations and improve productivity through **economies of scale**. By the 1870s, the opportunities created by an expanding economy gave rise to an industrial revolution. Entrepreneurs, engineers, and scientists developed new technologies that enabled manufacturers to produce new and better products at lower cost and much higher volume.

Mass production required not just better machines but also a reorganization of production. Before the Civil War, a typical American business consisted of an entrepreneur/owner and a relatively small number of employees. However, the complexity and size of mass production required efficient organization to coordinate the actions of hundreds and in some cases thousands of workers. The solution to this challenge emerged in the form of an increasing division of labor and hierarchical bureaucracies in which each person had a narrow and well-defined task. A worker might spend the entire day repeatedly performing one simple movement. This deskilling of labor meant that workers became increasingly interchangeable; many of the skills required for factory work could be learned in a few days.

The rise of large corporations also caused the gradual disappearance of small businesses in the manufacturing sector. In major industries, a few large corporations displaced hundreds of small, independent firms as the economies of scale associated with mass production prevented small businesses from matching the prices and marketing networks of large corporations. As corporations grew, their need for **financial capital** exceeded the capabilities of any single bank. The stock and bond markets channeled money from all over the world into American corporations, but financial markets also reinforced industrial concentration. Investors and banks were eager to provide money to large corporations with established products, solid reputations, and the cost advantages conferred by economies of scale. In contrast, small businesses often failed for lack of credit.

Economies of scale were not the only cause of industrial concentration. Owners of corporations relied on aggressive and often ruthless tactics to crush competitors and capture markets. With virtually no regulation of business behavior, corporations engaged in **collusion, mergers, predatory pricing**, and **interlocking directorates**. In addition, some corporate leaders, eventually known as "robber barons," actually violated the law to achieve their ends. John D. Rockefeller (1839–1937) hired mercenaries to physically assault the employees of competing railroad companies. Other tactics to ruin competitors and gain market share included stock manipulation, spreading false rumors, prohibiting retailers from selling a competing product, and **tying contracts**. The American economy was no longer based on small businesses competing through efficiency and innovation. Corporate behemoths now engaged in ruthless attempts to gain control over markets and restrict competition.

The federal government responded to public outrage over the abuse of business power. The Interstate Commerce Commission was created in 1887 to regulate railroads. The passage of the Sherman Act in 1890 created the first **antitrust law** in the United States, but, if anything, it accelerated business concentration. The Sherman Act prohibited "conspiracy in restraint of trade or commerce," but the law could be evaded by merging with or acquiring competing firms. The Supreme Court effectively endorsed the concentration of business power when it ruled that manufacturing was different from commerce and therefore not subject to antitrust laws. After that ruling, the American Sugar Refining Company promptly bought controlling interest in its four largest competitors.

Industrial workers were not the only Americans concerned about the growing power of large corporations. Farmers and even small business owners felt squeezed by big banks, railroads, and the power of elites in both business and government. This resentment manifested itself in the formation of The People's Party (better known as the Populists) in 1891. Although primarily a rural southern and midwestern movement, the Populists built an alliance between farmers and urban factory workers. William Jennings Bryan (1860–1925), the leader of the Populists, became the Democratic Party's presidential candidate in 1896 but lost the election to William McKinley (1843–1901), who was generously supported by the captains of industry.

The changing structure of competitive capitalism affected its performance. Beginning in 1873, the US economy entered a period of economic turmoil that lasted until 1896. Six **recessions** occurred during that period, four of which entailed declines in business activity of more than 25 percent. The downturns were usually triggered by the failure of a large bank and an ensuing financial panic, but deeper forces were at work. Shrewd business owners recognized that economies of scale would virtually ensure industry dominance for the firm that expanded most rapidly. Economies of scale gave the largest firm in an industry a **competitive advantage** over its rivals due to lower per-unit costs. With more profit, the firm could fund further expansion and gain even greater dominance.

As business owners rushed to expand as quickly as possible, the growth of productive capacity eventually outstripped consumer demand. Moreover, owners financed most of the expansion with borrowed money, so they needed to operate their factories at full capacity in order to generate enough revenue to repay bank loans. With every firm in an industry engaged in a race to expand, output exceeded consumer demand despite downward pressure on prices. Eventually, goods remained unsold, businesses and banks failed, and the economy sank into another recession.

The growing dysfunction of competitive capitalism is a classic example of a collective action problem. In pursuing profit, each firm was motivated to expand as quickly as possible using borrowed money. But if all firms pursued this strategy, the result was **excess capacity**, overproduction, downward pressure on prices, and reduced profitability. Prices fell by more than 60 percent between 1873 and 1893. No single firm could solve the collective action problem by reducing production because other firms in the industry would continue to expand in their quest for competitive advantage. Some firms tried slashing prices in an attempt to draw customers away from competitors, but if other firms responded with similar price cuts, the resulting **price war** damaged all firms. As businesses endured falling profits, they defaulted on loan payments, causing banks to fail and creating a recession. With six major recessions in two decades, many Americans began to lose faith in their economic system. They felt vulnerable to economic forces over which they had no control. Success or failure increasingly seemed to depend more on wealth and power than on individual ability and effort.

ORGANIZED CAPITALISM 1897–1932

Trusts

Discontent with competitive capitalism was not confined to farmers and industrial workers. Business leaders realized that economic instability threatened profitability of the enormous **investments** required for mass production. They envisioned a reorganization of their industries to replace competition with cooperation by joining together with other firms in pools, associations, or trusts to plan and coordinate production. A trust was created when shareholders of corporations in the same industry surrendered their shares of stock in exchange for shares in a trust with a single board of directors. For example, John D. Rockefeller's Standard Oil trust enabled previous competitors in the oil industry to act as a monopoly and control the market for oil. In 1901, the financier J. P. Morgan acquired Andrew Carnegie's steel company and combined it with other steel producers to create US Steel, a virtual monopoly in the steel industry. This drive to replace competition with organization led to a dramatic restructuring of the American economy. In the four years between 1895 and 1899, more than 1,600 mergers occurred in manufacturing and mining, creating firms of unprecedented size and power.

Organized Labor

Mass production often entailed the replacement of skilled labor with machinery. Many of the remaining factory jobs were so rudimentary that workers lost bargaining power because they could be easily replaced. However, this homogenization of blue-collar workers also had the effect of creating a sense of solidarity as the workers recognized their common plight and their shared interest in forming labor unions.

Despite the founding of the AFL in 1886, the power of labor unions proved to be no match for business and government resistance to higher wages. Striking workers often faced violent reprisals from the local police, the National Guard, or Pinkerton detectives hired by employers to break up union activities. In 1914, the National Guard opened fire on and burned the tents of striking miners in Ludlow, Colorado, killing twenty-five people. Government was effectively barred from protecting labor unions because the commerce clause of the Constitution prohibited regulation of business activity unless it crossed state borders. Judges often demonstrated open hostility toward unions, sometimes requiring them to compensate businesses for any losses incurred during a strike. Union organizers faced harassment, blackballing, tarring and feathering, and even murder. By 1929, only 20 percent of the nonagricultural labor force belonged to unions.

Chronic surpluses of labor further weakened the power of unions. Employers could pick and choose from a growing pool of job seekers due to the displacement of industrial workers by machines, massive immigration to the United States from southern and eastern Europe, and a steady exodus of farmers from rural areas to the cities. Employers often preferred to hire immigrants who were grateful to have jobs and less likely to join unions. Hiring workers who spoke different languages was a conscious strategy to undermine solidarity among employees that might lead to unionization. With surplus labor, employers had little incentive to raise wages even though labor productivity was rising due to improving technology and economies of scale.

Expanding Government

The period in American history from the 1890s to the 1920s is known as the Progressive Era. As the trend toward industrial consolidation continued unabated, reform-minded politicians and activists sought to curb the excesses of unbridled capitalism. Journalists known as "muckrakers" conducted investigations to expose both corporate and government corruption. Upton Sinclair's (1878–1968) book *The Jungle* described the unsanitary operations of the Chicago meatpacking industry. Ida Tarbell's (1857–1944) scathing magazine articles about Standard Oil led to the government-imposed dispersion of that trust into thirty-three smaller companies in 1911.

Among Progressives, a schism developed over government's role in regulating business. Despite his reputation as a "trust buster," Theodore Roosevelt (1858–1919) regarded large corporations as the natural consequence of economies of scale. If large corporations increased efficiency, then they should not be broken up. Roosevelt advocated the creation of a government agency to work cooperatively with businesses in each industry to promote the public interest. Participation by businesses would be voluntary, but refusal could result in prosecution under anti-trust laws.

Woodrow Wilson (1856–1924), on the other hand, claimed that close cooperation between government and big business would result in businesses controlling the regulating agencies and using the power of government to advance their own interests. For Wilson, vigorous enforcement of antitrust laws was necessary to prevent concentrated business power from arising in the first place. In 1914, a new antitrust law, the Clayton Act, effectively "put teeth in the Sherman Act" by prohibiting **price discrimination**, tying contracts, and interlocking directorates. In the same year, the Federal Trade Commission was established to monitor and regulate business practices.

The onset of World War I in 1914 settled the debate over breaking up corporations. The entire US economy had to be mobilized for the war effort, and government needed the cooperation of large corporations to prepare for battle. At that time, government lacked the administrative capacity to handle the task of coordinating the economy and therefore created the War Industries Board (WIB). The WIB was staffed largely with businessmen and representatives of various trade associations who volunteered for public service. Unlike government bureaucrats, these business people possessed the detailed knowledge and expertise to plan for maximum industrial output. The WIB had responsibility for setting prices and production quotas, allocating raw materials, and settling labor disputes.

Because the government lacked information about industrial capacity and costs, it usually accepted any recommendations made by the WIB. Cooperation between business and government created opportunities for corporations to abuse their power, and indeed many suppliers of war materials made fortunes. But output increased by 20 percent, and victory was secured by 1918. The success of the WIB persuaded many leaders in government and industry that cooperation and planning were the keys to a stable and prosperous economy. Competition was denigrated as cutthroat, ruinous, chaotic, and wasteful. The new vision of organized capitalism relied on experts applying scientific principles of management and organization to determine which business practices and forms of organization would best promote the public interest.

This vision of government and private businesses jointly coordinating economic activity bears some resemblance to **fascism**. Although fascism did not actually materialize until the mid-1920s in Italy, fascist ideas appealed to some American leaders in both business and government. The US dime minted from 1916 to 1945 displayed a *fasces* on the reverse side. The 1921 insignia for the Militia Bureau (forerunner of the National Guard) depicted an eagle with wings spread and two crossed *fasces* over its breast. The official seal of the US Senate included a pair of crossed *fasces*, and two *fasces* flanked the flag behind the podium of the House of Representatives. The prevalence of the fascist symbol attested to the growing popularity of suppressing market competition and relying instead on cooperation between government and business to organize and coordinate the economy.

The Demise of Organized Capitalism

At the end of World War I, the government disbanded the WIB. Without the stimulus of war production, a severe recession ensued as industrial output fell by 35 percent and unemployment rose to nearly 12 percent by 1921. The Progressive Era had ended, and under President Calvin Coolidge (1872–1933), government withdrew from active intervention in the economy. The "Roaring 20s" was a decade of highly unbalanced growth as the stock market soared to previously unimagined heights while farmers, miners, factory workers, and small businesses failed to share in the gains. Low prices for agricultural products caused a mass exodus of farmers from rural areas into cities where competition for jobs drove industrial wages even lower. By 1929, the degree of inequality in the distribution of wealth and income reached historic highs.

In late 1929, an event shook the global economy as the US stock market lost half its value in a two-month period. Reflecting the belief that excessive competition was undermining corporate profitability, President Herbert Hoover (1874–1964) encouraged businesses in each industry to form trade associations in order to plan production and self-regulate. Government would serve as a partner, facilitating the operation of these associations, but Hoover was a firm believer in private enterprise and would not accept any significant government control of business activities. He rejected proposals to revive the economic planning that had been so effective during World War I, calling such proposals "socialistic."

As the collapse of the stock market ushered in the Great Depression, the Hoover administration attempted to bolster **aggregate demand** with increased spending on public works projects. To maintain a balanced federal budget, the administration also increased taxes on wealthy individuals and corporations. In 1930, Congress enacted the Smoot-Hawley tariff to discourage imports and thereby increase demand for domestic products. Toward the end of his administration,

Hoover approved the creation of the Reconstruction Finance Corporation to lend money to state governments and banks. None of these programs prevented the economy from continuing its downward spiral.

REGULATED CAPITALISM 1933–1979

The New Deal

The election of Franklin Roosevelt (1882–1945) marked the beginning of a new form of capitalism. When Roosevelt took office in 1933, the official unemployment rate was approaching 25 percent, and an estimated additional 10 percent of the labor force had simply given up the search for a job. The stock market had lost 87 percent of its value since 1929. Roosevelt promised a New Deal, but he lacked a clear plan of action because the cause of the Depression was not fully understood. One explanation blamed excessive competition, which kept prices low and reduced profitability. To address this problem, Congress created the Agricultural Adjustment Administration (AAA) and the National Recovery Administration (NRA).

In an effort to increase farm prices, the Agricultural Adjustment Administration paid farmers to reduce crop production and destroy livestock. At a time when many Americans faced unemployment and hunger, millions of piglets and pregnant sows were slaughtered to raise the price of pork so that farmers could earn enough to survive. In the manufacturing sector, the NRA resembled the WIB of World War I. Conceived by Gerard Swope (1872–1957), the president of General Electric, the NRA encouraged the formation of self-governing business associations resembling **cartels**. These associations enabled firms in each industry to cooperate with one another in setting prices and levels of output in a profitable manner. Most business leaders welcomed the idea of self-regulation but resisted any government control of their decisions. Yet, as the experience of the

Figure 6.1 Unemployed men queued outside a soup kitchen in New York City during the Great Depression. © Shutterstock/Everett Historical

WIB demonstrated, business cooperation and self-regulation without government involvement opened the door for **opportunism** and abuses of power.

A second explanation for the Great Depression blamed the growing imbalance between the **market power** of large corporations and the relative weakness of labor. This imbalance created increasing inequality as profits soared while wages and farm income remained stagnant. Excessive inequality, in turn, led to inadequate consumer spending because most of the increasing income was going to affluent households who saved a large portion of it. To address this problem, the NRA mandated minimum wage standards and gave labor unions the right to bargain collectively with employers. As was the case with the WIB during World War I, planning and cooperation between government and business bore a resemblance to the economic policies of fascism. Indeed, the director of the NRA, General Hugh Johnson (1881–1942), had a picture of the Italian dictator Benito Mussolini (1883–1945) hanging in his office.

The NRA quickly proved to be ineffective. The federal government simply lacked the personnel and information to coordinate and monitor business associations in each industry. Moreover, business standards and codes typically reflected the self-interest of corporations rather than government authority. Corporations took advantage of their newly granted powers of self-government to raise prices and to drive smaller firms out of business. In 1935, the Supreme Court declared the NRA to be an unconstitutional delegation of government authority to the private sector.

After the failure of the NRA, the next major attempt at economic stimulus was the Works Progress Administration (WPA) in 1935. Because businesses failed to increase employment opportunities, the government became the employer of last resort. The federal government hired millions of Americans to build roads, bridges, dams, public buildings, and even to engage their talents as artists, musicians, and actors. The Civilian Conservation Corps (CCC) hired young people and unemployed workers to plant trees, improve national parks, and build levees. The 1935 Social Security Act ensured some degree of financial security for retired Americans, and the Fair Labor Standards Act of 1938 established a minimum wage, the forty-hour workweek, extra pay for overtime work, and restrictions on child labor.

Keynesian Economics

As the Great Depression continued, the British economist John Maynard Keynes (1883–1946) developed a dramatically different approach to understanding the problem of instability in a capitalist economy. The revolutionary nature of Keynes' ideas is evident in the contrasts between pre-Depression economic theory and Keynesian economics. Before the Depression, higher wages were regarded as a threat to profitability and therefore an obstacle to investment and growth. Keynes argued that higher wages would permit workers to buy more goods, thereby increasing demand and causing businesses to expand production and employment. Before the Depression, conventional economic wisdom called for the government to maintain a balanced budget, spending no more than it collected in taxes. Keynes, in contrast, advocated **deficit spending** during recessions to maintain sufficient demand. Before the Depression, concentrations of wealth were considered essential to generate the **savings** needed to fund new investment and growth. Keynes argued that too much saving resulted in too little spending and therefore slower growth. Finally, pre-Depression economics viewed government assistance to the poor and unemployed as undermining self-reliance and encouraging laziness. Keynesian economics, on the other hand, supported such assistance to place money in the hands of people who would spend rather than save.

World War II forced the United States to engage in a full-blown experiment with Keynesian economics because defeating fascism required an unprecedented increase in government spending. At the time, the size of the military was relatively small, so a substantial buildup was required in preparation for war. In addition, the government provided free food, oil, and military equipment to its Allies under the Lend-Lease program. With the prospect of strong demand for their products, businesses began expanding production and hiring workers. By the time the United States actually entered the war in 1941, the Depression had ended and full employment prevailed. Keynesian economics, it seemed, had been vindicated.

The Capital-Labor Accord

The Wagner Act of 1935 restored the right of collective bargaining and created the National Labor Relations Board to protect unions from harassment and intimidation by employers. A new nationwide union, the Congress of Industrial Organizations (CIO), was established in 1938. Like the AFL, the CIO was an umbrella organization, but the separate unions were **industrial unions** rather than craft unions. Industrial unions have greater bargaining power because they represent workers of all occupations within a single industry such as automobiles, trucking, mining, or steel. By the late 1940s, more than fifteen million workers, or a third of the nonagricultural labor force, belonged to unions.

After a series of devastating wildcat strikes during the Depression, corporate leaders sought to secure peace with labor unions. In 1950, the United Automobile Workers (UAW) negotiated a contract with General Motors that became known as the Treaty of Detroit. General Motors agreed to provide health insurance, pensions, and annual cost-of-living adjustments to wages, and the UAW guaranteed no strikes during the length of the contract and no interference with managerial decisions. This contract established a model for labor relations in America. For the first time, many corporate leaders viewed labor unions as beneficial to business. Union contracts created stability, gave corporations certainty about future labor costs, and prevented wildcat strikes.

Even if corporate leaders were unaware of Keynesian economics, the Depression demonstrated that low wages create inadequate demand for consumer goods. A consensus among influential executives viewed wage-cutting as a short-sighted strategy that might benefit a single employer but ultimately harmed all firms. With their substantial market power, corporations felt confident that the cost of higher wages could be offset either by increasing productivity or by raising prices. Because the United States remained the only major industrial country in the world with its productive capacity fully intact at the end of World War II, US firms could also rely on strong demand for exports to bolster their profits.

The Business-Government Accord

If government spending on the war ended the Great Depression, what would happen when the spending ended and millions of soldiers returned home looking for work? Visionary leaders in both business and government began laying the groundwork for new institutions to secure a prosperous peacetime economy. The Employment Act of 1946 committed the government to use fiscal and monetary policy to "provide maximum employment, production, and purchasing power." For businesses, this commitment created confidence that government would ensure adequate demand for their products, either directly or by stimulating the private sector. Government also signaled its commitment to private enterprise with assurances of noninterference in the internal operations of businesses.

In return, businesses accepted corporate taxes and regulations designed to promote the public interest. In many cases, businesses actually welcomed these regulations because they solved collective action problems. For example, if a single firm voluntarily reduced its pollution, the additional cost would place that firm at a competitive disadvantage. But if all firms were required to reduce pollution, the goal of a cleaner environment could be achieved without causing any single firm to lose competitive advantage. Increased regulation also became more feasible because the Supreme Court loosened its interpretation of the "commerce clause" of the Constitution. The Court accepted the argument that virtually all commerce creates effects spilling across state borders and therefore is subject to federal regulation.

The Citizen-Government Accord

Another pillar of the postwar economic system was an implicit pact between citizens and their government. Government would ensure citizens of substantial security against the dynamic and sometimes harsh effects of capitalism by providing social security benefits, support for labor unions, a minimum wage law, welfare programs, the GI Bill offering free college education to all returning veterans, occupational safety laws, and farm price supports. In return, citizens would reject political extremism and accept the private ownership and control of the means of production.

Bretton Woods

The Great Depression and World War II caused a significant decline in international trade. In 1944, representatives from the industrialized, noncommunist nations met in Bretton Woods, New Hampshire, to forge a new international financial system. They agreed to maintain fixed exchange rates between currencies and to use the US dollar rather than gold to settle debts between countries. To persuade foreign governments that the dollar could be trusted, the United States pledged that dollars held by foreign central banks could be redeemed for gold at any time. The Bretton Woods agreement also permitted **capital controls** that enabled nations to restrict the movement of financial capital across national borders. By creating confidence in the stability of the international financial system, the Bretton Woods agreement stimulated trade and investment around the world.

Culture

World War II brought deep changes to American culture. Millions of people who might otherwise have spent their lives on farms or in small towns were drawn into large-scale organizations either as soldiers or as factory workers producing the weapons of war. They learned how to function within large groups to achieve goals that no single person could accomplish. They became accustomed to chains of command and divisions of labor. Author William Whyte (1917–1999) described this new American in his 1956 best-selling book *The Organization Man*. Americans had been chastened, if not traumatized, by the Depression and war, and now they focused on doing their jobs well to gain economic security for their families.

World War II also brought millions of women into the labor force to replace men fighting in Europe and the Pacific. A government ad campaign featuring "Rosie the Riveter" was designed to persuade women that building military hardware in factories was consistent with femininity. As the war ended and GIs returned home looking for work, the popular media once again promoted the role of women as mothers and homemakers, but the trend toward financial independence was irreversible and would eventually give rise to the women's liberation movement in the 1960s.

Another cultural change emerging in the 1960s was consumerism. As both corporate and government leaders accepted the Keynesian notion that consumption is essential to sustaining economic prosperity, the discipline and prudence associated with saving and investment gave way to self-expression through consumption and leisure (Bell 1976). Advertisers were only too happy to encourage immediate gratification of every desire as the cultural legacy of Puritanism gave way to a new hedonism.

*   *   *

With the pillars of regulated capitalism in place, the US economy entered a nearly three-decade expansion known as "the golden age of capitalism." Wages and consumer spending were bolstered by strong labor unions, collective bargaining, minimum wage laws, and other regulatory protections of the rights of labor. To ensure adequate demand so that businesses could afford to pay higher wages, the government supplemented private spending with public spending on national defense, expanding public education, support for research and development, construction of the interstate highway system, and exploration of outer space. The government also caused private spending to increase through social security, farm price supports, and welfare programs to redistribute income toward lower-income families who were more likely to spend the additional money. When recessions did occur, and there were three during the 1950s, they were relatively short and mild. A broad and thriving middle class emerged, closing the prewar gap between a small group of wealthy elites and a mass of low-wage workers.

The Demise of Regulated Capitalism

In 1963, John Kennedy (1917–1963), who had been taught Keynesian economics at Harvard, proposed a major reduction in income taxes to stimulate the economy. Although he was assassinated shortly thereafter, the Johnson administration enacted tax cuts the next year. Lyndon Johnson (1908–1973) was even more aggressive than Kennedy in applying **fiscal policy** to boost the economy. He declared a War on Poverty in an effort to ameliorate the plight of poor Americans by expanding the economy to the point of full employment. His Great Society programs entailed major increases in government spending at the same time that spending on the Vietnam War was escalating. The expansion of government spending, much of it financed through sale of government bonds, overstimulated the economy and contributed to a problem that would damage Western economies for the next decade—**inflation**.

Despite a recession in 1969–70, prices continued to rise. At the time, economists were puzzled because weak demand during a recession should have kept prices in check. However, a new type of inflation had emerged. Previous bouts of inflation typically occurred during wars when spending on military equipment created excessive demand that pulled prices up (hence the name *demand-pull inflation*). But this new inflation was caused by rising production costs pushing prices upward (hence the name *cost-push inflation*). When another recession struck in 1973, prices continued to rise. The combination of simultaneous stagnation and inflation came to be known as **stagflation**.

Capitalism becomes unstable when profits are declining or are expected to decline. Beginning in the late 1960s, corporate profits fell due to increasing costs of production. The causes of rising costs included government regulations, increasing market power, rising labor costs, declining productivity, increasing foreign competition, depreciation of the dollar, inflationary psychology, and Keynesian policies.

Government Regulations

The very success of regulated capitalism in generating a broad middle class created a generation of young people who came to maturity without ever experiencing the trauma of depression and war. These "baby boomers," born between 1946 and 1964, felt secure enough about their own futures to turn their attention toward social justice and quality of life. Their numbers and energy were sufficient to ignite broad social movements in support of civil rights, women's liberation, peace, consumer safety, and environmental protection. Many of their demands for social change became institutionalized in the form of new laws and regulations. In fact, more new government regulations were added during the administration of Richard Nixon (1913–1994) than at any time since the New Deal. New agencies included the Environmental Protection Agency (EPA), the Occupational Safety and Health Administration (OSHA), and the Consumer Product Safety Commission. Complying with the new regulations imposed significant costs on businesses.

Increasing Market Power

A wave of corporate mergers during the 1960s created larger firms with greater control over their industries. As a result, the United States developed a **dual economy** consisting of a primary sector with large corporations and labor unions and a secondary sector composed of small businesses and nonunionized workers. Corporations and unions in the primary sector had substantial **market power** and used it to raise prices and wages. Resource and capital goods industries such as oil, steel, and heavy machinery tend to be most concentrated; therefore, their market power forced corporations in the consumer products and service industries to pay higher prices for resources and equipment. Another source of rising costs was the 1973 decision by the Organization of Petroleum Exporting Countries (OPEC) to quadruple the price of oil in retaliation for US support of Israel. Virtually every business uses oil in one way or another, and the impact of OPEC's action increased costs throughout the economy.

Rising Labor Costs

By the 1960s, members of labor unions had become solidly middle class and expected continually rising wages and better working conditions. Low unemployment and high union membership enhanced union bargaining power, so many of their demands were met. Corporate leaders accepted wage increases, confident that the additional cost could be offset by increased productivity or higher prices.

Declining Productivity

Growth in output-per-man hour began declining in the late 1960s. Corporate executives accustomed to operating in oligopolistic markets with limited competition chose to pay dividends to shareholders rather than reinvest profits in modernizing their plant and equipment. Cultural factors also played a role in declining productivity. Along with political activism, "baby boomers" developed a "counterculture" that challenged conventional institutions such as a strong work ethic and deference to authority.

Increasing Foreign Competition

World War II destroyed many factories in Germany and Japan, but as those countries rebuilt, they installed the most up-to-date technology. By the 1970s, they were producing goods with superior quality and lower prices. As a result,

US firms lost both international and domestic market share. Increased international competition also reduced the ability of US firms to pass on higher production costs by raising prices.

Depreciation of the Dollar

As US exports declined and imports rose, a growing deficit in the **balance of trade** meant that foreign central banks ended up holding a surplus of dollars. Under the Bretton Woods system, these excess dollars could be redeemed for gold, and between 1944 and 1971, the United States lost 60 percent of its gold reserves at Fort Knox. In 1971, President Nixon announced that the United States would no longer redeem dollars for gold and would allow exchange rates between the dollar and foreign currencies to fluctuate. The dollar was devalued by 10 percent and subsequently continued to depreciate. A weaker dollar meant that imported raw materials became more expensive, which only added to the problem of rising production costs. In 1974, the United States began lifting controls on the movement of financial capital across national borders so that money could flow freely into or out of the country. These actions effectively ended the Bretton Woods system.

Inflationary Psychology

As inflation continued year after year, Americans developed **inflationary psychology**. Because they expected continuing inflation, business and unions redoubled their efforts to raise prices and wages in order to keep up with the rising cost of living. A **wage-price spiral** developed in which rising prices caused unions to demand higher wages, and higher wages caused businesses to raise prices. By 1980, the annual rate of inflation hit 13 percent. At that rate, prices would double every five and a half years.

Keynesian Policies

By using Keynesian **fiscal policy** and **monetary policy** to ensure adequate demand for business products, government inadvertently encouraged unions and businesses to raise wages and prices. Yet any efforts to reduce government spending or tighten the money supply would, at least in the short term, result in declining output and higher unemployment. Keynesianism was in disarray. It could fight inflation by reducing government spending, or it could fight recession by increasing government spending, but it could not do both at the same time.

As stagflation worsened, Americans were enmeshed in another collective action problem. Raising prices was in the self-interest of each business, and raising wages served the interests of each labor union. But the aggregate result of these actions was inflation, which nobody wanted. Any effort by a single business or union to exercise restraint in raising prices or wages would be futile unless everyone else did the same. However, the American economic system, with its strongly individualistic culture, had no institutional means to foster the cooperation needed to halt inflation voluntarily. With the economy floundering and Americans increasingly disillusioned with government, a new form of capitalism was imminent.

NEOLIBERAL CAPITALISM 1980-2008

During the 1970s, conservative economists developed theories demonstrating that government intervention was the primary, if not sole, cause of regulated capitalism's problems. They proposed dramatic reductions in the size of government—less government spending, lower taxes, fewer regulations, elimination of social programs, privatization of government services, and an end to the active use of fiscal and monetary policy to stabilize the economy. These economists and their supporters in politics and academia are referred to as neoliberals because their proposed policies are very similar to those of the classical liberals of the eighteenth and nineteenth centuries. Neoliberal capitalism represented an effort to repeal the New Deal of the 1930s and return to the days of unfettered private enterprise with minimal government intervention. In fact, many of the economic theories on which neoliberal capitalism was based were simply revised versions of pre-Keynesian economic theory. With the election of Ronald Reagan (1911-2004) in 1980, these theories were put into practice.

Monetarism

The basic tenet of monetarism is that inflation and recession are caused solely by changes in the money supply. According to monetarist economists such as Milton Friedman (1912-2006), the Federal Reserve (Fed) caused the Great Depression by failing to create enough money. As inflation accelerated in the late 1970s, monetarists urged the Federal Reserve to clamp down on the money supply, even if such action caused soaring **interest rates** and a recession. The Fed followed their advice, and interest rates rose to 20 percent. By 1981, the unemployment rate approached 11 percent as the economy sank into the worst recession since the Great Depression. With demand plummeting, businesses and unions could no longer raise prices and wages, and inflationary psychology ended. The economy recovered by 1982 and would not experience another recession until the early 1990s.

New Classical Economics

New classical economics is an updated version of the classical economics of the nineteenth century. It holds that free markets perform admirably in coordinating economic activity and that government intervention is usually harmful. New classical economists blame unemployment on rigidities in labor markets (e.g., labor unions and minimum wage laws) that prevent wages from falling to an equilibrium level at which every person seeking work would find a job. Unemployment caused by market rigidities was called the **natural rate of unemployment** and any attempts by government to reduce unemployment below the natural rate were claimed to be futile due to **rational expectations**. In this context, rational expectations were formed when citizens observed that government stimulation of the economy caused inflation. Any additional stimulus would lead workers to expect more inflation and therefore demand higher wages to keep up with anticipated increases in the cost of living. Higher wages, in turn, deterred employers from hiring additional workers, so the net effect of government stimulation of the economy would be more inflation and no reduction in unemployment.

Supply-Side Economics

Keynesian economics is sometimes referred to as "demand-side economics" because it emphasizes the role of demand or spending in maintaining high levels of output and employment. In contrast, most economists before the Great Depression focused primarily on the supply of resources as the essential determinant of economic growth. In other words, they believed that any nation with free markets and ample supplies of land, labor, capital, and entrepreneurship will prosper because abundant supplies of resources keep business costs low. Low costs, in turn, encourage businesses to increase production and employment.

Supply-side economics is simply a restatement of this pre-Keynesian orthodoxy. Its adherents claim that the only way government can stimulate the economy is to reduce business costs. The only business costs that government can significantly affect are the costs of business taxes, compliance with regulations, and labor. Therefore, supply-side economists advocate tax cuts, deregulation, and the elimination of rigidities in labor markets (e.g., labor unions and minimum wage laws) that keep wages above their equilibrium level.

Not all neoliberals are supply-siders, but others support tax cuts as a strategy to "starve the beast" by cutting off government revenue. Non-supply-siders anticipate that with less tax revenue, government would be forced to reduce or eliminate many of its functions. In contrast, supply-side economists claim that tax cuts would actually increase government revenue and therefore shrink budget deficits for two reasons. First, tax cuts allow individuals and businesses to keep more of their earnings and therefore provide greater incentives for productive activity and enlarge the tax base. Second, tax cuts enable individuals and businesses to save more money, which creates pools of financial capital for investment. As businesses invest in additional productive capacity, they create more jobs, the economy flourishes, the tax base grows, and more revenue flows into government coffers. Critics call this policy *trickle-down economics* because businesses and wealthy households are the direct beneficiaries. The rest of the population gains only if the lower taxes result in increased saving and investment in expanding businesses and creating jobs.

Although both Keynesian and supply-side policies support tax cuts as a method to stimulate the economy, the cuts are aimed at very different groups. Keynesians cut taxes for middle and lower-income groups most likely to spend their tax savings and thereby increase demand. Supply-siders, on the other hand, aim the bulk of tax cuts at upper-income households and businesses more likely to save and invest any reduction in their taxes.

Deregulation

From the neoliberal perspective, most government regulations harm the economy. If the additional costs of complying with regulations are passed on to the consumer by raising prices, the result is inflation. On the other hand, if businesses cannot raise prices, the additional costs reduce profitability, thereby restricting businesses' ability to expand and create jobs. In addition, the complexity of government regulations may deter entrepreneurs from starting businesses.

In the Reagan administration, many of the appointees to top positions in federal agencies shared the neoliberal opposition to regulation. They often required their agencies to use cost-benefit analysis to demonstrate that a proposed regulation created greater benefit to society than its cost both to government in implementing and monitoring the regulation and to firms in complying with the regulation. Besides their ideological predisposition, these bureaucrats faced personal incentives to deregulate because of what is known as the "revolving door" in Washington. Individuals who worked for several years in a regulatory agency that actively pursued deregulation could expect lucrative job offers in the industries under their purview. The revolving door also worked in reverse. Lobbyists for a particular industry were appointed to high positions in the agency responsible for that industry's regulation. This mutually beneficial relationship between industries and their regulatory agencies led some economists to propose that the agencies had been "captured" by private interests. Deregulation was pursued most aggressively in the airline, energy, trucking, telecommunications, and financial industries.

Privatization

Neoliberalism presumes that government is less efficient than the private sector in providing goods and services. Government lacks the disciplining pressure of competition to keep costs low and quality high. With its ability to both borrow and create money, government has an essentially unlimited budget, which makes waste and inefficiency inevitable. Neoliberals contend that whenever possible, responsibility for the goods and services currently provided by government should be turned over to private businesses. Examples of privatization include postal delivery of packages, the provisioning of military bases, garbage collection, and janitorial services for public buildings. In addition, governments are experimenting with private prisons, private courts, and private airports.

Stronger Businesses

The government pursued the neoliberal goal of boosting profits to spur economic growth by intentionally strengthening the power of US firms. Lax enforcement of antitrust laws led to a wave of mergers and acquisitions in the 1980s. Business lobbyists wrote legislative bills that their allies in Congress then submitted for passage. Lobbyists and other strong supporters of business were appointed to cabinet positions and other high-level offices in government. As a result, groups such as the National Association of Manufacturers, the US Chamber of Commerce, and the Business Roundtable gained greater access to the political process.

Corporations and wealthy individuals used their growing profits to fund "think tanks" such as the Cato Institute, the Manhattan Institute, the American Enterprise Institute, the Heritage Foundation, the Rand Corporation, the Hoover Institution, Americans for Prosperity, and the Club for Growth to defend neoliberal policies and to educate Americans about the virtues of free enterprise.

Weaker Labor

In 1981, the union representing the nation's air traffic controllers went on strike. President Reagan ordered the controllers to return to work within forty-eight hours or else lose their jobs. When the union refused to concede, more than eleven thousand controllers were fired and banned for life from working in that occupation. This action sent a strong message to all unions that strikes and excessive wage demands would not be tolerated. To further undermine union bargaining power, neoliberals supported **right-to-work laws** banning mandatory union membership as a condition for employment. Currently, twenty-four states have right-to-work laws. In addition, neoliberal politicians have refused to approve nominations to the National Labor Relations Board, crippling that agency's ability to monitor labor relations. More generally, neoliberals believe that unions would never have gained power without the support of government, so their goal is to remove all regulations favoring labor unions. The success of neoliberal policies in undermining labor unions is reflected in declining union membership. Only 6.6 percent of private sector workers currently belong to unions compared to 24 percent in 1973.

Social Policy

Neoliberals oppose virtually all social welfare programs. They argue that high levels of government spending result in either growing budget deficits or higher taxes. In addition, they believe that benefits received from government reduce individuals' incentive to work by rewarding idleness, undermining self-reliance, and creating a cycle of poverty in which children growing up in government-supported households fail to develop the work habits and motivation needed to succeed. Neoliberals would replace Social Security with individual retirement accounts. They favor school vouchers to enable families to send children to any school of their choice, thereby undermining public education or at least creating competition in education to force public schools to improve the quality of their teaching and curriculum. Neoliberals call for reducing Medicare and Medicaid through reliance on private medical savings accounts that grant tax exemptions to individuals who place money in accounts designated solely for paying healthcare expenses. The common theme underlying all these proposals is to replace government authority with individual self-reliance in the market.

Culture

Beginning in the 1980s, American culture became increasingly antagonistic and polarized. On one side of the "culture wars," an alliance formed between neoliberals calling for a return to free markets and social conservatives seeking the restoration of "traditional American values." On the other side, progressives defended the separation of church and state, women's reproductive rights, greater social justice, and cultural diversity.

The alliance on the political right faced a dilemma. The neoliberal defense of individual self-interest and free markets clashed with conservative values such as stable communities, censorship, right to life, traditional gender roles, and patriotism. In fact, the most conservative regions of the country tended to be hit hardest by market forces associated with globalization. To maintain the alliance, neoliberals sought to convince social conservatives that government, not the market, was the source of their dissatisfaction. Neoliberals targeted certain "wedge issues" such as gun control, abortion, and civil unions to divert the public's attention away from economic hardship.

As the culture wars developed, the media and political parties discovered that wedge issues provided fertile ground for boosting ratings and soliciting campaign contributions. They fanned the flames of anger and frustration until many citizens felt that the survival of the nation was at stake. In this context, the political process became increasingly dysfunctional as both sides in the culture wars refused to cooperate or compromise. Attempts at institutional reform to improve the economy were stymied by political gridlock.

The culture wars are a symptom of a deeper problem afflicting American culture—the loss of **social capital**. American culture has always been highly individualistic, and that trait has been invaluable in fostering risk-taking and innovation. But the downside of individualism is a lack of trust, cooperation, and social cohesion. As the most litigious society in the world, the United States squanders resources on frivolous lawsuits. America has more prisoners and guns per capita than any other nation. The lack of social capital detracts from the productive potential of the economy.

The Demise of Neoliberal Capitalism

Three changes during the late twentieth century reinforced the neoliberal project of shrinking government to reduce production costs and increase profitability.

Collapse of Communism

As the Soviet Union and its Eastern European satellite states abandoned communism in 1989–91, their resources became available to the rest of the world. In particular, Russian exports of oil and natural gas restrained increases in the prices of those resources. The fall of communism also bolstered neoliberalism by further discrediting government intervention in the economy.

Globalization

Advancing technologies in information processing, telecommunications, and transportation increased the efficiency of virtually every industry. Businesses gained the ability to coordinate global operations while taking advantage of lower costs outside the country. Relocation and outsourcing became standard practices as US corporations moved facilities and transferred jobs overseas to reduce production costs. With capital and natural resources flowing freely to their most profitable use and with labor unions on the decline, workers in the United States were powerless to resist these changes. As a result, wages in the United States remained stagnant despite strong productivity growth and high corporate profits. The first group to feel the brunt of global competition was workers without specialized education or training because their jobs could be performed by foreign workers at a fraction of the pay. However, with improving educational systems in nations such as China and India, US companies are outsourcing skilled jobs in industries such as customer service, data processing, medical records, and legal services.

Deregulation of Financial Markets

Before the 1980s, corporate shareholders rarely challenged the prerogatives of corporate executives in making business decisions. However, the growth of mutual funds, hedge funds, and private equity funds empowered fund managers to demand changes in corporate practices. The power of fund managers stemmed from their ability to sell massive quantities of stock in those corporations failing to meet profit expectations. Chief executive officers came under increasing pressure to maximize short-term profitability, and with little control over revenue, they focused on cutting costs. Corporations not fully committed to cost reduction and efficiency became targets for hostile takeovers by corporate raiders. Cost-cutting strategies worked well for raising productivity and profits, but layoffs only added to unemployment and downward pressure on wages. Additional pressure for cost-cutting was created as countries around the world removed **capital controls** on the free flow of financial capital across national borders. Competition to attract capital caused nations to vie with one another in deregulating financial markets, cutting taxes, and weakening labor unions.

* * *

As a result of these changes, neoliberalism became a victim of its own success. The combination of stagnant wages and robust growth meant that nearly all the gains from increased productivity accrued to owners of capital. The degree of inequality in the distribution of income and wealth reached levels not seen since 1929. Under these conditions, neoliberal capitalism began to falter. Three factors contributed to its demise.

Inadequate Demand

Aggregate demand comes from four sources—consumer spending, government spending, investment spending, and spending by foreigners on our exports. Neoliberals believed that by reducing production costs (including wages), any decline in spending by consumers and government would be more than offset by increases in investment and exports. However, businesses were reluctant to invest in expanding productive capacity when stagnant wages were restricting consumer spending. Moreover, stagnant wages did little to improve US exports, which were competing with Asian goods produced with even cheaper labor. US manufacturers faced increasing difficulty in selling their goods and therefore had little incentive to increase employment or output.

Increasing Debt

Despite stagnant wages, consumer spending could be increased by expanding the availability of credit. As unemployment remained stubbornly high in the early 2000s, The Fed increased the money supply in order to keep interest rates low and encourage borrowing. However, its actions were not the primary cause of credit expansion during this period. With virtually no controls on the flow of financial capital, money poured into US financial markets from around the world, causing the stock market to climb steadily after 2001. Fund managers and banks found themselves with excess financial capital and a lack of profitable investment opportunities in businesses producing goods and services. As a result, they began steering financial capital into consumer credit and home mortgages. Lenders were so eager to find outlets for the pool of financial capital that they often ignored the creditworthiness of borrowers. Credit cards were available to nearly every applicant, and the infamous "NINJA" loans were offered to those who had "No Income, No Job, and no Assets." Debt kept the economy afloat temporarily, but eventually interest on debt crippled the economy. Money that could have been used to purchase goods and services was instead channeled back into the hands of lenders who then searched for new borrowers.

The expansion of debt was facilitated by **leverage** as individuals and businesses used current assets as collateral to borrow more money. Homeowners used the equity in their homes as collateral to secure additional loans, and investors relied on borrowing from brokerage firms and banks to purchase more shares of stock. The downside of leverage is that if asset values decline (e.g., a sinking stock market or falling home values), the borrower's losses are magnified in proportion to the amount of leverage.

Inequality

Excessive inequality also undermined the economy. Affluent households tend to spend a lower percentage of their income, so as income became more concentrated, the percentage of total income spent for consumption declined. As happened during the Great Depression, **underconsumption** caused business inventories to increase and eventually reduced employment and output. Inequality also destabilized the economy because the growing wealth of corporations and affluent households formed a pool of financial capital seeking profitable investment opportunities. However, with low wages restraining consumer spending, the sectors of the economy producing goods and services offered few opportunities for investors. Lacking any incentive to expand production, many corporations used their profits to buy back existing shares of stock or to increase dividends to shareholders, both of which only contributed to growing inequality.

By 2007, consumer debt reached such proportions that increasing numbers of households failed to make monthly payments on mortgages, credit cards, and automobile loans. A growing inventory of unsold homes was the first indication of danger on the horizon. As the housing bubble burst, investors holding shares of corporate stock and risky financial assets began selling, and the value of those assets plummeted. The combination of falling asset values and increasing defaults on loans brought major banks to the brink of collapse. With fear and panic spreading, banks stopped making loans, credit markets froze, and the US economy sank into the worst recession since the Great Depression.

Neoliberalism failed because its success in reducing production costs and increasing profits suppressed consumer spending and created a pool of financial capital that exceeded the capacity of the economy to absorb for productive use. When owners of capital could not find satisfactory rates of return in manufacturing, they turned to speculation, resulting in asset bubbles that inevitably burst. Neoliberals forgot the two most important lessons of the Great Depression; first, business profitability depends on adequate demand for products as well as low production costs, and second, unregulated financial markets are inherently unstable. The result of this amnesia was the Great Recession of 2008.

A NEW DIRECTION?

The election and reelection of Barack Obama in 2008 and 2012 seemed to indicate a major departure from neoliberalism. However, a divided Congress has effectively prevented the government from pursuing any bold initiatives other than healthcare reform. The two major political parties offer diametrically opposed programs to revive the economy. Republicans continue to embrace neoliberalism, confident that the economy will surge as the size and scope of government is minimized. Democrats remain committed to a significant role for government in improving the performance of the economy.

Understanding the contemporary debate about the future of the US economy requires an appreciation of the historical evolution of capitalism. Regulated capitalism failed because rising costs compressed profits, whereas neoliberal capitalism failed because profits were so high that they could not be profitably reinvested in improving productivity and creating jobs due to underconsumption. The neoliberal vision of resurrecting competitive capitalism by minimizing government failed because it ignored the concentration of power in the economy. Although regulated capitalism contained institutions to restrain power, neoliberal capitalism removed many of the restraints and thereby revived the worst aspects of organized capitalism in which powerful interest groups increase their wealth by manipulating both the market and government. The similarities between the eras of organized capitalism and neoliberal capitalism are striking.

Both led to increased corporate power, less effective regulation, increasing in-equality, growing debt, inadequate consumer spending, and a resulting economic crisis. Organized capitalism culminated in the Great Depression and neoliberal capitalism led to the Great Recession.

Despite its flaws, neoliberal capitalism has two advantages in debates over the future direction of the US economic system. First, its emphasis on freeing individuals and businesses from government constraints resonates with Ameri-can cultural values of individualism and self-reliance. No other nation in the world is considering as pure a version of neoliberalism as is being advocated by the Republican Party in America. Second, globalization is generating strong pressures on all nations to remove political and cultural constraints on the op-eration of markets.

There is potential common ground between neoliberal and regulated capi-talism. The government spending that Keynesians insist is necessary to sustain aggregate demand could be directed toward projects that raise productivity, pro-tect the environment, create jobs, and disperse the benefits of economic activity across the population. Programs fitting this description include spending on education, healthcare, vocational training, scientific research, innovation, devel-oping alternative energy sources, rebuilding infrastructure, and promoting com-munity development. All these programs bridge the divide between neoliberal supply-siders and Keynesian demand-siders by using government spending to increase productivity, employment, and output.

Unless the economy is growing, increased government spending requires either higher tax rates or increased borrowing which enlarges the **national debt**. Given the political obstacles to either of those options, the US Federal Reserve has chosen to stimulate spending through "quantitative easing" (QE), which in-volves purchases by the Fed of both government and private securities from com-mercial banks to increase bank reserves for lending. QE has been conducted in three phases. QE1 pumped an additional $1.4 trillion into the economy in 2009, QE2 created an additional $600 billion in 2010, and QE3 began with monthly infusions of $40 billion in 2012, rising to $85 billion in 2013, then dropping back to $65 billion and eventually ending in 2014. Despite concerns about the inflation-ary impact of increasing the money supply, prices have remained quite stable and the unemployment rate has fallen from a high of 10 percent in 2009 to 5.1 percent in 2015. However, a substantial portion of this decline is attributable to individuals dropping out of the labor force. Since the Great Recession of 2008, the **labor force participation rate** has fallen from 66 percent to 63 percent.

Policies to stimulate spending and improve productivity need not imply a larger or more intrusive government. Many functions currently performed by government are wasteful or beneficial only to certain special interest groups. By distinguishing between the positive role played by government in improving economic performance and the predatory aspects of government policies, political leaders and voters can assess the efficacy and legitimacy of alternative institutions in meeting a nation's objectives. Democracy is not simply the clash of competing interests but a process by which citizens cooperate with one another to achieve goals unattainable through the private pursuit of self-interest.

REFERENCES

Bell, Daniel. 1976. *The Cultural Contradictions of Capitalism*. New York: Basic Books.
Bowles, Samuel, Richard Edwards, and Frank Roosevelt. 2005. *Understanding Capitalism: Competition, Command, and Change*, 3rd ed. New York: Oxford University Press.
Shaw, Archer H., ed. 1950. *The Lincoln Encyclopedia*. New York: Macmillan.

ADDITIONAL READING

Alperovitz, Gar. *America Beyond Capitalism: Reclaiming Our Wealth, Our Liberty, and Our Democracy*. Hoboken, NJ: John Wiley & Sons, 2005.
Baker, Dean. *The United States Since 1988*. New York: Cambridge University Press, 2007.
Bellah, Robert N., *et al. Habits of the Heart: Individualism and Commitment in American Life*. New York: Harper & Row, 1985.
Eberly, Don. *American Promise: Civil Society and the Renewal of American Culture*. Lanham, MD: Rowman & Littlefield, 1998.
Ellis, Christopher, and James A. Stimson. *Ideology in America*. New York: Cambridge University Press, 2012.
Eisner, Marc Allen. *The American Political Economy: Institutional Evolution of Market and State*. 2nd ed. New York: Routledge, 2013.
Gilens, Martin. *Affluence and Influence: Economic Inequality and Political Power in America*. Princeton, NJ: Princeton University Press, 2014.
Gordon, John Steele. *An Empire of Wealth: The Epic History of American Economic Power*. New York: HarperCollins, 2004.
Gosling James J., and Marc Allen Eisner. *Economics, Politics, and American Public Policy*. 2nd ed. New York: Routledge, 2013.
Heilbroner, Robert, and Aaron Singer. *The Economic Transformation of America: 1600 to the Present*. 4th ed. New York: Harcourt, Brace, Jovanovich, 1998.
Hunter, James Davison. *Culture Wars: The Struggle to Define America*. New York: Basic Books, 1991.
Lehne, Richard. *Government and Business: American Political Economy in Comparative Perspective*. 3rd ed. Los Angeles: CQ Press, 2013.
Lind, Michael. *Land of Promise: An Economic History of the United States*. New York: HarperCollins, 2012.
Liu, Eric, and Nick Hanauer. *The Gardens of Democracy: A New American Story of Citizenship, the Economy, and the Role of Government*. Seattle, WA: Sasquatch Books, 2011.
McGerr, Michael. *A Fierce Discontent: The Rise and Fall of the Progressive Movement in America 1870–1920*. New York: Oxford University Press, 2005.
Perrow, Charles. *America: Wealth, Power, and the Origins of Corporate Capitalism*. Princeton, NJ: Princeton University Press, 2005.
Prindle, David F. *The Paradox of Democratic Capitalism: Politics and Economics in American Thought*. Baltimore, MD: Johns Hopkins University Press, 2006.

Pryor, Frederic L. *The Future of U.S. Capitalism*. New York: Cambridge University Press, 2002.

Rosenberg, Samuel. *American Economic Development Since 1945: Growth, Decline, and Rejuvenation*. New York: Palgrave Macmillan, 2003.

Seavoy, Ronald. *An Economic History of the United States*. New York: Routledge, 2006.

Tocqueville, Alexis. *Democracy in America*. New York: Penguin Classics, (1835) 2003.

Wilensky, Harold L. *American Political Economy in Global Perspective*. New York: Cambridge University Press, 2012.

Wright, Erik Olin, and Joel Rogers. *American Society: How It Really Works*. New York: W. W. Norton, 2010.

Chapter 7

THE BRITISH ECONOMIC SYSTEM

"It has been said that democracy is the worst form of government except all the others that have been tried."

WINSTON CHURCHILL (1874–1965),
British Prime Minister

The British nation formed in 1066 when William the Conqueror (1028–1087) invaded England from Normandy and united various tribes and regions under a single government. Wales was annexed in 1536, Scotland in 1707, and Ireland in 1801. The British economic system was mercantilist from the sixteenth to the eighteenth centuries, but by the late eighteenth century, conditions were ripe for the emergence of the first capitalist system in the world. Britain possessed ideal geographical conditions for industrialization, with plentiful deposits of coal and iron ore, an extensive coastline with good harbors, and the advantage of being an island nation less vulnerable to military attacks.

Markets for land, labor, and capital developed slowly for several centuries prior to **capitalism**. The enclosure movement forced peasant farmers off the land and, along with a growing population, created an abundant supply of labor for the emerging factories. Privatization of common land and the sale of church and royal property provided the basis for a thriving market in land. The market for financial capital was less developed. Although trading in stocks and bonds occurred in London as early as 1690, the early British banking system focused almost exclusively on London and foreign trade. As a result, bank loans were difficult to obtain up to the nineteenth century. Overall, though, entrepreneurs had relatively easy access to the resources needed for manufacturing and commerce.

During the seventeenth century, the English Civil War and the Glorious Revolution circumscribed the power of the state. Merchants, investors and, entrepreneurs could be confident of secure property rights and freedom from arbitrary taxation. The mercantilist economic system was designed to enhance state power by strengthening the economy, so the British government focused on creating ideal conditions for industry and commerce to flourish.

Culturally, the Enlightenment and the Protestant Reformation laid the groundwork for a secular society promoting scientific curiosity and individual initiative. The writings of Adam Smith reflected a growing belief that the pursuit of self-interest and accumulation of wealth contributed to the prosperity of the nation. Unlike other European countries in which vestiges of feudalism still posed both ideological and social barriers to business activity, Britain had several centuries of experience with manufacturing and commerce prior to the emergence of capitalism. The birth of capitalism was facilitated by securing international trade routes through British military dominance. The British navy defeated the combined navies of France and Spain at the Battle of Trafalgar in 1805 to gain control of the high seas, and the British army defeated Napoleon's French army at the Battle of Waterloo in 1815. With complete freedom to import and export, Britain was poised to become "the workshop of the world."

COMPETITIVE CAPITALISM 1800–1932

The Industrial Revolution

Beginning around 1760, a wave of technological innovations led to dramatic increases in the productivity of British manufacturing. Although the Industrial Revolution was based partly on abundant supplies of land, labor, capital, and entrepreneurship, this "supply-side" explanation overlooks the role of demand in the emergence of capitalism. Ample supplies of resources created prosperity in state-centered economic systems such as empires or **mercantilism** because the state could direct the resulting surplus to any purpose it chose. But in a capitalist economic system, resources are not utilized for production unless the resulting goods can be sold at a profit. Demand, whether from consumers, the state, foreigners, or other businesses, is a necessary condition for production.

Britain was fortunate to possess both ample resources and growing demand for its products. Improvements in agricultural productivity increased the availability of food, which, along with progress in disease control and public sanitation, increased the population of consumers needing food, clothing, housing, and other basic necessities. In addition, a vast colonial empire opened markets for British exports around the world. As the Industrial Revolution increased the efficiency of production, British goods became less expensive and of higher quality than those produced in other nations, so demand for British goods rose steadily. This strong demand created profitable opportunities, and British entrepreneurs responded with a series of innovations.

Expansion of the textile industry marked the beginning of the Industrial Revolution. Previously, production of cloth took place in family homes. A merchant would buy bales of raw wool and deliver them to designated families who would spin and weave the wool into cloth. This "putting-out system" later gave way to the factory system, which brought workers together under a single roof. Productivity increased due to a division of labor, **economies of scale**, and the ability of employers to monitor work effort. Technological innovations such as James Watt's steam engine, James Hargeraves' spinning jenny, and John Kay's flying shuttle increased output dramatically as human and animal muscle were replaced with water and steam power. Each innovation spurred additional inventions because increasing the speed of any single stage in the manufacturing process was pointless unless other stages were improved as well.

Britain was the first nation to industrialize; therefore, most of its companies were small and owned by a single family. Entrepreneurs personally identified with their businesses and were very cautious about expanding too rapidly. Not only were bank loans difficult to obtain, but owners hesitated to borrow money for fear of losing control of the business to lenders. As a result, expansion was usually financed with retained earnings and later with issues of stock. In short, the slow development of the British banking system coupled with the prudence of early entrepreneurs kept British businesses relatively small.

Unorganized Labor

An abundance of urban labor created by the exodus of peasants and farmers from the countryside kept wages for unskilled workers near a subsistence level, providing just enough money to stay alive and raise a family. The English economist Thomas Malthus (1766–1834) argued that wages above a subsistence level would lead to rapid population growth and even larger supplies of labor that would push wages down to a subsistence level. Another English economist, David Ricardo (1772–1823), restated Malthus's claim in the form of an "Iron Law of Wages." Under the influence of Malthus and Ricardo, British business leaders and politicians came to regard subsistence wages as the inevitable consequence of the human tendency to overpopulate.

Many of the employees of the early factories were skilled craftsmen. Their knowledge and skills gave them considerable power over the organization of production and the pace of work. Employers sought to reduce this power by introducing labor-saving technology and reducing work processes to repetitive motions that could be performed by unskilled labor. Skilled workers responded by forming craft unions, but their power was limited due to the passage in 1799 of the Combination Acts, which placed severe restrictions on the ability of workers to organize and bargain for higher wages. Although the government repealed the Combination Acts in 1825, picketing and strikes were still forbidden.

The plight of unskilled workers was much worse. Women and children worked alongside men for twelve to sixteen hours per day in hot, noisy factories with poor ventilation and lighting. Workers were often housed in nearby dormitories with poor sanitation, barely edible food, and straw on the floor as beds. The rapidly moving wheels and gears of crude factory machinery occasionally ensnared human limbs or hair, resulting in serious maiming or even death. These conditions led to a number of riots as workers developed deep resentment and hostility toward their employers. One group, the Luddites, blamed machinery for eliminating jobs and responded by breaking into factories at night and smashing the machines. In 1842, a group called the Chartists attempted to increase the political power of workers by submitting a petition with one million signatures to

Parliament seeking extension of voting rights for every man over the age of twenty-one. The petition was rejected, and workers remained without a full voice in politics until 1918 when Parliament passed the Representation of the People Act.

Resistance to extending the right to vote was based on the belief, shared by most economists and business people at the time, that low wages were essential for economic growth. By keeping production costs to a minimum, low wages allowed businesses to earn greater profit, which could be reinvested in expanding productive capacity and creating more jobs. The upper classes believed that full democracy might jeopardize the process of capital accumulation by enabling workers to enlist the power of the state to secure higher wages, which would reduce profits and slow the engines of growth.

Free Trade

Britain was the home of classical economics (or "political economy" as it was called at the time). The essential policy recommendation of Smith, Malthus, and Ricardo can be summarized by the French phrase laissez-faire ("let it be" or "leave it alone"). They advocated abolishing mercantilist restrictions on commerce so that the market would be the primary institution for guiding economic activity. They supported free trade not only within the nation but also between nations. Ricardo developed the theory of **comparative advantage** to demonstrate that if each nation specialized in producing those goods for which its resources were best-suited, free trade would result in increased consumption for every nation involved.

The idea of free trade appealed to virtually all sectors of British society with any political influence. Merchants and manufacturers assumed that their technology and business experience were superior to those in other nations and therefore welcomed the opportunity to compete without government interference. Britain's prosperity had already attracted many foreign merchants, manufacturers, and bankers who naturally resisted mercantilist restrictions on the flow of goods and money across borders. Even the landowning aristocrats offered little resistance to free trade. Some of them were investors in business ventures, and none of them fully realized the extent to which capitalism would demolish the old social order on which their privileges rested.

As the nineteenth century proceeded, the remnants of mercantilism were gradually dismantled. The 1846 abolition of the Corn Laws, which imposed **tariffs** on imported grain as a means of protecting farmers and landowners, signaled the triumph of manufacturing interests over agricultural interests. The growing power of manufacturing interests also led to the 1834 Poor Law Amendment Act, which increased the supply of labor by requiring anyone seeking public assistance to enter a poorhouse where they were available to employers for temporary work. Food and living conditions in the poorhouses were worse than could be obtained with the lowest paid jobs, so public assistance did not eliminate the incentive to work. Another method for motivating people to work in the factories was severe punishment for minor crimes such as vagrancy and petty theft.

The British Empire

One aspect of mercantilism did survive. As a relatively small island with limited resources, Britain continued to build its colonial empire. The domestic economy relied on raw materials from throughout the Empire to produce finished products for sale in a similarly wide market. As an imperial power, Britain exerted considerable control over the prices of both its resource imports and manufactured exports, resulting in immense profits from foreign trade. By the middle of the nineteenth century, the British Empire encompassed more territory than any previous empire in history. At its peak in 1922, it covered 25 percent of the Earth's land area and included 20 percent of the global population. The British Empire was so extensive that it was referred to as "the empire on which the sun never sets." However, unlike earlier empires, the British Empire was not a state-centered economic system. By now, the market was the primary **governance structure**.

Culture

The early years of industrialization had a profound and lasting impact on British culture. As the emerging capitalist class gained political and economic power, the landowning aristocracy responded with disdain. They scorned the nouveau riche (newly rich) who had gained wealth within a single generation. The successful entrepreneurs, many of whom rose from modest backgrounds, could match the wealth of the aristocrats, but most never gained acceptance into elite circles because they had not mastered the finer points of social decorum. The aristocracy strove to defend its status through enforcement of an informal code of manners, dress, and speech, and any hint of a working class accent or improper table manners would exclude a person from fashionable society.

Industrialization also affected social relations between workers and capitalists. The brutal conditions of factory work and the slums in which workers lived bred class tensions and hostile labor relations. The roots of the militancy of British labor unions in the twentieth century lie in the nineteenth-century treatment of workers as simply productive commodities rather than human beings.

The Demise of Competitive Capitalism

In the latter part of the nineteenth century, the British economy began a gradual decline that continued until, by the 1970s, Britain was called "the sick man of Europe." In many respects, the same institutions that contributed to Britain's success as the first capitalist economic system subsequently became impediments to further development. A lack of domestic investment, the increasing militancy of organized labor, deteriorating social conditions, and the commitment to free trade all contributed to the growing obsolescence of British institutions.

Lack of Investment

As the first country to industrialize, Britain became the first country to experience obsolete technology. By the late nineteenth century, when businesses in other countries were constructing new factories with the latest technology, British firms failed to make the necessary investments. To be competitive in the late nineteenth century required substantially larger firms than in the early years of capitalism. Without **economies of scale**, smaller British firms could not match the prices of rival foreign firms in new industries such as steel, chemicals, and electrical equipment. These industries required massive investments in factories and equipment, a task that proved beyond the financial capabilities of small British firms and the underdeveloped British banking system.

The unwillingness or inability to start new businesses and expand existing firms was partially attributable to the fact that by the late nineteenth century, many of the early entrepreneurs had died and bequeathed their businesses to family members. These heirs tended to view the businesses more as sources of income than as part of their personal identity. They often mimicked the leisurely lifestyles of the aristocracy and neglected costly but much-needed investments in modernizing factories. If these heirs had been more dependent on external financing, lenders would have demanded greater attention to profitability. But, absent the disciplining influence of bankers and investors, owners could rest on their inherited fortunes.

The lack of domestic borrowing by businesses caused British banks and investors to focus on international financial markets. Low wages in the British colonies created attractive investment opportunities, so **financial capital** tended to flow out of Britain instead of funding improvements in domestic industry. The size of this drain on financial capital is demonstrated by the fact that in 1914, Britain accounted for half of all foreign investment in the world. The British Empire also drained capital by forcing Britain to engage its army and navy to suppress indigenous uprisings and movements for independence in the colonies. Administering and policing this empire absorbed funds and productive citizens who might otherwise have engaged their talents in the domestic economy.

Labor Resistance

With few legal protections against unsafe working conditions, long hours, and low wages, workers became increasingly hostile toward owners and managers. By the 1850s, skilled workers began to form craft unions. To overcome the weakness associated with separate unions for each skill, hundreds of different labor unions formed a confederation called the Trades Union Congress (TUC) in 1868.

In 1884, Sidney and Beatrice Webb (1859–1947 and 1858–1943) established the Fabian Society, a political organization aimed at improving the lives of workers by moving Britain toward socialism through peaceful, democratic means. The Fabians advocated a national insurance program to protect individuals against unemployment, sickness, and loss of income after retirement; more **public goods** such as parks, museums, recreation areas, and schools; heavy taxation of rent; and nationalization of industries such as transportation, banking, communications, utilities, and mining. In 1900, the Fabian Society became the Labour Party, which, by 1918, advocated the abolition of capitalism. The Labour Party won its first national election in 1924 under the leadership of Ramsay MacDonald

(1866–1937). Although the conservative Tory Party won the next election, the Great Depression (called the Great Slump in Britain) of the early 1930s increased membership in and public support for both labor unions and the Labour Party.

Deteriorating Social Conditions

As the number of factories and coal mines increased, so did the **negative externalities** associated with heavy manufacturing. With virtually no government regulation, industrial cities deteriorated. Beggars proliferated, some of them maimed for life by accidents in the factories. Public health declined as evidenced by a resurgence of cholera and tuberculosis. Those miners who escaped frequent cave-ins or explosions were doomed to early deaths from lung disease.

The government severely restricted the right to vote, so citizens had virtually no recourse for addressing their grievances. Even after Parliament passed the Reform Act of 1832, the requirement of property ownership left only 20 percent of adult males eligible to vote. Journalists and writers increasingly publicized the dark side of industrialization. Charles Dickens (1812–1870) chronicled the stark social conditions of mid-nineteenth century Britain in novels such as *Oliver Twist* and *Hard Times*. Political leaders could not ignore the devastation being wrought by industrialization, and they gradually began to respond with laws concerning child labor, the length of the work day, factory inspections, and occupational safety.

The British Parliament at that time allowed the House of Lords to veto any legislation proposed by the House of Commons. Because members of the House of Lords were appointed rather than elected, government decisions remained, to a significant extent, insulated from democratic pressures. That situation would not change until the Parliament Act of 1911, after which Prime Minister David Lloyd George (1863–1945) succeeded in introducing legislation creating unemployment insurance, public housing, and other reforms aimed at benefitting the working class.

Free Trade

Whereas German and American firms were protected by tariffs on imports, the commitment to laissez-faire left Britain's relatively small companies vulnerable to international competition. By the late nineteenth century, British businesses were losing **competitive advantage** against larger foreign firms with economies of scale and supportive governments. Free trade had worked well when Britain dominated the global economy, but the combination of small firms, lagging innovation, and protective trade barriers in other countries caused British industries to encounter increasing difficulty in exporting.

The reluctance to abandon free trade, even when it became clear that the British economy was suffering, can be explained partly by the ideological legacy of classical economics and Ricardo's theory of comparative advantage. However, some segments of British society still benefitted from free trade. With their worldwide investments, British banks could potentially profit more from the success of

German or American firms than from British firms. The refusal to abandon free trade was based partly on the growing political power of the British financial sector.

WELFARE CAPITALISM 1932-1978

The Great Slump and World War II transformed the British economic system by enlarging the role of the state and strengthening the sense of national community. The Labour Party regained power in 1929, and when the Great Slump hit, Prime Minister Ramsay MacDonald responded with pre-Keynesian orthodoxy. He slashed government spending and raised taxes in order to balance the government budget. The government began providing unemployment benefits in 1931, but they were meager and lasted only fifteen weeks. As the unemployment rate rose to 20 percent, public anger over the Labour Party's inability to restore prosperity led to a Conservative Party victory in 1935 and control of government that would last until the end of the war.

To mobilize all available resources for the war effort, the British government relied on comprehensive planning to allocate investment funds and rationed virtually all consumer products. Conservative prime minister Winston Churchill (1874–1965) rallied British citizens by appealing to their duty as citizens to serve the nation. Ironically, Churchill's success in fostering a sense of social solidarity among the British people, along with the demonstrated efficacy of government in organizing the war effort, led to a resurgence of the Labour Party, which took power in 1945 under Clement Atlee (1883–1967). The Labour Party embarked on a bold program to create a mixture of socialism and capitalism. Government took ownership of some industries and closely regulated others. An array of public programs provided social benefits to all citizens, while government took responsibility for managing the macro economy to maintain high levels of employment.

The Welfare State

The goal of achieving full employment reflected a dramatic change in the accepted role of government in a capitalist economy. Prior to the Depression, most citizens regarded finding a job as a personal responsibility. Unemployment was often blamed on individual laziness, and the hardships associated with unemployment were widely accepted as necessary to provide the incentive for individuals to increase their productivity and discipline themselves to become contributing members of society. These attitudes changed with the Great Slump as millions of able-bodied people, desperate to work, could not find jobs. The British increasingly came to view unemployment as a failure of the economic system rather than the fault of individuals.

In 1942, a government-appointed commission headed by Sir William Beveridge (1879–1963), president of the London School of Economics and Political Science, issued a report recommending national healthcare and pension programs, unemployment compensation, family allowances for second and third children, and broader educational opportunities. Family allowances for child support began in 1945, and the National Health Service offered free medical care to all citizens beginning in 1948. These programs provided benefits to all citizens regardless of income in order to foster broad political support for the welfare state and to create a sense of social solidarity among British citizens.

Churchill and the Conservatives regained power in 1951, but even the Conservatives accepted the welfare state. The Great Slump and World War II created widespread disillusionment with the free market, and Britain emerged from the war with a strong sense of national solidarity. All citizens had sacrificed in the collective effort to defeat the Nazis, so now all deserved to live with dignity and a degree of economic security. In addition, the vestiges of medieval values in conservative thought created a sense of noblesse oblige ("nobility obliges") among the British upper classes. Just as the lord of the manor had a duty to prevent undue hardship among his serfs, Conservatives accepted a moral responsibility to care for the less fortunate. They viewed the welfare state as a new form of community to encourage the revival of feudal values such as chivalry and paternalism. Conservatives also anticipated that by providing adequate housing, nutrition, and healthcare, the welfare state would improve the productivity of the British labor force. Finally, Conservatives expected the welfare state to maintain social order and diminish the appeal of socialism by alleviating poverty.

Nationalization of Industry
In the late 1940s, the government nationalized the railroad, coal, steel, gas, electricity, bus, airline, trucking, and healthcare industries, as well as the Bank of England. In many cases, these industries were on the brink of bankruptcy, so the government takeover was effectively a bailout of the owners and an effort to preserve jobs. A subsequent wave of nationalization occurred in the early 1970s as the government took control of British Aerospace, British Petroleum, British Leyland, Jaguar, and Rolls Royce. Again, most of these companies were near bankruptcy, so shareholders did not object to nationalization.

Organized Labor
By the mid-twentieth century, the powerful TUC represented millions of workers. Unlike other European countries, Britain did not experience destruction of its labor unions during World War II. Furthermore, the combination of lost lives during the war and the absence of any significant influx of refugees after the war meant that labor was relatively scarce, giving unions substantial bargaining power during the postwar era. The TUC pushed for and obtained wage increases by posing the threat of a mass strike by workers from many different occupations. The government and business leaders tried to restrain wage increases by establishing nationwide labor negotiations in which government, employers, and the TUC participated. However, these efforts failed in part because the TUC, as an umbrella organization, could not force individual unions to comply with collective agreements.

To secure labor peace, British companies had previously ceded some control over the workplace to shop stewards who could veto proposed changes in production. By the 1970s, as the deterioration of the global economy created renewed pressures on British firms to reduce production costs, a wave of strikes and work stoppages erupted as managers challenged the prerogatives of shop stewards, and unions resisted any modernization that would result in layoffs or obsolescence of job skills. Unions in the state-owned sector of the economy became particularly aggressive because nearly every employee belonged to a union. Members believed that government could afford to pay higher wages by increasing subsidies or by raising prices for the products of nationalized industries. In the private sector, the presence of many different craft unions made labor relations difficult because a single union could block agreements acceptable to all other unions in an industry.

Stop-Go Cycles

In 1947, the Labour Party passed the National Economic Development Act calling for development councils in each industry. These councils provided a forum in which representatives of business, labor, and government jointly engaged in **indicative planning** to improve the performance of the economy. However, both business and labor groups opposed planning, viewing it as an effort by government to restrict their ability to gain higher wages and profits. The Labour Party eventually abandoned the idea of planning when its leaders concluded that the policies recommended by British economist John Maynard Keynes (1883–1946) could be more effective than planning in achieving full employment, stability, and greater equality. With Keynesian policies, the government controlled **aggregate demand** through appropriate **monetary policy** and **fiscal policies** rather than by directly influencing business decisions.

However, Britain's heavy reliance on international trade and lending undermined the effectiveness of Keynesian policies. When the government stimulated aggregate demand to bring the economy near full employment, inflationary pressures led to increased imports and reduced exports. The resulting balance of trade **deficit** put downward pressure on the British pound as foreigners sold the pounds they received from exporting to Britain. Because many of Britain's former colonies and trading partners held large reserves of pounds, any **devaluation** of the pound would impose losses on the treasuries of those countries and undermine confidence in the stability of British financial markets. To reduce balance of trade deficits, the British government consistently chose to intentionally slow the economy rather than devalue the pound. This pattern of intermittent stimulation and slowing was called a **stop-go cycle**, with a complete cycle averaging about five years. The slowdowns were painful for people who lost their jobs and for businesses. They also discouraged investment by creating uncertainty about the future course of the economy.

Incomes Policy

The dilemma created by stop-go cycles led British policymakers to search for a better method to achieve the goals of full employment and price stability. They needed to control wage increases during periods of economic expansion to prevent **inflation** and to stabilize the balance of trade. To achieve these goals, the government established the National Incomes Commission in 1961. The Commission monitored and publicized wage increases, hoping that public opinion would serve to restrain further increases. However, this **incomes policy** failed to dampen wage demands. Workers had sacrificed wage increases during and after World War II, and they believed that they deserved to share in the prosperity of the postwar era. An incomes policy also failed due to a **collective action problem**. Unless all unions simultaneously agreed to wage restraint, any single union foregoing a wage increase would be hurt by continuing inflation. In other words, no single union could voluntarily sacrifice to control inflation without suffering economic loss.

Another attempt at an incomes policy occurred in 1965 with the establishment of the National Board for Prices and Incomes. It met with similar failure. By the early 1970s, the government tried once more to restrain wage and price increases by proposing a social contract in which both labor unions and employers would agree to cooperate in controlling inflation. Not only did the social contract fail, but an unintended consequence occurred. Once the government became involved in determining wages and prices, both business and labor fought even more vigorously to advance their separate interests while rejecting government pleas for restraint. Labor unions became increasingly antagonistic toward the government, even when the Labour Party held power.

Indicative Planning

Despite the failure of planning in the immediate postwar era, in 1962, the government established the National Economic Development Council to provide a venue in which representatives of business, labor, and government could formulate plans to modernize British industry. In 1964, the Labour Party created the Department of Economic Affairs with responsibility for drawing up a national plan to direct government assistance to particular industries. This assistance might take the form of subsidies, protection against imports, or creating quasi-cartels to limit competition and improve profitability by colluding to set prices and establish production quotas.

British planning was designed not only to improve the competitiveness of British industry but also to achieve greater social equality. The government formulated regional development programs to benefit the poorest areas of the country. When individual firms or industries received government assistance, aid was typically directed toward declining sectors and struggling firms. Several rationales supported these egalitarian policies. First, sectors having difficulty might be **infant industries** needing temporary assistance until they could grow and mature sufficiently to become competitive in international markets. Second, aid might facilitate **learning by doing**, allowing firms sufficient time to gain the experience, knowledge, and skills essential for profitability. Third, the Labour Party believed that assisting less developed parts of the country was essential to achieving social justice. Finally, Keynesian economics supported greater equality to place more money in the hands of low-income families who would spend it and stimulate the entire economy.

However, by pursuing egalitarian **industrial policies**, the British shielded the weakest sectors of the economy from the disciplining forces of the market. A dynamic economy needs the process of creative destruction as resources shift from declining sectors to growing sectors. Markets accomplish this process by reducing profitability in declining sectors so that owners of resources voluntarily relocate their assets to more productive uses. If government resists this process by aiding the least profitable sectors, the entire economy may gradually suffer a loss of efficiency and competitiveness.

Another problem with planning as practiced in Britain stemmed from the individualistic nature of British society. Class hostility, coupled with distaste for government authority dating back to the Middle Ages, made cooperative planning very difficult. As was the case with an incomes policy, both business and labor refused to cooperate with any plan contrary to their self-interest. The Conservative Party objected to planning on the grounds that it violated property rights and individual freedom. The Labour Party objected to any planning that benefited the more profitable sectors of the economy, pushing instead for planning as a means of promoting greater social equality. The government tried to work cooperatively with business and labor, but in the process opened the door for lobbying by groups determined to promote their own interests.

Culture

The legacy of class antagonism created during nineteenth-century industrialization had a lasting effect on British culture. The aristocratic upper class generally disdained business and the open pursuit of wealth. No British university offered a graduate degree in business until the 1960s, and Oxford University did not offer a Master in Business Administration (MBA) program until 1996. British universities traditionally emphasized the classics, history, and literature instead of applied fields such as business, science, and engineering.

Class hostility also affected labor relations. Workers felt resentment and cynicism toward employers and authority figures. Britain's economic decline during the twentieth century only reinforced these attitudes. Former industrial centers such as Manchester, Birmingham, and Liverpool deteriorated into bleak, decaying cities offering few prospects for upward mobility. The lack of opportunity spawned pessimism about Britain's future.

The Demise of Welfare Capitalism

Having unsuccessfully tried Keynesian policies, stop-go cycles, income policies and indicative planning, the British government had seemingly exhausted its alternatives for improving the performance of the economy. In the early 1970s, the entire global economy weakened, with Britain experiencing greater hardship than most other developed nations. The annual rate of inflation reached 23 percent in 1975. Unemployment increased, government budget deficits swelled, and labor unions threatened mass strikes if employers did not meet their demands. A strike by coal miners in 1973 led to such severe energy shortages that virtually the entire economy was reduced to a three-day workweek for months. In 1976, Britain became the first developed nation to receive a loan from the International Monetary Fund and had to make significant cuts in government spending in order to obtain the loan. These cuts resulted in a wage freeze for public employees, who reacted with a series of work stoppages. The country verged on breakdown as hospitals closed, corpses remained unburied in cemeteries, and uncollected garbage piled up in the streets.

The Labour and Conservative parties offered widely contrasting explanations for Britain's economic woes. From the Labour perspective, capitalism was to blame for economic stagnation. Excessive inequality in the distribution of income and wealth led to reduced aggregate demand, dampened the productive energy of both the poor and the rich, and created class antagonism that fueled the militancy of British labor unions. The Labour Party also blamed capitalism for the lack of investment in British industry as private investors sought higher rates of return in other countries. The Labour solution to **stagflation** called for greater social equality and increased government control over the allocation of capital.

Conservatives relied on an entirely different narrative, blaming stagflation on the socialist aspects of Britain's economic system. Welfare programs and high taxes were undermining individual initiative by destroying the incentive to engage in productive activity. By demanding excessive wage increases, militant labor pushed up production costs and blocked efforts to raise productivity. Inefficient state-owned enterprises absorbed government funds that could have been used more productively in the private sector.

As the economic crisis deepened, public opinion swung in favor of the Conservative Party. A majority of citizens came to view labor unions as a threat to the economy and increasingly perceived government as weak and incapable of resisting the demands of powerful interest groups seeking greater benefits than they could obtain through the market. The Conservative Party proposed to strictly limit government's role in the economy and allow the market to operate more freely.

NEOLIBERAL CAPITALISM 1979–1996

The Conservative Party gained a majority in Parliament in 1979, and Margaret Thatcher (1925–2013) became prime minister. Thatcher's program was based on the same neoliberal economic theories that provided the ideological foundations for the Reagan revolution in the United States. **Neoliberalism** called for privatization of government functions, tight monetary policy, tax reform, efforts to weaken labor unions, and cuts in social welfare programs. The immediate results of these policies were negative. **Gross domestic product** (GDP) fell by more than 2 percent in 1980 and dropped further the following year. The number of unemployed workers rose from one million in 1979 to more than four million in 1984, with the unemployment rate peaking at 13 percent in 1985. However, in the late 1980s, economic performance improved as rising levels of investment led to higher growth rates.

Privatization

The nationalized sector of the British economy reached its peak in the late 1970s when it accounted for 11 percent of GDP, 8 percent of employment, and 20 percent of investment. Since then, approximately fifty major British companies have been transferred from public to private ownership by selling shares of stock to private investors. Many former government functions have been turned over to private contractors, and subsidies for the remaining state-owned firms have been virtually eliminated. In almost every case, privatization has resulted in lower production costs, but part of that reduction is attributable to the fact that employees of the newly privatized firms earn significantly lower wages than were paid to unionized workers in state-owned firms.

The British government developed methods to privatize industries with characteristics of **natural monopolies** such as railroads, electrical power, and communications. The government split the different components of these industries into separate private firms. For example, although railroad tracks are a natural monopoly, ownership of trains can be divided among several firms who then compete against one another. Similarly, long-distance telephone lines are a natural monopoly, but competition can be fostered by giving several private firms access to the lines.

Monetarism

In the late 1970s, neoliberal economists in both Britain and the United States began a sustained intellectual effort to discredit Keynesianism and revive the free-market ideas associated with Adam Smith. In Britain, this updating of classical economics was called **monetarism**. Monetarist economists claimed that the Bank of England could control inflation, promote full employment, and improve the efficiency of the economy simply by maintaining a rate of growth of the money supply equal to the real growth rate of the economy. With growth in the money supply limited, excessive wage demands by labor unions would theoretically cause unemployment rather than inflation, so unions would be harming themselves by demanding wage increases in excess of productivity gains. Moreover, if limiting the growth of the money supply prevented inflation, unions would no longer need wage increases because the cost of living would be stable. With wage restraint, monetarists assumed that employers would hire more workers and unemployment would drop. In short, the monetarists claimed that stopping inflation through a tight **monetary policy** would eventually promote full employment.

The initial impact of monetarism was drastic. Tight monetary policy caused interest rates to soar to 17 percent and triggered a **recession**. However, within a few years, weak **aggregate demand** brought inflation under control, unions moderated their wage demands, and the economy began to grow at a modest pace.

Tax Reform

Another aspect of the effort to move Britain away from its prior commitment to egalitarianism was tax reform. Britain had a steeply progressive income tax as well as a tax on real property (e.g., houses, boats, automobiles) that was also progressive because affluent households typically own more real property. These taxes reflected the Labour Party's belief that redistribution of income and wealth creates positive economic effects by increasing consumer spending and by giving dignity to the lives of the poor to motivate them to become productive citizens. Conservatives, on the other hand, argued that concentrated wealth and income promoted a high level of **saving** from which **investment** funds would flow. Without high levels of saving and investment, capital accumulation would slow, the entire economy would stagnate, and all citizens would be hurt. Based on this reasoning, Conservatives set out to shift the burden of taxation away from the rich. The highest marginal income tax rate was lowered from 83 percent in 1979 to 40 percent by 1989. The regressive **value-added tax** was increased from 8 percent to 15 percent. Taxes on cigarettes, alcohol, and gas all rose. In place of the progressive tax on real property, the government initiated a regressive **poll tax** that took the same amount from all adults regardless of their income. Public opposition to the poll tax was so vehement that the government ended it in 1993.

Weaker Labor

The National Union of Mineworkers initiated a strike in 1984. After twelve months of confrontations between striking miners and police, the union eventually withdrew its demands and work resumed. This event marked the beginning of a new era in British labor relations. The Thatcher government reduced the power of labor unions by enacting laws limiting the right to strike, to appeal firings, and to bargain for closed-shop agreements. The Trade Union Act of 1984 made union officials responsible for any losses imposed on firms by picketing or secondary strikes. It also required votes by union members to authorize strikes. Besides hostility from government, other factors contributing to the weakening of labor unions included the shift away from the heavily unionized manufacturing sector toward the service and "high-tech" sectors, increasing international competition, and reduced public sympathy for unionized workers. Whereas union members constituted 55 percent of the labor force in 1979, that number has fallen to less than 30 percent today. As an indication of labor's lack of power, Britain did not enact a minimum wage law until 1999.

Social Policy

Dismantling the welfare state was a top priority for the Thatcher administration. Neoliberals claimed that overly generous welfare programs sapped the vitality of the British economy by undermining incentives to work and by keeping taxes high. Recipients of welfare, they argued, developed a sense of entitlement to their benefits and felt no compulsion to seek employment. Despite the ascendency of neoliberal ideas, the size of the welfare state remained largely unchanged as politicians from both the Labour and Conservative parties recognized the popularity of social benefits and hesitated to make deep cuts. However, they did shift benefits away from supporting the unemployed to providing incentives for seeking employment. Manpower training programs paid high school dropouts who enrolled in vocational training and gave subsidies to employers to hire young workers. Older workers were offered incentives to take early retirement in order to open more jobs for young people. Finally, Britain instituted a workfare program in which unemployed citizens were placed in **public sector** jobs such as raking beaches, sweeping sidewalks, and picking up litter.

Culture

After the economic traumas of the 1970s, popular sentiment was decidedly pessimistic, particularly among young people. Job prospects were so dismal that only 37 percent of British students pursued any education beyond high school. Many citizens believed that Britain had seen its best days and faced an inevitable state of decline. However, having survived the 1970s and early 1980s, the British exhibited a renewed sense of national pride and optimism about the future. These changing attitudes contributed to the restoration of a growing economy.

As an island nation, Britain has always maintained a cultural identity separate from mainland Europe. The British have refused to adopt the euro currency, and a 2012 poll revealed that 56 percent of British citizens favored withdrawing from the European Union (EU). Initial proposals to construct a tunnel under the English Channel (the "chunnel") linking Britain to mainland Europe were met with widespread opposition. Economic theory strongly suggests that nations benefit from widening their markets, and this cultural sense of national superiority may simply be an obsolete legacy from the old British Empire. Nationalist sentiments also threaten the unity of Britain itself; Scottish voters narrowly defeated a referendum to secede from Britain in 2014.

Britain has experienced a steady flow of immigrants from former British colonies and more recently from other EU nations. In London, more than one-fourth of the population consists of immigrants from Africa, Asia, or the Caribbean region. However, ethnic and racial diversity have created a backlash, particularly among lower-class white males who view immigrants as threats to their job prospects.

The Demise of Neoliberal Capitalism

As desperate as the British people were to resolve the economic crisis of the late 1970s, the majority of the population never fully embraced neoliberalism. Margaret Thatcher's free-market policies marked a sharp departure from Conservative Party orthodoxy with its acceptance of a moral obligation to care for the less fortunate members of society. Attempts to cut welfare programs were met with strong public opposition. Many employed workers felt economically insecure and close enough to poverty that they valued the social safety net provided by welfare and social insurance programs. The National Health Service had nearly universal support.

Neoliberal policies also lost popularity as it became apparent that they contributed to growing inequality. Affluent households prospered with lower taxes and less regulation of business and financial markets. At the same time, workers experienced cuts in social programs and the displacement of high-paying jobs in manufacturing by low-paying jobs in the service sector. Margaret Thatcher offended the British sense of national community when she stated in 1987 that "there is no such thing as society, there are individual men and women, and there are families."

When the economy dipped back into recession in 1989, Conservative politicians sensed that their party's electoral prospects would be jeopardized if Thatcher remained prime minister. With urging from Party leaders, she resigned in 1990 and was succeeded by John Major. Lacking Thatcher's pure vision of a free market with minimal government intervention, Major pursued a moderately conservative program. Rather than cutting social benefits, his administration reformed their delivery by introducing market forces. For example, students were permitted to choose their schools, and schools were funded based on how many students they attracted. Physicians in the National Health Service were allowed to compete for patients, and their income depended on the number of patients they served.

Popular support for the Conservative agenda continued to erode, and in 1997, the Labour Party won the general election by the largest margin since the 1832 Reform Act extended the right to vote. During its two decades out of office, the Labour Party transformed itself. Under the leadership of Tony Blair, the Party renounced its socialist roots in the Fabian Society, committed itself to private enterprise, and sought to minimize the need for welfare programs by promoting economic growth.

A NEW DIRECTION?

Tony Blair based his 1997 campaign on the promise of a "third way," steering a middle course between neoliberal capitalism and welfare capitalism. Under Blair's leadership and that of his successor, Gordon Brown, the Labour Party remained in power until 2010. The British Third Way represented an acknowledgment that without a thriving economy, the goal of social justice can be realized only by redistributing income from one group to another. Given Britain's long history of individualism and class antagonism, the social conflict created by redistribution endangered the stability of the economy. In many respects, the British Third Way resembled neoliberalism more than welfare capitalism. Blair stated in 1998 that "government should not hinder the logic of the market." In other words, the role of government would be to complement and support the market rather than resist it.

The Third Way exhibited numerous similarities with the neoliberal agenda. In fact, Blair left most of Thatcher's economic reforms in place. Government functions continued to be privatized, although at a slower pace. If a government service was not privatized, efforts were made to create private firms to provide the same service in order to foster competition between the public and private sectors. Welfare and unemployment benefits were reduced, with strict conditions for eligibility and requirements for job training. To compensate for a shrinking social safety net, the Labour Party increased funding for manpower programs such as vocational training, job search assistance, relocation assistance, and wage subsidies for companies hiring unemployed workers. Funding was also increased for research and other forms of **infrastructure** to improve the productivity of British businesses.

Whereas neoliberals argued for cuts in social programs to discourage idleness and force individuals to seek employment, the Third Way entailed programs to provide welfare recipients with opportunities for "social inclusion" through productive work. The Third Way retained the Labour Party's concept of a national community with government having a responsibility to promote the well-being of citizens. However, that responsibility now took the form of creating opportunities for advancement rather than compensating people and businesses for failure in the market. In other words, government would focus more on ensuring equality of opportunity rather than equality of outcome. The British Third Way also called for fiscal responsibility in the form of balanced government budgets. Blair pledged that the government would borrow money only to invest in public infrastructure, not to fund current expenditures. He also promised that government debt would increase no faster than GDP.

The British Third Way has had mixed results. The Great Recession of 2008 hit Britain particularly hard because its economy depends so heavily on the financial sector. The Conservative Party regained control in 2010 under the leadership of David Cameron but has initiated no major economic reforms since then. Like other developed nations, Britain is deeply affected by globalization and competition from low-wage countries in Asia. As the manufacturing sector shrinks, desirable jobs are disappearing and being replaced by lower-paying service sector jobs. At present, wages in Britain are lower than wages in other major European nations. With wages growing at an annual rate of 1.25 percent and inflation at 2 percent, real wages are actually declining in Britain.

Britain has been slower than other northern European nations in recovering from the 2008 recession. It did not reach prerecession levels of GDP until 2014, which meant no net growth for nearly seven years. The Cameron administration has recently taken steps to stimulate the economy with an expansionary monetary policy. Because Britain did not adopt the euro, the Bank of England has not been constrained by the tight monetary policy pursued until recently by the European Central Bank. The government also offers first-time home buyers interest-free mortgages, which had the effect of driving housing prices up 10 percent in 2014.

Although growth in the housing and financial sectors caused GDP to rise by 3.2 percent in 2014, the manufacturing sector remains stagnant. Productivity has not increased for the past five years, and unemployment stands at 6.4 percent. Exports are being hampered by a 10-percent appreciation of the pound in 2013. However, despite these challenges, the British economy is currently growing faster than its counterparts in mainland Europe.

ADDITIONAL READING

Allen, Robert C. *The British Industrial Revolution in Global Perspective*. New York: Cambridge University Press, 2009.

Blair, Tony. *The Third Way: New Politics for the New Century*. London: Fabian Society, 1998.

Booth, Alan. *The British Economy in the Twentieth Century*. New York: Palgrave, 2001.

Giddens, Anthony. *The Third Way: The Renewal of Social Democracy*. Cambridge: Polity Press, 1998.

Hall, Peter. *Governing the Economy: The Politics of State Intervention in Britain and France*. New York: Oxford University Press, 1986.

Hay, Colin. *The Failure of Anglo-liberal Capitalism*. Basingstoke, UK: Palgrave Macmillan, 2013.

Mathias, Peter. *The First Industrial Nation: The Economic History of Britain 1700–1914*. New York: Routledge, 2001.

Mokyr, Joel. *The Enlightened Economy: An Economic History of Britain 1700–1850*. New Haven, CT: Yale University Press, 2012.

Pope, Rex. *The British Economy Since 1914: A Study in Decline?* New York: Addison Wesley Longman, 1998.

Rubinstein, W. D. *Capitalism, Culture and Decline in Britain 1750–1990*. New York: Routledge, 1993.

Sawyer, Malcolm, ed. *The UK Economy*. 15th ed. New York: Oxford University Press, 2001.

Wiener, Martin. *English Culture and the Decline of the Industrial Spirit 1850–1980*. Cambridge: Cambridge University Press, 1982.

Chapter 8

THE FRENCH ECONOMIC SYSTEM

"How can anyone govern a nation that has two hundred and forty-six kinds of cheese?"

CHARLES DE GAULLE (1890–1970),
French President

The French have a saying—"the more things change, the more they remain the same" (plus ça change, plus c'est la même chose). This adage aptly describes the French economic system. In the past two centuries, France has experienced five democratic republics, three monarchies, two empires, one fascist regime, and several provisional governments. Yet throughout this political turmoil, the economic system exhibited a remarkable continuity. The state has always played a powerful role; the labor force is fragmented yet adversarial; and businesses, with a few notable exceptions, are smaller than their foreign counterparts.

The unique character of the French economic system dates back to its transition from feudalism to capitalism. The combination of the Hundred Years War (1337–1453), several famines, and the Black Death (bubonic plague; 1348–1350) caused the French population to decline from seventeen million in 1320 to only twelve million in 1450. Facing shortages of labor and the growing attraction of cities, many feudal lords were forced to renegotiate the status of their serfs in order to keep them on the manor. By the end of the fifteenth century, serfdom had largely been replaced by free peasants paying rent for the use of land or hired as wage laborers. Over the next two centuries, rapid population growth led to increasing subdivision of land holdings as feudal lords dissolved their manors into small plots to be sold or rented.

Small-scale agriculture lacked **economies of scale** and therefore suffered from low productivity. To make matters worse for the peasant farmers, the lords still managed to extract a substantial part of the economic surplus through various taxes, tolls, and fees. French agriculture failed to thrive because the surplus supported the aristocracy rather than being invested in land improvements, **physical capital**, and technological innovation. This pattern of development contrasted sharply with British agriculture where the enclosure movement forced tenant farmers to leave the land, opening the way for large-scale agriculture focused on efficiency and profitability.

165

The development of the French state also followed a very different path than the British one. By the end of the seventeenth century, the power of the British monarch had been substantially limited by the English civil war of 1649, the Glorious Revolution of 1688, and the power of Parliament. In contrast, the French state was becoming increasingly powerful during the same period. Earlier French kings lacked power because many feudal lords retained virtual **sovereignty** over their territories. With the lords extracting most of the surplus from producers, the king was continually engaged in a struggle to gain control of sufficient resources with which to fight wars, establish colonies, and provide **public goods**. In the seventeenth century, Cardinal Richelieu (1585–1642), prime minister under King Louis XIII, centralized power by bringing the aristocracy, most of whom were descendants of feudal lords, under the king's control. In some cases, this consolidation of power entailed armed conflict.

Louis XIV (the Sun King) continued the power struggle by changing the tax system. Previously, the king gained a share of the surplus by taxing the aristocracy who extracted surplus from the peasants. Now, the peasants would pay a tax (taille) directly to the king, who then shared part of the **revenue** with the aristocracy. This change in the tax system made the aristocracy financially dependent on the king, effectively centralizing all power in his hands. Louis XIV could plausibly claim, "I am the state" ("l'état c'est moi").

Louis XIV's Minister of Finance, Jean-Baptiste Colbert (1619–1683), actively used the increasing power of the state to promote economic development. The French term for centralized state supervision of the economy is "dirigisme," but the goals and policies were similar to **mercantilism**. The state established royal factories to manufacture high-quality goods such as porcelain, textiles, silk, leather goods, furniture, and clocks that could be exported to other countries. High **tariffs** on imports protected farmers and industry from foreign competition. The government introduced new technologies imported from Britain and gave subsidies and interest-free loans to private manufacturers to make French exports more competitive in international markets. The army and navy were strengthened for the purpose of establishing colonies in North America, the Caribbean, and India to serve as suppliers of raw materials and consumers of French goods. The government required craftsmen and artisans to join guilds in order to tax membership dues. Colbert unified the domestic French market by eliminating many tariffs and tolls between regions. These reforms all had the purpose of increasing economic activity to generate more tax revenue for the state.

Colbert introduced two additional policies to increase tax revenue. First, jobs in the government were sold to the highest bidder, who would then use the power attached to the office to collect tolls and other fees from citizens. Second, a policy called "tax farming" allowed private individuals to become tax collectors. These tax farmers would use intimidation and coercion to extract as much money from citizens as possible and then keep a portion of the proceeds for themselves.

By the middle of the seventeenth century, France had the largest **gross domestic product** (GDP) of any European nation. However, it also had by far the largest population, with about twice as many people as Britain. Thus **per capita GDP** was quite low, and income was very unequally distributed. Tariffs on imported agriculture products kept domestic farm prices sufficiently high that farmers could support themselves, but rapid population growth kept per capita rural incomes from rising. The concentration of political power resulted in a steady flow of wealth toward the aristocracy and nobility in Paris, as exemplified by Louis XIV's construction of the magnificent Palace of Versailles in 1682.

The tariffs and subsidies that protected domestic farmers and manufacturers from international competition also removed the pressure to innovate and become more efficient. With farmers remaining in the countryside, the supply of urban labor was insufficient to support the growth of industry. Whatever profits did arise in commerce and manufacturing were often directed toward buying public offices, government bonds, or land, all of which typically offered higher **rates of return** than could be gained by investing in businesses.

The Seven Years War (1756–1763) with Britain resulted in the loss of France's colonies in North America and a further deterioration of government finances. The added expense of aiding the Americans in their war of independence (1775–1783) created a fiscal crisis for the French government. The king needed to raise taxes and called for a meeting of the legislature to establish new tax policies. From that meeting emerged the French Revolution (1789–1799). In the assembly hall, advocates of abolishing the monarchy and the privileges of the aristocracy sat on the left side of the room, and those who favored retaining the king and preserving the aristocracy occupied the right side. This seating arrangement is the source of the terms *left-wing* and *right-wing* in political discourse.

Initially, the Revolution was led by moderate members of the business class, or bourgeoisie, and liberal aristocrats who wanted economic reforms and a constitution to place limits on the power of the king. They succeeded in eliminating domestic tariffs and other barriers to trade within France, abolishing the guild system and royal factories, and establishing a unified system of weights and measures and a common currency. They also removed many mercantilist restrictions on industry and commerce and declared France to be a republic governed by elected representatives. Finally, they abolished the institution of primogeniture, which required that family property be inherited solely by the eldest son. This reform subsequently caused the division of family farms into smaller plots, which suppressed agricultural productivity and farm incomes.

In 1793, the Revolution devolved into a Reign of Terror, with mob violence aimed at all wealth and privilege. A group called the Jacobins, led by Maximilien de Robespierre (1758–1794), gained power and proceeded to redistribute much of the aristocrats' land to peasant farmers. Peasants vented their centuries of pent-up rage by burning the castles of many aristocrats. In Paris, those citizens deemed to be counterrevolutionary faced decapitation by the guillotine. An estimated 1,200 individuals, including King Louis XVI, Queen Marie Antoinette, and even Robespierre met that fate.

Figure 8.1 A Parisian crowd watches public executions using the guillotine.
(© Getty Images/UniversalImagesGroup)

By the end of the French Revolution, most of the land owned by the Catholic Church and the nobility had been confiscated and tax farming had been abolished. Perhaps the most significant development, however, was a continuation of royal efforts to centralize political power. Just as French kings had removed many of the privileges of feudal lords and aristocrats to eliminate any challenges to royal authority, the leaders of the Revolution sought to eliminate all local power that might obstruct their goals. In addition to the abolition of guilds and the confiscation of Church property, local networks and associations were suppressed to establish a centralized government administered by honest and competent civil servants and headed by a strong leader able to suppress factions pursuing their own interests at the expense of the public interest.

This vision of a "benign dictator" came to fruition when Napoleon Bonaparte (1769–1821), a military general, led an overthrow of the state (coup d'état) in 1799 and had himself crowned as Emperor of France in 1804. Although Napoleon actively attempted to improve the French economy, his frequent military campaigns, in places such as Egypt and Russia, hindered development. In 1806, he announced the Continental System, an effort to exert French control over the European economy by prohibiting all trade between Britain and the mainland. The British responded with a naval blockade that deprived France of access to resources from North America and French colonies in the Caribbean. In short, Napoleon's ambitions for dominating Europe took precedence over and sometimes conflicted with his domestic efforts to improve the economy.

Since Napoleon's defeat by the British at the Battle of Waterloo in 1815, the French economic system has consisted of a core set of institutions, including a strong and active government, fragmented labor, and small businesses. One explanation for this continuity is that the French have never reached consensus on the meaning of the revolution of 1789. Was it a bourgeois revolution in which manufacturers and entrepreneurs threw off the stifling regulations imposed by mercantilism? Was it a proletarian revolution in which rural peasants and urban workers rose up in protest against a rigid class system that offered them little opportunity for advancement? Or was it an effort by elites in the military and aristocracy to wrest control of the state away from an ineffective monarch and install a strong leader who would restore national unity and elevate France to a dominant position in Europe? These three themes recur during the subsequent two centuries of French economic history.

STATE CAPITALISM 1815–1944

In 1815, France was predominantly a land of peasant farmers. In fact, rural residents accounted for more than half the population well into the twentieth century. The Revolution did not significantly change the lives of most citizens; the economy continued to consist primarily of small farms, small shops, and small manufacturers. France never experienced an "industrial revolution" in which the economy underwent a rapid transformation and acceleration of growth. Even by 1906, only 25 percent of the labor force worked for businesses with more than fifty employees.

France faced several major obstacles in making the transition from an agricultural economy to an industrial economy. It lacked any significant deposits of coal and iron ore, more than a million French soldiers were lost in the Napoleonic wars, and much of the remaining population stayed on farms rather than migrating to cities. Farmers could make enough money to survive, but their meager existence led to low birth rates. The French population increased by just 40 percent during the nineteenth century. The comparable values during the same period were 350 percent in Britain and 250 percent in Germany.

In World War I, France lost 1.4 million soldiers and another five million were wounded. However, in the decade after the war, France's economy grew faster than any other European nation. The 1919 Treaty of Versailles required Germany to pay reparations for the damage inflicted on other nations, and France used this money to fund public investments in infrastructure. France also regained the province of Alsace-Lorraine, which had been lost to Germany in 1871. That region was particularly important for its deposits of coal and iron ore.

Industrial Policy

After the French Revolution, the government continued to play an active role in promoting economic development. High tariffs protected French farmers and manufacturers from foreign competition. Beginning in 1842, the government initiated a partnership with private firms to construct a nationwide railway system. This large increase in spending, coupled with the widening of markets due to improved transportation, created a period of prosperity that lasted until the 1860s. However, after tariffs were reduced, France's small and relatively inefficient firms and farmers could not compete in international markets. A serious **recession** ensued, and when the global economy slid into a two-decade-long stagnation in 1873, France reverted to protectionism.

The French economy began to rebound in the 1890s. The government nationalized the entire railroad system and by the 1920s was entering into public-private partnerships in which the state held shares of stock in private companies. Despite attempts to encourage private entrepreneurship, the results were usually disappointing. The legacy of protective tariffs and government control had left French businesses ill-equipped to cope with the challenges of open competition. They remained comfortable with the status quo and reluctant to innovate or invest in expansion to improve efficiency.

Unorganized Labor

The combined legacies of royal absolutism and Napoleon's centralization of power left local organizations, including labor unions, fragmented and weak. Labor strikes were illegal until 1864, and labor unions were not permitted until 1884. With no unions to express their grievances, workers occasionally resorted to sabotage and riots. To halt the production process, workers tossed a wooden shoe (sabot) into the fast-moving machinery, hence the term *sabotage*.

The absence of labor unions caused worker discontent to be channeled into the political process. France experienced two more revolutions in the nineteenth century. After Napoleon's defeat in 1814, the monarchy was restored, and subsequent kings attempted to roll back the liberal reforms of the French Revolution. By 1830, only landowners were permitted to vote, and freedom of the press was routinely violated. A revolution in that year deposed one king, but continued repression led to a second revolution in 1848 and the establishment of the Second Republic headed by Napoleon's nephew.

At the end of the Franco-Prussian War (1870–71), workers in Paris revolted by erecting barricades, seizing control of the city, and establishing the Paris Commune. They elected a city council that claimed authority to rule all of France. This attempt at **social anarchism** was short-lived as the army forcefully crushed the uprising seventy-two days later.

In 1895, various labor unions formed the General Confederation of Labor (Confédération Générale des Travailleurs [CGT]). This organization was subsidized and controlled by the state and functioned primarily to link job seekers with job openings. However, workers did gain some favorable legislation in the form of disability insurance in 1898, a ten-hour workday in 1904, and a week-long annual holiday in 1906.

Labor unions made significant gains between 1936 and 1938 when the government enacted legislation establishing a minimum wage, a forty-hour work-week, paid vacations, insurance for healthcare and old age, and the right of unions to organize, bargain collectively, and strike.

Culture

Intellectual life is an essential part of French culture. Citizens routinely read and discuss the works of French philosophers and social theorists. Many of the cultural beliefs and values shaping the French economic system are based on the ideas of the nation's great social theorists. Jean-Jacques Rousseau (1712–1778) preceded the French Revolution, but his ideas have had a continuing influence on French attitudes toward government, individual freedom, and social equality. Rousseau claimed that inequality of wealth creates social conflict as the wealthy use their power to control government and oppress fellow citizens. Conflict, in turn, causes individuals to focus on their self-interest as they seek security from oppression.

Rousseau believed that greater social equality would lead to cooperation in promoting the common good. In such a society, the laws enacted by the state would reflect the "general will" (volonté générale) of all citizens rather than the private interests of powerful groups. These laws would expand human freedom by enabling individuals to build communities based on shared interests rather than a clash of private interests. In short, Rousseau argued that substantial social equality is necessary for both individual freedom and close-knit communities. The motto of the French Revolution—liberty, equality, fraternity (liberté, égalité, fraternité)—preserves his legacy.

Two French sociologists developed ideas that have also continued to shape the nation's path of development. Henri de Saint-Simon (1760–1825) and Auguste Comte (1798–1857) each claimed that a small group of highly trained scientists and engineers could guide the national economy toward growth and prosperity in much the same way that expert managers can improve the operation of a single firm. Their ideas would provide the intellectual foundations for the use of economic planning in France.

French culture is imbued with socialist, communist, and anarchist ideas and values. Many of the most prominent leftist theorists were French. François Babeuf (1760–1797) espoused communism a century before Karl Marx. In fact, Marx was influenced by reading the works of French socialists while living in Paris from 1843 to 1845. Pierre-Joseph Proudhon (1809–1865) is regarded as the principal founder of social anarchism with his motto "property is theft." Georges Sorel (1847–1922) developed the idea of anarcho-syndicalism in which worker-owned factories would form networks and associations to coordinate their activities and manage the economy. All these writers condemned private property and markets for undermining the natural harmony and unity that should exist among humans. Their ideas are reflected in the French mistrust of free markets, competition, and big business.

The Demise of State Capitalism

The Great Depression spread to France in 1932 as exports and tourism declined sharply. Production dropped 25 percent from its 1929 level, and unemployment rose to 15 percent. Unemployment would have been worse, but growth during the 1920s was so strong that French firms hired workers from Poland. As the Depression worsened, Polish workers were sent home and therefore did not affect the French unemployment rate. A conservative government held office at the time and, following conventional economic wisdom, adopted an austerity program of cuts in government spending to maintain a balanced budget. The economy failed to respond as output and unemployment remained at their 1932 levels for the next three years.

As the Depression persisted, most leftists in France concluded that capitalism had failed, leaving only two alternatives—**socialism** or **fascism**. After Hitler took power in Germany in 1933, the different factions on the French political left (e.g., socialists, communists, and anarchists) united into a coalition called the Popular Front and won the 1936 election. President Léon Blum (1872–1950) was a moderate socialist committed to gradual change, but the German invasion of France in 1940 put an end to all reforms.

Despite its revolutionary tradition, France contained a number of powerful right-wing groups. Most notable was Action Française, founded in 1899, which was antidemocratic and favored restoring the monarchy and the power of the Catholic Church. Other openly fascist groups welcomed the rise of Hitler in Germany as the solution to France's drift toward socialism. After the German army captured Paris in 1940, Hitler saw no need to conquer the rest of the nation. Instead, the Germans allowed right-wing French leaders to establish a "puppet government" in the city of Vichy in southern France. The Vichy regime was led by Philippe Pétain (1856–1951), a general in the French army, who collaborated with the Nazis in controlling southern France and suppressing any resistance. Following the Nazi economic model, the Vichy regime abolished labor unions and relied on government planning to coordinate all major production. As the growing need for manpower in the German army depleted the German labor force, the Vichy regime conscripted French workers and deported them to work in German factories. By 1944, 15 percent of the German labor force consisted of French workers.

PLANNED CAPITALISM 1945–1982

As World War II ended, French leaders were determined to fashion a new economic system. Impressed by the strength of the German economy that enabled Hitler to capture their country in little more than a month, they attributed that feat to economic planning by the state. The challenge was to engage in economic planning while simultaneously protecting democracy, civil liberties, and individual freedom.

Popular opinion remained decidedly leftist. Many of the major industrialists such as Louis Renault (1877–1944) had cooperated if not collaborated with the German occupation, thereby further tarnishing the image of capitalism. In contrast, French communists led the resistance against Nazi occupation and emerged from the war as heroes with considerable political influence.

The French refer to the next three decades (1945–1975) as the Thirty Glorious Years (Les Trente Glorieuses). A 5 percent average annual growth rate during the 1950s and 1960s was higher than any other industrialized nation except Japan. Recovery from the war was aided by $2.3 billion of aid from the United States under the Marshall Plan plus the cancellation of another $2.9 billion of American loans. The Marshall Plan served the dual purpose of helping Europe recover from the war and making Europe less susceptible to socialism and communism. However, the coalition government that led France after the war included significant numbers of both socialists and communists. Despite their similarities, French socialists and communists were bitter rivals, and the communists were expelled from the coalition in 1947.

Industrial Policy

In 1945, the French government began nationalizing select businesses and industries. It confiscated Louis Renault's automobile company as punishment for producing more than 30,000 vehicles for the German army. Most other nationalizations occurred in potential **natural monopolies** such as railways, airlines, buses, seaports, coal, oil, natural gas, and electricity. In addition, the government took ownership of the central bank (Banque de France), the three largest commercial banks, and thirty-four insurance companies. Additional nationalization continued until 1958, when state-owned enterprises accounted for 20 percent of industrial output. The government compensated the previous owners of nationalized firms with government bonds.

In 1947, the French began formal planning of the economy. Jean Monnet (1888–1965), who oversaw the development of the planning process, sought to combine the strengths of both market and state by designing a planning apparatus to enhance the efficiency of the market while avoiding the cumbersome bureaucracy typically associated with planning. Unlike planning in China or the former Soviet Union, French **indicative planning** did not set mandatory production targets for businesses. Instead, the plan provided businesses with forecasts of future economic trends, giving them the knowledge and confidence to expand productive capacity.

In 1958, General Charles de Gaulle (1890–1970) was elected president. The conservative de Gaulle was just as supportive of planning as the communists and socialists, but he had a different vision. He wanted France to become a great industrial power, and to accomplish that goal, he suppressed wages in order to enlarge the surplus that could be used to develop a select group of firms with potential for global dominance. These "national champions" in the petrochemical, electronics, data processing, aeronautics, and pharmaceutical industries received subsidies, tax breaks, export assistance, and preferential credit. To create additional economies of scale, the government encouraged mergers and cooperation between firms.

The plan was formulated through a lengthy and detailed process known as *concertation*. Relying on approximately thirty commissions devoted to different sectors of the economy, the planning agency conducted extensive dialogues with representatives of business, labor, farmers, consumers, environmentalists, senior citizens, and women. As a result, the plan became more than simply a technical forecast of available resources and future output. It presented a vision of the future incorporating goals such as environmental protection, cultural preservation, and social justice.

Although compliance with the plan was voluntary, the government had various tools at its disposal to create incentives for compliance, including exemptions from price controls and regulations, tax credits, subsidies, loans, government contracts, import licenses, and accelerated depreciation allowances. Beginning in the late 1970s, the government initiated "development contracts" whereby businesses would commit to certain aspects of the plan in exchange for low-interest loans, tax breaks, and other concessions.

Organized Labor

At end of World War II, France's largest labor federation, the CGT, was aligned with the French Communist Party. Another group, the French Democratic Labor Confederation, maintained close ties to the Socialist Party. Popular support for labor unions was increasing in part due to public hostility toward major industrialists for having collaborated with the Germans during the war. However, when a conservative government took office in 1954, the state intervened in collective bargaining to prevent excessive wage gains. Hostility between government and labor unions was exacerbated during the 1960s and 1970s when planning policy was explicitly designed to suppress wages in order to stimulate the growth of large corporations. Labor leaders were often excluded from planning dialogues because both employers and government officials mistrusted the pervasive anticapitalist sentiments among workers.

France had five rival labor federations, which further eroded the power of labor unions. Because these federations competed with one another for membership and influence, each one sought to have an affiliated union in every major industry. As a result, labor's unity in the collective bargaining process was undermined; up to five different unions might bargain with a single employer. The unity of labor was also weakened by the CGT's frequent refusal to accept compromise agreements between other unions and employers.

With five different labor federations, French unions faced a collective action problem. Wage stability is a **public good** in the sense that all individuals benefit from noninflationary growth, but each labor union had an incentive to become a free rider by enjoying the benefits of other workers' wage restraint while aggressively seeking higher wages for its own members. Stated differently, although wage restraint would prevent inflation if all unions acted in a coordinated manner, any single union agreeing to wage restraint was likely to be hurt by inflation as other unions continued to push for higher wages. The lack of coordination among the five labor federations discouraged wage restraint because any federation agreeing to moderate wage demands would be challenged by rival federations for selling out its members.

Given the hostility between the French government and labor unions during the 1970s, the government eventually chose not to deal directly with unions in wage negotiations. Instead, the government relied on price controls, anticipating that firms would resist demands for higher wages if they could not pass the additional cost on to consumers through higher prices. The government also resorted to periodic **devaluation** of the franc to maintain competitive export prices and to reduce real wages by causing the prices of imported goods to rise.

Despite the efforts by French labor unions to gain higher wages, their power to do so remained relatively weak. A lack of unity and coordination undermined bargaining strength, and the communist and socialist federations often focused more on gaining control of the state than on securing immediate gains in wages and working conditions. Only about 10 percent of the labor force belonged to unions, and white-collar and public sector workers were more unionized than blue-collar workers. However, although labor was fragmented in terms of its collective bargaining power, unions were able to organize extremely effective general strikes against government policies.

Culture

Living in the country that gave birth to the Enlightenment in the seventeenth and eighteenth centuries, the French have a strong belief in the capacity of human reason to improve the functioning of society. They view planning as an effort to impose order and purpose on the chaotic and impersonal forces of competitive markets. Unlike other cultures in which beliefs about religion and politics are considered private matters, the French love to challenge each other's deepest beliefs. This capacity for conversation is evident in the planning process, which entails endless hours of dialogue between major interest groups in the effort to reach consensus about the desired course of economic development.

Despite the efforts of planners to modernize the economy by promoting large corporations, the French retain nostalgia for an earlier era of small, family-owned businesses and shops. A typical Parisian might purchase bread and pastries at one shop, meat and cheese at another, and fruits and vegetables at a third, all within easy walking distance. The shopper might have a personal relationship with the baker, the butcher, and the grocer. Many French citizens blame large supermarkets, chain stores, and discount warehouses for eliminating jobs and undermining French culture. In response to this public sentiment, government planners included provisions for supporting small businesses. Even today, French firms are, on average, smaller than their counterparts in other industrialized nations.

In May of 1968, university students in Paris boycotted classes to protest what they perceived to be the authoritarian and hierarchical nature of higher education in France. An estimated eleven million workers around the country joined them in a nationwide general strike that nearly brought the economy to a halt. Both students and workers demanded a voice and self-determination (autogestion) in governing their universities and workplaces. After two weeks of violent confrontations between police and protesters, the strike ended when the French Communist Party declared that France was not yet ready for a socialist revolution and urged workers to return to their jobs. However, the disruption was sufficient to topple the government as President de Gaulle resigned the following year.

The Demise of Planned Capitalism

As the global economy suffered from stagflation in the mid-1970s, the French economy was weakened by both rising oil prices and increased competition from Japan and other emerging Asian nations. In 1974, newly elected President Valéry Giscard d'Estaing pledged to reduce the role of planning and government intervention in the economy. Because the economy was in a recession, the government had fewer resources to allocate and therefore less power to secure compliance with a plan. Also, government planning of the economy meant that politicians, not the market, bore much of the blame for recession. By reducing government control over the economy, politicians hoped to minimize their responsibility for poor economic performance. Also, France's increasing involvement in the global economy meant that planners could no longer control or make accurate predictions about the future course of the French economy. Just as domestic markets create competitive pressures on individual firms, national governments found themselves increasingly unable to resist the power of global markets.

Another factor contributing to the downfall of planning was the government's preferential treatment of "national champions" at the expense of small businesses and workers. As long as the economy remained healthy, French citizens accepted the use of public funds to stimulate private businesses because everyone seemed to benefit. However, as recession and inflation grew worse, the French public increasingly resented the special privileges and favors bestowed on big business. Instead, political support grew for assistance to smaller firms and social programs to benefit citizens directly.

The problems facing planning were compounded in 1979 when France entered the European Monetary System and accepted a fixed exchange rate between the franc and other European currencies. This decision limited the government's ability to stimulate the economy because expansionist policies tend to create inflationary pressures, and inflation leads to **balance of trade** deficits and downward pressure on the currency. With devaluation no longer an option, the government had to shift its focus from stimulating growth to controlling inflation.

The French experience with planning provides valuable lessons about the difficulties facing government efforts to coordinate economic activity. Planners typically form cooperative alliances with industry leaders to facilitate compliance with the plan. But the closer these ties become, the greater the likelihood that the planning process will be biased in favor of particular industries or sectors. In France, this problem was exacerbated by the fact that senior officials often alternated between jobs in the private sector and high-level government positions. Moreover, the leaders of government and business often had personal ties based on having attended the same elite universities and mingling in the same social circles. Over time, the planning process lost much of its legitimacy because the public perceived a coalition of elites in business and government supporting policies that benefited each other.

Although the job of planners is easier if public input is kept to a minimum, more widespread participation tends to promote the legitimacy of the process and adherence to the plan. Yet opening the planning process to public input allows groups to exert influence that may serve only their own narrow interests. In other words, a less accessible planning process would shield planners from outside influence and permit them to objectively promote the good of society as a whole, but too little democratic input jeopardizes public confidence in the fairness and legitimacy of the plan. Finding the right balance between reliance on the scientific expertise of planners and creating an open forum in which every citizen can potentially participate was a constant challenge.

In 1981, the French elected a socialist-communist coalition government headed by François Mitterand (1916–1996). The government quickly enacted an array of new policies, including a 28 percent increase in government spending on social programs, a 38 percent increase in the minimum wage, higher taxes for corporations and the wealthy, increased social security benefits, an increase from four to five weeks of annual paid vacation for workers, a reduction of the workweek from forty to thirty-nine hours, 50,000 new public sector jobs, subsidies for hiring and training young workers, and a lower retirement age. The government also nationalized twelve large conglomerates and thirty-eight banks by exchanging government bonds for shares of stock. Thirteen of the largest twenty firms and 90 percent of the entire banking sector were now owned by the state. France had the largest state-owned sector in Europe, accounting for approximately 25 percent of industrial output.

The reaction from investors, both domestic and foreign, was swift and negative. Domestic investment declined by 10 percent, and **financial capital** flowed out of the country. At the same time, the global economy entered the worst recession since the Great Depression. As French exports plummeted, the balance of trade deficit grew. Declining tax revenue caused the government's budget deficit to swell. Unemployment rose to 9 percent and the annual rate of inflation reached 14 percent.

Realizing that efforts to move toward socialism were unsustainable, Mitterand reversed direction and adopted an austerity program with cuts in government spending, lower taxes for business, higher taxes for individuals, a wage-price freeze, and three devaluations of the franc over a two-year period. In addition, a tight **monetary policy** caused interest rates to rise, which stemmed the outflow of financial capital and reduced inflation. Finally, Mitterand privatized the state's holdings in the banking industry and reduced subsidies to other state-owned enterprises.

In retrospect, the brief attempt at moving toward socialism was a final effort to salvage a planned economy. But globalization now gave investors the power to effectively veto any policy they disliked by moving financial capital out of the country. Ironically, a socialist government oversaw the decline of planning and a transition toward greater reliance on markets and private enterprise.

WELFARE CAPITALISM 1983–1995

Mitterand remained president of France until 1995, but after 1982, the Socialist Party abandoned its advocacy of state-ownership of enterprises and continued the process of privatization and deregulation. This rejection of socialism was accelerated in 1986 when a coalition of moderates and conservatives gained a majority of seats in the legislature, and a conservative, Jacques Chirac, became prime minister. This split government, which the French call "cohabitation," prevented both socialists and conservatives from fully implementing their agendas. Instead, the two sides reached a compromise—the socialists would essentially abandon planning and reduce government's role in the economy, while the conservatives would accept an expansion of welfare programs. Rather than attempting to control the market, the government would allow the market to operate with less regulation and then provide social benefits to those who fared poorly. The size of the state budget as a percentage of GDP actually grew, but spending was now directed less toward regulating the market and more toward ameliorating the condition of less successful citizens.

Industrial Policy

In 1986, Prime Minister Chirac reduced the Planning Commission's budget and staff. Although planning continued, it no longer entailed a blueprint for the future course of the entire economy. Planning was now done simply to improve communication between different sectors of the economy so that business leaders and politicians had better information for decision-making.

Beginning in 1988, the planning process expanded to include dialogue with business leaders and government officials from other nations within the European Community. However, once France became a member of the European Union (EU) in 1992, the significance of planning again declined because member states of the EU lost considerable sovereignty in controlling the future of their economies. EU guidelines required conformity to common policies in agriculture, social security, the **value-added tax**, and interest rates.

Industrial policy after 1982 consisted of a steady rollback of government's role in the economy. Reforms included the lifting of most price controls, elimination of the tax on wealth, reducing the top marginal income tax rate from 65 percent to 50 percent, cuts in government subsidies, relaxed regulation of state-owned enterprises, and the privatization of sixty-five state-owned enterprises. Government officials instructed the remaining state-owned enterprises to make decisions based on profitability rather than adherence to the government's plan. Financial markets were deregulated in 1985, and capital controls on the flow of financial capital in and out of the country ended soon thereafter.

Works Councils

Mitterand's administration passed legislation to strengthen the bargaining power of labor unions at the firm and industry level. The government required all firms with fifty or more employees to establish and fund a "works council" to serve as a forum in which workers could voice their concerns over work conditions. In addition, state-owned enterprises were required to fill one-third of the seats on their boards of directors with employee representatives. Any firm planning to reduce its labor force was required to submit a document to its works council outlining provisions for the affected workers such as early retirement plans, retraining, and placement services. If the council rejected the plan, the issue could be taken to a court of law for final resolution.

Social Policy

Prior to 1983, social benefits in France were minimal as the government devoted funds to subsidies and other aid to businesses. In contrast, the advent of welfare capitalism witnessed an array of programs to benefit those who were marginalized in the economy, including youth, people with disabilities, immigrants, seniors, single parents, and those lacking employable skills or unable to find jobs. During the late 1980s, France devoted 33 percent of its GDP to social programs, a higher percentage than any nation except the Netherlands and the Scandinavian countries. Social programs were funded primarily through payroll taxes paid by both employers and employees.

In contrast to the United States and Britain, where funding for welfare programs often becomes a major source of political conflict, in France, most conservatives support social benefits as a means of ensuring that all citizens have a sense of belonging to the national community. Social exclusion and marginalization are widely viewed as contributing to crime, ethnic and racial hostility, and political extremism.

Most French social programs remain in effect today. Comprehensive national health insurance covers most physicians' fees, hospital bills, and prescription drug costs. Low-income households receive free health insurance. The government heavily subsidizes university education, resulting in annual tuition of only about $300. Prenatal and maternity costs as well as day care expenses are also subsidized, and families receive allowances for child rearing. When a person dies, the family receives more than $6,000 to pay for funeral expenses. Eligibility for social security is universal for people older than age sixty-five. Unlike the United States, social security benefits do not depend on an individual's work history or marital status.

In labor markets, workers may apply for early retirement at age fifty-five to receive close to a full pension. Only one French worker in three is still employed at age sixty. The government subsidizes jobs for youth in the public and nonprofit sectors to provide job experience and skills. Benefits for unemployment, sickness, and disability are quite generous. After losing a job, unemployed workers are eligible to receive approximately 60 percent of their former pay for as long as five years. In the late 1980s, several new social benefits were created for people whose income fell below a specified level. These "means-tested" benefits include housing allowances, income supplements for single parents, and in-home assistance for the elderly.

Culture

Centuries of state regulation of the economy have affected French culture. Shielded from competitive market forces, many French citizens view unbridled capitalism as a threat to their nation and lifestyles. They believe that free markets lead to low wages, little leisure time, low quality of goods, and domination of the economy by large corporations. Even small business owners and farmers may vote for socialist candidates because they resent the power of big businesses.

Conservatives join with socialists in supporting government efforts to protect French culture from commercial and foreign influences. The government restricts the use of English words in French publications, limits the number of foreign radio and television programs, and discourages the construction of large stores and franchises to preserve small retail shops.

The French people pride themselves on appreciation of the nonmaterial aspects of life such as leisure, intellectual development, and the arts. They tend to have a much more positive attitude toward government than is found in Britain or the United States. When the government nationalized businesses, many French citizens viewed this action as recovering the fruits of their labor that had been stolen by monopolists. Regulations on business were regarded as protection from exploitation. The French generally approve of governmental authority to control market forces so that individuals can enjoy the freedom to pursue their private lives in a stable and secure economic environment.

Partly out of concern about a slowing rate of population growth, France has adopted relatively open immigration policies, particularly for citizens of its former colonies in Africa and Asia. However, the influx of foreigners has created significant social tensions as growing numbers of French citizens view immigrants as undermining traditional French culture, burdening welfare programs, and contributing to crime. The National Front, an ultraconservative political party led by Marine Le Pen, has ties to neo-Nazi and anti-Semitic groups and is fueling ethnic conflict by blaming immigrants for France's economic problems. The growing influence of the National Front was demonstrated when it received 25 percent of the vote in the first round of the 2015 election. A resurgence of neo-Nazi groups has led to assaults on minorities and desecration of Jewish cemeteries and synagogues.

The Demise of Welfare Capitalism

The cost to government of supporting the array of social programs under welfare capitalism was enormous. When the shift to welfare capitalism occurred in 1983, the government expected that deregulating the economy would unleash market forces and lead to rapid growth and job creation. A growing economy, in turn, would reduce the need for social benefits and provide additional tax revenue to pay for social programs. Unfortunately, these projections did not materialize. A global recession in the early 1990s kept unemployment high, resulting in expansion of social benefits.

The recession was not the only cause of stagnation in the French economy. The payroll tax that funded social programs was close to 33 percent (compared to 20 percent in Britain and 6 percent in the United States), which discouraged job creation. Increasing globalization was undermining the French economy as more efficient producers in other countries gained **competitive advantage** over smaller, less innovative French firms with higher labor costs. Finally, EU policies regarding the size of government budget deficits forced the French government to reduce spending on social programs.

A NEW DIRECTION?

When the French elected conservative Jacques Chirac as president in 1995, the country appeared to have turned a corner toward a more neoliberal form of capitalism. Chirac promised to increase the competitiveness of the economy by reducing state ownership and control of business, by cutting social programs, and by deregulating labor markets. However, two years later, Chirac was forced to accept another *cohabitation* as the socialists regained control of the legislature and Lionel Jospin became prime minister. The turn toward neoliberalism was dealt another setback by the 2012 election of socialist François Hollande as president. He canceled tax cuts for the wealthy, proposed raising the top marginal income tax rate to 75 percent, and restored full pensions at age sixty. In reaction, foreign investment in France dropped by 77 percent in 2012.

French citizens remain sharply divided over the roles of market and state and the appropriate synthesis of the two. They continue to value an active state to shield them from market forces, but they also recognize the necessity to become more efficient in order to thrive in the global economy. Labor relations exemplify the effort to both regulate and unleash market forces simultaneously. In 1999, France reduced the workweek from thirty-nine to thirty-five hours for firms with more than twenty employees and for all firms by 2002. This change reflected a cultural preference for leisure but was also intended to reduce unemployment by having more employees working fewer hours. However, without wage reductions or increases in productivity, the shorter work week would increase per-unit labor costs and make French goods less competitive in international markets. To prevent this, the government has also taken steps to reduce labor costs by increasing the "flexibility" of labor markets, meaning that wages are allowed to rise or fall in response to changes in the supply of or demand for labor and firms can more easily hire or fire workers.

French labor markets have historically been quite inflexible. Not only does the high payroll tax discourage hiring, but discharging workers often entails a lengthy process that may lead to court hearings and costly severance packages. As a result, French firms are reluctant to hire new employees. In recent years, more than 80 percent of new jobs are temporary contracts of three months or less. Labor unions and employers reached an agreement in 2013 permitting companies to reduce working time and salaries when demand is weak. In exchange, workers are eligible for a longer period of unemployment compensation. The government also enacted a twenty-six billion dollar payroll tax credit to reduce the cost of hiring new workers.

Although membership in labor unions has declined to only 8 percent in the private sector, French workers continue the revolutionary tradition of taking direct action to address their grievances. In 1995, when President Chirac announced plans to reduce pensions for railroad workers and cut social security benefits, workers organized nationwide demonstrations and shut down the mass transit systems for three weeks until the government conceded. More recently, fishermen used their boats to blockade harbors, Air France workers occupied airport runways to prevent planes from flying, truckers blocked highways, and farmers hijacked trucks carrying produce into France and dumped the contents. Workers have even resorted to "bossnapping," which entails holding an executive hostage until their demands are met.

These confrontational actions have an institutional basis. France lacks the cooperative labor relations found in nations such as Germany and Sweden where peaceful negotiations usually resolve conflicts. The hostility between workers and both employers and the government dates back to the French Revolution and has been sustained by strong left-wing elements within labor unions. Also, because France has greater income inequality than any other European nation, workers refuse to accept the sacrifices (e.g., wage cuts and reduced benefits) sought by government and employers to make the economy more competitive. Ten percent of French households own 50 percent of the nation's wealth, and taxes on property, inheritance, and capital gains are all quite low. In these circumstances, workers typically vote for socialist candidates who pledge to place a greater tax burden on the wealthiest groups in society.

The law enacted in the early 1980s requiring French firms with fifty or more employees to fund works councils and meet stringent requirement for layoffs has had a perverse effect. Many small firms stop hiring at forty-nine employees or else the owner establishes a second business with additional workers. As a result, firms remain small and fail to achieve potential economies of scale. However, this problem is gradually being resolved as foreign investors buy French firms and proceed to shed redundant workers, streamline operations, and close obsolete plants. The movement of global capital is accomplishing what the French government could not by forcing firms to become bigger, more efficient, and therefore more competitive in international markets.

The lingering effects of the 2008 global financial crisis continue to suppress growth. The economy is stagnant with an unemployment rate of 11 percent compared to less than 6 percent in the United States and Germany. Youth unemployment is 25 percent, and many young people are leaving the country in search of better job opportunities. The government has seemingly exhausted its active policies to combat slow growth with more spending. EU rules require that government deficits not exceed 3 percent of GDP, although France was allowed a deficit of 4.1 percent of GDP in 2014 in recognition of its efforts to achieve more flexible labor markets. Similarly, France's **national debt** is currently 91 percent of GDP; EU guidelines call for a maximum of 60 percent, so additional deficit spending is virtually prohibited. The government already employs 25 percent of the labor force, and government spending as a percentage of GDP is 56 percent compared to 49 percent in Britain and 47 percent in Germany.

France faces a dilemma. Neoliberal capitalism is so unpopular that even conservatives oppose it. Yet the pressures created by global competition are steadily eroding welfare capitalism and the protections created by centuries of state intervention. With voters nearly evenly divided between socialists and conservatives, governments often consist of tenuous coalitions unable to embark on any clear strategy for improving the economy. Attempts by conservatives to impose austerity are met with active resistance, while expansions of the welfare state by socialists are blamed for reducing the competitiveness of French firms. Indeed, the Socialist Party has become so sensitive to voters' concerns about the growing size of government that President Hollande has responded to economic stagnation with an austerity program of tight monetary policy and cuts in government spending. The French economy has failed to rebound, experiencing two recessions in the past five years and currently teetering on the brink of a third recession.

ADDITIONAL READING

Angresano, James. *French Welfare State Reform*. 2nd ed. New York: Anthem Press, 2011.

Dormois, Jean-Pierre. *The French Economy in the Twentieth Century*. New York: Cambridge University Press, 2004.

Forbes, Jill, Nick Hewlett, and Francois Nectoux. *Contemporary France*. 2nd ed. Reading, MA: Longmans, 2001.

Hall, Peter. *Governing the Economy: The Politics of State Intervention in Britain and France*. New York: Oxford University Press, 1986.

Hayward, Jack. *Fragmented France: Two Centuries of Disputed Identity*. New York: Oxford University Press, 2007.

Hazareesingh, Sudhir. *How the French Think: An Affectionate Portrait of an Intellectual People*. New York: Basic Books, 2015.

Heywood, Colin. *The Development of the French Economy in the Twentieth Century*. New York: Cambridge University Press, 1995.

Jenkins, Cecil. *A Brief History of France*. London: Constable & Robinson, 2011.

Kresl, Peter Karl, and Sylvain Gallais. *France Encounters Globalization*. Northampton, MA: Edward Elgar, 2002.

Lebovics, Herman. *Bringing the Empire Back Home: France in the Global Age*. Durham, NC: Duke University Press, 2004.

Levy, Jonah D. *Tocqueville's Revenge: State, Society, and Economy in Contemporary France*. Cambridge, MA: Harvard University Press, 1999.

Safran, William. *The French Polity*. 5th ed. White Plains, NY: Longman, 1998.

Schmidt, Vivian A. *From State To Market? The Transformation of French Business and Government*. New York: Cambridge University Press, 1996.

Steele, Ross. *The French Way: Aspects of Behavior, Attitudes, and Customs of the French*. New York: McGraw-Hill, 2006.

Vail, Mark I. *Recasting Welfare Capitalism: Economic Adjustment in Contemporary France and Germany*. Philadelphia: Temple University Press, 2009.

Chapter 9

THE GERMAN ECONOMIC SYSTEM

"If you invest all your energy in economics, world commerce, parliamentarianism, military engagement, power and power politics . . . there won't be any left for the other direction. Culture and the state—let us be honest with ourselves—are adversaries."

FRIEDRICH NIETZSCHE (1844–1900),
German philosopher

The Holy Roman Empire (800–1806) represented an effort to create a unified European state. However, the actual authority of that state was quite limited. To gain financial and military support from feudal lords and princes, the emperor gave them virtual **sovereignty** over their local jurisdictions. After the Thirty Years War (1618–1648), the Empire fragmented into approximately 360 self-governing states, many of them little more than small cities surrounded by rural land. Lacking effective central government, the region had few **public goods** such as uniform weights and measures, commercial laws, common currencies, or agreements on taxing authority. Without this essential **infrastructure**, the economy failed to develop, and central Europe remained largely feudalistic until the end of the eighteenth century.

In 1806, the French general Napoleon Bonaparte (1769–1821) defeated the two most powerful states in central Europe—Prussia and the Austrian Empire. This defeat marked the official dissolution of the Holy Roman Empire, but to govern the region more effectively, Napoleon consolidated thirty-nine small states into the Confederation of the Rhine. Under French rule, central Europe finally began to modernize with the introduction of commercial laws, public education, and civil rights. Serfdom ended in 1807 in Prussia and in 1832 in Saxony. However, the aristocratic landlords (Junkers) retained ownership of the land, and the serfs became tenant farmers whose lives were little different than before. They continued to turn over a significant portion of their crops to the Junkers in exchange for use of the land. In the cities, feudal guilds continued to suppress competition and innovation until the 1850s.

The Junkers were skeptical about industrialization because they wanted peasant farmers to remain on the land and pay rent rather than relocate to cities for work in factories. In addition, they viewed business owners (the bourgeoisie) as disrupting the traditional social order by focusing on self-interest and profit rather than the strength and unity of the nation. The Junkers feared that capitalism would lead to conflict between the social classes and dissolution of national power.

When the British finally defeated Napoleon at Waterloo in 1815, representatives from European nations met in Vienna to redraw national boundaries. In an effort to create a balance of power between nations, Prussia was given control of much of the territory of the Confederation of the Rhine. At the time, the lingering vestiges of feudalism and the dominance of the aristocratic Junkers left Prussia considerably less developed than either Britain or France. However, two actions by the government set the stage for industrialization. In 1834, Prussia established a customs union (Zollverein) to create a common currency and to eliminate the many internal **tariffs** that impeded the flow of commerce throughout the country. During the 1840s, the government oversaw the completion of a nationwide network of railroads by providing grants, subsidies, favorable tax treatment, and guaranteed profitability for private rail companies. These two projects widened the market, leading to greater regional specialization, **economies of scale**, and gains in productivity. By stimulating the demand for steel and coal, the expansion of railroads also triggered development in those industries.

In 1848, Prussian workers and many middle-class professionals, seeking more genuine democracy and civil rights, attempted a revolution. After weeks of street fighting, police and militia suppressed the uprising. Therefore, unlike Britain, France, or the United States, Prussia entered the industrial era with aristocratic rule still intact. Under the leadership of Otto von Bismarck (1815–1898), himself a Junker, Prussia expanded its territory by waging and winning wars against Austria in 1866 and France in 1870. Having achieved domination in central Europe, Bismarck established the German Empire (Deutsches Reich) in 1871.

STATE CAPITALISM 1871–1932

Major industrialization did not occur in Germany until the 1880s, a full century after Britain's industrial revolution. As a late capitalist country, Germany had the advantage of adopting British technology and learning from Britain's mistakes. German economists such as Wilhelm Roscher (1817–1894), Karl Knies (1821–1898), and Gustav Schmoller (1838–1917) formed what came to be known as the German Historical School. Claiming that each nation has a unique history and culture and therefore needs to fashion its own economic policies, they rejected the laissez-faire stance of classical economics in Britain. Although German economists favored the reduction of trade barriers within the nation, they called for tariffs on imports to protect Germany's **infant industries** from competition with more mature industries in Britain and the United States. German economists also sought to avoid the negative effects of industrialization in Britain, including dangerous working conditions, low wages for workers, and a banking system that failed to provide sufficient **financial capital** for businesses. Based on these concerns, the German government would play an active role in steering the development process by consciously structuring markets to limit competition.

Developmental State

The German Empire was a constitutional monarchy with an emperor (Kaiser), a chancellor, and a parliament (Reichstag). Chancellor Bismarck's overriding goal was to unify the nation by avoiding class conflict between workers, business owners, and landowning aristocrats. He viewed democracy as a necessary evil to instill patriotism by giving the German people a sense of inclusion and belonging. Despite universal male suffrage and regular elections to select representatives to the Reichstag, the German constitution granted little power to the legislature. The Kaiser, the Chancellor, and their Junker supporters effectively ruled the country. Bismarck expressed his contempt for democracy by saying "the great questions of the time will not be resolved by speeches and majority decisions . . . but by iron and blood."

To dampen conflict between the social classes, Bismarck offered benefits to each group. He raised agricultural prices to gain support among the Junkers and farmers. To appeal to business owners, Bismarck imposed tariffs on imports and reduced internal barriers to commerce. In 1889, he granted workers the first collective bargaining laws and comprehensive social security system in the world.

In contrast to the laissez-faire policies in Britain, Germans viewed state power as essential to harmonize conflicting class interests. They mistrusted the free market, believing that efficiency depended more on a stable social order than on competition. Viewing unfettered competition as a recipe for chaos, the state encouraged cooperation and collusion among firms in the same industry. The state also supervised labor relations to avoid strikes and played an active role in determining which industries received **financial capital** for expansion.

Another significant role for the state was providing the **infrastructure** essential to economic development. These projects reached far beyond transportation and communication systems. Germany was one of the first countries to adopt a uniform commercial code requiring common weights and measures across industries. The government established chambers of commerce and industry throughout the country to develop standards for industrial production, assist small businesses, and provide vocational training. Germany was also the first nation to develop a comprehensive public education system and pioneered in polytechnic schools that emphasized applied research. Some of the earliest professional scientific associations in the world arose in Germany, serving as consulting agencies for German businesses and promoting the discovery and dissemination of technical knowledge. A state corporation (the Seehandlung) demonstrated new technologies and established model factories in textiles, chemicals, mining, and luxury goods to encourage potential entrepreneurs.

Beginning in 1884, Germany attempted to establish a colonial empire by acquiring colonies in central and southern Africa and the South Pacific. However, Bismarck was focused on maintaining domestic stability, so imperial conquests were never a high priority. As a consequence, Germany did not experience the burdens of maintaining a large empire that were beginning to drain the British economy at the time.

Cartels

Shortly after the founding of the German Empire in 1871, a global **recession** threatened the profitability of Germany's newly emerging industries. To gain economies of scale and greater control over prices, firms in the major industries began to cooperate to suppress competition. Initially, this effort took the form of industry associations designed to share information and coordinate strategies. The government actually encouraged this collusion, and when the Imperial Court ruled in 1897 that **cartels** were legal, monopolization accelerated. Cartels reduced competition by establishing production and sales quotas for each member firm, controlling both resource prices and product prices, and conducting marketing efforts for the entire group of firms. In 1900, 275 cartels existed throughout Germany. By 1908, the number of cartels had grown to five hundred, and the electrical equipment and chemical industries each consisted of only two massive firms.

German banks also became instrumental in creating cartels. German firms in the steel, mining, chemical, and electrical equipment industries needed large production facilities to achieve economies of scale and compete with foreign producers. The large start-up costs of building steel mills or chemical factories required extensive borrowing of financial capital, and banks were the primary source of credit.

At the time, German banks engaged in both commercial banking (lending to individuals and businesses) and investment banking (buying and selling corporate stock for themselves and clients). As partial owners of private businesses, these "universal banks" had a strong interest in ensuring that firms in which they held stock had access to financial capital. To cement the close relationship between firms and their banks, bank executives often served on the boards of directors of German companies. Moreover, these executives wielded disproportionate power because they had proxy voting rights for all the shares of stock owned by individual shareholders and held by the bank. Not surprisingly, banks wanted their client firms to prosper and so favored cartelization and **vertical integration** to reduce competition. Cartels also reduced the risk of **overinvestment**, which could occur if firms simultaneously expanded operations until productive capacity exceeded demand. The government favored cartels because they suppressed competitive pressures to cut prices during recessions and therefore preserved jobs. The success of cartelization was demonstrated by the fact that the German economy grew faster than either Britain or France between 1870 and 1913.

Organized Labor

The first socialist political party in the world, the Social Democratic Party of Germany (Sozialdemokratische Partei Deutschlands [SPD]), was established in Prussia in 1863. In 1878, Anti-Socialist Laws banned meetings of socialists, shut down sympathetic newspapers, and outlawed labor unions. Despite this repression, SPD candidates ran as independents for seats in the Reichstag, receiving 27 percent of the vote in 1890 and 33 percent in 1903. By 1912, the SPD was the largest faction in the Reichstag. Support for **socialism** became so prevalent among Germans that some regional governments resorted to manipulating the voting process by weighing the votes of members of the upper classes more heavily than the votes of workers. The Anti-Socialist Laws were lifted after Bismarck's death in 1890, and membership in labor unions expanded rapidly. In 1897, numerous industrial unions joined together to form the Free Association of German Trade Unions.

In Britain, socialist ideas did not become influential until nearly a century after the Industrial Revolution. By then, the bourgeoisie (i.e., business people and professionals) held a firm grip on political power. However, in Germany, the challenge of socialism arose simultaneously with industrialization, and the bourgeoisie had not yet gained political dominance over the aristocratic Junkers. This unique timing of historical events led to considerable social tensions. Whereas the British bourgeoisie focused on overthrowing aristocratic rule by eliminating all remnants of feudalism and mercantilism, the German bourgeoisie were more concerned about the rising threat of socialism. As a result, they formed a political alliance with the Junkers that came to be known as "Iron and Rye," the two major products of the industrial bourgeoisie and the landowning Junkers. This anti-socialist alliance would have serious repercussions over the next several decades. The German bourgeoisie made a fateful decision to choose authoritarian government over competitive capitalism, valuing social order above democracy and civil liberties. They feared that the only alternative was a socialist revolution.

Social Policy

By the late 1700s, Prussia introduced universal public education for children from ages six to thirteen, nearly a century earlier than in Britain. Prussia also pioneered in establishing polytechnic schools in the 1830s, which became technical universities after 1868. During the 1880s, Chancellor Bismarck directed more public funds into education, particularly university training in science, math, and engineering. According to Bismarck, "the nation that has the schools has the future." By the early twentieth century, Germany had the best educated citizens in the world, and its universities attracted students from many countries, including the United States. Some of the most prominent early economists in the United States received their training from German universities.

Bismarck's antipathy toward socialism persuaded him that the government must go to extraordinary lengths to assure workers that they were an integral part of German society and would be treated fairly. In 1884, he established the world's first social security programs with compulsory national insurance against sickness and accidents. Old-age pensions were guaranteed to all citizens in 1889. After Bismarck's death, additional social programs included occupational health and safety laws, mandatory factory inspections, and benefits for widows and orphans. In short, Germany established the first welfare state.

The purpose of these generous social benefits was threefold. First, Bismarck sought to unite the different social classes by ensuring that all citizens were benefiting from the growth of the German economy. He believed that social cohesion was essential to building a strong nation capable of winning the competitive economic battle with other nations. Second, Bismarck hoped that social benefits would soften the harsh edges of capitalism and undermine support for socialism. Finally, after the failed revolution of 1848, a mass emigration of German workers to the United States noticeably diminished the labor force. Bismarck hoped that social welfare programs would compensate for low wages and keep German workers from leaving the country.

Culture

German culture in the early nineteenth century developed, in large part, as a backlash against the Enlightenment and the French Revolution. Philosophers, writers, and poets such as Georg Hegel (1770–1831), Johann Fichte (1762–1814), Friedrich Schelling (1775–1831), and Johann von Goethe (1749–1832) rejected the Enlightenment's celebration of human rationality and the universal rights of man. They blamed these values for contributing to the violence and anarchy of the French Revolution and called instead for the preservation and celebration of traditional German culture. Whereas the Enlightenment prized human intelligence and scientific pursuits, German philosophers defended the spiritual and mystical aspects of culture. They claimed that each national group (Volk) had its own spirit (Geist). To protect German culture from foreign influences would require that individuals forego the pursuit of narrow self-interest. True freedom, they claimed, could be achieved only by fulfilling one's moral obligations as a virtuous citizen of the state. The idea that individual freedom is possible only within a stable and orderly state would reverberate for the next century and a half as German culture was hostile toward liberal values such as individualism, free markets, and democracy. Hegel claimed that the Prussian monarchy was the most perfect form of government and that historical change had come to an end.

The Demise of State Capitalism

By 1900, the German economy had become the strongest in continental Europe and was rapidly closing the gap with Britain. However, despite Bismarck's efforts to promote national unity, hostility seethed between the social classes. The Junkers, still a powerful political force, viewed both capitalism and democracy as threats to traditional German culture and national strength. Small business owners faced increasing difficulty in remaining profitable. Their costs rose due to tariffs on imported raw materials, wage gains secured by labor unions, and the **market power** of cartels and banks. At the same time, competition from large department stores suppressed their prices. Jews were prominent in labor unions, banks, and department stores, which meant that the frustrations of small proprietors were manifested in a rising tide of anti-Semitism.

Although Germany entered World War I (1914–1918) inadvertently, the nation took full advantage of the opportunity to expand its borders. The intense nationalism that Bismarck had fueled to unite the nation was now directed toward conquering all of Europe. During the war, the government took full control of the economy, shutting down many small businesses in order to shift workers to weapons production. The government also rationed consumer goods, imposed prices controls, and required most able-bodied noncombatants to work in war-related industries. To prevent disruptive labor conflicts, the government supported the right of workers to unionize and collectively bargain so that disputes could be settled through **mediation** rather than strikes.

In 1918, as it became clear that Germany was losing the war, groups of soldiers and workers established local revolutionary councils inspired by the socialist revolution that had occurred in Russia a year earlier. As these councils spread from city to city with very little violence, Kaiser Wilhelm II abdicated the throne, and Germany's political leaders ordered the army to surrender. Because the surrender occurred while German forces still occupied France and Belgium, rumors spread that the army could have been victorious had it not been "stabbed in the back" by revolutionary forces within Germany. This sense of betrayal fueled right-wing passions and poisoned German politics for the next decade.

In 1919, a constitutional convention assembled in the town of Weimar to establish a new republic. In the subsequent election, the SPD received 38 percent of the vote and other socialist parties captured an additional 25 percent. The SPD remained the largest party in the Reichstag until 1932, but it faced strong opposition from both communists on the left and nationalists on the right. The Weimar Republic faced seemingly insurmountable obstacles. The Treaty of Versailles ending World War I imposed harsh punishment for German aggression. Germany not only lost substantial territory and resources but was required to pay reparations of more than 132 billion marks to its European neighbors as compensation for the damage inflicted during the war. To ease the burden of reparations, the government printed more currency, resulting in **hyperinflation**. In 1919, the US dollar exchanged for 8.2 units of the German currency, the Papiermark. By 1923, a dollar exchanged for more than four trillion Papiermarks. At that point, the government introduced a new currency, the Reichsmark, and the central bank severely tightened credit to control **inflation**.

The class tensions evident before the war only intensified. Widespread suffering and deprivation during and after the war caused many workers to resent both business and political elites for profiteering through generous government contracts as well as black market activities. The upper classes, in turn, accused workers of betraying their country by supporting socialism. The rising level of anger manifested itself in violent street fights, assassinations, and destruction of property as activists on both the political left and right fought for power. To ease the tensions, politicians began a concerted effort to rebuild national unity by blaming Germany's problems on "outsiders," including foreigners, Jews, gypsies, Slavs, communists, and any other group perceived as non-Germanic or unpatriotic.

Recognizing that the burden of reparations was destabilizing Germany, the United States began making loans to enable Germany to pay reparations to Britain and France. These countries, in turn, returned the money to the United States in payment for their wartime debts. In effect, the United States canceled debts owed by Britain and France to revive the German economy, but more than altruism lay behind this strategy. Having witnessed the recent revolution in Russia, the United States was concerned that continued turmoil in Germany would provide fertile breeding grounds for the spread of communism. The US loans contributed to a period of relative prosperity in the late 1920s, but the crash of the US stock market in 1929 triggered a global depression that caused the German economy to collapse. By the end of 1932, the rate of unemployment in Germany had risen to 33 percent.

GERMAN FASCISM 1933–1945

The Nazi Party

With their economy in shambles and their nationalist pride battered by military defeat and the punishment of reparations, the German people craved a strong leader who could restore the nation's glory. Yet forming a governing coalition was nearly impossible—forty different political parties vied for power. One party, The National Socialist German Workers Party (the Nazis) led by Adolf Hitler (1889–1945), attracted increasing numbers of followers by skillfully tailoring its message to appeal to different classes. For workers who wanted socialism, Hitler promised jobs as well as expanded pensions and social benefits. Even the name of Hitler's political party, National Socialist German Workers Party, was designed to attract workers sympathetic to socialism. In actuality, however, the Nazis later rounded up socialists and communists for execution.

For small business owners, Hitler proposed interest-free loans and government confiscation of department stores, which would then be divided and leased to single proprietors. Large business owners were attracted by Hitler's strong anticommunism and his promise to suppress the increasing militancy of labor unions. The aristocratic Junkers were drawn in by Hitler's vision of a Third Reich to restore the lost glory of the Holy Roman Empire and the German Empire. To appeal to both Junkers and peasant farmers, Hitler proposed price supports for agricultural products. Germans from all levels of society were eager to believe that a strong leader could restore their nation's strength and vitality.

By 1933, Hitler's growing popularity and his apparent ability to transcend conflicting class interests persuaded President Paul von Hindenberg (1847–1934) to appoint him as chancellor. The following year, the Nazis gained control of the legislature with 44 percent of the vote. The validity of that election is questionable because the Nazis engaged in a campaign of ruthless violence to intimidate potential political rivals. But with Nazi party members controlling the legislature, Hitler quickly dispensed with democracy, abolished all opposition political parties, and appointed himself leader (Führer) of the German people.

Economic Planning

Under Nazism, the German form of fascism, a totalitarian state planned and co-ordinated the activities of privately owned businesses. The Nazi economic program was designed to create a totally unified national economy in which the state directed resources toward politically established priorities and eliminated the perceived failures of capitalism such as instability, wasteful competition, class conflict, and shortsightedness. To facilitate planning by the state, all major industries were required to form cartels. Hitler eliminated labor unions in 1934 and required all workers to join the German Labor Front, which had no independent bargaining power. To deal with inflation, Hitler mandated a price freeze in 1936.

Although businesses remained in the hands of private owners, the government required full cooperation between businesses and the state in setting prices, production quotas, and guidelines for the use of resources. Business owners willingly cooperated because reduced competition virtually guaranteed their profitability. In fact, some of the major industrialists served a dual role as both entrepreneurs and government planners. They might manage their factory for one week and spend the next week in Berlin with other industrialists working in the National Economic Chamber to formulate detailed plans for the entire economy. These plans covered the level and direction of investment spending, provision of credit, allocation of raw materials and labor, and production of consumer goods. Plans were implemented through the use of quotas, rationing, wage and price controls, taxes, and tariffs. In addition, the government established ministries to coordinate production in each industry and strengthened existing cartels by forcing small businesses to merge with large corporations. In agriculture, for example, all aspects of food production from farmers to grocers were organized into a single cartel. In exchange for meeting production quotas, producers received subsidies, guaranteed prices, and protection from imports.

Culture

Hitler was one of the first modern leaders to fully realize the importance of culture in creating a strong nation and vibrant economy. The Nazis engaged in elaborate propaganda campaigns, including massive public rallies complete with torchlight parades, flags, group singing, and political orations. Symbols such as the swastika and the outstretched-arm salute were designed to develop unquestioning loyalty to the Führer. Parades of soldiers and armaments displayed military prowess and assured the German people of their collective strength. The government told the German people that they were Aryans, a race superior to all others. Young people were organized into highly disciplined groups such as Hitler Youth, where Nazi ideology was taught at an early age.

The Nazis built impressive architectural structures as symbols of national strength. Public works projects such as a system of nationwide highways (autobahns) employed thousands of workers and contributed to a sense of national unity. Recognizing the potential power of mass media, Hitler relied extensively on film to convey his political message. However, not everyone was persuaded. A steady flow of Germany's most talented citizens left the country and later made major scientific and cultural contributions in their new homelands.

By 1937, Germany had full employment, and industrial output had doubled since 1932. Hitler's impressive accomplishments gained a number of foreign admirers, including King Edward VIII of Britain as well as the aviator Charles Lindbergh and writers T. S. Eliot and Ezra Pound of the United States. At a time when other nations were still mired in the Depression, Germany appeared to have fashioned an enviable new economic system.

The Demise of German Fascism

Beneath the façade of German prosperity lay ominous trends. Most civil rights were suspended, and real wages were lower than they had been in the 1920s. Shortages of food and other essential supplies necessitated rationing. To divert attention from economic hardship, Hitler played on the xenophobia and anti-Semitism that had become endemic in German culture. This intentional cultivation of ethnic hatred served to unite the German people against a common enemy. The persecution of Jews and other minorities began with violent harassment and later evolved into murder and deportation to concentration camps for mass extermination. The Holocaust resulted in the death of more than six million Jews in Europe, and the German army killed another nine million non-German civilians and prisoners of war.

The first sign of German aggression was the 1938 invasion of the Sudetenland, a part of Czechoslovakia home to many ethnic Germans. When other nations failed to react, Hitler launched an intense war (Blitzkrieg, or lightning war) against Poland in 1939. The Soviet Union had already signed a nonaggression pact with Germany, but France and Britain declared war. The German army and its allies in Italy, Spain, and Portugal quickly gained control over all of central and western Europe except Britain. British prime minister Winston Churchill pleaded with US president Franklin Roosevelt for assistance, but the devastation of World War I had left most Americans opposed to involvement in foreign wars. Two events in 1941 led to Germany's eventual defeat. First, Hitler made the mistake of invading the Soviet Union, where the German army would be turned back at the Battle of Stalingrad. Second, Germany's ally, Japan, bombed the US naval base at Pearl Harbor, causing the United States to finally commit itself to the war effort. With the Soviet army advancing from the east and the Allies attacking from the west, Germany was defeated in 1945.

At the end of the war, the Allied powers divided Germany into four zones controlled separately by the United States, Britain, France, and the Soviet Union. Berlin, the capital, lay entirely within the Soviet zone; therefore, that city was also divided into four zones. The Allied occupation forces faced a dilemma in determining the fate of Germany. On one hand, they wanted to prevent Germany from ever regaining the capacity to wage war and considered plans to deindustrialize the country by making it an agrarian buffer zone between the Soviet bloc and

Western Europe. The Soviets actually pursued this strategy in their zone by dismantling factories and shipping moveable assets back to the Soviet Union. The Allies focused instead on arresting top Nazi leaders and placing them on trial for war crimes.

However, a second consideration soon overshadowed the desire to punish Germany. The Allies feared that an impoverished Germany would be vulnerable to communism and that a concerted effort to capture and punish all Nazi leaders might effectively destroy the structure of authority in German society. With these concerns in mind, the Allies decided to leave much of the existing power structure intact, restoring many managers and politicians to their former positions despite connections to the Nazi Party. In some cases, high-ranking Nazis were placed on Allied payrolls to assist in the restructuring effort. Others were allowed to escape to countries such as Argentina, Brazil, and even the United States.

A question about German fascism inevitably arises. Could fascism have succeeded as an economic system if Hitler had not engaged the nation in war and the extermination of minorities? Most economic historians would answer in the negative. The expansion of output and employment in the mid-1930s resulted from an easy **monetary policy** and massive government spending on military preparations and public works projects. When this stimulus created inflation, the government imposed a price freeze. Without market-determined prices, planners faced no constraints in directing resources toward politically determined priorities, and Hitler's top priority was the domination of Europe. Hitler's purported rationale for war was that Germans needed more living space (Lebensraum) and access to additional resources. However, both war and the campaign against minorities served to channel the frustrations of the German people toward an external enemy, thereby creating a sense of shared purpose and national identity. Without this contrived sense of community, fascism would not have achieved its relative economic success prior to 1939. As long as the German people believed their efforts would save the nation from external enemies, they toiled in the factories and tolerated hardship and deprivation. But without war, the internal tensions and class conflict would almost certainly have resurfaced.

ORGANIZED CAPITALISM 1946–1997

The American Occupation

The aftermath of World War I had demonstrated the unintended consequences of punishing Germans for their transgressions. Beginning in 1948, the United States initiated the Marshall Plan, providing $12 billion over the next four years for rebuilding Europe. The Marshall Plan ultimately served US interests by preventing the spread of communism and developing strong trading partners. Despite the devastation of war, Germany stood well-poised to stage a quick economic recovery. Allied bombings intentionally spared manufacturing areas, so at the end of the war, German industrial capacity was 20 percent larger than at the beginning of the war. The human skills and knowledge that had fueled industrialization remained intact, so economic growth began anew.

The rebuilding of Germany took an unexpected turn in 1949, when the zone controlled by the Soviet Union formed a separate nation called the German Democratic Republic (East Germany), which would remain within the Soviet sphere of influence for the next forty years. The remaining three zones, along with the sectors of Berlin controlled by the West, became the Federal Republic of Germany (West Germany), with its capital in the city of Bonn. The old capital, Berlin, lay entirely within East Germany, which meant that West Berlin was now geographically isolated from the rest of West Germany. In 1948, the East German government attempted to gain control of West Berlin by prohibiting land travel between West Berlin and West Germany. The United States responded with a massive airlift to supply food and provisions to the people of West Berlin until the East Germans lifted the blockade a year later.

Many of the American economic advisors in postwar Germany had experience working in Roosevelt's New Deal. They believed that a major factor contributing to the rise of fascism was the concentration of economic power in the hands of cartels. The owners of these cartels were willing to sacrifice democracy and civil rights in order to protect their profits by maintaining social order. With encouragement from US advisors, Germany adopted antitrust laws similar to those in America. A Federal Cartel Office was established, and most existing cartels were declared illegal.

The Economic Miracle

Industrial production in West Germany grew by 24 percent in 1949 and continued to expand at an annual rate of 10 percent through the 1950s. This economic miracle (Wirtschaftswunder) occurred under the political leadership of a new political party, the Christian Democratic Union (Christlich Demokratische Union [CDU]) , headed by Konrad Adenauer (1876–1967) and his Economics Minister, Ludwig Erhard (1897–1977). They envisioned a middle path between free-market capitalism and socialism, hoping to achieve the efficiency and dynamism associated with markets while providing an array of social insurance programs designed to ensure basic economic security for all citizens. Due to housing shortages, rent controls were prevalent, and the government engaged in some planning of the steel, mining, and energy industries.

However, the economic miracle resulted from more than just effective government policies. The inflow of twelve million refugees from the East and the virtual absence of labor unions created a surplus of labor, keeping wages at their Nazi-era level. With low labor costs and plentiful business opportunities in rebuilding war-ravaged cities, the German economy was profitable for both domestic and foreign investors. Even the wartime destruction of **physical capital** worked to Germany's advantage because renovated factories could be equipped with the latest technology. With wages stagnant and productivity rising, high levels of profit could be reinvested in expanding productive capacity.

Business Associations

Many of the institutions associated with organized capitalism in Germany still exist today. Despite Allied efforts to decartelize the German economy, Germans continue to believe that a high degree of cooperation between firms within an industry improves economic performance by stabilizing prices, reducing duplication and waste, and facilitating research and development. Most industries have networks and associations to facilitate communication between firms, coordinate decision-making, and negotiate with government policymakers and labor unions. An umbrella organization, the Federal Associations, includes forty-seven different employer associations representing more than 80 percent of all private employers.

Another organization, the Federation of German Industry, was established in 1949 and consisted of thirty-nine industrial associations. It planned industry-wide investment to avoid excess capacity, engaged in collaborative research, gathered and publicized statistics, developed proposals for public policies, and lobbied government for approval of those policies. The overlap between organized capitalism and fascism is evidenced by the fact that the Federation of German Industry was modeled after the planning process instituted for Hitler by the steel magnate Alfried Krupp (1907–1967).

Business associations in Germany take on some of the functions typically performed by government. They establish production standards, fund vocational training, share technology, and provide potential investors with information about the financial performance of member firms. Within an association, firms may own shares of each other's stock, which increases the willingness to pool resources for research and marketing.

Small and medium-sized businesses (Mittlestand) constitute a significant portion of the German economy, employing nearly 65 percent of the labor force and accounting for half of all business sales. Like larger firms, they are highly organized in employers' associations to facilitate communication and collective bargaining with labor unions. Firms are required to belong to a regional chamber of commerce, which has authority to establish business hours, issue licenses and permits, and resolve disputes between member firms within their region.

Corporate Governance

Large German firms have a unique form of corporate governance in which virtually every group with a stake in the company's performance has a voice in decision-making. These "stakeholders" include banks, managers, workers, and the government.

Banks

German law permits banks to purchase shares of stock in corporations. German banks also act as brokerage firms. Most shareholders deposit their shares with a bank, which then possesses proxy rights to vote in corporate decisions. As a result, banks hold majority interest in most large corporations and effectively control the management. Bank officers often sit on the supervisory boards of German corporations and occasionally serve as board chairmen. This close relationship between corporations and their banks effectively insulates corporate decision-making from pressures normally created by individual shareholders who seek maximum short-term profit. German firms excel in technological innovation because they are willing to incur short-term costs to develop new technologies and products that will eventually result in greater profitability over the long run. Unlike American corporations, in which executives know that any failure to meet short-term profit expectations will result in a selloff of the company's stock, German corporations enjoy **patient capital**; banks continue to provide credit as long as they have confidence in the long-term viability of the firm. The presence of patient capital also discourages hostile takeovers and makes firms less likely to lay off workers during downturns in the economy.

Managers
Before making major decisions, German managers typically build a consensus among employee representatives, bank officials, major shareholders, suppliers, and customers. The need for consensus encourages firms to share information and conduct transparent operations. The incentive to provide accurate information is the potential loss of reputation for any firm that misleads its stakeholders. German managers enjoy an advantage in building consensus because they are typically promoted from the scientific/technical departments of their firms as opposed to the financial/marketing/legal areas. Their detailed knowledge of the firm's production process commands the respect of all stakeholders.

Workers
The institution of codetermination (Mitbestimmung) gives workers a voice in the management of their companies. Laws require all firms with more than 2,000 employees to fill half the positions on their supervisory board with representatives of labor. Supervisory boards meet several times each year to oversee company policies. In firms with fewer than 2,000 but more than 500 employees, one-third of the positions on the board are held by labor representatives. In addition, all firms with more than five employees must establish a works council (Betriebsrat) to convey workers' concerns to management and to facilitate discussions concerning plant closings, job evaluations, overtime schedules, recruitment, dismissals, training, and safety. The inclusion of workers in the decision-making process has created a more cooperative labor force that shares management's focus on long-term profitability. Both management and labor remain relatively insulated from opportunistic pressures to defect from established agreements by the transparency of the decision-making process and by the involvement of both parties.

Government
German corporations are subject to extensive government regulations regarding product quality, environmental protection, and worker health and safety. Rather

than objecting to government control, German managers view regulations as solutions to **collective action problems**. In the absence of regulation, each firm has an incentive to gain a **competitive advantage** by cutting costs. But cost-cutting may result in unsafe working conditions, lower quality products, lower wages, less on-the-job training, and more environmental pollution. By prohibiting these forms of cost-cutting, regulations create a level playing field on which firms compete through technological innovation, superior product quality, and customer service rather than lower prices. With less competitive pressure to reduce costs and prices, German firms can invest more in developing their human resources, technology, and products.

Organized Labor

After the end of World War II, American advisors urged the German government to revive the labor unions previously abolished under Nazism. Within a short time, seventeen **industrial unions** emerged, including both blue-collar and white-collar workers. In 1949, these unions became affiliated with the nationwide German Trade Union Federation (Deutscher Gewerkschaftsbund). The next year, Germany began industry-wide coordinated wage bargaining in which government officials met with representatives of both labor unions and the Confederation of German Employers' Associations (Bundesvereinigung der Deutschen Arbeitgeberverbande, or BDA) to negotiate an annual wage package effective for all firms in an industry. The government also coordinated negotiations in different industries to maintain uniformity in wage increases across the economy.

This centralized bargaining process solved another collective action problem. If each union were to bargain separately with each employer, unions would have an incentive to aggressively seek higher wages using threats of strikes and work stoppages to reinforce their demands. A single union is not concerned with possible inflationary effects of higher wages because it represents only a fraction of the total labor force. But when all unions bargain collectively, they realize that excessive wage demands are likely to result in inflation or reduced profitability and slower economic growth. Therefore, coordinated wage bargaining leads to greater wage restraint on the part of unions.

Despite this restraint, German workers have secured some of the highest levels of pay and benefits in the world. They receive thirty-nine paid holidays per year, and some of the large unions have negotiated a 38.5-hour workweek. In addition, employers and unions have agreed to regulations that make layoffs rare. High wages and job security could potentially undermine profitability, but German firms have managed to thrive by raising worker productivity through extensive training and the development of more efficient technology. German labor unions welcome new technology because their members have considerable job security and are confident that they will be able to bargain for wage increases to match the increased productivity associated with improved technology.

Germany places strict limitations on the right to strike. A strike cannot be declared until after the current contract has expired, the national union approves, and at least 75 percent of members approve in a secret ballot. These legal restrictions, coupled with the generally cooperative nature of German unions, have resulted in one of the lowest strike rates of any country in the world.

By the early 1960s, the economy was expanding so rapidly that the unemployment rate fell to 1 percent and labor shortages developed. To supplement the labor force, German firms began hiring "guest workers" (Gastarbeiters) from Turkey, Yugoslavia, and other southern European countries. These workers, typically young, single men living in company dormitories, often sent a portion of their wages back to families in their home country or else accumulated savings in hopes of bringing their families to Germany. After the global recession of the mid-1970s, the demand for labor weakened and the government banned the recruitment of workers from outside the European Community. However, Germany continues to experience a significant flow of immigrants due to its policy of granting asylum to political refugees. That policy, coupled with generous social programs, makes Germany a haven for immigrants from Eastern Europe and the Middle East seeking to escape poverty and oppression. Today, foreign workers fill many of the unskilled and less desirable jobs in Germany.

Industrial Policy

Germany's economic system is highly organized and structured by an array of institutions. These include public ownership of some firms, macro policy, development banks, policies to promote saving, and vocational training.

Public Ownership

Germany's **public sector**, although smaller than in most other European countries, has in the past included the entire railroad system, the radio, telephone, and television industries, plus utilities such as electricity, gas, water, and sanitation. The government also owned substantial portions of the aluminum, iron ore, ship building, and coal industries, as well as some banks and 20 percent of Volkswagen, the automobile manufacturer. However, the worldwide trend toward privatization of public enterprises has taken hold in Germany. Recent privatizations include Germany's major airline, Lufthansa, and its largest telephone company, Deutsche Telekom.

Macro Policy

The experience with hyperinflation during the 1920s left Germans with a strong determination to maintain price stability. Prior to the creation of the European Union (EU), major responsibility for this goal lay with the German central bank (Deutsche Bundesbank). The central bank consistently maintained a tight **monetary policy** aimed at stabilizing both domestic prices and the value of the German mark. Until 1966, Germany rejected the use of Keynesian **fiscal policies** to stimulate aggregate demand, but when the SPD regained power in 1967, **countercyclical fiscal policy** became an accepted part of the government's management of the economy. Even with this change, however, the Bundesbank could offset any inflationary pressures resulting from fiscal stimulus by pursuing a tight mone-tary policy.

The SPD continued to govern for the next sixteen years under the leadership of Willy Brandt (1913–1992) and Helmut Schmidt (1918–2011), but in 1982, the more conservative CDU, led by Helmut Kohl, gained control. Like his contempo-raries, Margaret Thatcher in Britain and Ronald Reagan in the United States, Kohl sought to reduce the role of government in the economy. However, Kohl's agenda was more moderate than the neoliberalism of Thatcher and Reagan. Cuts in government spending were mild, privatization was less extensive, and most welfare and social insurance programs remained intact.

Development Banks

The German government promotes economic growth by providing low-interest loans to private firms through regional development banks. The government sub-sidizes the loans, and the banks keep part of the subsidy. Banks are considered less likely than government agencies to be influenced by political considerations in allocating loans. The development banks also gain a voice in decision-making within the firms receiving aid.

Promotion of Saving

Germany has developed several policies to encourage saving, particularly by low-income families. All citizens can avoid taxation on a portion of their income by depositing money in accounts that prohibit withdrawals for seven years. In addi-tion, all interest income is tax-exempt except for wealthier citizens. Long-term capital gains also enjoy tax-exempt status in order to discourage investors from engaging in short-term speculation in the stock market. Finally, government subsidies allow low-income families to receive higher interest rates on savings accounts and to purchase shares of corporate stock at lower prices.

Vocational Training

Germany has the most extensive vocational education and apprentice system in the world. The Federal Labor Agency sends counselors to every ninth grade class in the country to expose students to career opportunities through pamphlets, films, and visits to businesses. After the tenth grade, compulsory education ends, but approximately 60 percent of students choose to enter an apprentice system in which they attend school for two days a week to receive vocational training and spend the remaining three days working in their chosen field. Apprentices are paid a small wage funded partially by government but mostly by employers who recognize the value of developing a skilled labor force.

After completing a three-year program, passing an examination, and obtain-ing a license, young Germans are well-prepared for full-time employment. More than 50 percent remain with the firm where they served their apprenticeships. With a highly educated and skilled labor force, German industry has focused on products requiring sophisticated technical knowledge such as cameras, clocks, watches, optical equipment, musical instruments, and engines. These high-quality products have made Germany a successful exporter in the global market.

Other countries such as the United States and Britain offer much less vocational training because the cost is usually borne either by the government or by students themselves. Private firms are typically unwilling to fund vocational training because they have no assurance that students will join their company after graduation. Moreover, students may be reluctant to pay for specific training in a particular industry because they have no assurance that jobs will be available. Taxpayers resist subsidizing vocational training because the benefits accrue primarily to students and the employers. Vocational training poses a collective action problem. Nobody has a strong incentive to fund the training, yet everyone benefits by having a skilled labor force.

Germany solves this collective action problem by coordinating the actions of employers, workers, and students. The industry-wide business associations supervise and subsidize vocational training, preventing individual firms from becoming free riders who enjoy the benefits of vocational training without paying the cost. Employers virtually guarantee job opportunities to graduates of vocational training, so students are willing to invest their time in acquiring very specific skills needed by a particular industry. Labor unions also contribute to the cost of vocational education so that each generation of workers, having benefited from training in the past, bequeaths a similar advantage to the next generation. As a result, the interests of all parties are advanced more effectively than if each had acted in pursuit of narrow self-interest.

Reunification

In 1989, after the Soviet Union granted greater autonomy to its Eastern European-satellite states, the East German government removed a wall that had been constructed through the city of Berlin in 1961 to prevent East Germans from escaping to the West. In 1989, the East German government removed the so-called Berlin Wall, which had been constructed in 1961 to prevent East Germans from escaping to the West. In 1990, East and West Germany reunited as a single nation. The state-owned enterprises (SOEs) in the east were transferred to a public holding company as a prelude to privatization. To make the SOEs more attractive to private investors, the holding company took responsibility for firms' debts and any additional expenses associated with meeting the former West Germany's environmental standards. When possible, property was returned to former owners or their descendants, although settling disputed claims became exceedingly difficult due to successive confiscations by the Nazis, then the Soviets, and ultimately the East German government. When no rightful owner could be found, assets were simply sold to investors, most of whom had been West Germans.

Given the primitive condition of East German factories, the bids from private investors were quite low. In fact, 40 percent of the SOEs taken over by the holding company simply closed. The **revenue** from the sale of SOEs did not even cover the holding company's assumption of debt and cleanup expenses, resulting

Figure 9.1 Berlin's Brandenburg gate, completed in 1791, was part of the wall built in 1961 to prevent East Germans from escaping to the West. (© Shutterstock/Thorsten Schier)

in nearly $200 billion of additional debt for the German government. New owners were required to sign contracts requiring them to renovate the firms, to retain a specified number of employees, and to remain in operation for a specified number of years. The privatization process was completed by the end of 1994.

At reunification, the West German currency (Deutschemark) replaced the East German currency (Ostmark). The conversion ratio varied depending on the type of financial asset, but the average ratio was approximately 1.8 Ostmarks per Deutschemark. Prior to the monetary union, the unofficial exchange rate stood at 20 Ostmarks per Deutschemark, so the 1.8 to 1 conversion ratio represented a tremendous windfall gain for East Germans. Since reunification, the German government has attempted to modernize the eastern part of the country by developing public infrastructure such as rail lines, airports, highways, and communications systems. An income tax surcharge ("solidarity tax") funded approximately $100 billion of aid to the eastern part of the country each year from 1995 to 2005.

Culture

Despite the evolution of Germany's economic system from state capitalism to fascism to organized capitalism, several fundamental cultural values and institutions have remained relatively constant. All three systems were highly structured with many rules and regulations, and all three emphasized social order, deference to authority, and individual security. These deeply embedded characteristics of German culture date back to feudalism. During the Thirty Years War (1618–1648), opposing states could not afford to pay armies, so soldiers extracted compensation by looting and pillaging. The devastation resulted in the deaths of an estimated ten million people, or a third of the population of the Holy Roman Empire. For innocent citizens, the only hope for protection lay in the army of the local feudal lord, thus creating a strong respect for and deferential attitudes toward rulers with sufficient power to offer protection. Even in times of peace, recurring crop failures, famines, and marauding tribes made citizens dependent on feudal lords for their personal security.

Germany's late industrialization resulted in further threats to social order as the appeal of socialism led workers to challenge the status quo. Both aristocratic Junkers and business owners concluded that a powerful government with control over the economy was the only alternative to a socialist revolution. This cultural predisposition toward stability, order, and security is reflected in the structure of the German economic system. German businesses are highly organized to protect themselves against the vicissitudes of the market. Workers form labor unions that cooperate with employers to promote stability and growth. Banks and investors tend to be highly risk-averse and demand transparency and sharing of information by firms.

More than other developed nations, Germany tends to codify informal social rules into enforceable laws. Laws prohibit mowing lawns on Sunday and squeezing tomatoes in grocery stores. Other laws specify how often hedges must be trimmed and how to hang curtains in windows. The result of all these rules and regulations is a remarkably clean, tidy, and organized society. Gardens are manicured, houses and cars well-maintained, and streets and sidewalks free of dirt and litter. The downside of this emphasis on order and conformity is that the German economy lacks the flexibility and dynamism that comes from risk-taking. Germans largely prefer the security of salaried positions with well-established firms to the risk associated with entrepreneurship. German law discourages entrepreneurship by prohibiting new firms from seeking financial capital through the sale of stocks and bonds during the first year of their existence. The government assumes that banks are more prudent than individual investors in assessing the potential profitability of a start-up company.

The Demise of Organized Capitalism

After performing admirably from the end of World War II through the 1980s, the German economy began to falter in the 1990s. Reunification drained financial resources from the western part of the country, and an aging population placed increasing strains on government's ability to maintain the array of social benefits. However, the fundamental cause of a slowing economy was globalization. Germany's organized capitalism was carefully structured to solve collective action problems by creating institutions to limit competition and promote cooperation. But globalization exposed German firms to competition from firms in low-wage countries, primarily in Asia, intent on challenging the dominance of German exports. Exports accounted for one-third of the German GDP, but high prices made them increasingly noncompetitive as Asian companies developed automobiles, motorcycles, cameras, and stereo equipment of equal if not superior quality at lower prices.

Faced with global competition, the institutions of organized capitalism became dysfunctional. German firms could no longer provide high wages and generous fringe benefits without losing sales to lower-priced foreign competitors. Government faced increasing difficulty in providing social benefits as recession and unemployment reduced tax revenue. Banks and private investors became less willing to provide patient capital to German firms when they could earn higher rates of return abroad.

Two additional factors placed increasing competitive pressure on the German economy. First, the formation of the EU in 1993, along with the adoption of the euro in 1999, led to reduced trade barriers and exposed firms in all member nations to intensified competition. Germany's high-priced goods now competed directly with lower-cost items produced in nations such as Spain and Italy. Second, the establishment of the World Trade Organization in 1995 reduced trade barriers around the world.

A NEW DIRECTION?

In 1998, Germans voters returned the SPD to power under the leadership of Gerhard Schroeder. The SPD formed a coalition with the Green Party, an environmentally oriented organization founded in 1983. At the time, this political realignment seemed to indicate a rejection of Helmut Kohl's attempt to steer the economy in a neoliberal direction and an affirmation of Germany's organized capitalism and welfare state. However, Schroeder signaled his intention to change the economic system, calling for a Neue Mitte (New Center) between the organized capitalism of the past and neoliberal capitalism.

Beginning in 2001, the German economy stagnated with virtually no growth for the next four years. Part of the problem was a global recession that hit the export-dependent German economy particularly hard, but high labor costs and expensive social benefits were steadily eroding Germany's competitive advantage in the global economy. In 2003, Chancellor Schroeder announced Agenda 2010, a program designed to improve the competitiveness of the German economy by the year 2010. To the chagrin of many Social Democrats, Agenda 2010 called for neoliberal reforms, including tax cuts for the wealthy, reductions in social benefits, and measures to increase the flexibility of labor markets by reducing the power of labor unions, cutting unemployment benefits, and making it easier for firms to fire workers.

These proposals were so unpopular that mass protest demonstrations involving several hundred thousand citizens occurred in major cities. The Social Democrats received only 21 percent of the vote in the 2004 election, and the CDU regained control of the government under the leadership of Angela Merkel. The more conservative CDU might have been expected to embark on an even more stringent neoliberal agenda, but Chancellor Merkel has proceeded cautiously. Virtually every major institution of the German economic system has been changed in a neoliberal direction, but the institutions have not been abandoned. Firms may now negotiate directly with their labor representatives to revise agreements reached through industry-wide bargaining. Criteria for eligibility to receive unemployment compensation and welfare benefits have been tightened.

Firms have gained greater leeway in shedding unneeded workers and relocating production to other countries. Labor unions have lost power as indicated by the fact that only 18 percent of the labor force is now unionized compared to 35 percent in the 1980s.

As German firms obtain more of their financing from global capital markets rather than domestic banks, they are pressured to focus on short-term profitability to keep investors satisfied. Indeed, any firm not keeping the price of its stock sufficiently high is vulnerable to acquisition by a foreign firm. Foreign ownership undermines the German tradition of cooperation and sharing of information between firms in the same industry. Foreign shareholders are more likely to oppose the influence on corporate decision-making of other stakeholders such as workers, banks, and government. Even German banks are now enmeshed in global capital markets and therefore pressured to maximize profit by providing credit wherever they can earn the highest rate of return.

The results of Germany's turn toward neoliberalism remain inconclusive. Unemployment initially shot up to 12.5 percent in 2005, and the global recession of 2008 caused a 5 percent drop in Germany's GDP. The economy has remained weak since the recession as Chancellor Merkel and the CDU have pursued a policy of austerity by reducing government spending to eliminate deficits in the budget and by encouraging the European Central Bank (ECB) to pursue a tight monetary policy. The government's budget has been balanced or had a surplus since 2012.

According to Keynes, a policy of austerity is entirely inappropriate during the recovery from a recession, but Germans never fully accepted Keynesian economics for several reasons. First, the collective memory of hyperinflation during the early 1920s made Germans reluctant to engage in expansionary fiscal and monetary policies even during recessions. Second, German culture frowns on debt as evidenced by the fact that the same word (schuld) means both debt and sin. Third, as Germany was recovering from World War II, a conscious decision was made by Chancellor Adenauer and Economics Minister Erhard to structure the economy around export industries. The Germans feared that Keynesian policies to stimulate consumer demand with higher wages and to increase government spending might result in higher prices for German products, thereby restricting the ability to export.

The proponents of austerity argue that balancing the budget and reducing public debt are essential to restore "investor confidence" and thereby ensure that financial capital will be available for economic expansion. They claim that governments, like private households, cannot continue to spend and borrow without dire consequences. By creating confidence among investors that government has its financial affairs in order, austerity should cause increased spending on physical capital that will more than compensate for reduced spending by consumers and government. As yet, though, investors remain cautious until they perceive increased demand for business products.

The focus on austerity has taken a toll on the German economy. In late 2014, Germany barely avoided entering its third recession since 2008. Budget cuts have undermined the quality of Germany's physical and social infrastructure as highways and bridges built during the Economic Miracle of the 1950s are now rapidly deteriorating and funds for education and research are slashed. Yet German citizens continue to support the government's policies as Chancellor Merkel's approval ratings are nearly 80 percent and the SPD received only 25 percent of the vote in the 2013 election. However, other European nations are rebelling against the EU-imposed restrictions on monetary and fiscal policy. In response, ECB president Mario Draghi announced in 2015 that the bank would begin a policy of "quantitative easing" similar to that pursued by the US Federal Reserve in the aftermath of the Great Recession. The ECB will purchase sixty billion dollars of private and government bonds per month until late 2016, for a total monetary infusion of more than one trillion dollars.

Germany's insistence on a policy of austerity to preserve its ability to export raises the possibility of another collective action problem. A single nation can prosper with a strong export sector leading to surpluses in its balance of trade, but if all European countries pursue the same policy, low levels of spending may create stagnation throughout the region. Germany is essentially imposing austerity on the rest of Europe through its influence over the ECB and by linking bailouts to Greece and other southern European nations to their commitments to reduce government spending. With the entire continent pursuing a policy of austerity, the overall unemployment rate in the EU remains at 11.2 percent, growth is at a virtual standstill (GDP grew by 0.1 percent in 2013), and the threat of deflation looms. The decision by the ECB to initiate quantitative easing was undoubtedly motivated by these statistics.

Although growth increased slightly in 2015, the German economy faces several major obstacles. Germany's ability to export is being hampered by not only the weakness of its trading partners in the EU but also by slowing economic growth in Russia and China. A nation whose economy is centered around exports cannot thrive when much of the rest of the world is experiencing stagnation. Moreover, Germany's commitment to cooperating in the imposition of trade sanctions against Russia as punishment for its invasion of Ukraine is dampening exports and reducing access to oil and natural gas. In addition, energy prices in Germany are likely to rise as the government responded to the 2011 nuclear meltdown in Fukushima, Japan, by immediately shutting down eight of the nation's seventeen nuclear power plants. The rest are scheduled for closure by 2022, meaning that Germany will be increasingly reliant on more expensive energy sources. The impact of losing 25 percent of Germany's production of electricity is currently mitigated by the decline in oil prices, but those prices will inevitably rise in the future. Finally, Germany's demographics do not bode well for the future. The median age is forty-six, and the birth rate is relatively low, meaning that the portion of the population dependent on social security and other social benefits will be expanding. At current rates of population growth, both France and Britain will surpass Germany in population size by 2040.

On the positive side, Germany continues to benefit from its system of vocational training, which is responsible for the fact that unemployment among youth is significantly lower than in other EU nations. The overall rate of unemployment is only about 6 percent despite a virtual lack of growth. The German economy also benefits from close ties with eastern European countries such as Hungary, Poland, the Czech Republic, and Slovakia. Many German firms are either relocating or outsourcing production to take advantage of low wages in these nearby nations. Another benefit comes from the depreciation of the euro to near par with the US dollar, which has the effect of making German exports more competitive in global markets. The euro has lost nearly a third of its value since the Great Recession of 2008. Finally, recognizing that Germany needs to become less dependent on exports and generate more internal demand, the government in 2015 initiated the first nationwide minimum wage at 8.50 euros per hour.

ADDITIONAL READING

Barkai, Avraham. *Nazi Economics: Ideology, Theory, and Policy.* New Haven, CT: Yale University Press, 1990.

Blair, Tony, and Gerhard Schroeder. *Europe: The Third Way/Die Neue Mitte.* London: The Labour Party, 1999.

Braun, Hans-Joachim. *The German Economy in the 20th Century.* New York: Routledge, 2000.

Evans, Richard J. *The Coming of the Third Reich.* New York: Penguin Books, 2005.

Gerschenkron, Alexander. *Economic Backwardness in Historical Perspective.* Cambridge, MA: Harvard University Press, 1962.

Glossner, Christian L. *The Making of the German Post-War Economy.* New York: I. B. Tauris, 2013.

Hagen, William W. *German History in Modern Times: Four Lives of the Nation.* New York: Cambridge University Press, 2012.

Harding, Rebecca, and William E. Paterson. *The Future of the German Economy: An End to the Miracle?* New York: Manchester University Press, 2000.

Herrigel, Gary. *Industrial Constructions: The Sources of German Industrial Power.* New York: Cambridge University Press, 1995.

Siebert, Horst. *The German Economy: Beyond the Social Market.* Princeton, NJ: Princeton University Press, 2009.

Smith, Eric Owen. *The German Economy.* New York: Routledge, 1994.

Streeck, Wolfgang. *Re-Forming Capitalism: Institutional Change in the German Political Economy.* New York: Oxford University Press, 2009.

Tooze, Adam. *The Wages of Destruction: The Making and Breaking of the Nazi Economy.* New York: Penguin Books, 2006.

Chapter 10

THE SWEDISH ECONOMIC SYSTEM

"In the good home, equality, consideration, cooperation, and
helpfulness prevail. Applied to the great people's and citizen's
home, this would mean the breaking down of all social and
economic barriers that now divide citizens into the privileged
and the unfortunate, the rulers and the subjects."

PER ALBIN HANSSON (1885–1946),
Swedish Prime Minister

Imagine living in a country with the fourth highest **per capita gross domestic product** (GDP) in the world, 2 percent unemployment, 5 percent annual growth of GDP, virtually no poverty, low crime rates, free education through graduate school, free healthcare, a pristine environment, no engagement in war since 1814, an honest and competent government, and a strong sense of social responsibility on the part of both corporations and labor unions. Sweden fit that description in the late 1960s. The performance of the Swedish economic system inspired curiosity and admiration around the world. Yet twenty years later, the country verged on financial collapse and eventually abandoned some of the key institutions that contributed to its previous success. Although Sweden is a relatively small country in terms of population, its bold experimentation in fashioning a unique economic system provides important lessons for all nations.

Sweden became an independent nation in 1523 with a king and a parliamentary form of government. A considerable portion of its original territory was lost in 1809 when Russia captured the eastern section, which is today Finland. Sweden is endowed with abundant natural resources, including high-quality iron ore and copper deposits, extensive hardwood forests, and numerous rivers and waterfalls for generating hydroelectric power. Located in the northernmost region of Europe, Sweden's challenging cold climate and its relative isolation led to an ethnically and culturally homogenous population sharing the same religion (Lutheran), values, and ancestry. This homogeneity fostered a strong sense of social solidarity.

The most notable feature of early Swedish economic history is the absence of feudalism. Unlike most of the rest of Europe, Sweden's location, forbidding climate, and poor soil made it unattractive to the Roman Empire and other potential

208

conquerors. Although political institutions and authority certainly existed within Sweden, leaders were selected by democratic consensus rather than by hereditary rights. In 1335, King Magnus Erickson (1316–1374) abolished any vestiges of serfdom or slavery, so the vast majority of peasant farmers owned their land and enjoyed freedom from oppression. However, survival in the harsh climate required considerable cooperation and collective action such as working together in communal fields. Early industrial development centered around mining and logging. Manufacturing typically occurred in small factories or workshops that often provided housing, healthcare, education, and pensions for employees. In the cities, guilds controlled most economic activity until the government abolished them in 1846. At that time, Sweden was a poor, agrarian country with high unemployment and considerable poverty.

ORGANIZED CAPITALISM 1870–1931

Industrialization in Sweden began around 1870 with expanding exports of iron ore and timber to other European countries. By this time, the communal fields in the countryside had been privatized, so displaced farmers migrated to cities seeking employment in the new factories. The resulting surplus labor depressed wages and left many workers in poverty. Approximately 1.3 million Swedes (25 percent of the entire population) emigrated, mostly to America, in search of better opportunities. The government had neither the administrative capacity nor the financial means to offer much assistance, so citizens began forming associations, clubs, and cooperatives designed to protect and advance their economic interests. In 1899, forty consumer cooperatives joined together to form the Cooperative Union, a national organization that operated retail stores and offered insurance policies.

As industrialization progressed, the government gradually began to promote development and provide citizens with a social safety net. In addition to public investments in **infrastructure** such as railroads and harbor construction, the government enacted a few **tariffs** to protect Sweden's **infant industries** and granted subsidies to stimulate research and development of new products and technologies. As a "late capitalist" country, Sweden had the advantage of access to **financial capital** and technology from more developed countries. A social security system was instituted in 1913, and welfare programs began in 1918. One of the purposes of welfare programs was to persuade impoverished Swedes to remain in the country rather than emigrate.

World War I provided a tremendous boost to the Swedish economy. As a neutral country, Sweden was able to sell its exports to all combatants, and the high demand for steel and timber led to rising prices and large profits for Swedish firms. However, the end of the war brought economic disaster as the devastation of the German economy caused a sharp decline in Swedish exports. To make matters worse, a global **recession** in 1920–21 resulted in an unemployment rate of 30 percent and a drop in output of 25 percent.

The Swedish Social Democratic Party (Sveriges Socialdemokratiska Arbetarepartiet [SAP]), which was founded in 1889 with the avowed purpose of establishing socialism, won its first election in 1920 with Hjalmar Branting (1860–1925) serving as prime minister until 1923. Despite its commitment to socialism, the SAP initiated no major changes in the economy and lost the 1923 election to a liberal-conservative coalition that ruled until 1932.

From early in the industrialization process, the Swedish economy exhibited a high degree of concentration. To compete in international markets, Swedish businesses needed the **economies of scale** associated with large size. Because Sweden's population was relatively small, two or three large corporations in an industry could meet the entire nation's demand for a product. The Swedish government had no desire to break up large corporations because the economy depended on exports, and economies of scale were essential to keeping export prices low.

However, the considerable **market power** enjoyed by Sweden's large corporations gave them the upper hand in wage negotiations with workers. As a result, workers began organizing labor unions. Sweden's ethnic homogeneity facilitated the recruitment of new union members as organizers appealed to workers' sense of belonging to a large family united for mutual protection. In 1898, various **industrial unions** joined together to establish the Swedish Trade Union Confederation (Landsorganisationen [LO]), which staged a general strike in 1902 demanding higher wages and universal suffrage. Employers responded to the growing mobilization and militancy of the labor force by forming the Swedish Employers' Confederation (Svenska Arbetsgivareföreningen [SAF]).

The Demise of Organized Capitalism

In the first two decades of the twentieth century, Sweden endured more labor strikes than any other European country. The concentration of power among both workers and employers led to repeated confrontations, stalemates, and occasional violence. When the Great Depression hit Sweden in 1930, exports declined by 34 percent as other nations enacted trade barriers to protect their own industries. Faced with declining sales, Swedish companies began cutting wages and discharging workers. The government devalued the Swedish currency (krona) by 25 percent in an effort to boost exports, but a weaker currency meant that imports became more expensive, contributing to further declines in workers' standard of living.

The Depression also triggered another catastrophic event for the Swedish economy. Ivar Kreuger (1880–1932) had built a multinational business empire by borrowing money from banks and private investors. His primary business was manufacturing matches, and his company controlled about 70 percent of global match production at the time. However, the Depression revealed that Kreuger's empire was a giant Ponzi scheme, using money from new loans to repay old loans. His bankruptcy resulted not only in his suicide but also the near-collapse of the Swedish banking system and stock market. Another factor contributing to the demise of organized capitalism was an event during a protest march by striking workers. Police opened fire on the marchers, killing several people. The ensuing public outrage left Swedes ready to vote for fundamental institutional changes.

WELFARE CAPITALISM 1932–1991

As the SAP prepared for the 1932 election, it relied on the ideas of Swedish economists Gunnar Myrdal (1898–1987) and Ernst Wigforss (1881–1977). Prior to the work of British economist John Maynard Keynes, Myrdal and Wigforss claimed that inadequate demand was the cause of recessions. The party platform called for **deficit spending** on public works projects such as schools, hospitals, roads, railways, and harbor construction to compensate for inadequate spending in the private sector. The SAP also advocated a higher minimum wage, unemployment compensation, agricultural price supports, and additional welfare programs to increase demand by placing money in the hands of the people most likely to spend it. These proposals appealed to the Swedish people as the SAP won the election in coalition with the Agrarian Party and remained in power for the next forty-four years. Prime Minister Per Albin Hansson (1885–1946) urged Swedes to think of the nation as the "people's home" (folkhemmet) in which all citizens had a mutual responsibility to care for one another as if they were family members.

The SAP made no effort to nationalize private businesses. In fact, the percentage of businesses owned by the state, which has remained relatively constant over the decades at about 5 percent, consists mainly of utilities and mass transportation. Another 5 percent of businesses are cooperatives, leaving 90 percent in private hands. So, contrary to popular perception, Sweden is not a socialist country. Instead, it has sought to develop a "middle way" between capitalism and socialism by pursuing the egalitarian goals of socialism while attempting to harness the dynamism and efficiency of private enterprise. The SAP's commitment to private ownership was reconfirmed in 1982 when it privatized several shipbuilding and steel companies that had been previously nationalized by the conservative party in order to rescue them from bankruptcy.

During the 1930s, the government's efforts to sustain **aggregate demand** through both deficit spending and a **devaluation** of the currency succeeded in reducing the severity of the Great Depression in Sweden. Output fell by only 10 percent and unemployment never exceeded 12 percent (compared to 25 percent in the United States and 33 percent in Germany). By 1936, industrial production was 50 percent higher than in 1929 and unemployment had fallen to 5 percent. However, Sweden could not rely exclusively on demand stimulation to buoy its economy. In addition to the debt burden created by continual deficits in the government's budget, the assurance of strong demand encouraged businesses and labor unions to raise prices and wages. Sweden could not tolerate significant inflation due to its dependence on exports. Inflation would reduce exports, leading to **balance of trade** deficits and loss of jobs.

The SAP sought to control inflation by relying on the cooperative nature of the Swedish people. Fighting inflation poses a **collective action problem**. Without cooperation and coordination, individual labor unions and corporations have no incentives to restrain wage and price increases because their individual restraint would have no effect on inflation unless all other unions and corporations exercised similar restraint.

Fighting unemployment also poses a collective action problem. The self-interest of employers motivates them to pay low wages and lay off any redundant labor. Yet if all employers pay low wages and fire workers, two potential problems arise. First, consumer demand may be insufficient to keep the economy growing, and second, workers may respond to low wages with strikes or reduced productivity. Having witnessed the consequences of labor unrest prior to the Depression, the Swedish government sought to resolve these collective action problems by developing institutions to enable labor unions to bargain for wages sufficiently high to sustain consumer demand and labor peace yet not so high as to erode business profitability or cause inflation.

Organized Labor

The LO and the SAF were already well-established organizations in Sweden, where they represented more than 50 percent of all workers and most large employers. In 1938, under the threat of government intervention in labor negotiations, the LO and SAF met in the city of Saltsjobanden and agreed to standardized procedures for collective bargaining. First, all disputes would be settled through consultation and negotiation rather than strikes. Second, employers would provide "just cause" for any layoffs and would fund state-run unemployment compensation programs. Third, the LO and SAF would engage in annual centralized collective bargaining to reach agreements on wage increases, working hours, and fringe benefits that were binding on all parties. Finally, the Saltsjobanden Accord established a policy of "wage solidarity," assuring equal pay for equal work throughout the economy regardless of the productivity or profitability of different industries. Workers in more profitable industries were expected to restrain their wage demands so that workers with similar jobs in less profitable industries could receive similar wages. Largely as a result of centralized collective bargaining and wage solidarity, Sweden experienced no major strikes between 1940 and 1970.

World War II provided a huge stimulus to the economy as neutral Sweden once again supplied both the Allies and Germany with iron ore and machine parts. As the war ended, Sweden feared a recurrence of the deep recession following World War I. However, with no damage to its own productive capacity, the nation was able to provide equipment and materials to rebuild war-torn Europe, and the economy boomed.

In the postwar era, labor negotiations became even more centralized. Wages were, for the most part, determined by negotiations at the national level in which representatives of both labor and employers negotiated with one another in the presence of government mediators. This bargaining process included not only the LO, representing blue-collar workers, but also the Central Organization of Salaried Employees, the Swedish Confederation of Professional

Associations, and the Federation of Government Employees, representing white-collar workers.

Strong demand for exports after World War II placed strains on the policy of wage solidarity. Firms in the export sector of the economy grew so rapidly that they needed to offer higher wages to attract more workers. However, such actions would undermine wage solidarity and threaten the cooperation between unions that was essential to maintaining wage stability throughout the economy. In 1951, two economists working for the LO proposed a solution to this dilemma.

The Rehn-Meidner Model

Two economists, Gosta Rehn (1916–1996) and Rudolph Meidner (1914–2005), claimed that a continued policy of wage solidarity would actually improve the efficiency of the economy. The previous argument for wage solidarity was that the creation of a sense of solidarity and fairness among all workers would keep wages and prices from rising too quickly. Rehn and Meidner added another claim—if similar jobs were paid the same in all industries, then industries with higher productivity would be more profitable than industries with lower productivity. Capital markets steer financial capital toward the most profitable industries; therefore, resources would flow out of low-productivity industries such as tex-tiles, clothing, and footwear into high-productivity industries such as shipbuild-ing, petrochemicals, and steel. In other words, by preventing high-productivity industries from bidding up wages, the policy of wage solidarity would keep wages in those industries relatively low, leading to higher profits and expansion. Over time, the Swedish economy would transition away from less productive indus-tries as resources flowed toward more productive industries.

The decline of less productive industries would cause many workers to lose their jobs, so the Rehn-Meidner model also included policies to assist laid-off workers in finding new employment. The government established programs to hire workers in public sector jobs; to create job placement services; and to provide subsidies for vocational training, job searches, and moving expenses. In addition, corporations were given tax incentives to reinvest their profits, expand produc-tive capacity, and create new jobs. Underlying the Rehn-Meidner model was an ethical proposition—if the economy as a whole improves by closing factories and laying off workers in less productive industries, then the burden of job loss should be borne by society as a whole rather than by individual workers who lose their jobs. The LO adopted the Rehn-Meidner model in 1962.

Over the years, Sweden developed additional policies to stabilize the econ-omy and minimize unemployment. Employers received subsidies for retraining their workers or offering them incentives for early retirement. Beginning in 1955, corporations were permitted to reduce taxes on up to 40 percent of their profits by placing the money into a reserve fund held by the Swedish central bank (Riksbank). Firms needed government approval to take money out of the fund, so government gained some control over the timing of investment spending. The goal was to reduce investment spending during economic expansions, when it might overstimulate the economy and eventually lead to **excess capacity,** and to increase investment during recessions when additional spending would sustain aggregate demand and reduce unemployment. The government also controlled construction permits, issuing more permits during recessions, and gave loans and subsidies to industries threatened by international competition. These policies contributed to annual growth rates in excess of 5 percent and unemployment rates of around 2 percent during the 1950s and 1960s.

Large Corporations

Sweden's small size meant that if corporations grew large enough to compete in international markets, they became **oligopolies** in the domestic market. **Concentration ratios**, the percentage of industry output controlled by the four largest firms in an industry, averaged more than 80 percent in major industries. Economic concentration was further increased by a single company, Investor AB, that held controlling interest in many of the largest Swedish firms. These firms accounted for one-third of Sweden's GDP and employed approximately 25 percent of the labor force. A single family—the Wallenbergs—owned 40 percent of Investor AB. Even today, wealth is highly concentrated in Sweden. One percent of households own about 75 percent of stocks, and 90 percent of households own none. Sweden has more billionaires per capita than does the United States.

The power of Sweden's oligopolies has traditionally been limited by two factors. First, competition from imported goods forces Swedish producers to remain competitive in terms of price and quality. Second, Swedish citizens have the alternative of buying from the many consumer cooperatives in the country. Half of Swedish households belong to the Kooperativa Förbundet (KF), a nationwide confederation of thirty-nine consumer cooperatives with more than three million members. As the largest retailer in Sweden, KF encompasses cooperative insurance companies, automobile dealerships, department stores, and grocery stores. The very size of KF gives it bargaining power in purchasing goods from manufacturers.

Social Policy

During the 1960s and 1970s, Sweden devoted a higher percentage of its GDP to government expenditures on social programs than any other developed nation. Generous social benefits, coupled with wage solidarity, gave Sweden the most equal after-tax distribution of income and the lowest rate of poverty in the world. Students enjoyed free education through graduate school and received monthly stipends to cover living expenses for any education beyond high school. The educational system provided the same quality of education to all students, and the high quality of public schools made private schools unnecessary.

Healthcare benefits, including dental care, treatment by physicians, hospitalization, and prescription drugs, were free and available to all citizens. Partly because of the excellence of Swedish healthcare, the country stood second only to Japan in average life expectancy and low infant mortality rates. The government covered all childbearing expenses as well as many childcare fees. For each child born, the government provided 450 days of paid leave from work to be divided between the parents in any manner they chose until the child reached eight years of age. During the first 360 days, the parents received 90 percent of their working income, and the last 90 days were subsidized at the same rate for all households. In addition, families received an annual allowance to defray childrearing expenses for each child younger than sixteen years of age. Each worker received twenty-four days of fully paid sick leave per year. In-home assistance for the elderly and marital counseling were provided free of charge. In an effort to achieve gender equity, the government provided grants to pay vacation expenses for nonworking spouses.

All citizens older than age sixty-five received a pension equal to two-thirds of their annual income during their fifteen highest paid working years. The funding for this pension came solely from employers. Unemployment benefits covered 90 percent of a worker's previous earnings for a period of ten months. Welfare programs were available for citizens unable to earn a living. In addition to cash allowances, indigent families could apply for housing benefits, stipends for each child, and day care for children.

Swedes justified their generous welfare state on both moral and economic grounds. Many Swedes viewed the country as one big family and therefore felt a moral obligation to ensure that all citizens were cared for and secure. Beyond that, they also believed that providing social benefits represented an investment in **social capital** that improved the economy by creating increased trust and cooperation. They assumed that citizens who feel valued and supported by their nation would reciprocate with increased productivity and cooperation in moderating wage and price increases. When individuals trust that others will cooperate, collective action problems become easier to solve. For example, Sweden had to maintain price stability to keep its export industries competitive in international markets. But price stability is a **public good** because everyone benefits from it, although individual businesses and labor unions have no incentive to restrain their prices and wages unless others do the same. Through centralized collective bargaining, this collective action problem was solved, but mutual trust between business, labor, and government was essential to secure the necessary cooperation.

Swedes also believed that greater equality generated through social programs would benefit the economy by reducing crime and the waste of human resources associated with poverty and unemployment. In addition, programs providing education, retraining, and counseling represent investments in **human capital** and therefore contribute to increased productivity. Government spending on the development of human capital may actually reduce the need for spending on unemployment compensation and welfare.

Culture

The prevalence of trust, solidarity, and cooperation in Sweden, coupled with a strong work ethic, provided the cultural basis for the impressive performance of the Swedish economy. Far from resenting the taxes needed to fund the welfare state, most Swedes viewed high taxes as their contribution to maintaining the "people's home" or folkhemmet. In fact, the Swedish word for tax (skatt) also means "treasure." Citizens shared their treasure and believed that all individuals, including themselves, benefited as a result. Sweden's ethnic homogeneity contributed to public acceptance of the welfare state. Welfare benefits were viewed not as money taken from "us" and given to "them" but as compensation to those members of the national community who were unfortunate enough to bear the burden of unemployment so that labor markets could remain flexible and dynamic.

The strong sense of social solidarity in Sweden explains an 80 percent turnout for national elections. Laws against trespass are limited, so hikers in the countryside are free to cross property lines. The dominant religion, Lutheranism, treats all people as equal in the eyes of God and thus supports the egalitarian and consensual nature of Swedish society. However, most Swedes rarely attend religious services.

Despite a cultural predisposition to form social groups and to favor an active government, Swedes also value individual autonomy and have a reputation for being reserved in social interactions. This apparent paradox can be resolved by understanding that Swedes view groups and government as expanding their freedom and opportunity by solving collective action problems and by providing resources for the development of individual capacities. For example, free day care allows both parents to work full time. Social psychologists suggest that when a culture emphasizes group activity, individuals need to protect their privacy as a haven from the social pressures of collective existence.

Critics of Swedish culture have charged that economic security and equality lead to a bland existence due to the lack of opportunities to take risks and earn high rewards. They point to high divorce and suicide rates as evidence of a general malaise in Sweden. However, an alternative explanation is that Swedes divorce more frequently because generous social programs reduce the financial pressures to remain in a failing marriage and because Swedish culture attaches less social stigma to divorce. Similarly, Swedes do not regard suicide as shameful for family members, so self-inflicted deaths that might be reported as accidents in other countries are acknowledged as suicides in Sweden.

The Demise of Welfare Capitalism

The oil crisis initiated by the Organization of Petroleum Exporting Countries (OPEC) in 1973 marked the beginning of the end of welfare capitalism in Sweden. The **stagflation** that afflicted Western nations throughout the remainder of the 1970s was particularly challenging for Sweden because of its heavy reliance on exports. In 1976, the SAP lost its first election since 1932 to a coalition of centrist and conservative parties. However, the popularity of the welfare state forced even a conservative government to maintain most social benefits. When the SAP regained office in 1982, it initiated reforms in the welfare state, but significant change would not come until the system reached a crisis in 1991. The demise of welfare capitalism occurred as a result of several changes.

End of Capital Controls

Under the Bretton Woods system established at the end of World War II, flows of financial capital across national borders were restricted. When Sweden abolished **capital controls** in the mid-1980s to attract more foreign capital, corporations and affluent citizens could avoid high taxes by moving money and production facilities overseas. This massive "capital flight" drained the Swedish economy of an essential resource.

International Competition

By the 1980s, Japan and Germany had grown into economic powerhouses, and both nations were export-oriented. In addition, low-wage producers throughout Asia flooded global markets with low-priced goods. As a result, Swedish corporations faced downward pressure on both prices and profits. To maintain profitability, they reduced production costs by relocating some operations abroad and by pushing for greater flexibility in labor markets so that wages could be reduced and redundant labor laid off.

Growth of Government

As economic growth slowed, declining tax revenue and rising claims on social benefits created a fiscal crisis for the Swedish government. Any government facing a weak economy confronts two options. Either it can pursue a policy of austerity by reducing spending in order to balance the government budget, or it can accept a growing budget deficit as necessary to maintain aggregate demand and prevent the economy from sliding even deeper into recession. Based on the success of demand stimulation during the Great Depression, Sweden again chose the latter option. The government increased spending and created public sector jobs to employ citizens who were losing their jobs in the private sector. It also granted new subsidies to industries such as shipbuilding, steel, and wood products. By 1981, government expenditures and transfer payments accounted for more than 65 percent of the GDP.

Funding for these additional programs required higher taxes. During the 1960s, taxes took only 27 percent of national income, but that number rose to 42 percent in 1975 and 52 percent by 1990. In 1983, the top marginal income tax rate stood at 84 percent, and corporations paid a tax on profits of more than 50 percent in addition to a payroll tax of 35 percent on their wage costs. Consumers faced not only a personal income tax but also a **value-added tax** (VAT) of 19 percent on the sale of most goods and services. The composition of government spending also changed. Whereas social spending during the 1960s had been aimed primarily at education and healthcare, both of which contribute to the formation of human capital, much of the additional government spending after the mid-1970s went toward welfare, subsidies, and administrative costs, which had little effect in raising productivity and improving economic performance.

The Swedish government subsidized weak industries in the belief that tax revenue from those industries was essential to funding the welfare state. However, the subsidies merely masked the growing inability of Swedish firms to compete in global markets. Acknowledging this, the government began facilitating the transition of capital and labor to new industries such as chemicals, pharmaceuticals, telecommunications, and engineering, hoping to achieve **comparative advantage** due to Sweden's highly educated labor force. This policy yielded some promising results, but a recession in the late 1980s offset any gains in tax revenue from new industries. The government finally conceded its financial inability to continue the generous social benefits and labor market interventions of previous decades.

Loss of Trust and Cooperation

As long as the Swedish economy prospered, virtually all citizens benefited from the unique institutions of centralized collective bargaining, wage solidarity, and the welfare state. However, these institutions relied on high levels of trust and cooperation. Workers trusted that if they restrained wage demands, corporations would reinvest increased profits in the Swedish economy and create more jobs. Workers also trusted that if they maintained high productivity by working diligently, they would share in a growing economy. Corporations trusted that if they refrained from raising prices, other firms would do the same to prevent inflation. Citizens trusted that government would use their taxes to promote the well-being of the Swedish people. When the economy faltered in the mid-1970s, this trust and willingness to cooperate eroded. Individuals, unions, and corporations began to defect from cooperative agreements, seeking to protect themselves from the consequences of a stagnant economy.

Decline of Work Ethic

One manifestation of defection on the part of individuals was a declining sense of social responsibility that obligated people to work hard, fulfill their civic duties, and care for their fellow citizens. These social norms formed the foundation of the Swedish economy, and as they dissipated, the economy suffered. For example, workers began to abuse the generous provisions for paid sick leave. In the late 1980s, the average Swedish worker took thirty-five days of sick leave per year, and Sweden was devoting 3 percent of its GDP to sick pay.

The declining work ethic can be understood with reference to the concept of a hierarchy of needs developed by psychologist Abraham Maslow (1908–1970). With a prosperous economy supported by a generous welfare state, Swedes felt secure in meeting their needs for survival and safety, leaving them free to focus on higher needs for love, social esteem, and self-actualization. Too often, however, these nonmaterial needs conflicted with productivity. For younger workers, who had grown up knowing only prosperity and economic security, rates of absenteeism were 50 percent higher than for older workers.

The welfare state undermined civic virtue in other ways as well. High taxes pushed significant amounts of economic activity into the **underground economy** as citizens engaged in barter or failed to report income to the government. After paying high taxes to fund numerous social programs, many citizens felt no further obligation to demonstrate concern for the well-being of others. For example, the bonds between generations weakened as Swedes devoted less time to elderly parents. Paradoxically, the welfare state, which arose on the basis of social solidarity, eventually undermined community spirit and fostered increasing individualism.

Demands for Socialism

One sign of worker defection from the cooperative agreements underlying the Swedish economic system was an effort by labor unions and factions within the SAP to move beyond welfare capitalism to socialism in which workers collectively owned the means of production. In 1975, the economist Rudolph Meidner proposed a plan in which all firms employing fifty or more workers would be required to issue new shares of stock each year equal to 20 percent of their pretax profit. These shares would be placed in a union-controlled fund so that unions would gradually gain majority interest in firms, and workers would effectively own and control the nation's productive assets. Despite strong opposition from employers, the government enacted a milder version of the Meidner Plan in 1983. The revenue from a tax on both profits and payrolls was divided among six regional, union-controlled funds that purchased shares of corporate stock. However, no single fund was permitted to acquire more than 8 percent of a company's stock, meaning that workers collectively could not gain controlling interest in any firm.

Another change that increased workers' influence over corporate decision-making occurred in 1977 with the passage of a law requiring firms to establish "works councils" of elected worker representatives who consulted with management on a wide range of issues, including working hours, safety conditions, training, and potential plant closings. In addition, every firm with more than twenty-five employees was required to have two union representatives on its board of directors. These changes may have been welcomed in a more cooperative environment; however, Swedish employers viewed them as hostile attacks on the prerogatives of management and another example of defection from the agreements reached in the 1938 Saltsjobanden Accord.

Breakdown of Wage Solidarity

The policy of wage solidarity was designed to equalize wages for similar work across all industries. By keeping wages in high-productivity industries lower and wages in low-productivity industries higher than they would have been without the policy, profits would increase in high-productivity industries. As a result, high-productivity industries would expand, whereas low-productivity industries would contract, and overall productivity would rise.

However, wage solidarity required a high degree of trust and cooperation because many of the parties involved had incentives to pursue their short-term self-interest. Workers in high-productivity industries could gain higher wages by bargaining separately with their employers. Similarly, firms in high-productivity industries could attract more skilled workers by raising wages. Employers in low-productivity industries could increase profits by cutting wages. Wage solidarity began to crumble as loss of trust undermined cooperation between labor unions and employers. The first signs of defection occurred in expanding industries needing to increase employment. Because employers were prevented from paying higher wages to attract additional workers, they offered shorter hours, longer vacations, and opportunities for overtime work, all of which had the effect of driving up per-unit labor costs and creating an inflationary bias in the economy.

Workers also began to defect from wage solidarity. Labor unions divided into four separate federations—two for blue-collar workers in the public and private sectors and two for white-collar workers in the public and private sectors. Public-sector employees had no incentive to restrain their wage demands because they faced no competitive pressures from global markets. White-collar employees in the private sector, believing their skills to be more valuable than average, began aggressively demanding higher wages. The policy of wage solidarity was gradually abandoned and replaced with negotiations based on profitability and productivity in each industry.

Breakdown of Centralized Collective Bargaining

By 1983, the entire process of centralized wage negotiations began to break down; several large unions representing highly skilled workers and employer groups representing "high-tech" firms boycotted the negotiations and met separately. The "high-tech" firms claimed a need for greater wage flexibility in order to respond to the pressures of international competition. As labor unions began negotiating separately with employers, no single union felt constrained in its wage demands, and labor costs began to increase dramatically. With its heavy dependence on exports, Sweden's balance of trade turned negative, which contributed to an economic crisis in 1991. By that date, any remnants of centralized wage bargaining were gone as the employers' federation refused to participate.

The demise of wage solidarity and centralized bargaining in Sweden provides an instructive lesson in labor relations. As long as mutual trust existed between labor, business and government, wage restraint could be achieved. But if any one of the parties abandoned the trust, a downward spiral developed. When government ended its commitment to full employment and a social safety net, unions no longer felt secure and demanded higher wages. With unions no longer cooperating in restraining wages, Swedish corporations began shifting operations abroad, further undermining the trust between labor and management and leading to even more aggressive bargaining by unions. Inflationary pressures created by higher wages reduced Swedish exports, resulting in lower profits for corporations and less tax revenue for government. The government was then forced to further reduce spending on social programs and the downward spiral continued.

Financial Deregulation

In 1985, the government enacted legislation removing many of the regulations on the financial sector, including banks and capital markets. The goal was to make

Sweden more attractive to international investors, but the result was catastrophic. Banks took full advantage of deregulation by expanding credit so rapidly that a speculative bubble developed in the stock market and real estate. The bubble burst in early 1990, and bank losses were so severe that the financial sector nearly collapsed. The government took control of 25 percent of all bank assets, and two banks were nationalized at a cost of $18 billion, or about 4 percent of the GDP.

The financial crisis spilled over into the real economy, leading to a serious recession and negative growth for the next four years. Housing prices dropped by 25 percent, and the commercial real estate market lost 42 percent of its value. In terms of job loss, the recession of the early 1990s was worse for Sweden than the Great Depression. The Social Democrats lost the 1991 election and were replaced by a coalition of four conservative parties led by Carl Bildt. Unlike the conservative government that held office from 1976 to 1982, the new coalition pledged to make fundamental reforms in the Swedish economic system.

A NEW DIRECTION?

Although the Social Democrats regained power in 1995, they were a changed party. Prime Minister Göran Persson, the leader of a faction within the party known as "renewers," pushed the party to endorse reforms aimed at reducing social benefits and increasing incentives to work. In 2006, the Social Democrats again lost power, defeated this time by the Moderate Party. The SAP received only 35 percent of the vote, its worst showing since before the Great Depression. However, in 2014, the Social Democrats once again regained control of the government. Despite the turnover in political administrations, Sweden has undertaken substantial reforms to its economic system since the crisis of 1991.

Taxes

Tax reforms reduced the progressivity of the tax system. The top marginal income tax rate, which had been 84 percent in 1983, is now 56 percent, and the top rate on corporate profits has been reduced from 50 percent to 22 percent. Between 2005 and 2008, the inheritance tax, the wealth tax, and taxes on residential property were all eliminated. To recoup some of the lost tax revenue, the regressive VAT that consumers pay on the purchase of goods and services rose from 19 percent to 25 percent (except for 12 percent on food and other essential goods), and formerly exempt categories of spending such as entertainment, public transportation, telecommunications, and personal services became subject to the VAT.

Another aspect of tax reform has been the growth of what economists call **tax expenditures**. When the tax system contains provisions for deductions, credits, and other loopholes, the effect on the public budget is the same as if government had given subsidies to the affected parties. When the reduced progressivity of the tax code is coupled with tax expenditures, income is actually being redistributed from poor to rich, not vice versa. The primary goals of tax reform have been to make Sweden more appealing to investors, to increase the incentives for productive activity, and to reduce the incentives for tax avoidance and evasion.

Government Spending

The Swedish government has become a paragon of fiscal responsibility. The ratio of government spending to GDP has dropped from 67 percent in 1993 to 49 percent. The government budget has been in surplus every year since 1998 except in 2004, and as a result, the **national debt** as a percentage of GDP has dropped from 70 percent in 1993 to 35 percent. Several changes place restraints on government spending. Since 1996, the legislature (Riksdag) sets an annual ceiling for government spending and a target for the rate of inflation. The Swedish Fiscal Policy Council, a group of independent experts, then audits the government's budget to determine whether it is designed to promote economic growth and ensure the long-term financial viability of the government.

Social Benefits

Most social benefits have become less generous, and the criteria for eligibility have been tightened. Unemployment benefits are now lower than in most other developed nations. To reduce the cost of social benefits, the government allows private businesses to compete with government agencies in providing healthcare, education, child care, and elder care. In the cases of education and healthcare, citizens receive vouchers to be redeemed for services with either a public or private provider. A voucher system creates competition between public and private providers in order to reduce cost and improve quality.

The Meidner Plan

The conservative government elected in 1991 scrapped the Meidner Plan that placed shares of corporate stock into regional funds controlled by labor unions. The shares were transferred to government agencies and subsequently sold to private investors in order to generate funds to finance research and promote economic growth.

Industry-Level Labor Negotiations

Although centralized wage bargaining was abandoned in the late 1980s, the government initiated industry-level negotiations in the 1990s covering about half of all workers. The goal was to restrain wages through cooperation between unions in the same industry.

Financial Reform

Two notable reforms occurred in the financial sector of the economy. The Swedish Central Bank, the Riksbank, is now completely independent of the government so that monetary policy has become, in principle at least, free from political pressures. The Riksbank can now pursue unpopular policies (e.g., raising interest rates) to fight inflation. The second reform occurred in 1991 when the government abolished the investment reserve fund that permitted corporations to reduce taxes by placing part of their profits in a fund held by the Riksbank. That fund enable the government to control the timing of investment spending in order to stabilize the economy, but the conservative administration insisted on reducing government involvement in private decision-making.

*   *   *

The initial impact of these reforms was negative. To protest cuts in government spending, public employee unions of physicians, postal workers, teachers, and transit workers staged major strikes, which crippled the economy. Between 1990 and 1993, the unemployment rate rose from 1.5 percent to 8 percent while GDP fell by 5 percent. However, between 1993 and 2010, the Swedish economy grew at an average annual rate of 2.7 percent compared to 1.9 percent for other countries in the European Union.

Although Sweden's reforms have moved the nation closer to neoliberal capitalism, the welfare state is still very much alive, particularly with regard to benefits aimed at the parents of young children. Maternity leaves from work last for a full year with 75 percent of salary. At least one month of that year's leave must be taken by the father. Workers have ninety days of sick leave to care for sick children, and the government continues to provide subsidized day care and family allowances for each child up to the age of sixteen. Universal free healthcare and education are still intact. Swedes remain convinced that an extensive welfare state is essential to supplement and improve the functioning of a market economy.

Despite tax cuts on income and assets, Sweden's tax burden as a percentage of GDP is 47 percent, the second highest of any nation after Denmark. The government still employs 30 percent of the labor force. Sweden has the most unionized labor force in the world, with 67 percent of blue-collar and 73 percent of white-collar workers belonging to labor unions. (Even soldiers, teachers, and physicians have their own unions.)

The fact that the Swedish economy has outperformed most other developed nations since 1993 defies the neoliberal claims that high taxes, a large government, generous social benefits, and powerful labor unions are obstacles to economic growth. In the words of former prime minister Göran Persson, "a bumblebee, with its overly heavy body and little wings . . . should not be able to fly—but it does."

The Swedish experience provides several valuable lessons for other nations. First, high taxes do not necessarily discourage productive activity. In fact, the opposite may be true. Sweden has one of the highest **labor force participation rates** in the world, and many workers hold two jobs in order to bolster household after-tax income.

Second, in assessing the role of government in the economy, the most important factor is not the size of government but the specific roles that government plays. A small government can suppress growth if it acts as a **predatory state** extracting wealth to benefit government officials and their allies in the private sector. A large government can stimulate growth with policies that supplement and support the market by providing infrastructure, solving collective action problems, and maintaining stability.

Third, social benefits can be so generous that they undermine individual initiative and responsibility. However, some social benefits are consistent with maintaining incentives to work. Sweden's social benefits are now aimed more at assisting citizens to become productive members of society rather than consigning them to idleness and dependency. Most social benefits target areas where positive **externalities** and the **free-rider problem** prevent the market from responding fully to essential public needs (e.g., education, healthcare, and child care). The Swedish government has managed to maintain extensive social benefits despite budget cuts by improving the efficiency of delivery and by eliminating or reducing benefits such as unemployment compensation that do not improve productivity.

Fourth, national governments cannot ignore competitive market forces from outside the country. Sweden's cooperative institutions worked remarkably well before globalization reduced barriers to the free flow of capital, resources, and goods around the world. However, faced with competitive market pressures, the Swedish economy faltered, and the nation was forced to scale back its commitment to equality and security for all citizens.

Fifth, nations can improve their competitiveness in the global economy in two ways. The neoliberal approach calls for gaining **competitive advantage** by lowering production costs through tax cuts, deregulation, reducing social benefits, and weakening labor unions. Sweden has moved in the direction of neoliberalism, but its primary focus has been on enhancing competitiveness through improving infrastructure and **human capital** through education, healthcare, and funding for research. Increasing skills, knowledge, creativity, innovation, entrepreneurship, and social mobility all raise productivity and improve competitiveness. Much of Sweden's current success is attributable to its strength in fields such as information technology, software development, and telecommunications. All these industries are based on one primary resource—human knowledge. Swedes believe that a degree of economic security encourages entrepreneurs to undertake the risk of starting new businesses because social benefits create a safety net that reduces the cost of failure.

The strength of Sweden's new form of capitalism was demonstrated by its remarkable resilience after the global recession of 2008. By 2010, the economy was growing at an annual rate of 5.5 percent, a figure significantly higher than in other industrialized nations. Sweden learned valuable lessons from the recession of 1990–94 that helped to mitigate the effects of the Great Recession. After the near-failure of the banking system in 1990, bankers were much more cautious in their lending than in the United States and other countries. Also, the government's commitment to fiscal discipline led to budget surpluses leading up to the Great Recession. With its fiscal house in order, the Swedish government was able to respond quickly to provide additional stimulus to the economy. In addition, much of that stimulus was applied through what economists call "automatic stabilizers." With Sweden's extensive array of welfare programs, as soon as citizens began losing jobs, spending on social benefits automatically increased. The government did not need to engage in lengthy debates about approving a stimulus package and developing projects to receive funding. Finally, Sweden's decision not to adopt the euro and to keep its own currency, the krona, proved to be beneficial. As Swedish exports began to decline during the recession, the krona depreciated, making exports less expensive to foreigners and sustaining economic growth.

Sweden provides testimony to the importance of community and consensus-building in a healthy economic system. Despite the breakdown of centralized collective bargaining, wage solidarity, and other forms of social cooperation, the degree of social cohesion and cooperation in Sweden remains high. In the past, this feature of Swedish culture could be explained by ethnic homogeneity, but as a result of extensive immigration, 25 percent of the current population is non-Scandinavian. Yet, labor unions, corporations, government, and citizens continue to exhibit a high degree of social responsibility and commitment to maintaining a high quality of life for the "people's home."

ADDITIONAL READING

Bergh, Andreas. *Sweden and the Revival of the Capitalist Welfare State*. Northampton, MA: Edward Elgar, 2014.

Bosworth, Barry, and Alice Rivlin, eds. *The Swedish Economy*. Washington, DC: The Brookings Institute, 1987.

Gylfason, Thorvaldur, ed. *The Swedish Model under Stress*. Stockholm: SNS Forlag, 1997.

Hort, Sven, E. O. *Social Policy, Welfare State, and Civil Society in Sweden: Vol. I: History, Politics, and Institutions*. 3rd ed. *1884–1988*. Lund, Sweden: Arkiv Academic Press, 2014.

——. *Social Policy, Welfare State, and Civil Society in Sweden: Vol II: The Lost World of Social Democracy 1988–2015*. 3rd ed. Lund, Sweden: Arkiv Academic Press, 2014.

Kent, Neil. *A Concise History of Sweden*. New York: Cambridge University Press, 2008.

Magnusson, Lars. *An Economic History of Sweden*. New York: Routledge, 2000.

Millner, Henry. *Sweden: Social Democracy in Practice*. New York: Oxford University Press, 1989.

Olsen, Gregg J. *The Struggle for Economic Democracy in Sweden*. Brookfield, VT: Avebury, 1992.

Pontusson, Jonas. *The Limits of Social Democracy: Investment Politics in Sweden*. Ithaca, NY: Cornell University Press, 1992.

Schon, Lennart. *An Economic History of Modern Sweden*. New York: Routledge, 2012.

Sejersted, Francis. *The Age of Social Democracy: Norway and Sweden in the Twentieth Century*. Princeton, NJ: Princeton University Press, 2011.

Steinmo, Sven. *The Evolution of the Modern State: Sweden, Japan, and the United States*. New York: Cambridge University Press, 2010.

Tilton, Tom. *The Political Theory of Swedish Social Democracy: Through the Welfare State to Socialism*. New York: Oxford University Press, 1990.

Chapter 11

THE RUSSIAN ECONOMIC SYSTEM

"Whoever does not miss the Soviet Union has no heart. Whoever wants it back has no brain."

VLADIMIR PUTIN,
Russian President

For seventy-four years (1917–1991), Russia was the largest republic in the former Soviet Union, spanning eleven time zones and accounting for 88 percent of the land area and 91 percent of industrial output. However, the country had a long history prior to its inclusion in the Soviet Union, and it is once again an independent nation engaged in a very difficult transition from **communism** to **capitalism**. For nearly a decade after the end of communism, the Russian economic system performed so poorly that standards of living actually declined. Although growth has been stronger in the twenty-first century, **per capita gross domestic product** (GDP) remains quite low. The dissatisfaction among Russians with their new economic system was reflected by the 20 percent of votes going to the Communist Party in a 2011 general election. To understand the difficulties facing capitalism in Russia today requires knowledge of its imperial and communist past.

PRE-COMMUNIST RUSSIA 1721–1916

Although nominally an empire established in 1721 by Tsar Peter the Great (1672–1725), Russia was essentially a feudal economic system until the late nineteenth century. A relatively small aristocracy owned most of the land. Agricultural labor was performed by peasant farmers whose status was not much different from the serfs of medieval Europe. Due to the poor quality of soil throughout much of Russia, agricultural productivity remained low, and peasants were required to turn over at least half of their harvest to absentee landowners. As a result, what little surplus the economy produced was devoted to luxury consumption by the aristocrats and the monarchy rather than being directed toward investment in agriculture, manufacturing, or **infrastructure**.

When Peter the Great toured western Europe, he recognized Russia's failure to keep pace with economic development in other countries. To accelerate industrialization, he imported technology from the West, established state-owned manufacturing firms, and moved the imperial capital westward from Moscow to St. Petersburg in an effort to open Russia to European influences. However, these reforms did little to change the lives of peasants who comprised 90 percent of the population.

In 1861, Tsar Alexander II (1818–1881) attempted to lift Russia out of its feudal past by emancipating the peasants from their obligations to landowners. Since the fifteenth century, many Russian peasants had formed communal farms (mirs) to gain **economies of scale** and reduce the risk of crop failure on any single plot. The monarchy offered mortgages to enable peasants to buy land, but for most families, group ownership was the only financially feasible strategy and communal farms persisted as the dominant form of agriculture.

Alexander II also initiated a vast railroad system to widen the market for agricultural goods. By the late nineteenth century, Russia had become the largest grain exporter in the world. To promote Russian industry, the government used money from exports to purchase modern capital equipment from abroad. The government also encouraged economic development through subsidies and low taxes for industry, protective **tariffs**, and violent suppression of any labor unrest. French and English investors were attracted by these policies as well as Russia's ample resource base and cheap labor. By the onset of World War I, Russia had become the fifth largest manufacturer in the world.

The Demise of the Russian Empire

Only the urban elite and foreign investors were benefitting from development. Due to high taxes and heavy debt, peasants continued to barely subsist. In addition, industrial workers were paid abysmally low wages due to virtually limitless supplies of labor escaping rural hardship to seek employment in the cities. Outraged by the growing disparity of wealth and income, some Russian intellectuals were attracted to anarchism, socialism, and communism. Social anarchists such as Peter Kropotkin (1842–1921) and Mikhail Bakunin (1814–1876) envisioned self-governing local communes that controlled their own production. In the 1880s, a group called the Narodniki claimed that rural communes could serve as the basis for a new communist economic system. By this time, however, the writings of Karl Marx (1818–1883) were circulating in Russia, and the leading Russian Marxist, Georgi Plekhanov (1856–1918), argued that Russia first needed to experience capitalist industrialization before making the transition to socialism and then communism.

The political group that ultimately changed the course of Russian history was the Social Democratic Party, which held its second convention in London in 1903 to escape tsarist repression. At that meeting, a schism developed between two groups within the Party. The Mensheviks, led by Alexander Kerensky (1881–1970), advocated liberal reforms such as parliamentary democracy, open elections, and labor unions. The Bolsheviks and their leader, Vladimir Ilyich

Ulyanov (1870–1924), who adopted the pseudonym Lenin, called for total revolution led by a "vanguard party" of Marxist intellectuals and culminating in communism.

The monarchy was aware of growing discontent among citizens. During the early twentieth century, Tsar Nicholas II (1868–1918) used censorship, a pervasive secret police, and an internal passport system to suppress dissent. In 1905, a peaceful protest march in St. Petersburg resulted in hundreds of deaths as the tsar's palace guards opened fire on the crowd. The massacre, which came to be known as Bloody Sunday, turned public opinion against the tsar. Workers called a general strike and formed councils (soviets) to direct their protest activities. In an effort to appease citizens, the tsar permitted the formation of an elected parliament (Duma), but it remained largely symbolic and had little power to influence government policies. Public discontent festered for another decade until the hardships brought on by World War I created the conditions for revolution.

Russia entered the war as an ally of France and Britain and lost more than two million soldiers in battles against the German army. In addition to casualties, the war caused nationwide food shortages and high prices, and it intensified pressure on workers and peasants to increase production. In February, 1917, after a month of demonstrations and riots, the Mensheviks seized control of the government and the tsar abdicated the throne. When the Mensheviks decided to continue Russia's participation in World War I, Lenin saw his opportunity. Living in exile in Switzerland, Lenin had been directing and funding the revolution from a distance. The German government, hoping that revolution would end Russia's involvement in the war, gave Lenin forty million marks and arranged safe railway passage back to St. Petersburg. As Lenin stepped off the train, he promised Russians that they would get "peace, land, and bread." In October, 1917, with growing support from urban industrial workers, the Bolsheviks overthrew

Figure 11.1 Lenin addresses a crowd in Red Square. (© Getty Images/Heritage Images)

the provisional government established by the Mensheviks and began the process of building the first communist economic system in the world.

SOVIET COMMUNISM 1917–1991

War Communism

Given the chaotic conditions in Russia, the Bolsheviks quickly discovered that controlling the government did not necessarily mean controlling the country. A significant number of Russians, particularly the aristocratic landowners and industrial capitalists, opposed the Bolshevik revolution. With substantial wealth at their disposal, they organized a White Army to challenge the Red Army of the Bolsheviks, and a civil war ensued for the next three years. The Bolsheviks also faced hostility from Western nations, which became apparent when France, Britain, and the United States sent a small, multinational military expedition into Russia in an effort to thwart the revolution. The Red Army successfully repelled the invasion.

To cope with both internal and external threats to the revolution, Lenin established War Communism in 1918. The most pressing economic issues were providing food for urban workers and transporting raw materials to the factories. With the economy in turmoil, Lenin decided that reliance on money and markets could not move resources quickly enough. He opted instead for forced requisition. The Red Army was ordered to confiscate food supplies from the more prosperous farmers (kulaks) and deliver it to cities for distribution. The Bolsheviks nationalized nearly all businesses and required all able-bodied citizens to work. To ensure that the basic needs of citizens were met, food, housing, electricity, and transportation were rationed by the government free of charge.

After three years of War Communism, the Bolsheviks had solidified their rule, but the economy was in shambles. In the absence of markets or any sophisticated planning techniques, factories experienced chronic shortages of raw materials and other inputs. The kulaks reacted to the confiscation of their crops by hiding food to sell in the black market or by ceasing production altogether. The resulting food shortages in the cities forced urban workers to roam the countryside in search of sustenance. By 1920, the economic disarray had become so severe that industrial output fell 20 percent below its 1917 level.

The New Economic Policy

Lenin changed course in 1921 with the New Economic Policy (NEP). The Bolsheviks abandoned forced requisition in favor of taxing a fixed percentage of farmers' output. The state retained control over only the "commanding heights" of the economy, including core industries such as metals, banking, communications, transportation, and energy. Small businesses were leased to private entrepreneurs, larger businesses were granted independence to maximize profit, and citizens were permitted to start new businesses as long as they hired no more than twenty employees. Workers could choose their jobs, and wages were determined by market forces of supply and demand.

The economy responded favorably to the NEP, but Lenin's death in 1924 triggered a power struggle within the Bolshevik party over the future course of the Soviet Union. Leon Trotsky (1879–1940) criticized the Bolshevik leadership for centralizing political authority and insulating itself from democratic input. Trotsky wanted to eliminate both the market and the centralized state by relying on local councils (soviets) to coordinate production. In contrast, Nikolai Bukharin (1888–1938) claimed that the NEP's emphasis on entrepreneurship and profit-making should be expanded in order to unleash the human energy associated with the pursuit of self-interest. Bukharin urged Soviet citizens to "get rich." A third viewpoint came from Evgenii Preobrazhensky (1886–1937), who believed that rapid industrialization was the key to economic success and that strong government control of the economy was necessary to transfer the surplus produced in agriculture into capital accumulation in the manufacturing sector. This transfer would be accomplished through price controls—farmers would receive low prices for their products and pay high prices for manufactured goods.

Within this struggle for power, Yossif Dzhugashvili (1878–1953), who adopted the pseudonym Stalin, skillfully played the opposing sides against each other. He allied himself with Bukharin to undermine Preobrazhensky and to have Trotsky exiled from the country and later murdered in Mexico. Stalin then turned against Bukharin and by 1927 held absolute power over the entire nation. Within a short time, Stalin adopted policies nearly identical to those advocated by Preobrazhensky. Anticipating that the kulaks would resist governmental efforts to transfer agricultural surpluses to manufacturing, Stalin ordered the collectivization of agriculture. He consolidated more than twenty-five million peasant farms into about 200,000 large, state-owned collective farms (kolkhoz). The opposition to collectivization was fierce, but in the end, Stalin's only concession was to allow farmers to keep small plots of land for personal gardening.

Central Planning

Beginning in 1928, the Soviet Union instituted comprehensive five-year economic planning by the State Planning Committee (Gosplan). The Committee decided what goods to produce and then issued output targets or quotas to the state ministries in charge of each industry. The ministries, in turn, formulated specific targets for individual state-owned enterprises (SOEs). The Soviet economy industrialized swiftly during the 1930s, but development was achieved at a horrible price. Through the planning process, resources were diverted from consumption to capital formation, so the standard of living of the average Soviet citizen remained dismal. Loyal communists viewed this deprivation as the sacrifice required to construct a new society that would someday deliver abundance for all. However, acceptance of deprivation was reinforced by a reign of terror. Anyone who criticized or resisted the state received brutal punishment. Many kulaks were either murdered by roving bands of communists or sent to forced-labor camps (gulags). Stalin periodically initiated purges of suspected "enemies of the people," and many officials in the higher echelons of the military and bureaucracy, including Bukharin and most of the top Bolshevik revolutionary leaders, were executed after sham trials. In addition, secret police and informants kept the entire population in a constant state of fear. In all, millions of Soviet citizens were either shot or sent to the gulags. The Stalinist rationale for this iron-fisted repression was that the Soviet people must act as a unified body to ensure the success of communism.

The initial results of central planning were impressive. Western nations remained mired in the Great Depression, but the Soviet economy grew at an annual rate of 10 percent during the decade of the 1930s. The ability of central planners to mobilize and direct resources to targeted projects enabled the Soviet Union to function much like a giant military organization. By tolerating no dissent and restricting consumption, the government accomplished the transition from an agrarian to an industrial economy more quickly than had any other nation in history. The high growth rate was also attributable to a highly motivated labor force. Material incentives for work were minimal; therefore, the willingness to engage in long hours of difficult labor was based on both hope and fear—hope for a future communist society in which all citizens lived freely and comfortably, and fear of execution or imprisonment in the forced-labor camps. The reliance on punishment to enforce work and solidarity was vividly illustrated by the Red Army's practice of immediately executing any soldier attempting to desert.

World War II (called The Great Patriotic War by Russians) devastated the Soviet Union. As the German army advanced eastward in 1941, the Soviets practiced a "scorched earth" policy, destroying any resource that could possibly be used by the Germans. The Red Army burned crops and either dismantled factories for relocation east of the Ural Mountains or razed them altogether. Although the Germans never entered the major cities of Moscow and Leningrad (formerly St. Petersburg), fierce fighting reduced other cities such as Stalingrad to rubble.

The German defeat at Stalingrad marked the turning point in the war, after which the Red Army began a westward drive, ending with the capture of Berlin in 1945. As the Germans retreated, they flooded mine shafts, destroyed buildings, killed livestock, blew up railroad tracks and roads, and burned fields and forests. At the end of the war, the western part of the Soviet Union, where much of the most fertile land and industrial capacity was located, had been reduced to a wasteland. Twenty million Soviet citizens lost their lives during the war, and most of the economic gains made during the 1930s were lost.

By the 1950s, problems with central planning were becoming increasingly apparent. The directives from central planners were typically expressed as physical quotas, and plant managers engaged in opportunism by pursuing their self-interest. A common ploy was to understate a factory's productive capacity in order to receive a lower and therefore more easily met quota. Alternatively, a manager might submit an exaggerated estimate of the resources required to meet the quota. With plentiful resources, the quota could be easily surpassed, and the manager would receive a bonus. Managers also cultivated political connections in order to influence planners to reduce quotas and make bonuses more easily attainable.

Because managers' bonuses were based on production and not on actual sales of products, there was no incentive to produce high-quality products desired by consumers. For example, if a factory manufacturing windows were given a quota expressed in weight, the manager might order the production of thick, heavy windows. On the other hand, if the quota were expressed in square feet, the manager might produce thin, flimsy windows. Managers also routinely engaged in black market activities arranged by expediters (tolkachi) to sell surplus resources or purchase resources needed to meet their targets. With such extensive illegal activity, bribery became a normal part of doing business in the Soviet Union.

The Nomenklatura

A new class system emerged within the Soviet Union. Soviet leaders accepted the need for salary differentials to provide incentives for workers to acquire certain skills, to enter selected industries or professions, or to relocate to particular regions of the country. However, the major source of growing inequality in the Soviet Union was the system of nomenklatura wherein the Communist Party appointed members to fill the top positions in government, industry, and academia. Absolute loyalty to the Party was a prerequisite for attaining these positions, and generous rewards were attached to them. In addition to high salaries, the nomenklatura could shop at special stores (barioskas) where prices were less than half the normal level, goods were of better quality, and imported luxury items were available. The elites might be provided with chauffeured limousines, spacious apartments in the city, and second homes in the country (dachas). They had access to special medical facilities, elite schools for their children, vacation resorts, and the best seats at cultural events.

The system of political appointments extended even deeper into the economy as patron-client relationships became pervasive. A person in power (patron) appointed subordinates (clients) whose prospects for advancement depended on their usefulness to the patron. The system of nomenklatura and patron-client relationships led to appointments and promotions based on obedience and blind loyalty rather than initiative, creativity, and productivity. As a result, inequality in the Soviet Union failed to provide the incentives essential to promoting productive activity and economic efficiency.

Social Policy

Life in the Soviet Union was not without its benefits. The government provided free healthcare, free education through the university level, and free child care for all citizens. In addition, Soviet citizens enjoyed good public transportation systems, subsidized housing, subsidized food prices, job security, and old-age and disability pensions. Street crime was virtually nonexistent because the penalties were so harsh. The large SOEs often provided their employees with housing and recreational facilities. Every able-bodied citizen was required to work, which meant that welfare programs and unemployment compensation were unnecessary. Despite this array of social benefits, the standard of living in the Soviet

Union remained low. Most families lived in small apartments in multistory complexes, few citizens had automobiles, the quality of healthcare was primitive by Western standards, and consumer goods were often shoddy and unappealing.

Culture

Culture develops very slowly over time and, once established, is highly resistant to change. The Bolshevik revolution transformed the Russian polity and economy, but the culture remained remarkably unchanged. In fact, several aspects of Russian culture under the tsars contributed to the rise of communism. The peasant communes (mirs) accustomed Russians to collectivism. The mirs had authority to discipline members, collect taxes, intervene in family disputes, and make production and distribution decisions for the entire group.

Russians have traditionally valued charismatic leaders and a strong state. Invasions over the centuries by Mongols, Poles, Swedes, Germans, French, and Lithuanians caused Russians to look to the state for protection. With no experience of the legacies left by the Renaissance, the Enlightenment, the Protestant Reformation, the scientific revolution, or struggles for democracy, many Russians held premodern worldviews right through the twentieth century. Having experienced only hardship and oppression, they tended to be stoic and fatalistic about their lives. Alienation and cynicism proliferated, which in turn, contributed to high levels of alcoholism, domestic violence, and disregard for the law.

The communal nature of Soviet society extended beyond state control of the economy. Cultural manifestations of a communal consciousness included such practices as clapping in unison at the same tempo to show appreciation at cultural events, sharing restaurant tables with strangers, publically scolding strangers for inappropriate dress, and demonstrating an eagerness to inform authorities of any suspected subversive activities. What Westerners would call snooping, Russians viewed as their civic duty to maintain an orderly society. The Communist Party had no difficulty in recruiting citizens to serve as informants in their apartment buildings or workplaces. The prevalence of spying and informants caused citizens to confine their true thoughts and opinions to the privacy of their families and close friends. Even telephone conversations were guarded because of the prevalence of wiretapping. Russians could be warm and gregarious in their homes, but they often behaved rudely in public, pushing and jostling to get into a crowded store or onto a bus.

The Demise of Soviet Communism

When Stalin died in 1953, his successor, Nikita Khrushchev (1894–1971), took significant steps to change the nature of the Soviet economic system. In 1956, he publically denounced Stalin's reign of terror and ordered that Stalin's body be moved from the hallowed Kremlin wall to a cemetery in a Moscow suburb. Most of the forced-labor camps were closed, and citizens were allowed greater freedom to choose their jobs and places of residence. Political authority over the economy was decentralized by shifting much of the responsibility for planning from

Moscow to a hundred regional economic councils. Bonuses for plant managers were based on profitability rather than fulfillment of quotas. The initial results of these reforms were promising—the quality of food and housing improved noticeably. The Soviet economy performed sufficiently well at this time that it became an appealing model for developing nations throughout the world. There was no inflation, standards of living were rising, and average life expectancy matched that of Western nations. Soviet scientists regularly won Nobel Prizes, and the Soviet Union successfully launched the first orbiting satellite and sent the first man into space in 1961.

Despite Khrushchev's reforms, economic growth slowed during the 1960s. The decentralization of planning created regional rivalries as local planners, politicians and plant managers colluded to manipulate production targets and thereby keep more resources and output within their region. When Khrushchev was forced to resign in 1964, his joint successors, Leonid Brezhnev (1906–1982) and Alexei Kosygin (1904–1980), promptly abolished the regional economic councils and restored much of the centralized planning process. For the next two decades, Soviet leaders vacillated between markets and planning. A wave of market-oriented reforms would be followed by reassertion of state control, but neither strategy improved the performance of the economy.

Several factors contributed to slowing growth rates. The most accessible natural resources had been tapped during the early years of industrialization, so locating new reserves required the diversion of labor and capital to activities such as exploration, drilling, and transportation. Also, whereas Stalin had intentionally suppressed consumption to make resources available for industrialization, subsequent Soviet leaders recognized the need to provide citizens with improved standards of living. However, shifting resources toward the production of consumer goods caused lower rates of capital formation in heavy industry. Finally, central planning itself became increasingly cumbersome and inefficient. As the economy grew and production became more complex, the potential for errors in the planning process increased. One small miscalculation could create a bottleneck that would slow production in many related industries.

The decline of the Soviet economy accelerated during the 1980s as the nation lagged behind other industrialized countries in technological innovation. Whereas the impressive economic performance of the 1930s was based on mobilizing previously untapped resources, additional growth required technological change to improve the productivity of existing resources. Soviet plant managers had little incentive to innovate or improve product quality because doing so would require a diversion of resources from meeting current quotas and therefore jeopardize their bonuses.

Weakness in the Soviet economy also reflected changing attitudes among workers. By the 1980s, the original generation of committed communists was gone. Most of the threats of punishment had been lifted, and the dreary quality of life in the Soviet Union had effectively ended any hopes of a "workers' paradise." Cynicism and apathy prevailed as citizens endured the frustrations of dealing with shoddy products, cramped living quarters, long lines at stores, wiretaps on telephones, and the constant fear of being labeled dissidents. The government tried to sustain faith in communism by pointing to crime, racism, and decadence in Western nations and by preventing access to foreign magazines, newspapers, music, and television that might fuel desires for Western lifestyles. However, this censorship only made Western culture more attractive, particularly among youth.

Another popular explanation for the demise of communism remains controversial. In the early 1980s, the United States initiated a significant increase in military spending. The Reagan administration proposed a Strategic Defense Initiative to protect the United States against incoming missiles armed with nuclear warheads. At the time, the United States was spending 6 to 7 percent of its GDP on national defense. In an effort to match US military capabilities, the Soviet Union was spending 13 to 14 percent of its smaller GDP on defense. This diversion of resources away from civilian production prevented Soviet standards of living from rising and therefore, the argument goes, contributed to the fall of communism. However, data shows that the level of Soviet defense spending did not increase during the 1980s. Instead, the increase occurred in the late 1970s, prior to the Strategic Defense Initiative. The Soviet military buildup is better explained by internal factors such as paranoia about foreign attacks and the political power of the Soviet defense industry.

When Mikhail Gorbachev became the leader of the Soviet Union in 1985, he remained committed to government ownership of the means of production. However, he wanted to capture the dynamism and efficiency of markets by abolishing mandatory output quotas and allowing managers of SOEs to decide what goods to produce, how to produce them, what price to charge, and how many workers to hire. This policy of restructuring (perestroika) encouraged individual initiative by providing incentives for more efficient production. Also, individuals were allowed to purchase their own houses, and small private businesses were permitted to open in the service sector. In 1988, private banks appeared for the first time since the revolution.

Gorbachev also called for openness and transparency (glasnost) in government affairs. Ideally, perestroika and glasnost would reinforce each other, as transparency in politics would make restructuring the economy more feasible by exposing corruption, waste, and mismanagement. However, glasnost unleashed decades of repressed anger and resentment. For the first time, citizens were permitted to openly discuss government policies and vent their frustrations. The newly independent media began publicizing issues such as alcoholism, suicide, corruption, police brutality, abuse of dissidents, and pollution. Glasnost brought the shortcomings of Soviet communism into full public view.

The effort to restructure the economy also failed to improve economic performance. Perestroika gave plant managers a great deal of latitude in making economic decisions, but this freedom simply opened the door for increased corruption and opportunism. Seeking to maximize personal gain, managers diverted resources to black markets often controlled by criminal gangs. Gorbachev had unleashed the powerful motive of self-interest, but without essential political and cultural institutions such as well-defined property rights, respect for the rule of law, and a culture of trust and honesty, self-interested behavior degenerated into chaos. Employees and managers stole goods from their workplaces to furnish their homes or to sell on the black market. Businesses deposited some of their **revenue** in foreign banks accounts to avoid taxes or diverted production to small enterprises operating in the black market.

Perhaps the final nail in the coffin of Soviet communism was a growing perception among the nomenklatura that their interests would be better served by a full-scale transition to capitalism. Although this group comprised the privileged class under communism, their standards of living were low compared to their counterparts in the West. Furthermore, the egalitarian ideology of communism discouraged them from openly displaying and enjoying their privileges. Privatization of state-owned assets appealed to the nomenklatura because they possessed the knowledge and personal connections to become wealthy in a new capitalist society. As private property owners, they would no longer be subject to the whims of political superiors, and they could bequeath assets to their children.

By 1990, popular opposition to communism was coalescing under the leadership of Boris Yeltsin (1931–2007). Gorbachev was now caught in the middle between hard-liners within the Communist Party who opposed change and Yeltsin supporters. In August of 1991, the hardliners staged a coup in an effort to reverse Gorbachev's reforms. Although the coup failed within days, the Soviet Union was now irreversibly weakened. Individual republics began declaring their independence, Gorbachev resigned, and on January 1, 1992, the Soviet Union officially ceased to exist.

STATE CAPITALISM 1992–PRESENT

Shock Therapy

Almost immediately after the dissolution of the Soviet Union, Russia embarked on a program designed by economist Yegor Gaidar (1956–2009) to complete the transition from communism to capitalism in 500 days. The program, popularly referred to as "shock therapy," called for the elimination of price controls, privatization of SOEs, an end to central planning, reduction of government subsidies, free international trade, and the convertibility of the Russian ruble into foreign currencies. The immediate impact was **hyperinflation** along with increased unemployment and falling standards of living. Raw materials could now be exported, and their prices quickly rose toward international levels, causing a chain reaction as firms at each stage of the production process attempted to raise prices to cover their higher costs. Bottlenecks developed when firms were unable to afford more expensive inputs or to raise price without losing customers. During the four years following the introduction of shock therapy, industrial output fell by nearly 60 percent, and 40 percent of the population lived in poverty. The rate of inflation in 1992 was 2,500 percent. Conditions became so dire that the average life span of Russian citizens actually declined.

With both the government and SOEs lacking cash or credit, barter often became the only method for making exchanges. Businesses sometimes traded their products to obtain raw materials and other inputs. Similarly, instead of paying wages to workers, businesses simply gave them some of the firm's products. For example, a worker in a tire factory might be paid with new tires. Workers then attempted to sell the products, often standing alongside highways with their wares on display, to obtain money for food and other necessities.

The government privatized SOEs as quickly as possible because (1) it could no longer afford to subsidize them and (2) rapid privatization would make the transition to capitalism irreversible. Initially, much of the privatization was spontaneous, as plant managers claimed ownership of their factories. However, this process amounted to little more than theft as many managers enriched themselves by selling the firm's assets. In response, the government established the State Property Management Agency to privatize SOEs in an orderly and transparent manner.

In principle, the assets of SOEs belonged equally to every citizen, so fairness seemed to dictate an equal distribution of assets. However, any viable plan to disperse state property needed the support of the still-powerful nomenklatura as well as the workers in SOEs. To gain their support, a complicated process developed in which small SOEs employing fewer than 200 people were auctioned to the highest bidder, usually the current management. For larger firms, the government had to walk a fine line between gaining support from the nomenklatura and creating an image of fairness in the public eye. The former goal was achieved by giving current managers and workers preferential access to a portion of shares of their firm at discounted prices. The public's demand for fairness was addressed by disposing of the remaining shares through a voucher system. All citizens received vouchers that could be sold for cash, put into a mutual fund that purchased stock in a variety of companies, or used to buy shares of stock in a particular enterprise through public auction.

Despite the egalitarian intent of a voucher system, the result was highly concentrated ownership of productive assets. Many citizens did not understand the program, resulting in vouchers being sold for a few rubles or traded for a bottle of vodka. People who chose to participate in public auctions were at a distinct disadvantage because they lacked information about the actual worth of companies. Also, auctions were often manipulated in favor of politically powerful groups. After the auctions were concluded, the collective wealth of the Russian people ended up largely in the hands of the nomenklatura, the very individuals most privileged under communism. By 1994, the voucher system had privatized approximately 16,000 SOEs, or about 60 percent of all industrial assets. The most notable exceptions were utilities and firms in the energy, defense, and natural resource sectors.

At this point, the government was so desperate for money that it could not pay public employees or provide essential social services. To raise revenue, more SOEs were sold in auctions. In addition, the government borrowed money from banks using the assets of remaining SOEs as collateral. The auctions resulted in SOEs being purchased at bargain-basement prices by the only groups with significant amounts of money—the former nomenklatura, organized crime syndicates, and foreign investors. When the government defaulted on many of its bank loans, banks took over the SOEs used as collateral, thereby gaining ownership at a fraction of the firms' true value and further concentrating the ownership of the nation's productive assets.

Financial-Industrial Groups

By the mid-1990s, many Russian firms were weak and unstable, making their survival doubtful. To assist large businesses, the government established financial-industrial groups (FIGs) by offering tax incentives to firms that would cooperate in forming **cartels**. The largest FIGS were centered around a major bank that served as a source of credit for firms in the organization. Some FIGs were conglomerates consisting of firms from different industries, whereas others were horizontally integrated within a particular industry. FIGs provided firms with a supportive structure within which they had access to credit and technical expertise and were subject to tighter external supervision. FIGs captured some of the benefits of central planning, but the planning was carried out on a much smaller scale by private owners rather than government bureaucrats. As in any system that replaces competition with organization, the potential danger posed by FIGs lay in their power to manipulate the government in pursuit of their private interests. The 1990s witnessed a Russian state largely under the control of private concentrations of power. The FIGs used their political power to avoid taxes, and the government, with insufficient tax revenue, could no longer enforce laws or provide basic social services.

Financial Markets

As part of the perestroika reforms of the late 1980s, the Soviet State Bank (Gosbank), which controlled financial policy within the Soviet Union, was divided into a central bank and three state banks specializing in financing agriculture, industry, and public infrastructure. The Central Bank of Russia conducts monetary policy through regulation of credit and **interest rates**, as well as licensing and regulating the approximately 2,000 commercial banks. A stock exchange opened in 1991.

Obtaining a bank loan in Russia often requires knowing a politically connected person who will vouch for the borrower's reliability. Russian banks have no deposit insurance, so some citizens have lost their savings due to bank failures. In the period following the collapse of communism, the combination of high inflation and **depreciation** of the ruble caused savings held in rubles to lose most of their value. Consequently, many Russians are reluctant to put their money in banks. Wealthy Russians often deposit money in foreign banks both to protect its value and to avoid taxes.

A global financial crisis spread to Russian financial markets in 1998. Foreign investors withdrew large amounts of money, the government defaulted on $40 billion worth of bonds, and the ruble lost 60 percent of its value. The devalued ruble provided a stimulus to the economy as Russian exports became more competitive in international markets and Russian citizens purchased more domestic goods in place of expensive imports. Increased sales of Russian goods, in turn, created more tax revenue, enabling the government to restore some essential social services.

Predatory State

During the 1990s, the Russian state became so weak and underfunded that it was forced to strike deals with the new private owners of large firms in major industries—particularly oil, natural gas, and precious metals—to gain financial and political support. The owners (often called "oligarchs") were rewarded with political connections leading to government contracts and other benefits. This system, sometimes called "crony capitalism," resulted in alliances between the state and private interest groups. Businesses captured the power of the state to gain advantages in the market, and the state granted favors in exchange for revenue to fulfill its functions. For example, the government might give a subsidy to a firm in exchange for an agreement to fund a health clinic or sponsor a sports team.

Linkages between the oligarchs and organized crime syndicates date back to the operation of black markets in the Soviet Union. After the collapse of communism, crime syndicates often established businesses to serve as covers for their illegal operations, and some oligarchs did not hesitate to use syndicates to carry out murders, kidnappings, bribery, and extortion to gain greater control over productive assets.

When Vladimir Putin became president in 2000, he was determined to confront the oligarchs and break the dependency of the state on private interest groups. He struck an agreement with prominent industrialists—the state would not interfere with their businesses if they would agree to end efforts to control government. To increase the independence of the state, Putin sought to enlarge the tax base. Many firms and wealthy citizens were refusing to pay taxes because they doubted that the state had sufficient power to enforce compliance with tax laws. To combat tax evasion, the government assembled teams of heavily armed commando squads to break into the businesses and homes of tax delinquents and confiscate cash or property. To set an example for oligarchs who challenged state authority, the government took over the largest oil company in the nation and imprisoned its owner, Mikhail Khodorkovsky, for ten years. Putin also extended government's power over businesses by appointing members of his administration to the boards of directors of major Russian companies.

Under Putin, the Russian economy initially experienced a minor boom. Inflation, which had been a major problem during the 1990s, was finally subdued, and in the decade from 1999 to 2008, real growth of the GDP averaged 6.7 percent. The global financial crisis of 2008 caused a **recession** in Russia, but since 2010, the economy has been growing at about 1 to 2 percent annually. However, these statistics mask more fundamental problems facing Russia. The economy has been buoyed by exports of oil, natural gas, and precious metals, but in the future, these resources will be gradually depleted. In addition, global efforts to reduce carbon emissions from burning fossil fuels may reduce the demand for Russia's natural resources and thereby threaten the future viability of its economy.

Putin's efforts to strengthen the power of government pose a dilemma. The more powerful the state becomes, the greater the incentives for private interest groups to engage in **rent seeking** by influencing state policy. With government desperate for revenue to build infrastructure and provide social services, the offers of bribes and other forms of influence-buying are nearly irresistible. But the result is government policy that serves the narrow interests of the rent seekers rather than promoting overall economic development. In attempting to build a **developmental state**, Putin runs the risk of perpetuating a **predatory state** in which both government officials and business leaders use the power of the state for personal enrichment.

A predatory state can be avoided either by reducing the power of the state so that rent seekers have little incentive to seek favors or by insulating the state from public input. Putin is clearly pursuing the second alternative, but in his quest to increase state autonomy, he is also suppressing freedom of the press and closing off access to government by civic associations and other political parties. In short, Putin is weakening democracy in order to protect the state's independence and ability to pursue what he believes to be the public interest.

Putin's strategy may be acceptable to the Russian people who have historically demonstrated a preference for strong leaders instead of the cumbersome process of democracy. However, the appeal of a strong state insulated from popular input is based on a view of government as a "benevolent dictator," acting as a unified body to advance the public interest. But democratic governments include representatives of different interest groups who, whether accepting bribes or not, have contradictory agendas for advancing the nation. The attempt to shield government from outside influence removes the disciplining effect of public opinion, thereby allowing politicians to remain unyielding in their policy proposals. Factional disputes within the government may result in political gridlock and an inability to pursue any clear-cut agenda.

Social Policy

Discontent runs rampant in Russia today. Standards of living for many citizens are below the levels achieved under communism, and lack of government funds has led to reductions in social benefits. In 1993, unemployment benefits were established, but they provided only 15 percent of the average wage. Privatization of SOEs has resulted in massive layoffs, but the government offers little in the way of retraining or assistance with job searches. At times since 1991, the government has been so underfunded that physicians, teachers, and soldiers remained unpaid, and retirees did not receive their pensions. The social safety net in Russia is so meager that poverty, malnutrition, and inadequate healthcare contribute to an average life expectancy in Russia that is ten years shorter than in the United States. Poor nutrition, along with alcoholism and stress, is steadily eroding the quality of the Russian labor force. The birth rate has dropped dramatically as families either cannot afford or choose not to rear children under these conditions. The combination of a falling birth rate, rising death rate, and emigration from Russia has reduced the total population by nearly five million people since 1991.

Culture

Russia's difficulty in finding the right balance between state and market is partially attributable to a culture that remains deeply enmeshed in the past. Markets can be created by establishing property rights, and states can be changed by enacting different laws and policies, but culture is extremely resistant to change from above. The attempt to use "shock therapy" to achieve a quick transition from communism to capitalism suffered from the same fallacy that undermined the early attempts at communism in 1918—a mistaken notion that a new economic system can be created simply by changing control over property. Economic systems are deeply embedded in cultural institutions that shape behavior and beliefs, and those institutions resist rapid change. Several cultural legacies of tsarism and communism continue to pose obstacles for the development of capitalism in Russia.

Anticapitalist Attitudes

The Russian people harbor deep suspicion of the new capitalists. Any Russian older than age forty grew up under communism and was taught that profit comes from exploitation of labor, that entrepreneurs are "sharks" preying on their fellow citizens, and that competition and self-interest are antisocial. These negative views of business may have been reinforced since the collapse of communism as many oligarchs and criminal syndicates used their power to enrich themselves through both legal and illegal means. Today, only 7 percent of Russians engage in entrepreneurial activity. Most university graduates pursue employment in government or as managers in large corporations.

Weak Civil Society

Ironically, communism destroyed community in Russia. Stalin feared that any organized group could potentially challenge the power of the state, so he eliminated all civic organizations and interest groups not directly tied to the Communist Party. For example, churches in Moscow were razed and replaced with subway stations. Communism reduced Soviet society to a mass of individuals with few social ties outside families other than their status as "comrades" unified under the rule of the state. Due to secret police surveillance, the pervasive presence of informants, and wiretapping, citizens could trust nobody beyond their families and perhaps a small circle of close friends. Because many Russians regarded the authority of the state as illegitimate, they felt justified in circumventing the law to meet their needs. Even today, cheating, bribery, extortion, and engaging in the black market are widely accepted practices despite threats of severe punishment.

Communism eroded the **social capital** and **cultural capital** that function as prerequisites for a healthy economic system. The legacy of that destruction is a widespread lack of trust, honesty, and respect for the law. In both government and the private sector, many individuals will use any means necessary to survive and gain a measure of security. When opportunistic behavior becomes so widespread, a collective action problem arises. Any individual who refrains from engaging in corruption, extortion, or cheating is at a disadvantage, so nobody has an incentive to change current practices. Successful entrepreneurs often face bogus accusations from competitors who file official complaints to put them out of business. The police may offer to drop charges in exchange for a bribe, but if the case goes to court, the entrepreneur's business is shut down until a court ruling is made.

Like the communist revolution of 1917, the transition from communism to capitalism was implemented from the top down, so average citizens played no role and had no effective voice in the process. As a result, most Russian citizens still view themselves as powerless to change their system. Having learned to endure oppression under communism, Russians have little experience with civic engagement and focus instead on surviving in a dysfunctional economic system.

Gender Roles

Communist ideology called for gender equality as both men and women were required to work. However, gender roles in the home remained very traditional. Russian women typically worked full time and were also responsible for homemaking and childrearing. The end of communism placed additional burdens on women and families due to reductions in social programs such as day-care centers and to the real possibility of being unemployed. Women are responding to this situation by delaying marriage; having fewer children; and, in some cases, leaving the country.

Women, whose educational attainment is equal to that of men, dominate the professions of law, medicine, and teaching. However, lawyers, physicians, and teachers in Russia are often paid less than many factory workers. The high-paid jobs in government and industry continue to be male-dominated. By keeping women in a subordinate status, Russia is failing to fully utilize its **human capital**.

The former Soviet republic of Ukraine lies immediately to the east of Russia. The "breadbasket" of the Soviet Union because of its extensive fertile land, it also has significant manufacturing. Russia has tried to keep the country within its sphere of influence, but after Ukrainian voters chose a president who favored joining the European Union (EU), Russia reacted with threats of invasion and actually annexed a portion of southeastern Ukraine known as Crimea in 2014.

The United States and the EU imposed restrictions on trade to punish this aggression, contributing to a virtual halt in economic growth in Russia.

ADDITIONAL READING

Alexeev Michael, and Shlomo Weber, eds. *The Oxford Handbook of the Russian Economy.* 2013.

Barnes, Andrew. *Owning Russia. The Struggle over Factories, Farms, and Power.* Ithaca, NY: Cornell University Press, 2006.

Bodin, Per-Arne, Stefan Hedlund, and Elena Namli, eds. *Power and Legitimacy: Challenges from Russia.* New York: Routledge, 2013.

Cohen, Stephen F. *Soviet Fates and Lost Alternatives.* New York: Columbia University Press, 2009.

Fish, M. Steven. *Democracy Derailed in Russia: The Failure of Open Politics.* Cambridge: Cambridge University Press, 2005.

Fitzpatrick, Sheila. *The Russian Revolution*, 3rd ed. New York: Oxford University Press, 2008.

Goldman, Marshall. *Petrostate: Putin, Power, and the New Russia.* Oxford: Oxford University Press, 2008.

Hanson, Philip. *The Rise and Fall of the Soviet Economy: An Economic History of the USSR 1945–1991.* London: Longman, 2003.

Harrison, Lawrence, and Evgeny Yasin. *Culture Matters in Russia—and Everywhere: Backdrop for the Russian-Ukraine Conflict.* Lanham, MD: Lexington Books, 2015.

Hedlund, Stefan. *Russian Path Dependence: A People with a Troubled History.* New York: Routledge, 2005.

Kotz, David and Fred Weir. *Revolution from Above: The Demise of the Soviet System.* New York: Routledge, 1997.

Robinson, Neil, ed. *The Political Economy of Russia.* Lanham, MD: Rowman & Littlefield, 2013.

Rosefielde, Steven, and Stefan Hedlund. *Russia since 1980.* New York: Cambridge University Press, 2009.

Sakwa, Richard. *Russian Politics and Society.* London: Routledge, 2008.

Taylor, Brian D. *State Building in Putin's Russia: Policing and Coercion after Communism.* Cambridge: Cambridge University Press, 2011.

Volkov, Vadim. *Violent Entrepreneurs: The Use of Force in the Making of Russian Capitalism.* Ithaca, NY: Cornell University Press, 2002.

Chapter 12

THE CHINESE ECONOMIC SYSTEM

"Americans are just beginning to catch up to the significance
of what's been happening in China, and I don't believe they've
caught up yet."

JEFFREY A. BADER, Former Senior Director
for Asian affairs, U.S. National Security Council.

C hina currently has the most dynamic economic system in the world, recording average annual growth rates of around 10 percent since the government began moving away from communism in 1979. At that rate of growth, **gross domestic product** (GDP) has doubled every seven years, enabling 500 million people to escape poverty in the past thirty years. However, standards of living for most Chinese remain quite low, with **per capita GDP** of about $12,000, just slightly higher than in Egypt or Peru.

In 2010, China surpassed Japan to become the second largest economy in the world and, if current growth rates continue, will surpass the United States in 2029. With one-fifth of the world's population (1.4 billion people), many of whom are living in rural areas and only marginally engaged in the modern economy, China's potential for additional growth is staggering. Yet serious challenges loom over the economy, and China's response will shape the future of the global economy.

PRE-COMMUNIST CHINA 1644–1948

The Chinese Empire was founded in 221 BCE and remained stable and relatively prosperous under seventeen different dynasties for more than 1,500 years. Government was highly centralized, with a competent bureaucracy administering public affairs. By the tenth century, when most of Europe was just emerging from the Dark Ages, China was the most advanced civilization on earth. Its dominance continued until about 1400, as the government used tax **revenue** to build **infrastructure** such as large-scale irrigation systems and roads. Evidence of China's technological superiority at the time includes the inventions of porcelain, gunpowder, the compass, casting of iron, woodblock printing, machines to spin thread, and paper currency.

In 1644, tribes from the northern province of Manchuria founded the Qing Dynasty. From that point onward, the Chinese economy deteriorated. At the same time, mercantilism was paving the way for the emergence of capitalism in the West. This simultaneous development in Europe and stagnation in China has been labeled "The Great Divergence."

Weaknesses of the Chinese Empire

What aspects of the Chinese Empire led to its downfall? Some of the usual explanations for the collapse of empires do not apply to China. Imperial overreach was not a factor. After early commercial forays into Southeast Asia, China largely withdrew from contact with other nations. Also, the rulers of the Chinese Empire did not oppress citizens or squander the economy's surplus on royal extravagance. Instead, government affairs were conducted by highly educated civil servants (mandarins) who attained their positions through competitive examinations and were devoted to maintaining peace, prosperity, and stability throughout the country. Although no clear consensus exists among historians on the causes of China's stagnation after the seventeenth century, several factors are relevant.

Chinese Culture

The Chinese Empire sought to supplement state power by creating a sense of national community among citizens. This strategy entailed strict adherence to ethical principles based on the teachings of Confucius (551–479 BCE). By emphasizing social obligations and duty to superiors, Confucianism was invaluable in creating stability and order, but the suppression of self-interest discouraged entrepreneurship, risk-taking, and accumulation of wealth. Merchants in China had low social status because they were perceived as self-interested and unwilling to work cooperatively with others as part of a community.

Political Unity

Unlike Europe in the Middle Ages, where rival states competed for military supremacy, China was a unified empire. With the exception of the Mongol invasion and subsequent rule of Kublai Khan (1215–1294), China faced no external threats. This lack of competition between states meant that Chinese rulers faced no pressure to develop more efficient economic and political institutions. A second problem created by political unity was the absence of an independent aristocracy to challenge and limit the power of the state.

Political Suppression of Commerce

Unlike mercantilist Europe, the Chinese Empire derived its tax revenue from agricultural production. With no wars to fight, the state had little interest in promoting commerce to gain more tax revenue. Market activity was tightly regulated, and the state allocated credit based on personal connections to government. By keeping commercial activity in the hands of loyal supporters, the rulers sought to prevent the accumulation of large fortunes that could potentially threaten the power of the state. The suppression of commerce was aided by the fact that many large-scale investment projects were **public goods** that no private entrepreneur could undertake. For example, Chinese agriculture depended on extensive irrigation systems which were constructed and maintained under the supervision of the government.

Isolationism

The Chinese economy also failed to thrive due to the decision by rulers to turn inward and withdraw from engagement with other countries. This isolationism resulted in both limited access to resources and reduced demand for Chinese goods that might have been exported. While European nations were engaged in exploration and colonization to open markets around the world, China was content to remain economically independent.

Population Growth

Much of China is arid and mountainous. After 1644, rapid population growth combined with a shortage of arable land and a stagnant economy caused living standards to steadily deteriorate. Surplus labor kept wages very low, which reduced the incentive to develop labor-saving technology and suppressed demand for consumer products.

Loss of Human Capital

Government suppression of business activity by the Qing Dynasty caused an outflow of entrepreneurial talent as Chinese business people spread out over Southeast Asia in search of better economic opportunities. The effects of this diaspora are still evident today as ethnic Chinese dominate commerce in many Southeast Asian countries. The suppression of business also impeded the formation of **human capital**. With a stagnant economy, jobs in government civil service offered one of the few pathways to success. Because government jobs required that candidates take competitive examinations testing their knowledge of Confucianism, intelligent and ambitious individuals were more likely to study Confucianism than to pursue a career in science or business. In fact, China largely missed out on the scientific revolution of the seventeenth and eighteenth centuries. Without a systematic method for conducting scientific experiments, the development of technology in China quickly fell behind European advances.

The Demise of the Chinese Empire

By the nineteenth century, the Chinese Empire was disintegrating for both internal and external reasons. Internally, increasing economic hardship created social unrest as manifested in religious uprisings, revolts against the government, and the formation of secret societies. The Taiping Rebellion, a civil war lasting from 1850 to 1864, resulted in twenty million deaths. Led by Hong Xiuquan (1814–1864), who claimed to be the younger brother of Jesus, the rebels gained control over half the nation and established their own capital city at Nanjing. To combat the rebellion, the Emperor encouraged provincial officials to organize their own armies, but these armies subsequently formed the power base for regional war-lords who challenged the authority of the Qing dynasty.

Externally, China was increasingly the target of Western **imperialism**. British traders wanted Chinese tea and silk, but the Chinese had no interest in ex-changing their goods for British textiles because they were capable of manufacturing their own fabrics. Needing a commodity that could be exchanged for tea and silk, the British began shipping opium from India into China. When the Chinese government objected and destroyed a large cache of opium in Canton, the British launched a military attack. In the Opium War of 1840–42, The British seized Hong Kong and forced the Chinese government to pay $27 million for the destroyed opium. In 1858, the British and the French again used military action to force China to accept opium in exchange for Chinese goods. Foreign troops occupied Peking, destroyed the royal palace, and extracted repa-ration payments to cover the cost of war. By the end of the nineteenth century, 10 percent of the Chinese population was addicted to opium.

China suffered further humiliation in a war with Japan in 1895 that resulted in the loss of the island of Formosa (now Taiwan). Reacting to continuing defeats by foreign imperialists, a group called the Boxers formed to defend Chinese cul-ture from foreign influences. The 1900 Boxer Rebellion resulted in the burning of foreign churches and embassies and the murder of missionaries and diplomats. Troops from the United States, Britain, Germany, France, and Japan entered China to suppress the rebellion and simultaneously laid claim to various Chinese islands and coastal enclaves to serve as entry points into the Chinese market.

The inability of the Chinese Empire to protect itself from foreign incursions led to increasing discontent, particularly among youth. In 1894, a medical stu-dent named Sun Yat-sen (1866–1925) founded a secret society with the intent of overthrowing the Qing dynasty. His efforts culminated in a successful revolu-tion in 1911 and the establishment of the Republic of China with its capital in Peking. The new government, however, was unable to secure effective control over the county and became the puppet of regional warlords determined to resist centralized political authority. Sun Yat-sen responded by founding the National-ist Party (Guomindang), which established a rival government in Canton. A civil war between the two opposing governments engulfed the nation for the next fifteen years.

The Chinese Communist Party (CCP) was founded in 1921, and the Soviet Union brought young leaders, including Mao Zedong (1893–1976), to Moscow for education and training. Mao believed that only communism could free China from domination by warlords and foreign imperialists. Sun Yat-sen also turned to the Soviet Union for support, and he was instructed to cooperate with the Communists in fighting the warlord-dominated government in Peking.

Sun Yat-sen died in 1925, but his successor, Chiang Kai-shek (1887–1975) initially agreed to work together with the Communists. However, by 1927, the Nationalists felt sufficiently confident in their control of government to turn against their allies. The Nationalists rounded up thousands of Communists for mass executions, forcing Mao and 90,000 of his followers to flee the cities. They were pursued by the Nationalists over a two-year period (1934–35) for 6,000 miles from southeast China to remote mountains in the northwest, where the Communists established an impregnable base of operations. This "Long March" was one of the epic events in Chinese history.

Taking advantage of China's internal turmoil, Japan invaded and took possession of the northeastern province of Manchuria in 1931. A long and brutal struggle between the Japanese and the Chinese ensued over the next fourteen years as the Japanese conquered most of northern and eastern China. The Chinese death toll from that war is estimated at more than twenty million people. In 1936, with the nation's independence at risk, Communists and Nationalists set aside their differences and united to fight the Japanese. However, as soon as World War II ended in 1945, the truce was broken, and civil war resumed in China. With their promise to redistribute land to peasants, the Communists rapidly gained support in rural areas. They captured cities by encircling them and cutting off food supplies. In 1949, the Communists won the civil war, and the Nationalists fled to the island of Formosa (now Taiwan), which had been reclaimed from Japan.

CHINESE COMMUNISM 1949–1978

The Communists inherited an economic system devastated by a century of civil wars, foreign invasions, and imperialism. Their initial policies were aimed at stopping inflation, confiscating the land of the warlords, and distributing land to the peasants who cultivated it. By 1952, eleven million acres of land had been distributed to 300 million peasants. The government also confiscated foreign-owned assets, but Chinese citizens were permitted to own businesses.

In 1953, China initiated its first five-year plan for the economy modeled after planning in the Soviet Union. The plan called for raising agricultural productivity and using the agricultural surplus to feed industrial workers and to export in order to gain **financial capital** for industry. The single-family farms established through land redistribution were too small to be efficient, so the government ordered the formation of mutual aid teams consisting of small groups of five to fifteen households sharing land, draft animals, and tools to work collectively.

A year later, the mutual aid teams evolved into agricultural cooperatives consisting of twenty to forty households with collective ownership of all capital. The purpose of forming larger production units was to increase productivity through cooperation, **economies of scale**, and the ability of the CCP to monitor work effort. The collective farms were required to pay taxes and to sell their goods to the government at low prices. The government sold the food at higher prices, using the tax revenue and profit to fund expansion of industry.

The first five-year plan also entailed the nationalization of most industry and the use of central planning to coordinate economic activity. The Soviet Union offered loans and sent more than 15,000 engineers and technicians to advise the Chinese in constructing and operating factories and power plants.

The Great Leap Forward

The Chinese economy remained sluggish, and by 1958, Mao became disillusioned with the Soviet model of development. Whereas the Soviets had focused on rapid development of heavy industry and large-scale manufacturing, China's major resource was labor. The second five-year plan, called the Great Leap Forward, continued to focus on raising agricultural productivity but dispersed industrial production by establishing small factories scattered throughout the countryside. This strategy sacrificed economies of scale to conserve on scarce capital and rely more heavily on China's plentiful labor.

To improve agricultural productivity, the government abolished privately owned farms, which, along with collective farms, were merged into 25,000 large communes—each with an average of about 5,000 households. The communes provided communal kitchens and free healthcare, senior citizen centers, schools, and nurseries so that working adults could devote full time to production. To decentralize industry and make it more labor-intensive, "backyard factories" were built on the communes to enable local production of steel, chemical fertilizer, cement, hydroelectric power, and tools. The effort to conserve capital was also evident in the construction of infrastructure such as roads, canals, and dams. Hundreds, and sometimes thousands, of people were gathered at the construction site with little more than picks, shovels, and baskets to move massive amounts of earth.

The labor-intensive strategy underlying the Great Leap Forward was based on more than just conserving scarce capital. Mao believed that the Chinese people had the potential to transform the country if they were fully mobilized and engaged in the effort. To this end, he sought to develop an entirely new culture based on selfless dedication to building a new society. Old cultural traditions such as festivals, religious rituals, and elaborate funerals and weddings were banned. Instead, the Chinese people were required to participate in political group discussions designed to instill a strong community spirit and willingness to sacrifice for the good of the nation.

Both subtle and overt coercion were used to "raise the consciousness" of the peasants. Public address systems carried a steady stream of Maoist ideology, glorifying communism and condemning bourgeois self-interest. Communist cadres used physical violence to punish anyone deemed to be counterrevolutionary. Party officials justified this use of force, insisting that only by working together for the common good could China escape its centuries-long poverty and oppression.

By 1960, the Great Leap Forward was clearly failing—mass starvation spread across the country. Natural disasters played a role as a combination of droughts, floods, locust infestations, and rats wreaked havoc on crops. However, Mao's policies were largely responsible for the famine. The relocation of peasants from agriculture to industry caused a drop in farm output. New, untested planting methods proved to be ineffective. In addition, the government established mandatory quotas for agricultural output, and farmers were allowed to keep only whatever surplus remained after they met the quota. The combination of misguided government policies and natural disasters eliminated the surplus, and at least twenty million people died from hunger as agricultural output fell by 30 percent between 1958 and 1960.

Although manufacturing output increased, the results were unsatisfactory. The quality of products coming from the small, communal factories was poor, and, without economies of scale, production methods remained highly inefficient. Also, China lacked sufficient transportation **infrastructure** to move resources and products quickly around the country, so shortages of parts and materials frequently halted production. Representatives from the Soviet Union were so dismayed by Mao's policies that they withdrew their advisors and technicians who, to compound the problem, took the blueprints and operating manuals for many of the power plants and factories with them. The Great Leap Forward was so disastrous that Mao was removed from his position as head of state. After 1961, some private ownership in agriculture was restored, communes became smaller, and farmers were allowed to sell their surplus crops in local markets.

The Great Proletarian Cultural Revolution

Mao was now in a power struggle for control of the country. In 1966, he initiated the Great Proletarian Cultural Revolution to energize the masses by leveling social distinctions and attacking anyone in a privileged social position. These elites included not only his rivals in the Communist Party, but also professors, lawyers, scientists, bureaucrats, writers, artists, and anyone who failed to openly support Mao's policies. Mao accused his opponents of being "capitalist roaders" trying to steer China toward capitalism's reliance on self-interest and markets.

Calling for permanent revolution, Mao ordered the relocation of many urban professionals to rural communes where they performed manual labor alongside the peasants. Factory managers were required to engage in menial tasks such as sweeping the shop floor. The teenage Red Guards harassed and humiliated professionals, intellectuals, and academics suspected of being bourgeois or counterrevolutionary. All high school graduates went directly to a factory or commune where their fellow workers decided who would go on to college based on job performance and "ideological correctness." Once in a university, students were required to combine periods of manual labor with their studies. A collection of Mao's ideas known as "The Little Red Book" became the source of all political wisdom.

Culture

In addition to attempting to eliminate class distinctions, Mao was determined to revolutionize China's culture, which was dominated by ancient rituals and traditions. He sought to erase past culture by ordering the destruction of historical artifacts, books, paintings, and religious sites. Even Confucianism was attacked for its emphasis on duty to the family rather than the state and its failure to promote economic development. Citizens were required to engage in sessions of "criticism and self-criticism" in which they pointed out the bourgeois tendencies of neighbors and coworkers and then confessed their own shortcomings.

The Demise of Chinese Communism

The Cultural Revolution was disastrous for the Chinese economy. Output fell 18 percent in 1967, and was no higher in 1969 than it had been in 1966. Mao's power within the Communist Party was again slipping as the failure of the Cultural Revolution emboldened rival factions to question his leadership. When Mao died in 1976, a power struggle ensued over the future course of the country. On one side was the Gang of Four, which included Mao's wife. They wanted to continue the emphasis on leveling class distinctions, suppressing bourgeois tendencies, and isolating China from the rest of the world. An opposing group, derisively called the "capitalist roaders," favored more pragmatic reforms relying on material incentives to reward productivity, greater decentralization of decision-making, and opening China to international trade. The capitalist roaders prevailed, and beginning in 1979 under the leadership of Deng Xiaoping (1904–1997), a series of major policy changes fundamentally reshaped the Chinese economic system and gradually introduced capitalism.

STATE CAPITALISM 1979–PRESENT

Transition from Communism to Capitalism

China and Russia both made the transition from communism to state capitalism, yet China now has the most dynamic economic system in the world while Russia has yet to thrive. Several factors have contributed to these diverging paths.

Pretransition Conditions

Differences in the economic systems of the Russia and China prior to the abandonment of communism may explain their contrasting achievements since the transition.

First, in the Soviet Union, political control was loosened before privatization of property began, so the government felt the need to privatize swiftly before popular discontent led to social disorder or a resurgence of support for communism. In contrast, the CCP maintained tight political control, enabling it to conduct gradual experiments with markets and privatization.

Second, China was less industrialized than the Soviet Union. Because of China's relatively primitive communication and transportation systems, its central planning never matched the Soviet Union in detail or scope. As a result, the transition to local control and decentralized decision-making was easier in China. Despite Mao Zedong's image as a communist hard-liner, his repeated efforts to foster local initiative and autonomy left a legacy of entrepreneurial energy that is contributing to the dynamism of China today.

Third, the Soviet Union's history of oppression by tsars, aristocrats, and then communist elites created widespread cynicism and antipathy toward government. In contrast, the Chinese Empire, whatever its failings in promoting economic development, was benevolent in its intentions, and the large majority of Chinese citizens remained loyal to the government even through the worst phases of communism. Mao remained highly popular until his death because the general populace viewed him as genuinely devoted to lifting China out of poverty and ending domination by foreigners. Public support allowed the government to experiment gradually with reforms designed to move toward capitalism.

Access to Financial Capital

Whereas Russia had virtually no economic ties with noncommunist nations when it began the transition to capitalism, China quickly established links with Western financial markets through the British colony of Hong Kong. Foreign investors preferred China's political stability to the often-chaotic transformation in Russia. Moreover, many of the most prominent business people throughout Southeast Asia were of Chinese descent and therefore eager to transmit technical expertise and investment funds back into China. Between 1982 and 1994, 70 percent of foreign investment in China came from ethnic Chinese outside the country.

Pace of Change

Unlike the shock therapy applied in Russia, the Chinese relied on gradual trial-and-error to guide their path toward a new economic system. The resulting differences are striking. Whereas Russia experienced sharp increases in unemployment and inflation, declining output, and general social distress, China's path to reform yielded annual growth rates of around 10 percent. A gradual transition allowed new economic institutions to develop, evolve, and gain popular support. Mistakes could be recognized before they threatened the stability of the entire system. China's gradual transition away from communism gave citizens a relatively stable economy in which to learn and adapt to the attitudes and skills required for success in the market. By contrast, the shock therapy applied in Russia assumed that citizens would immediately become effective entrepreneurs despite an economic climate of rising unemployment, falling standards of living, failing firms, and widespread crime and corruption.

Goals

Mikhail Gorbachev's failure to steer the Soviet Union toward a viable socialism led reformers in Russia to embrace the vision of a pure free-market system. Government officials consulted with Western free-market economists, who advised the immediate privatization of all property and minimal government intervention. These economists failed to consider the compatibility between free markets and Russia's political and social institutions. The Chinese government, on the other hand, did not fully embrace free markets and remained committed to fashioning economic institutions that were compatible with Chinese culture. Chinese reformers have been willing to try various forms of ownership and markets without being committed to either capitalism or socialism. In the words of Deng Xiaoping, "Black cat, white cat, what does it matter what color the cat is as long as it catches mice."

Strong State

Russia's focus on dismantling state power allowed organized crime syndicates and ruthless oligarchs to steal much of the newly privatized property and to continue to undermine the Russian economy. In contrast, the CCP has maintained firm political control over the country to ensure a stable and orderly transition away from communism.

Agricultural Reforms

China's transition to state capitalism began with reforms in agriculture. In 1979, a "household responsibility system" reduced the size of communal farms and provided incentives for individual households to increase productivity. Although land remained under state ownership, households leased plots for a period of fifteen years, ensuring that any gains in productivity would accrue to the producers. By the mid-1980s, 93 percent of China's farmland was cultivated by individual households who, in return for use of machinery and equipment, were obligated to sell 40 to 50 percent of their produce to the state at preset prices. Any excess could be sold in the market or to the state at a higher price.

In 1988, the contract period for leasing land was increased to thirty years, and government took on a larger role in providing agricultural infrastructure such as irrigation and transportation systems. With each passing year, the percentage of agricultural output sold at market prices has increased until it now stands at more than 80 percent.

Agricultural land is still owned by the state, but farmers have the right to sell their leases and to use the value of their land as collateral in obtaining bank loans. By allowing the sale of land leases, the government hopes that market forces will lead to farms of the most efficient size.

Township and Village Enterprises

During the early 1980s, the CCP began decentralizing political authority by giving local officials greater discretion in establishing policy. This local autonomy led to many experiments aimed at improving the productivity of the backyard factories that had been established in rural areas during the Great Leap Forward. Although formal ownership of these small manufacturing enterprises remained in the hands of local governments, private managers were given authority to decide what to produce, what resources and technology to use, and whom to hire and fire. Any profits remained in the local community and were used either for reinvestment or to provide public goods such as schools and health clinics. Other than preferential access to credit, these township and village enterprises (TVEs) received no government subsidies or bailouts, so if they failed to produce goods that consumers wanted, they faced the real prospect of bankruptcy.

By 1985, twelve million TVEs were the major source of new jobs and growth in China. TVEs served as incubators for entrepreneurs who subsequently started their own private businesses. Beginning in 1995, TVEs began to fail at a rapid rate, with 30 percent of them declaring bankruptcy within a two-year period. There were several reasons for this decline. Many managers found better opportunities for profit by starting their own private firms. In addition, by this time, the government was convinced that small businesses were more efficient under private ownership than public ownership and therefore made "credible commitments" to entrepreneurs that that their private property rights would not be violated. Finally, entrepreneurs were motivated to start their own businesses because they could keep all the profits rather than sharing them with the local government. Despite the rapid decline of TVEs, they served as an effective institution for facilitating the transition from collective ownership to private ownership.

Privatization

Private businesses were first permitted in 1978—but only for firms with fewer than eight employees. Deng Xiaoping signaled government approval of private ownership by saying "to get rich is glorious." Since then, the number of private firms has grown steadily, with the private sector surpassing the state sector in the mid-1990s and now accounting for nearly 70 percent of GDP. Most private businesses in China are retail stores and restaurants, but large manufacturing firms as well as joint ventures with foreign companies are also prevalent. They operate very much like private firms in the West, hiring and firing workers based on productivity, paying wages no higher than necessary to attract qualified workers, and seeking to maximize productivity and profit. In 1993, new laws regarding corporate governance and shareholder rights were patterned closely after US laws.

Sweeping generalizations about the relation between government and private businesses are difficult for two reasons. First, decentralization of political authority has led to different reforms in different regions. Local and provincial governments experiment with various forms of regulation, taxation, and provision of infrastructure. In general, however, a high degree of cooperation exists between the public and private sectors because both government and businesses recognize their mutual interest in economic growth. Rapid growth provides businesses with more profit and government with more tax revenue. Second, negotiations between business people and local government officials involve both formal rules and informal procedures. Property rights in China are best described as "fuzzy," and the rule of law is frequently open to exceptions. This reliance on personal negotiations has led to charges of "crony capitalism" as one business might be awarded a government contract or a low-interest loan after conversations with government officials. However, the Chinese have a very different perspective on the role of negotiations. They believe that face-to-face relations and getting to know people contribute to successful business relations by creating opportunities to assess the other person's character and to establish trust.

State-Owned Enterprises

Despite extensive privatization, China continues to maintain about 130 massive businesses owned by the state. These state-owned enterprises (SOEs) are found primarily in industries with extensive economies of scale, which might lead to natural monopolies even in a purely market economy (e.g., transportation, telecommunications, steel, ship-building, aerospace, nuclear energy, mining, oil, natural gas, utilities, banking, and insurance). Beginning with reforms in 1986, the government has attempted to improve SOE productivity by issuing four-year contracts to sell specific quantities of output and to remit a fixed portion of profits to government. Any excess output can be sold in the market, and additional profit can be used for employee benefits or reinvestment. SOEs purchase their resources through the market and charge prices for their products based on supply and demand.

Although output rose dramatically after these reforms, several undesirable effects also materialized. Setting production quotas provided incentives for managers of SOEs to maximize output, but quotas also created an incentive to understate productive capacity in order to persuade central planners to set a low quota. In addition, SOEs tended to exaggerate their need for resources because more resources increased the size of the surplus that could be sold in the market.

In 1992, a new round of reforms led to the privatization or closing of thousands of SOEs. By the mid-1990s, one-third of the surviving SOEs were still operating with negative profit, leading to additional closings and privatization. Some of the SOEs have been converted to employee stock ownership programs (ESOPs) in which workers hold shares of stock in the company and receive dividends proportionate with profitability. In 2007, the remaining SOEs were listed on the stock exchange so that private investors could purchase partial ownership.

Although relatively small in number, the remaining SOEs are so large that they account for 30 percent of all business activity. The government insists that SOEs will remain a fundamental part of the economy, but as the private sector grows, the SOEs will be under increasing pressure to improve productivity. The government is adding to this pressure by increasing the portion of SOE profits remitted to government from the current level of around 12 percent to 30 percent by 2020. This additional burden will result in one of two effects. Either more SOEs will be gradually privatized as they are forced to seek infusions of private capital or they will become more efficient and government will reap much of the additional profit.

Special Economic Zones

During the initial phases of economic reforms, nationwide reforms were considered too risky, so the Chinese government established special economic zones (SEZs) along the southeastern coast. Beginning with four cities in 1978, SEZs expanded to include all of coastal China plus the capital cities of each of the provinces. Within these zones, the government enacted new policies relating to foreign trade, labor markets, stock markets, SOEs, and foreign investment. The SEZs offer extremely low taxation of profits, less regulation, subsidized utility rates, and low rents to attract foreign investment and joint ventures between Chinese and foreign companies. With memories of past imperialism, the Chinese give preferential treatment to ethnic Chinese investors living outside of China, but they are also willing to negotiate with non-Chinese businesses.

The SEZs serve both economic and political purposes. One economic rationale for geographical concentration of business activity is that providing infrastructure such as transportation and communication systems is less expensive if businesses are in close proximity. Also, positive **externalities** are generated as firms benefit from each other's ideas and innovations. Politically, SEZs provide government officials with opportunities to assess the effects of market reforms on the quality of life before opening the entire country to such changes.

The downside of SEZs is the rising social problems that typically accompany rapid urban industrialization. More than 120 million people have migrated from rural areas to the coastal cities seeking work, and as a result, traffic congestion, pollution, unemployment, crime, and homelessness are all on the rise.

Financial Reforms

In the Maoist era, nearly all banking and finance was conducted through the People's Bank of China (PBC). After extensive financial reforms, the PBC now serves simply as the central bank issuing currency, supervising other banks and conducting monetary policy. The PBC relaxed controls on interest rates in 2013 and initiated deposit insurance in 2014. Government controls on the flow of financial capital in and out of the country have also been loosened. Four large state banks oversee the allocation of credit to SOEs, with each bank specializing in loans for construction, agriculture, foreign trade, and industry and commerce. These state banks collectively hold more than 80 percent of all bank assets. In addition, China has commercial banks that lend to private enterprises, state development banks for fast-growing regions, and local credit cooperatives.

The rationale for decentralizing the banking system was to introduce competitive market forces to create greater efficiency in the allocation of credit. However, the dominant state banks continue to base their lending on politically determined priorities rather than the credit worthiness of borrowers. For example, money may be lent to a failing SOE while profitable private firms have difficulty obtaining credit. Stock exchanges opened in 1990 in the cities of Shanghai and Shenzhen. Both Chinese citizens and foreigners may buy and sell stocks in Chinese companies, including state-owned enterprises (SOEs). However, only a portion of SOE shares are available for public sale so that the government maintains controlling interest. Selling shares of stock is simply a way for SOEs to raise additional financial capital.

Figure 12.1 The Shanghai skyline provides vivid illustration of modernization and growth in China. (© Shutterstock/smallhorse)

Trade Policy

Like most countries late to industrialize, China has used **tariffs** and **quotas** to protect itself against the perceived threat of imports from more mature industries in other nations. However, because their economy is centered around exports, the Chinese need open access to the markets of developed nations. This desire to export extensively while limiting imports has created considerable animosity in the West, where China is widely viewed as capturing market share with low prices based on cheap labor and lax environmental regulations. Beginning in the early 1990s, China responded to international pressure by reducing trade barriers and encouraging Western corporations to produce in China. By 2001, reductions in trade barriers were sufficient for China to gain admission to the World Trade Organization.

To offset the loss of its protective trade barriers, the Chinese government kept export prices artificially low by intentionally maintaining an undervalued currency. This was accomplished through government purchases of foreign currencies and financial assets. In 1994, China agreed to maintain a constant exchange rate between its currency, the yuan (or renminbi), and the US dollar, but this action simply prevented any further **depreciation**. Yielding to continuing pressure from the West, China announced in 2005 that the yuan would be tied to the value of a combination of different foreign currencies, and minor **appreciation** has occurred since then.

An appreciating yuan places additional pressure on Chinese industry to improve efficiency. Faced with virtually unrestricted foreign imports, Chinese industries such as agriculture, automobile manufacturing, telecommunications, and banking are particularly vulnerable. The Chinese government hopes to soften the impact of freer trade by encouraging foreign firms to enter into joint ventures with Chinese firms. The expectation is that infusions of foreign technology, capital, and marketing skills will revitalize Chinese production methods and create an internationally competitive economy.

The Chinese Communist Party

The CCP has been surprisingly flexible and pragmatic in steering the economy away from communism. The Chinese love adages, and the phrase that captures the CCP's approach to reform is "crossing the river by stepping on stones." The CCP keeps one foot on a stable stone (e.g., SOEs) while searching for the next one. The CCP may not have a clear vision of what lies on the other side of the river, but forward progress will continue as long as the results are positive.

The nature of the CCP is also changing as recruitment of new members is focused on young, highly-educated citizens. The eighty-seven million members include one-third of all private business people. Business leaders and professionals are generally supportive of the CCP, in part because they view membership as opening doors to connections and resources controlled by the Party. Unlike the Communist Party in the Soviet Union, in which promotions depended on ideological purity and agreement with one's superiors, individual advancement in the CCP is based on performance in promoting local economic growth and social stability. As a result, CCP officials have strong incentives to work cooperatively with private businesses. However, the reliance on negotiations and personal ties between government officials and private businesses creates the potential for widespread corruption. Party leaders have initiated efforts to combat corruption, resulting in numerous arrests and convictions.

Whereas Western nations tend to place high priority on the protection of individual rights, the CCP accepts individual rights only to the extent that they promote prosperity and stability. The rights of religious groups are respected as long as they do not attempt to proselytize or subvert the authority of the state. Freedom of speech and freedom of the press may be restricted if the government judges them to be destabilizing to social order. In 1978, citizens were permitted to express their ideas on posters hung on public walls in Beijing, but that freedom ended a year later when Deng Xiaoping was criticized by name. An expansion of civil liberties in the 1980s culminated in 1989 when approximately one million people gathered for six weeks in Tiananmen Square, the central public space in Beijing, to protest against government corruption and lack of full democracy. The event ended with 200,000 soldiers dispersing the demonstrators with tanks, tear gas, and gunfire, resulting in hundreds of deaths. Soon after, the government reversed its liberalization policies, claiming that strong political authority was needed to preserve social order. More recently, the government blocks material on the Internet deemed to be disruptive of Chinese society.

Social Policy

The effort to control population growth led China to impose certain restrictions on reproduction. Beginning in 1977, families were strongly discouraged from having more than two children, and in 1980, that limit was reduced to one. Couples who pledge to have only one child may receive bonuses from their employer, longer maternity leaves from work, more generous pensions, and access to higher-quality medical care and housing. Penalties for having more than one child include higher taxes, less desirable housing, and fines. Exceptions to the one-child rule are made for ethnic minority groups that might otherwise experience declining numbers.

In 1994, a new law banned marriages unless the man is at least 22 years of age and the woman at least 20. Cohabitation prior to marriage is not permitted. The government has the legal authority to enforce mandatory sterilization for persons carrying diseases or possessing genetic defects that could be passed on to children.

Efforts to control population growth have been so successful that unintended consequences have appeared. Because Chinese culture prizes male children over female children, parents whose first child would be female have sometimes opted for abortion or infanticide, hoping that they will have a male child next time. As a result, 17 percent more boys than girls are born, and millions of men are unable to find marriage partners. Another concern is the relative lack of young people to support an aging population. In recognition of these problems, the government loosened its one-child policy in 2013 so that any family in which at least one parent is an only child is permitted to have two children.

China's social programs are minimal because the SOEs traditionally provided their employees with housing, child care, healthcare, education for children, libraries, dining halls, and theaters. With the number of SOEs in sharp decline, the state has not yet filled the void in social services. A nationwide pension fund was only recently established.

A growing gap exists between those who are prospering in the new economy and those left behind. Poverty and homelessness exist, particularly in large cities where the poor are sometimes evicted from their homes and land to make way for new development. Until recently, migrants who moved to cities lost any entitlement to social services in order to discourage people from leaving rural areas unless they possessed employable job skills. However, China is growing so rapidly that labor shortages are developing. As a result, in 2013 the government extended social services to migrants in all except the largest cities.

Environmental sustainability is becoming increasingly problematic in China. With a strong central government, China has the administrative capacity to enact and enforce laws protecting the environment. However, CCP leaders have apparently chosen to give economic growth priority over environmental protection. The extent of pollution in China is evidenced by the fact that five of its cities rank in the top ten most polluted cities in the world. Air quality is often so bad that urban residents resort to wearing masks to cover their mouth and nose. Half the rivers are unfit for human use. The second largest lake in the country has been rendered unusable by algae bloom due to pollution.

Despite the obvious deterioration of the environment, political support for sustainability remains weak. Concern for the environment tends to increase after basic human needs have been met, but nearly a billion Chinese people remain in poverty. Local governments are reluctant to enforce the few existing environmental laws because they are in competition to attract new businesses by minimizing production costs. The national government is reluctant to impose any regulations that would increase production costs and therefore make Chinese goods less competitive in global markets. The CCP appears to assume that the Chinese people are willing to tolerate environmental degradation as the sacrifice required to achieve higher levels of consumption.

Culture

Over the centuries, ethnic Chinese who emigrated from China often prospered in their new locations, particularly in Southeast Asia. This raises an interesting question—does Chinese culture contribute to economic success? Clearly, Mao Zedong did not believe so; his Cultural Revolution attempted to erase the past and build a new society. However, there are several plausible links between Chinese culture and recent economic performance.

Confucianism, with its emphasis on selfless dedication to family and community, seems antithetical to entrepreneurship. However, Confucianism, along with Taoism and Buddhism, provides many Chinese citizens with a highly ethical philosophy of life. As a result, many of the **collective action problems** that arise when individuals focus exclusively on self-interest are more easily resolved in China. Individuals, businesses, and local governments are more inclined to cooperate in promoting the common good.

The Chinese word *guanxi* translates as relationships or connections between people. Due to guanxi, the Chinese are more likely to consider the needs of others when choosing a course of action. Guanxi creates trust, as manifested in the networks and communities formed between private businesses and between businesses and government officials. Networking allows small firms to gain economies of scale as they share market information and innovations in technology and product quality. Business owners trust that government officials are committed to helping them succeed and therefore cooperate with taxation and regulation. Government also trusts that businesses will act in a socially responsible manner. Of course, these trusts are sometimes violated, but the penalty can be a loss of guanxi and a resulting loss of access to information and favors.

Finally, Chinese culture may breed a complex combination of personality traits conducive to economic success. Because China was once the most advanced civilization on earth, citizens have a strong sense of national pride and even superiority. Unlike people in other developing nations, many Chinese view their current success as simply a restoration of their rightful place in the global economy. At the same time, the history of domination and exploitation by foreign powers left the Chinese with a sense of shame and inadequacy. This combined sense of superiority and inadequacy generates a powerful drive to excel.

Capitalism or Socialism?

We have labeled the Chinese economic system as "state capitalism," but it could just as easily be called "**market socialism**." Indeed, the CCP calls China a "socialist market economy." Yet with each passing year, privatization and market reforms push the nation further toward capitalism. Is a complete transition inevitable or will China remain a hybrid economic system and, more importantly, will this hybrid continue to generate the astounding growth rates of the past three decades?

CCP leaders are clearly committed to further expansion of the private sector and greater reliance on markets instead of planning. They recognize the importance of unleashing the powerful motive of self-interest, the role of competition in improving efficiency, and the importance of prosperity in maintaining social order and stability. Yet the CCP, using the metaphor of a "bird in a cage," also maintains a firm grip on the economy and on society. The market and individual rights have gained considerable latitude, but ultimately political considerations define the acceptable boundaries of individual freedom.

All capitalist economies constrain the market with politically determined rules and regulations, but the extent of state control is still greater in China than in Western nations. For example, to prevent a speculative bubble in housing prices, some cities restrict home ownership to no more than one per family. When the global financial crisis of 2008 threatened the stability of the Chinese economy, the government responded with a $586 billion stimulus package, which represented a significantly larger percentage of GDP than a similar program in the United States. Similarly, in response to a 27 percent drop in the Chinese stock market in June of 2015, the government ordered SOEs and government pension funds to buy stocks, reduced brokerage fees, and prohibited large shareholders from selling.

Despite more than three decades of robust economic growth, potential problems loom on the horizon as evidenced by a decline in the growth rate to less than 7 percent in 2015. Investment spending currently accounts for nearly half of China's GDP, potentially raising the problem of **excess capacity**. Unless exports or domestic consumption rise to provide additional demand for goods and services, new investment opportunities will dwindle, and the Chinese economy will become vulnerable to a financial collapse. Pressure from other countries to force an appreciation of the yuan will dampen the growth of exports, so China needs to transition from investment spending to domestic consumption spending as the major source of demand in the economy. Citizens can increase their consumption only to the extent that their incomes rise; therefore, higher wages are essential to China's continued growth. In 2013, the government acknowledged the need to stimulate consumer spending by raising the minimum wage by 20 percent to $270 per month, still less than one-fourth of the US minimum wage.

A second problem, known as the "middle income trap," could arise if wages increase too rapidly. Other developing nations have experienced robust growth until labor shortages led to rising wages, which reduced the country's **comparative advantage** in labor-intensive industries. At that point, exports weakened and growth slowed. So, China faces the challenge of finding the right balance between higher wages to fuel consumer spending and low wages to promote exports. Chinese manufacturing wages have risen by 12 percent annually since

2001, but they remain low by Western standards. Rising wages need not reduce a nation's ability to export if productivity is rising at the same time so that per-unit labor costs remain roughly constant. Labor productivity in China is increasing at 11 percent per year due primarily to the introduction of more automated production processes.

A third potential impediment to continued growth in China is the amount of debt accumulated by local governments and private businesses. One of the reasons that investment spending accounts for half of GDP is that credit is readily available. Interest rates are low due to the fact that the Chinese save 40 percent of their income. The past single-child policy and lack of pensions or social security meant that families needed to save to support themselves after retirement. Low interest rates, in turn, have encouraged Chinese firms and local governments to borrow extensively based on the expectation that rapid growth in demand will generate enough revenue to service their debts. Any significant slowing of growth could result in widespread defaults on debt payments and an ensuing financial crisis.

Rising inequality poses another potential problem for China. Beginning in 1979, the CCP pursued a conscious policy of uneven development by dividing the country into "three belts." The coastal provinces would specialize in export industries, finance, and trade; the central provinces would concentrate in agriculture and energy production; and the western provinces would emphasize mining and animal husbandry. This strategy was based on the theory of comparative advantage, which suggests that specialization and trade lead to increased efficiency. However, the result has been growing prosperity in the eastern regions, whereas the central and western parts of the country lag behind in development. This growing inequality potentially jeopardizes both economic and political stability. Economically, the lack of purchasing power in the interior provinces restrains consumer spending and economic growth. Politically, inequality is leading to rising social tensions as manifested in protest demonstrations against the government, acts of terrorism, and growing resentment and cynicism. In response, the CCP has recently changed its development priorities to channel more investment into the interior provinces. Even private businesses are expanding into the interior to take advantage of cheaper labor.

Critics of China have been predicting its imminent demise for several decades, and yet the economy continues to achieve phenomenal rates of growth each year. Growth will undoubtedly slow, as it has for all countries after the initial phases of industrialization. The challenge facing China's leaders is to adjust to slower growth while avoiding a financial collapse caused by overinvestment in productive capacity, excess debt, and speculation in the real estate and stock markets. Despite these potential pitfalls, the country's overall prospects remain bright. If China manages a "smooth landing" by stabilizing at a more sustainable rate of growth, its success will provide a model for other nations to study.

ADDITIONAL READING

Brandt, Loren, and Thomas G. Rawski, eds. *China's Great Economic Transformation.* New York: Cambridge University Press, 2008.

Coase, Ronald, and Ning Wang. *How China Became Capitalist.* New York: Palgrave MacMillan, 2012.

Dickson, Bruce J. *Wealth into Power: The Communist Party's Embrace of China's Private Sector.* New York: Cambridge University Press, 2008.

Fang, Cai, ed. *Transforming the Chinese Economy.* Boston: Brill, 2010.

Grivoyannis, Elias C., ed. *The New Chinese Economy: Dynamic Transitions into the Future.* New York: Palgrave Macmillan, 2012.

Guo, Rongxing. *An Introduction to the Chinese Economy: The Driving Forces behind Modern Day China.* Singapore: John Wiley & Sons, 2010.

Halper, Stefan. *The Beijing Consensus: How China's Authoritarian Model Will Dominate the 21st Century.* New York: Basic Books, 2010.

Harney, Alexandra. *The Chinese Price: The True Cost of Chinese Competitive Advantage.* New York: Penguin Books, 2009.

Huang, Yasheng. *Capitalism with Chinese Characteristics.* New York: Cambridge University Press, 2008.

McNally, Christpher A., ed. *China's Emergent Political Economy—Capitalism in the Dragon's Lair.* New York: Routledge, 2008.

Naughton, Barry. *The Chinese Economy: Transitions and Growth.* Cambridge, MA: MIT Press, 2007.

Pomeranz, Kenneth. *The Great Divergence: China, Europe, and the Making of the Modern World Economy.* Princeton, NJ: Princeton University Press, 2000.

Schell, Orville, and John Delury. *China's Long March to the Twenty-First Century.* New York: Random House, 2013.

Shoe, Jinghao. *Chinese vs. Western Perspectives: Understanding Contemporary China.* Lanham, MD: Lexington Books, 2014.

Starr, John Bryan. *Understanding China: A Guide to China's Economy, History, and Political Culture*, 3rd ed. New York: Hill and Wang, 2010.

Tong, Junie T. *Finance and Society in 21st Century China.* Burlington, VT: Gower, 2011.

Tsai, Kellee S. *Capitalism without Democracy: The Private Sector in Contemporary China.* Ithaca, NY: Cornell University Press, 2007.

Urio, Paolo. *Reconciling State, Market and Society in China: The Long March Toward Prosperity.* New York: Routledge, 2010.

Wright, Teresa. *Accepting Authoritarianism: State-Society Relations in China's Reform Era.* Palo Alto, CA: Stanford University Press, 2010.

Zhang, Jianjun. *Marketization and Democracy in China.* New York: Routledge, 2008.

Chapter 13

THE JAPANESE ECONOMIC SYSTEM

"The realization of the myth that if you entrust things to the
market mechanism, the invisible God's hand will bring about
a rational result is quite limited."
            NAOHIRO AMAYA (1925–1994), Former Vice-minister
            of Japan's Ministry of International Trade and Industry

Japan is a mountainous, volcanic archipelago consisting of four large islands
and more than 3,000 small islands stretching over 2,000 miles in the north
Pacific. The few natural resources it once possessed have been largely depleted. Its
land mass approximates the size of California, yet only 13 percent of the land is
arable, and the population is nearly half that of the United States. Despite these
challenges, Japan rose to become the second largest economy in the world until it
was surpassed by China in 2010.

Japan remained a quasi-feudal society well into the nineteenth century. In 1603,
Ieyasu Tokugawa established a military dictatorship, the Tokugawa Shogunate,
governed by a centralized bureaucracy overseeing 260 smaller domains controlled
by warlords (daimyo) and their warriors (samurai). The Tokugawa regime viewed
the numerous European missionaries and traders in Japan as a threat to its power
and so proceeded to close the country to foreign influences. Imports were virtually
banned, and Japanese citizens could not leave the country. A massacre of more than
20,000 Japanese Christians in 1637 was followed by the expulsion of all foreign
traders. The country remained relatively isolated for the next two centuries, allowing foreign traders access to only two ports.

A rigid caste system divided society into four hereditary groups—the samurai, peasants who worked the land, artisans, and merchants. The primary difference between European feudalism and Japan in the early nineteenth century was
the presence of a strong central government. The Shogunate taxed peasants up to
50 percent of their production and used the resulting **revenue** to pay stipends to
the daimyo.

This stable society was disrupted in 1853 when the American commodore
Matthew Perry led a fleet of US Navy warships into Tokyo Bay and forced the
government to open Japanese markets to Western commerce. Soon, traders from
Europe established markets in coastal cities. Angered by the weakness of the
Tokugawa state, a group of samurai staged a coup in 1868 and installed the

sixteen-year old Emperor Meiji as ruler. The new government initiated a program of rapid industrialization and militarization designed to strengthen Japan against foreign domination.

ORGANIZED CAPITALISM 1868–1935

Having suffered the humiliation of foreign invasion, Japanese leaders viewed economic development not as an end in itself but as a means to empower the state. The concepts of free markets and pursuit of self-interest remained antithetical to Japanese values that stressed group cooperation and hierarchical control. From the beginning of **capitalism** in Japan, the government promoted private businesses with various forms of aid, extensive **infrastructure**, and opening of foreign markets. These policies stimulated average annual growth rates in **real gross domestic product** (GDP) of around 4 percent during the late nineteenth and early twentieth centuries.

Zaibatsu

To promote rapid economic development, the Japanese government encouraged **vertical integration** and **horizontal integration** of firms, resulting in massive **conglomerates** of twenty to thirty firms known as zaibatsu. Each zaibatsu was led by a family-owned holding company, with the member firms connected through **interlocking directorates** and cross-holding of shares of stock. Only shares of minor subsidiary firms were sold to the public. Most zaibatsu also included a bank to provide credit for member firms. This unique corporate structure gave Japanese firms two advantages. First, cross-holding of stocks insulated firms from stock market fluctuations and hostile takeovers. This protection enabled Japanese businesses to make investments that, while not immediately profitable, paved the way for long-term growth. Second, the zaibatsu captured the benefits of both decentralized management of each firm and the power, efficiency, and stability associated with large size. If one firm in the zaibatsu encountered difficulty, other firms offered support.

Organized Labor

Despite the presence of powerful zaibatsu, nearly 80 percent of the industrial labor force worked in firms with fewer than 100 employees. The first small labor unions appeared around 1890 in the mining and textile industries. A metalworkers union formed in 1897 but succeeded in enrolling only 5 percent of the workers in that industry. The first nationwide union, the Japan Federation of Labor, was established as an umbrella organization in 1921. By 1923, it had a 100,000 members belonging to three hundred different unions.

Despite numerous strikes and labor riots, Japanese unions remained weak and ineffective. They faced opposition not only from employers but also from the government, which viewed them as a threat to national unity and economic development. Antiunion legislation made organizing unions difficult. Employers could fire a worker for joining a union or refusing to leave one. By 1931, only 8 percent of the labor force had been unionized.

Developmental State

To consolidate state power, the Meiji regime ordered the daimyo to move to Tokyo where they could be kept under surveillance. Having lost political power, many of the daimyo retired from politics and went into business. When the government replaced the samurai with a conscripted army, the former warriors received compensation for their lost status in the form of government bonds. Many of the samurai used these financial assets, along with preferential loans from government, to start businesses, and would subsequently become leading industrialists. This unique evolution of political leaders and warriors into business owners within a single generation explains a prevailing ethic of social responsibility among business leaders. As warriors and political leaders, the samurai and daimyo had been both servants of the state and protectors of their communities. This dual role carried over into business practices as notions of duty, patriotism, and honor took precedence over calculations of short-term profitability. Market behavior was embedded in a web of morality and social norms governing business decisions.

With political, economic, and military power concentrated in relatively few hands, Japanese leaders were able to fundamentally reorganize society within the span of several decades. Their efforts were heavily influenced by the economists of the German Historical School as the Japanese looked to Germany as a role model. Political and business leaders supported a central role for the state in leading the development process, and the government quickly established modern transportation, communications, legal, and financial systems.

In 1872, Japan created one of the world's first compulsory education systems for both male and female students. Soon after, Tokyo University and the Tokyo Institute of Technology were founded. The government sent some students to universities in Europe and the United States to gain technical knowledge and brought foreign experts to Japan to provide instruction in science, business administration, and manufacturing. Although teaching methods and course content were often adopted from the West, Japanese schools prepared students to serve the state by teaching the importance of morality, cooperation, and deference to authority.

In 1884, political leaders prepared a ten-year national development plan relying heavily on the state to initiate and lead the process of industrialization. The government owned and operated the iron, steel, telephone, telegraph, and railroad industries and established state monopolies in tobacco and salt. In addition, government-created producer associations took responsibility for coordinating the silk, banking, shipping, agriculture, and fishing industries. Other industries, such as chemicals, cement, munitions, coal mining, and petroleum received government subsidies and other forms of assistance. In one case, the government gave the Mitsubishi zaibatsu eleven steamboats so that it could challenge foreign shipping lines carrying goods into and out of Japan. In most years prior to World War I, government investment in the economy exceeded private investment.

Japan adopted a constitution in 1890 and held limited elections with strict requirements for eligibility to vote. A two-party political system emerged in 1925, and all males older than age twenty-five gained the right to vote. However, the Emperor and his advisors still held substantial power in formulating public policy. Virtually all Japanese leaders, whether in the military, politics, or business, were recent descendants of samurai warriors, so they shared common values and a commitment to defend Japan against foreign aggression by building a strong economy.

Government acted as a partner to encourage the formation and expansion of businesses. New entrepreneurs received training, technical assistance, and financial backing from the state. The government purchased machines from other countries so that Japanese engineers could study and imitate them. It constructed model factories so that potential entrepreneurs could gain experience and learn how to operate their own firms. These forms of assistance were welcomed by private business owners, who worked in close partnership with government officials. Both sides viewed unrestrained competition as wasteful and destructive and accepted government intervention as essential to achieving prosperity. With this consensus, little coercion was needed to carry out the government's vision of building a powerful state by promoting economic growth.

Imperialism

In the late nineteenth century, Japan carefully observed the economic systems of Western nations to learn from their success. At that time, the leading industrial countries were turning to **imperialism** to gain control of a wider array of resources and to open markets for their exports. In an 1895 war with China, Japan acquired the island of Formosa (now Taiwan). After defeating Russia in a war, Japan claimed Korea as a colony in 1910. During World War I, Japan's alliance with Britain enabled it to capture several German colonies in Asia.

World War I provided a tremendous stimulus to the Japanese economy as it began exporting military goods to Europe and consumer goods to the Asian countries whose trade with Europe was disrupted by the war. To succeed as an imperialist power, Japan needed a strong military, and as the twentieth century progressed, the country devoted an increasing share of its economy to military preparations. In 1931, the Japanese army invaded and conquered the northern Chinese province of Manchuria to secure access to iron ore and coal deposits. As an indication of the growing power and independence of the military, this invasion was executed without authorization from the Japanese government. Factions within the military expressed open hostility to the government and tried several times to overthrow it. The military scorned democracy, viewing political parties as serving the narrow self-interest of their constituents rather than uniting the country to become a great power.

Culture

The major Japanese religions are Confucianism, Shintoism, and Buddhism. They share a strong emphasis on the importance of community, hierarchy, and social harmony. The tenets of these religions suggest that human suffering is caused by selfish desires and that happiness lies in transcending the egotistical focus on self. The Japanese learn to function well in communities and to place group obligations above self-interest. They believe that only through involvement in and acceptance by a community can the individual find meaning, security, and happiness in life.

Hierarchy provides individuals with a clear understanding of their rights and duties. People in subordinate positions are expected to be respectful, deferential, obedient, and loyal to their superiors. Leaders also have obligations to respect and protect those under their authority. Hierarchy permeates Japanese society. Even today within the family, women remain subordinate to men and children to their parents. Workplace hierarchies are based on gender, educational attainment, and age, resulting in the virtual exclusion of women from the higher ranks of corporate management. The Japanese desire for harmony is revealed by the importance placed on building consensus prior to any important decision. Once consensus is reached, all affected groups are expected to cooperate.

The Demise of Organized Capitalism

The Great Depression crippled the Japanese economy. Between 1929 and 1931, exports dropped by 50 percent and the economy shrank by 8 percent. Amid the economic woes, Japan's fragile parliamentary democracy came under attack. In the early 1930s, two prime ministers were assassinated along with several other prominent political figures. The military, which had steadily gained political power since World War I, attempted a coup in 1931. Although the coup failed, it signaled the rise of ultranationalist groups within both the military and civil society, who viewed democracy as weak and incapable of forging a unified nation.

The government initially responded to the Great Depression by devaluing the currency (the yen) to stimulate exports. It also engaged in large-scale **deficit spending** to stimulate **aggregate demand**. Additional government support was given to the zaibatsu along with mandates to form **cartels** that would maintain profitability by reducing competition and **excess capacity**. These policies enabled Japan to emerge from the Great Depression by 1933. Growth became so strong that concerns about **inflation** caused the government to reduce military spending in 1936. However, these budget cuts only increased the military's hostility toward the government.

Despite the improving economy, political and social tensions were rising. The growing power and privileges of the zaibatsu created resentment among farmers and small businesses trapped between rising costs of production and weak demand for their products. By suppressing competition, the zaibatsu gained **market power** to raise prices, causing increased hardship for consumers. Some farmers were so desperate that they sold their daughters to brothels. The combination of class

CHAPTER 13 • The Japanese Economic System 269

hostility and the plight of small businesses and farmers created fertile ground for the rise of fascism.

JAPANESE FASCISM 1936–1945

Japan's version of organized capitalism paved the way for a quick transition to fascism. For decades, government and business had been working together to coordinate the economy and suppress the market while preserving private ownership of most businesses. Due to imperialism and World War I, the military played an increasingly powerful role in Japanese politics. Culturally, Japan remained ethnically homogeneous with a high priority on unity and harmony, so the concept of a national community with no internal divisions appealed to the Japanese. They readily accepted the vision of all citizens working together toward the common goal of promoting the country's economic and military power.

The transition to fascism occurred in several steps. A second failed military coup in 1936 further eroded the stability of the democratic government. In 1938, a National General Mobilization Law gave the government wider powers to direct the economy and was accompanied by a dramatic increase in military spending. In 1940, pressure from the army led to the replacement of the prime minister's entire cabinet. All political parties were eliminated and replaced by a single party. Labor unions were abolished and replaced with the Industrial Association for Service to Country. In an effort to unite other Asian nations against China, Japan created the Greater East Asia Co-Prosperity Sphere. Finally, Japan joined with Germany and Italy in forming the Axis to gain control of the entire Eurasian landmass.

Under fascism, the zaibatsu increased their size and power. By 1940, the four largest zaibatsu controlled 50 percent of the nation's production of machinery and equipment and 30 percent of mining, metals, and chemicals. Many of the families owning the zaibatsu supported the growing power of the military because they anticipated increased spending on military equipment, political stability, suppression of labor costs, and access to raw materials and markets for finished products throughout the Pacific basin.

The Demise of Japanese Fascism

The military occupation of the Chinese province of Manchuria, which began in 1931, developed into a full-scale war between Japan and China. By 1938, Japan controlled most of northern and central China. To punish this aggression, the United States and its allies froze Japanese assets in other countries and enacted an **embargo** to cut off Japan's access to resources throughout Asia. Threatened with loss of the resources essential to its economy, Japan took action to eliminate the US naval presence in the Pacific. On December 7, 1941, Japanese planes bombed the US naval base at Pearl Harbor, Hawaii. Within six months the Japanese army occupied Burma, Malaya, Singapore, the Philippines, and much of the Dutch East Indies. However, the bombing of Pearl Harbor proved to be a strategic blunder. The attack on Pearl Harbor brought the United States into World War II, culminating

Figure 13.1 The city of Hiroshima was leveled by a single atomic bomb.   (© Getty Images/The Asahi Shimbun)

in the dropping of two atomic bombs on the cities of Nagasaki and Hiroshima in 1945. Nearly 250,000 people died in the bombings and the immediate aftermath. Many more died later from radiation sickness. Less than a month after the bombings, Japan surrendered unconditionally, bringing an end to World War II.

PLANNED CAPITALISM 1946–1990

The American Occupation

World War II devastated the Japanese economy. Three million lives were lost, and firebombing and the atomic bombs destroyed major cities. Forty percent of infrastructure and industrial capital lay in ruins, the colonial empire was lost, and Japan's GDP was reduced to half its prewar level. The US forces that occupied Japan until 1952 were determined to change the Japanese economic system so that fascism and imperialism would not reappear. US advisors believed that the incestuous alliance between the zaibatsu and government had blocked the formation of a thriving middle class of small business owners, farmers, and professional workers. The lack of a middle class, in turn, explained the near absence of political opposition to the increasingly authoritarian and militaristic policies of the government.

To end the close relationship between big business and government, the United States ordered the dissolution of the zaibatsu by forcing more than 1,500 top executives into permanent retirement, ending the family-owned holding companies, and converting subsidiary enterprises into independent firms. For example, the Mitsui zaibatsu, which employed nearly two million workers, was divided into more than 180 separate firms. Labor unions that had been illegal since 1940 were reestablished and given the right to strike and to collectively bargain with employers. Extensive land reform broke up large farms and eliminated absentee owners in order to establish a class of independent farmers. A new constitution established a multiparty parliamentary democracy, gave women the right to vote, protected civil rights, and prohibited Japan from maintaining any significant military capability. Emperor Hirohito (1901–1989) was permitted to remain on the throne—but merely as a figurehead.

Keiretsu

Although the initial impetus of postwar reforms aimed at restructuring the Japanese economy by breaking up the zaibatsu, the beginning of the Cold War between the United States and the Soviet Union changed that policy. After 1947, rather than dispersing concentrated business power, the United States focused on creating a strong Japanese economy capable of resisting the spread of communism. To accomplish that goal, many of the business and government leaders previously forced into retirement were allowed to return to their positions. By the time the US occupation ended in 1952, the Japanese government had reverted to its prewar policy of encouraging vertical and horizontal integration so that groups of firms could gain strength by cooperating with each other.

Through lax enforcement of antitrust laws, government allowed corporations to reassemble large industrial groups called keiretsu. The keiretsu, although less vertically integrated than the zaibatsu, achieved horizontal integration by holding shares of each other's stock, using the same bank, sharing the same marketing networks, and establishing joint subsidiaries. Like the zaibatsu, the keiretsu were insulated from pressures to focus on short-term profitability because their loans were from banks that belonged to the same group and because their shares of stock were held by other firms in the group. As a result, the keiretsu focused on long-term investments in product development, **human capital**, and expanding their share of the market.

Cooperative Labor

Once labor unions again became legal in Japan, membership grew rapidly to more than six million by 1948. After some initial militancy and attempted strikes, the government purged communist elements from the unions, and labor relations became quite harmonious with very few strikes and low rates of absenteeism and turnover. Explanations for Japan's cooperative and highly motivated labor force involved several factors.

Enterprise Unions

More than 90 percent of unionized workers belonged to enterprise unions composed solely of workers in a single firm. Enterprise unions encouraged close consultation between management and workers, leading to a strong sense of identification with and loyalty to the firm.

Lifetime Employment

The largest Japanese companies, which employed about 25 percent of the labor force, were committed to retaining their employees until retirement. This practice began after World War II, when shortages of skilled labor motivated firms to offer job security in order to retain their best employees. During slowdowns in the economy, large companies rarely laid off workers. If changing technology rendered certain job skills obsolete, companies retrained their employees to work with new technology rather than replacing them with younger workers possessing more up-to-date skills and knowledge. In some cases, employers sent workers abroad for specialized training, confident that they would return to the company. Workers with lifetime employment were expected to retire at age fifty-five. If they needed additional income, they sought employment elsewhere, although large companies attempted to place their retiring workers in positions with subcontractors.

Lifetime employment offered many advantages to employers as well. Workers exercised greater restraint in their wage demands because they identified their interests with the long-term viability of the company. In addition, job security made workers more willing to accept labor-saving innovations, learn new skills, change work patterns, or transfer to different divisions within the company. Employers could also provide extensive on-the-job training without fear of losing workers to another firm. Finally, when companies made lifetime commitments to their employees, workers reciprocated with increased dedication and loyalty.

Seniority Wages
Wages for lifetime employees were based more on age and years of experience than on performance. Young workers typically began their careers earning low wages, but the prospect of rising wages as they aged created a strong incentive to assure the long-term survival of their company. If the company remained profitable, workers' best-paid years would be their final years before retirement. On the other hand, if a company failed, workers would lose their seniority and face the prospect of finding new employment at a significantly lower wage. Although basing wages on age rather than productivity may seem inefficient, Japanese culture emphasizes the importance of age as an indicator of wisdom and social status. To pay an older worker less than a younger worker would shame the older worker and damage his relationship with the firm. Less productive workers were offered counseling to improve their performance rather than a reduction in pay.

Semiannual Bonuses
Most large Japanese companies gave employees semiannual bonuses equal to about 25 percent of their wages. These bonuses were tied to the performance of the firm, so workers had a personal stake in the company's success. Bonuses also created greater flexibility in worker compensation, allowing firms to reduce costs by cancelling bonuses during **recessions** rather than by laying off employees.

Team Production
A significant portion of production in Japan was performed by work teams, with jobs rotating among team members. This system broadened workers' skills and increased firms' flexibility to shift workers to different tasks. Job rotation also made work less monotonous and offered opportunities to master new skills.

Team members monitored each other's performance, thereby improving quality control and minimizing shirking on the job. As a result, Japanese firms needed fewer managers than their counterparts in the West.

Salary Compression

The gap between the salaries of Japanese executives and the lowest wages was much smaller than in other industrialized countries. In fact, the pretax distribution of income in Japan was more equal than in Sweden. Greater equality fostered solidarity among employees and minimized resentment.

Fringe Benefits

Large Japanese companies provided an array of fringe benefits such as company uniforms; subsidized cafeterias; barbershops; medical facilities; educational subsidies for children of employees; dormitories at popular vacation destinations; auditoriums for cultural events; gifts for birthdays, weddings, and funerals; and facilities for social and recreational activities after work.

Culture

Japanese culture, with its emphasis on harmonious group activity, was well-suited to foster a strong work ethic. Japanese workers viewed work not simply as a source of income, but as a means to gain meaning and purpose in their lives. Their place of employment often became their community, with opportunities for recreation and socializing after the workday.

Although wages, working conditions, and job security were generally excellent for employees of large corporations, the same did not hold true for workers in smaller companies. In fact, large corporations kept their costs low by subcontracting much of their production to smaller firms. Costs remained lower at smaller companies because they lacked the **market power** of the keiretsu and received little assistance from government. Operating in competitive markets, small businesses provided few fringe benefits and paid wages typically 50 percent lower than those offered by the keiretsu.

Collective bargaining between labor unions and employers became increasingly organized over the years. In 1987, many Japanese labor unions joined together to form the Japanese Trade Union Confederation (Rengo), encompassing two-thirds of unionized workers. Representatives of Rengo and the Japan Federation of Economic Associations (Nippon Keidanren) met each spring to discuss and issue guidelines for wage increases consistent with projected growth and inflation. Subsequent negotiations at the industry level established benchmarks or guidelines to which settlements between enterprise unions and companies were expected to conform.

Industrial Policy

In competitive capitalism, the state ideally serves as a referee enforcing rules without favoring any particular interests. In contrast, the Japanese state actively influenced the structure and direction of the economy. Industrial policy in Japan consisted of a comprehensive set of government policies designed to supplement and in some cases counteract the market. Successful industrial policy requires a state not easily influenced by groups seeking to promote narrow self-interests. The Japanese government, with its hierarchical organization and commitment to national strength, possessed more power than any single interest group. It could therefore promote the national interest rather than being captured by special interests. Three of the most important aspects of Japanese industrial policy were selective targeting, promoting **saving**, and price supports.

Selective Targeting

In 1949, the Japanese government established the Ministry of International Trade and Industry (MITI) to oversee and coordinate the process of rebuilding the economy after the devastation of World War II. Rather than allowing free markets to determine which firms and industries would thrive, MITI targeted support for select industries deemed most likely to succeed or most crucial to building Japanese strength. This support took the form of **tariffs** on imports, subsidies, tax concessions, government contracts, preferential loans, government-financed research and development, exemptions from antitrust laws, import permits, licenses, and government allocation of raw materials and **foreign exchange**.

MITI sought to create **competitive advantage** for a relatively small number of Japanese industries so they could dominate global markets. Unlike **comparative advantage** based primarily on a country's endowment of resources, competitive advantage can be created by reducing production costs, stimulating product innovation, or improving product delivery. In the early 1950s, Japan relied on comparative advantage when it chose to take advantage of its cheap labor by specializing in labor-intensive goods such as handicrafts, textiles, and low-priced electronics. However, beginning in 1955, the Japanese used profits from those exports to acquire more sophisticated technology and to make the transition to high-quality, capital-intensive goods such as steel, ships, machinery, petrochemicals, and automobiles. In a free market, starting such industries would have been difficult because they would compete against mature industries in the United States and Europe. MITI relied on tariffs and subsidies to shelter and aid Japan's **infant industries** until they could develop sufficiently to match or exceed the efficiency of foreign competitors.

MITI also protected industries threatened with declining markets. In the short-run, if decline appeared inevitable, MITI cushioned the effects of plant closings and layoffs by permitting firms to form cartels and fix prices in order to maintain profitability. This intervention minimized unemployment and the **negative externalities** associated with plant closings. In the long-run, MITI planned for the transition to newer, more competitive industries.

The planning process was based on dialogue and consensus between industry leaders and government bureaucrats. Planning did not result in mandatory production goals but merely guided government policy and provided business leaders with more information about the future direction of the economy. The rationales for planning include the following:

- Although market participants are pressured to focus on self-interest and short-run profitability, planners can base their decisions on the long-run interests of the entire nation.
- Planners have access to information about the entire economy, whereas private decision-makers are typically aware only of conditions in their specific industry.
- By targeting aid, planners can limit the number of firms in an industry and avoid wasteful duplication.
- Aid from the government can accelerate the expansion of an industry, thereby securing significant **economies of scale**, a resulting competitive advantage, and the potential for global dominance.
- By selecting industries with both **backward linkages** and **forward linkages**, targeted aid to a few industries can stimulate the entire economy.
- Planners can undertake major projects needed for economic development whose profitability will not materialize for several years.

The actual record of MITI's performance was a mixture of spectacular successes and very costly mistakes. Automobiles and consumer electronics were two of the greatest successes. However, petrochemical and aluminum industries failed to thrive in Japan despite extensive support from MITI. MITI supported the development of the analog version of high-density television, but the digital version eventually became the world standard. MITI poured billions into an effort to make the Japanese microprocessor industry the global leader, but superior innovation by US firms eventually led to US dominance in that industry. Other failures included efforts to develop commercial aircraft and computer software industries.

Despite arguments in favor of government planning to support selected industries, the most powerful counterargument is that private investors have greater incentives to allocate **financial capital** efficiently because they personally reap the gains and suffer the losses resulting from their decisions. Also, although the government may possess extensive information about the overall economy, analysts employed by private brokerage firms might have more detailed information about any specific industry and therefore can steer financial capital to firms and industries with the greatest potential for growth and profitability.

Two other government agencies were also involved in planning the Japanese economy. The Economic Planning Agency used **indicative planning** to establish guideposts for production in each industry so that firms could be more confident in their knowledge of the future direction of the economy. The Ministry of Finance supervised Japan's central bank and therefore controlled **monetary policy**, credit allocation, and banking and foreign exchange regulation. The Ministry of Finance also formulated **fiscal policy** by drafting the national budget.

Promoting Saving

With a lack of natural resources, the Japanese realized that economic success would require large amounts of **financial capital** and high-quality **human capital**. Human capital was enhanced by excellent systems of public education and on-the-job training, but to promote the accumulation of financial capital, the Japanese government sought to increase the rate of saving. A variety of government and corporate policies led to a savings rate four times higher than in the United States.

- Tax policy promoted saving by increasing taxes on consumption and reducing taxes on income. During the late 1980s, Japan cut its top marginal income tax rate from 70 percent to 50 percent and its top corporate income tax rate from 42 percent to 37.5 percent. The absence of a capital gains tax on financial assets as well as additional loopholes in the tax code enabled wealthy households to reduce their average income tax rate to 22 percent.
- Japan's meager social security benefits and the practice of early retirement encouraged citizens to accumulate substantial personal savings in order to live comfortably after retirement.
- To ensure that personal savings would be channeled into productive investments, the Japanese postal service functioned as a bank. Households could give savings to their mail carriers for deposit in tax-free accounts at the post office. The postal service also sold annuities and life insurance. These funds went to government financial institutions such as the Japan Development Bank and the Export-Import Bank, which, in turn, provided low-interest loans to selected industries.
- Saving and investment by corporations increased due to government's supportive intervention, which reduced the risks associated with expansion and modernization.
- The corporate practice of giving workers semiannual bonuses tended to increase saving because workers received periodic income above and beyond their normal monthly expenditures.
- Japanese culture promoted saving by encouraging modesty and restraint in consumption spending. Most individuals owned small automobiles and homes. Ostentatious displays of wealth were considered socially inappropriate. As personal income rose rapidly, consumption spending grew more slowly, resulting in increased saving.

Price Supports

Japanese industrial policy used price supports for agricultural products to maintain parity between the incomes of farmers and those of industrial workers. These price supports, coupled with trade barriers on imported agricultural products, caused food prices to escalate. The government claimed that high food prices were necessary to maintain the economic viability of the agricultural sector in case the nation should ever be isolated by international conflict. However, price supports also ensured political support among farmers for the pro-business Liberal Democratic Party.

Despite an active and interventionist government, the size of Japan's public sector during planned capitalism remained the smallest relative to GDP among all developed nations. Government spending as a fraction of GDP stood at about 27 percent compared to about 32 percent in the United States. Most of this difference resulted from the fact that Japan spent only 1 percent of its GDP on national defense while the comparable figure for the United States was 7 percent. Japan had few state-owned enterprises, and those that existed tended to provide infrastructure such as railroads, airlines, telephones, and utilities. State monopolies in alcohol, tobacco, and salt once existed, but those industries were privatized in the 1980s. However, Japan Airlines and major radio and television networks continue to be owned by the government.

Social Policy

Under planned capitalism, the Japanese government devoted a relatively small portion of its budget to welfare, healthcare, and social security because families, communities, and businesses were largely responsible for social welfare. Many firms provided rent-subsidized housing, subsidized cafeterias at work, discount company stores, medical care, and cultural and recreational facilities. Old-age security was handled primarily through pension programs funded by employers or through mutual aid associations to which individuals contributed during their working years. Pensions and social security were less essential in Japan because more than half of all retired persons lived with their adult children.

Japan's educational system remains excellent. High school students attend classes fifty days more per year than their American counterparts. To graduate, students must pass rigorous national tests measuring educational attainment, yet 90 percent of Japanese students graduate from high school compared to 77 percent in the United States. Large Japanese corporations recruit exclusively from the top universities, causing intense competition for admission to those institutions.

Japan began universal healthcare coverage in the late 1950s. The government finances the healthcare system, but care is provided through private hospitals and clinics. Japanese citizens rank high on global measures of health, a fact often attributed to a low-fat diet centered around fish and vegetables. Average life spans in Japan are the longest in the world, but this longevity poses a problem for social programs. By the year 2050, more than one-third of the population will be sixty-five or older, placing increasing strains on the country's social security system and on business pension plans.

Culture

Japanese culture stresses the importance of harmony. An informal code of conduct requires that Japanese never damage the prestige and self-respect of others. Allowing others to "save face" is facilitated by hierarchy wherein individuals recognize the customary behavior attached to their social positions and do not challenge the authority of superiors. Japanese business people have some difficulty when negotiating with foreigners who use aggressive and confrontational tactics to maximize their gains. For the Japanese, aggression demonstrates disrespect and rudeness. On meeting a new client or supplier, Japanese business people immediately exchange business cards. The information on the card allows them to assess the other person's social status and to behave accordingly.

The Japanese value conformity, which in turn fosters self-discipline. An inability or unwillingness to conform indicates a lack of control over one's selfish instincts. A Japanese adage states that "the nail that sticks up will be pounded down." Conformity is instilled in youth by parents and teachers who demand deference to and respect for authority. Japanese religions teach that the pursuit of selfish desires leads to unhappiness. A meaningful and fulfilling life is achieved through the security and acceptance of belonging to close-knit communities. These cultural beliefs explain the loyalty and dedication exhibited by most Japanese workers toward their employers. They view their workplace as a community providing not just an income but also a sense of purpose and belonging.

The Demise of Planned Capitalism

Japan's average annual growth of GDP during the 1960s rose to an astounding 9.3 percent. That rate slowed to 4 percent during the 1970s and 1980s due in large part to Japan's dependence on increasingly expensive imported oil. Japan's success so impressed corporations around the world that they began imitating Japanese business practices such as quality circles and just-in-time inventory management. As the second largest economy in the world, Japan seemed on the brink of accomplishing through economic means the global domination it failed to accomplish through military means during World War II. However, that success ended abruptly in the early 1990s, as evidenced by the collapse of the Nikkei stock index from a high of 38,957 in 1989, to 14,000 in 1992, and to a low of 7,600 in 2003. Several factors contributed to the demise of Japanese planned capitalism.

Loss of Export Markets

Whereas Japan's postwar development was based on its ability to export due to low wage costs, by the 1980s, Japanese wages had become relatively high compared to those of other Asian countries such as China, South Korea, the Philippines, Taiwan, and Thailand. As a result, Japanese companies began outsourcing production, and those goods still made in Japan became less competitive in international markets. Another factor contributing to Japan's declining exports was growing resentment among its trading partners over Japanese protectionist trade policies. The United States threatened to set quotas on Japanese goods if the Japanese did not voluntarily reduce their exports. The French relied on the more subtle practice of delaying customs inspections of Japanese goods arriving in their ports. In 1985, after lengthy negotiations, Japan agreed to a substantial **appreciation** of its currency, which made its exports more expensive to foreigners.

Easy Monetary Policy

Fearing that restraints on the ability to export would cause a recession, the Bank of Japan increased the money supply to lower **interest rates** and stimulate private borrowing and spending. However, low interest rates also encouraged speculation in the booming stock and real estate markets, leading to a speculative bubble that could not be sustained. By 1989, the total value of stocks listed on the Tokyo Stock Exchange exceeded that of the New York Stock Exchange, and the average price/earnings ratio of Japanese stocks was 54 compared to 15 in the United States. The total value of Japanese real estate was four times greater than that of US real estate, even though the United States is geographically twenty-five times larger than Japan. When the Bank of Japan acted to slow speculation by tightening the money supply in 1989, the bubble burst. Within three years, real estate and stock prices fell by 50 percent, causing massive losses for investors, banks, and brokerage firms.

Restricted Consumption

The Japanese cultural predisposition to save rather than consume was key to providing financial capital during planned capitalism. A relatively low level of consumer spending was not a problem so long as strong demand for exports and high levels of business investment sustained **aggregate demand**. As exports and investment declined, the government encouraged consumer spending, but the cultural habit of thrift was resistant to change. As a result, the economy suffered from **underconsumption**. The precipitous drop in asset values between 1989 and 1992 further restricted consumption. Having lost a substantial portion of their wealth and concerned about job security, Japanese consumers grew pessimistic about the future and tightened their belts.

Deflation

Beginning in the early 1990s, the Japanese economy experienced recurring **deflation**. Prices dropped because of less expensive imports from other Asian countries, weak consumer demand, an aging population that spent less as it grew older, and cost-cutting by Japanese firms. Deflation tends to be a self-perpetuating phenomenon as the expectation of falling prices leads consumers to postpone spending in anticipation that their money will buy more in the future. Investment spending may also decline as businesses expect weak consumer demand for their products and therefore devote their financial capital to repaying debt rather than purchasing new physical capital. Lower levels of consumption and investment reduce aggregate demand and put downward pressure on prices.

Insolvent Businesses and Banks

The financial collapse of 1989–92 caused many businesses to become insolvent, meaning that they were unable to make payments on their bank loans. Banks could have removed these bad loans from their balance sheets, but doing so would have jeopardized the solvency of some banks. Instead, banks often chose to continue lending money to insolvent businesses so the borrowers could avoid defaulting on their previous loans. Banks hoped that an economic recovery would restore business profitability, but when recovery failed to materialize, many banks faced **insolvency**. The prospect of widespread bank failures exacerbated the crisis as Japanese citizens and businesses chose to deposit savings in foreign financial markets rather than Japanese banks.

During the 1990s and 2000s, the Japanese government introduced a variety of policies and reforms to revive the economy, but with little success. The government engaged in deficit spending to build infrastructure, including new bridges, highways, harbors, and railways. However, the declines in exports, consumption spending, and private investment were so severe that the fiscal stimulus had little impact on the economy. In 1996, Japan deregulated its financial markets, allowing open access by foreign investors. A mild recovery occurred in 1997, but an Asian financial crisis soon resulted in slumping exports and further weakness in Japan's stock market. By 1999, the government engaged in an all-out effort to provide stimulus through expansionary fiscal and monetary policies. Government spending increased, taxes were cut, the government bailed out fifteen major banks, and the Bank of Japan lowered the short-term interest rate to 0 percent. Unfortunately, the global economy entered a recession soon after and by 2001, the Japanese economy fell back into recession with rising unemployment and falling prices.

A NEW DIRECTION?

Japan's inability to restore prosperity in the twenty-first century has created considerable political instability. Since 2005, seven prime ministers have resigned, each having spent only about a year in office. Amid the political turmoil, several distinct changes in the structure and functioning of the Japanese economic system have emerged.

More Flexible Labor Markets

Despite two decades of low growth, unemployment in Japan rarely rose above 5 percent and was only 3.7 percent in 2013. Japanese firms have traditionally placed higher priority on their employees than on their shareholders, leading them to avoid layoffs even when profits are declining. Unlike France, where inflexible labor markets are caused by laws designed to protect workers from layoffs, Japanese firms voluntarily retain redundant workers. Instead of focusing on short-term cost-cutting, they consider the long-term consequences of layoffs in terms of undermining trust and morale among workers, affecting the ability to recruit new workers, and damaging the firm's reputation. Also, Japan's lack of social benefits means that workers who lose their job face real hardship.

Despite these considerations, the commitment to avoid layoffs has been undermined by prolonged stagnation. As Japanese firms struggle to regain profitability, they allow market forces to play a larger role in determining wage rates and job security. Moreover, the tradition of economy-wide and industry-wide wage negotiations is gradually being replaced by negotiations between individual companies and their unions. Lifetime employment has grown less common and workers are encouraged to take early retirement. Instead of linking wages to seniority, more firms are relying on merit-based pay. One-third of Japanese workers now hold part-time, temporary, or fixed-term jobs. The increasing reliance on part-time workers undermines the bargaining power of labor unions, which now include only 20 percent of the labor force.

Less Planning

In 2001, a new government agency, the Ministry of Economy, Trade, and Industry (METI), replaced MITI. The new agency is less involved in planning and managing the economy. Blatant protectionism is no longer feasible due to international trade agreements negotiated through the World Trade Organization. However, protection is still practiced in more subtle ways such as encouraging Japanese firms to use Japanese-made parts in manufacturing or forbidding large retail stores from opening in Japan. METI regards its role as facilitating the transitions dictated by market forces rather than opposing the market.

Abenomics

In 2012, Shinzo Abe became prime minister of Japan. Pledging to restore prosperity, he has initiated an array of reforms referred to as "Abenomics." At the heart of Abenomics lies a Keynesian stimulus package designed to boost aggregate demand and employment. In 2013, massive government spending on physical infrastructure led to a budget deficit equal to 11.5 percent of GDP compared to 4.3 percent in the United States. Japan's **national debt** is 240 percent of GDP, more than double that of any other developed nation. In addition, the Bank of Japan announced in 2014 that it would purchase $734 billion of government bonds and other assets with the intention of doubling the money supply within a two-year period.

Abenomics is intentionally designed to create inflation. With a target rate of 2 percent annually, the hope is that mild inflation will encourage both consumers and businesses to spend more because savings will lose value over time. Inflation should promote additional business borrowing and investment by pushing **real interest rates** close to or below 0 percent. The government also intends to stimulate exports by devaluing the yen, which has already depreciated by 25 percent since 2012. Finally, in an indication that Japanese leaders still rely on exports and investment spending rather than domestic consumption to boost aggregate demand, the national sales tax was increased from 5 to 8 percent in 2014 to offset a portion of the government's budget deficit created by the fiscal stimulus. An additional increase in the tax to 10 percent was scheduled for 2015, but the continuing weakness of economy prompted a postponement of the tax increase until 2017.

Cultural Changes

In a more market-centered economic system, the process of recovery from a financial collapse usually entails widespread business failures and personal bankruptcies. The economist Joseph Schumpeter (1883–1950) used the term "rubbish disposal" to describe the elimination of less efficient firms and less productive workers to clear the way for a new recovery. Yet the Japanese, with their strong ethic of obligation and duty to the community, remain reluctant to accept this harsh process. They feel a strong moral duty to prevent hardship and suffering among fellow citizens. Also, close personal ties between business and government leaders make austerity measures politically difficult to impose. Many of the most hard-hit industries, such as real estate, retailing, and construction, have been longtime contributors to the ruling Liberal Democratic Party, so the government is reluctant to pursue policies that might force some of these firms to declare bankruptcy or lay off workers.

A more market-oriented approach to economic recovery would require changes in Japanese culture, and this change is gradually occurring. Western values of individualism, materialism, enjoyment of leisure, and conspicuous consumption grow more prevalent in Japan with each passing generation. Advocates of these shifts in culture argue that the old values of conformity, loyalty, group discipline, and self-denial dampen individual creativity and initiative. However, many Japanese, particularly older generations, cling to the traditional values that they believe made Japan such a strong nation. They fear that widespread layoffs and bankruptcies will undermine the loyalty and work ethic that contributed to the high productivity of Japanese workers. Japan is clearly caught in a cultural dilemma, and the resolution may well determine whether the country is able to regain its previous levels of growth and prosperity.

ADDITIONAL READING

Alexander, Arthur J. *In the Shadow of the Miracle: The Japanese Economy since the End of High-Speed Growth.* Lanham, MD: Rowman & Littlefield, 2002.

Estevez-Abe, Margarita. *Welfare and Capitalism in Postwar Japan.* New York: Cambridge University Press, 2008.

Flath, David. *The Japanese Economy,* 2nd ed. New York: Oxford University Press, 2005.

Gordon, Andrew. *A Modern History of Japan: From Tokugawa Times to the Present,* 3rd ed. New York: Oxford University Press. 2013.

Karan, Pradjumna. *Japan in the 21st Century: Environment, Economy, and Society.* Lexington: University Press of Kentucky, 2005.

Kingston, Jeff. *Contemporary Japan: History, Politics, and Social Change since the 1980s,* 2nd ed. Malden, MA: Wiley-Blackwell, 2012.

Tansman, Alan, ed. *The Culture of Japanese Fascism.* Durham, NC: Duke University Press, 2009.

Vogel, Steven K., and Naazreen Barma. *Japan Remodeled: How Government and Industry Are Reforming Japanese Capitalism.* Ithaca, NY: Cornell University Press, 2006.

Chapter 14

NEWLY INDUSTRIALIZING ECONOMIC SYSTEMS: BRAZIL, INDIA, IRAN, AND SOUTH KOREA

"Economic development is something much wider and deeper than economics. Its roots lie outside the economic sphere, in education, organization, discipline, and, beyond, that, in political independence and a national consciousness of self-reliance."

E. F. SCHUMACHER (1911–1977),
British economist

This chapter examines the economic systems of four newly industrializing countries—Brazil, India, Iran, and South Korea. South Korea is the most developed of the four, whereas Brazil and India are often grouped together with Russia, China, and South Africa (hence the acronym BRICS) as rising economic powers. Iran is classified as a semideveloped transitional economy that has yet to achieve a clear path to self-sustaining growth as it attempts to combine modernization with adherence to traditional Islamic principles.

The developing nations of Latin America, Africa, the Middle East, and Asia face several common challenges in their quest to achieve successful economic systems. Most of them continue to bear the legacy of European or Japanese colonialism. The colonizing nations installed the **infrastructure** needed to extract natural resources (e.g., railroads; harbors; ports; security forces; and rudimentary communication, healthcare, and educational systems). However, their interest in economic development was secondary to the goal of accessing natural resources at the lowest possible cost and capturing markets for manufactured goods.

Colonization began during the era of **mercantilism,** when European nations sought to create empires by broadening the scope of their markets to create wealth that would fund a more powerful state. After the advent of **capitalism** in the early nineteenth century, colonization continued in the form of **imperialism** as competitive market pressures pushed both states and individual firms to seek opportunities abroad for profitable trade and investment. Whatever the benefits to the colonies, imperialism entailed a variety of practices that actually impeded economic development.

- Colonizers created alliances with particular ethnic groups or castes to "divide and conquer" the indigenous population. This discrimination created social conflict among groups and diverted energy from productive activities.
- The alliances between colonial governments and particular groups were often maintained by granting privileges and benefits such as government contracts or exclusive rights to produce a particular product. To gain access to these benefits, individuals and groups bribed government officials, leading to a heritage of pervasive corruption.
- Europeans unintentionally introduced diseases such as smallpox, malaria, and yellow fever that decimated native populations. In Central America, the indigenous population was reduced by 90 percent within a century after the arrival of Spanish conquistadors.
- Colonial governments often undermined traditional social structures and economic systems, leading to increased poverty, hunger, and insecurity.
- Colonizers established and reconfigured national boundaries with little regard for traditional ethnic groupings, leading to battles over control of territory.
- Colonial governments often discouraged or prohibited local manufacturing that might compete with exports from the mother country.
- The jobs created for indigenous people were mostly in primary industries such as agriculture, mining, logging, and rubber production. These jobs required few sophisticated skills; therefore, the colonizers had little interest in promoting literacy or other forms of human development.
- Colonization typically resulted in extreme inequality as colonizers claimed the best land and most valuable resources. For labor, they either relied on slavery or paid subsistence wages. Inequality thwarted economic development by weakening demand for local products and creating rigid social stratification with few opportunities for indigenous people.

By the twentieth century, colonial empires began to crumble in the face of various "national liberation movements." Despite successful struggles for independence, the long shadow of colonialism continued to block economic development. Former colonies had limited experience with democracy and self-government. Long-standing religious and ethnic conflicts flared as different groups battled for political power. With newly independent rulers often viewing themselves as successors to the privileges held by colonial governments, corruption was rampant. The centuries of repression left a deep mistrust if not hatred of foreigners and of capitalism that caused many former colonies to pursue paths of self-sufficiency or **socialism**. By attempting to minimize international trade and foreign investment, these countries ignored the insight of British economist Joan

Robinson (1903–1983): "The misery of being exploited by capitalists is nothing compared to the misery of not being exploited at all" (Robinson 1962, 45).

BRAZIL

As noted above, Brazil represents the "B" in the BRICS acronym, a term used to refer to a specific group of developing couintries considered to be on the threshold of economic maturity. In fact, Brazil's economy today is the seventh largest in the world.

Early History

As the only Portuguese colony in the Western hemisphere, Brazil inherited all the political and social challenges of its mother country. When Portugal claimed Brazil in 1500, it had only recently ended the struggle to drive the Moors out of the Iberian Peninsula and therefore was accustomed to military conflict, non-democratic government, and the imposition of Catholic orthodoxy. The Portuguese monarchy often rewarded high-ranking military officers with large plots of land (latifundios) in Brazil, which included the legal right to force local residents to work the land. Jesuits introduced Catholicism to Brazil, but because the Church was part of the ruling power structure, it did little to promote social **justice**. In fact, Jesuits led expeditions into the interior of Brazil to capture indigenous people to work as slaves on sugar plantations. The use of African slaves began around 1550, and by the time the country abolished slavery in 1888, Brazil had imported an estimated four million African slaves—ten times as many as were brought to the United States.

Independence in the Nineteenth and Twentieth Centuries

Brazil gained independence in 1822 but maintained its Portuguese heritage by establishing a kingdom that lasted until 1889 when the first democratic elections were held. Sugar plantations and discoveries of gold and other metals and minerals fueled the economy in the eighteenth century, but by the nineteenth century, coffee beans grown for export had become the leading industry. Large landowners and coffee growers controlled the government, exhibiting little interest in industrialization except to provide infrastructure for transporting their products to the coast for export. Other than enacting protective **tariffs** on imports in 1879, the government did little to promote domestic manufacturing, resulting in a relatively stagnant economy during the nineteenth century.

Brazil's economy depended heavily on **revenue** from exports; thus, the weakening of foreign demand during the Great Depression of the 1930s ultimately forced the country to confront its lack of industrial development. As the global depression caused the demand for coffee to drop, the loss of revenue left the country unable to pay for essential imported goods or to make payments on its foreign debt. With the economy in crisis, the army staged a coup in 1930 and installed Getulio Vargas (1882–1954) as president. Events in Europe at that time played an important role in shaping Brazilian politics. In 1933, just as Adolf Hitler assumed power in Germany, the Portuguese government established a quasi-fascist New State (Estado Novo) under the leadership of Antonio Salazar. **Fascism** appealed to many of the Brazilian coffee oligarchs and landed aristocracy who resembled the German Junkers insofar as their livelihoods depended on keeping rural workers on the land and opposing industrialization that might foster socialist organizations among workers.

In 1937, after rewriting the Constitution to give government increased authority over the economy, the Vargas regime replicated the Portuguese model by establishing a military dictatorship, also called the New State. The government suppressed freedom of speech and freedom of the press in order to quash political dissent and severely limited the rights of labor unions to organize and strike. However, unlike Hitler, Vargas had no intention of engaging in warfare to conquer other nations. Instead, his administration utilized its considerable power to restructure the economy. The government engaged in rudimentary economic planning, using public funds to build infrastructure and to make investments in private industry. To control the prices of exports, the government established marketing **cartels** in coffee, sugar, cocoa, and tea. The Vargas regime also established monopolistic, state-owned enterprises (SOEs) for oil production, mining, steel-making, and truck production. The rationale for SOEs was that these industries required such large initial outlays of capital that private businesses could not obtain sufficient financing.

Vargas, an ardent anticommunist, was also a nationalist whose foremost priority was to promote Brazil's economic development by reducing its dependence on exports. Like Bismarck in Germany, Vargas recognized the need to include all social classes in the benefits of economic growth. He instituted a minimum wage and a variety of social welfare programs resembling Franklin Roosevelt's New Deal agenda in the United States. These reforms made Vargas extremely popular with the Brazilian populace, so after relinquishing power in 1945, he was elected president in 1951. At that time, his administration initiated a development strategy known as *import substitution industrialization* (ISI).

The turn toward ISI was based on Brazil's experience during the Great Depression and World War II. Cut off from access to many foreign imports, Brazil was forced to produce more goods for itself, and the economy actually improved during that period. As a result, some Latin American economists concluded that foreign trade had been retarding the growth of developing countries. Brazilian economist Celso Furtado (1920–2004) and Argentine economist Raul Prebisch (1901–1986) were instrumental in developing **dependency theory**, which directly challenged the conventional economic wisdom that each nation should specialize in producing those goods in which it had **comparative advantage**. The theory of comparative advantage suggests that developing countries should specialize in primary industries such as agriculture and timber while trading with developed nations for manufactured goods. Prebisch argued that specializing in

primary industries would doom the developing countries to perpetual stagnation. The combination of competition among developing countries to export primary products and the relatively slow growth of demand for primary products
combine to suppress their prices. As a result, developed countries gain most of
the benefits of international trade. Furtado added the argument that successful
development requires both primary and manufacturing industries in order to
gain the benefits of **vertical integration** and **backward linkages** and **forward
linkages.** Specializing in only primary products would doom a country to
remain underdeveloped.

Relying on ISI strategy, the Brazilian government increased efforts to stimulate the formation of new manufacturing industries to produce previously imported goods. To thrive, these **infant industries** needed protection from imports
through tariffs, currency **devaluations**, and controls on access to **foreign exchange**
as well as government support in the form of **subsidies**, low-interest loans, tax
breaks, or, in some cases, public ownership. Ideally, after a period of government
support, the new industries would gain greater efficiency through **learning by
doing** and **economies of scale**, thereby enabling them to compete effectively
against industries in the more industrialized nations. ISI seemed to produce favorable results as Brazil enjoyed annual real growth rates averaging 8 percent from
1956 to 1962, but that performance was undoubtedly aided by the postwar recovery of the global economy.

In the late 1950s and early 1960s, left-wing administrations initiated reforms
designed to promote development by increasing demand and widening markets.
Widespread poverty in Brazil limited domestic consumer demand; therefore, the
government undertook land reform to break up large estates and provide farmers
with opportunities to become independent producers with sufficient income to
purchase Brazilian products. In 1962, Brazil and six other countries began the
Latin American Free Trade Association in an effort to increase the demand for
each country's products by widening markets.

The large landowners vehemently opposed land reform, and in 1964, the
army staged another coup to establish a military government (junta) that would
rule until 1985. This right-wing government continued ISI strategy but also focused on opening the country to foreign investment and increasing exports. The
result was Brazil's equivalent of the German Economic Miracle of the 1950s.
Annual growth averaged 4 percent between 1964 and 1967 but shot up to 11 percent between 1968 and 1973. Annual **inflation** fell from 64 to 24 percent. During
this period, the government continued to play a significant role in the economy,
providing subsidies; tax incentives; support for SOEs; and controls on wages,
prices, and availability of credit. The junta also imprisoned and tortured political
dissidents, censored the press, and deprived labor unions of the right to strike
and to collectively bargain. Despite the booming economy, **real wages** dropped
and inequality in the distribution of income increased.

When the Organization of Petroleum Exporting Countries (OPEC) quadrupled the price of oil in 1973, the Brazilian economy suffered. At the time, Brazil

had few oil fields, so higher oil prices caused a deteriorating **balance of trade**. Based on strong economic performance leading up to 1973, the government was able to borrow heavily from foreign lenders to pay for increasingly expensive foreign oil. As a result, Brazil's foreign debt increased from $12 billion in 1973 to $92 billion in 1980. To finance the debt as well as domestic development projects, the government engaged in **deficit spending** and increased the money supply. However, the fiscal and monetary stimulus, coupled with the rising cost of oil, resulted in runaway inflation. The annual rate of inflation rose from 16 percent in 1974 to 110 percent in 1980.

In addition to deficit spending and money creation, two other factors fueled inflation. First, in an effort to reduce its balance of trade deficit, Brazil periodically devalued its currency. Devaluation caused prices of imports to rise, adding to inflationary pressures. Second, the government began indexing wages, **interest rates**, rents, pensions, and taxes by raising these payments at the same rate as inflation. Indexing was intended to prevent workers, landlords, lenders, retirees, and the government from being hurt by inflation, but it virtually guaranteed that inflation would continue.

By 1979, Brazil had the largest **public sector** relative to **gross domestic product** (GDP) of any noncommunist nation. Twenty-eight of the thirty largest nonfinancial firms were SOEs, including the telecommunications industry, electricity, gas utilities, railways, petroleum, coal, and two-thirds of the steel industry.

Annual growth remained strong, at 7 percent, during the 1970s, but between 1980 and 1983, Brazil experienced its first recession since the 1930s as **real GDP** declined by 10 percent. Growth remained sluggish for the remainder of the decade, inflation averaged 400 percent per year, and real wages declined by 3 percent. Brazilians refer to the 1980s as "the lost decade."

In 1985, the military junta allowed legislators to elect a new president, but the first fully democratic election since the military coup of 1964 did not occur until 1990. By this time, disillusionment with ISI strategy had become widespread. Protecting domestic manufacturing industries insulated them from competitive pressures to reduce costs and innovate with improved products and technology. Also, the massive government support and periodic currency devaluations required to keep these industries afloat contributed to foreign debt and inflation. To replace ISI, administrations during the early 1990s enacted a series of reforms aimed at restoring growth and controlling inflation. Minister of Finance Fernando Henrique Cardoso initiated a program to reduce tariffs on imports and to sell $7 billion of assets in SOEs in the petrochemical, electricity, shipping, and fertilizer industries. To curb inflation, Cardoso developed the *Real* Plan (named after the new currency, the *real*) in 1994, calling for higher taxes to balance the government budget, further reductions in tariffs, and a new currency tied or "pegged" to the US dollar at a one-to-one ratio.

Based on the success of the *Real* Plan, Cardoso was elected president and began an even more aggressive program of market-oriented reforms. Before holding public office, Cardoso had been a highly respected sociologist and prominent dependency theorist, so his commitment to opening Brazil to foreign trade surprised many of his supporters. He continued the process of privatization by selling SOEs in the steel, mining, and telecommunications industries to private owners. To combat inflation, which had climbed to 4 percent per month, Cardoso began the gradual dismantling of indexation. This action caused hardship for groups previously protected from inflation but was essential to stabilize prices. He also initiated stronger protections for human rights, improvements in Brazil's educational system, and programs to alleviate poverty.

Cardoso's efforts to halt inflation exacted a toll on the economy. Setting the value of the *real* equal to the US dollar caused the *real* to be overvalued, which reduced the prices of imports and made Brazilian exports more expensive to foreigners. As imports rose and exports fell, growth came to a halt in 1998. The following year, a growing balance of trade deficit forced the government to devalue the *real* by 60 percent. Even with that action, the economy grew at a rate of only 1.3 percent in 2001. By the end of his eight years in office, Cardoso's popularity had plummeted.

Brazil in the Twenty-First Century

In 2002, Brazilians elected the openly leftist candidate of the Workers' Party, Luis Lula da Silva. Lula, as he was popularly known, had been the leader of the metalworkers union, but he continued Cardoso's commitment to privatization and anti-inflation measures. To promote social justice and strengthen consumer demand, Lula's administration increased the minimum wage, provided grants to low-income families, established a pension system for rural workers, and increased funding for education, healthcare, and other social services. The central bank began targeting a specified rate of inflation, announcing the rate in advance and then using **monetary policy** to achieve that rate. A contractionary **fiscal policy** resulted in government budget surpluses, and the government allowed the exchange rate between the *real* and foreign currencies to fluctuate within a specified range. The economy responded with strong growth from 2004 until 2010, attributable in part to rising exports of primary products to China and other rapidly growing Asian countries.

In 2010, Brazilians elected as president another candidate of the Workers' Party, Dilma Rousseff. She had been imprisoned during the 1980s for actively opposing the military regime and campaigned as a leftist. Since her election, economic performance has been disappointing, with growth falling to less than 3 percent in 2011, less than 1 percent in 2012, and near zero since then. Inflation has risen to 6 percent, and the Brazilian stock market has lost one-third of its value. Several interacting factors account for the sagging economy. First, the weak recovery from the global recession of 2008 has hurt Brazilian exports. In addition, declining exports caused the *real* to depreciate by 30 percent between 2011 and 2012, leading to losses for foreign banks and investors who held Brazilian financial assets. More generally, foreign investors have been hesitant to engage funds in a country led by an openly leftist government. Finally, with the country's commitment to relatively free trade, Brazil's manufacturing sector is being forced to make difficult adjustments to become competitive in global markets.

Rousseff narrowly won reelection in 2014 against a probusiness, free-market challenger. Her margin of victory resulted from overwhelming support in the poorer states of northeastern Brazil. The discontent of investors was reflected in a nearly 4 percent drop in the Brazilian stock market the day after her reelection. She has promised to work with opposing political parties to improve the business climate in Brazil and to restore growth.

As the seventh largest economy in the world, Brazil faces a promising future. Unemployment remains relatively low despite sluggish growth, the middle class is rapidly expanding, the agricultural sector is among the most efficient in the world, and the manufacturing sector has made great strides. Citizens have universal access to primary education and basic healthcare, although private clinics and hospitals provide more specialized care for those who can afford it. Illiteracy and malnutrition have been virtually eliminated among the younger generation. Culturally, Brazil has achieved a relatively harmonious multiethnic society.

However, certain challenges still face Brazil. Inequality of income and land ownership is higher than most other countries in the world. The top 10 percent of families receive 50 percent of the income, whereas the poorest 40 percent earn less than 10 percent. The prosperous, urbanized southeastern region of Brazil looks like a different country than the poor, rural northeastern states. Corruption in government remains an issue as Rousseff is accused of funneling money into her campaign from the state-controlled oil company Petrobras. Finally, despite Brazil's universal primary and secondary education, the country's universities cannot yet accommodate the large numbers of young adults whose skills will be needed to make the final transition to economic maturity.

INDIA

Today India ranks second to China in population and may well become the most populated country in the future. Like China, India was once among the wealthiest nations on earth. The Moghal Empire, which ruled most of the territory constituting modern India, may have been the richest empire in the world in 1700. However, this prosperity was accompanied by sharp inequality. While rulers and elites lived in opulence, the vast majority of the populace eked out a living in rural villages. Peasants often relied on communal ownership of land and pooled resources for agriculture and small-scale manufacturing. Villages collectively provided support for the elderly and disabled.

Early History and Caste System

A hereditary caste system, based on the Hindu belief in reincarnation, established the division of labor, with children following in the footsteps of their parents. The castes ranged from the highest level (Brahmin priests) to the lowest level of social outcasts called "Untouchables." The caste system served the function of maintaining social order by reducing conflict over social status and employment. Indian villages developed a system of reciprocal labor exchanges (jajmani). For example, a cobbler might make a pair of sandals in exchange for a blanket produced with a similar amount of labor by a weaver.

The Portuguese were the first Europeans to establish a colony (Goa) on the west coast of India in 1511. By 1600, the Dutch had gained control of ports in southern India, and the British and French followed shortly thereafter. The British monarchy granted a "crown charter" to the East India Company, giving it exclusive control over trade between Britain and India. By skillfully pitting local rulers against each other, the East India Company and the British government gradually gained political control over most of India. Major victories in battles between British and Indian armies in 1757 and 1764 resulted in the Moghal emperor ceding authority to the British. The British lacked the manpower to administer the entire colony; therefore, they allowed the Moghal ruler to remain on the throne as a figurehead and permitted local rulers to retain a degree of **sovereignty** within specified territories.

India Under British Rule

The economic impact of the British Raj (rule) on India has been much debated. Perhaps because India's large population offered so many potential customers for British exports, the British devoted more resources to developing India than was typical of other European colonizers. The British built substantial physical infrastructure, including railroads, telegraph lines, and roads. Under colonial rule, India gained a common currency, a modern judicial system, standardization of weights and measures, a competent civil service, and a financial sector of banks and capital markets. The British established universities in Bombay, Calcutta, and Madras in 1857, and they started an engineering school in 1886. Politically and culturally, British colonization created a sense of national identity in a country filled with many different ethnic and religious groups, lacking a unified language and never before ruled by a single government.

On the other hand, beneath all these benefits lay the British goal of extracting wealth from India. The British talked of their moral obligation to bear "the white man's burden" of civilizing the rest of the world, but the driving force behind British imperialism was economic gain. The British undermined the self-sufficient village system of labor exchanges by imposing taxes on rural peasants, thereby forcing them to work for wages in order to earn money to pay taxes. Given the unequal power and social status created by India's caste system, the penetration of markets into rural areas resulted in growing inequality of income and wealth. Wealthy landowners discovered that they could make more money by lending to peasant farmers at usurious interest rates than by investing to improve agricultural productivity. In fact, many small farmers who did own land would subsequently lose it to money lenders when they were unable to repay loans. One indication of the damage done by British imperialism is that the poverty rate and the number of deaths due to starvation actually increased as the nineteenth century progressed. Between 1820 and the end of British rule in 1947, the annual growth rate in real GDP averaged only a tenth of one percent.

The East India Company suppressed local manufacturing that might have competed with British exports. India's substantial textile industry exported processed cotton and silk prior to 1800. After Britain placed tariffs on Indian exports of textiles, India became a net importer of those goods. The British also relied on a "divide and conquer" strategy by training and employing only upper-caste Hindus for civil service and managerial positions. This discrimination sowed the seeds of ethnic and religious strife. In 1858, Indian troops (sepoy) under British command staged a mass uprising. The Sepoy Rebellion caused the British government to remove the Moghal emperor and take control of the country from the East India Company.

The Emerging Independence Movement and Gandhi

In the early 1920s, a young Hindu lawyer named Mohandas Gandhi (1869–1948) began performing acts of civil disobedience to protest British rule. Gandhi, known as "Mahatma" (Great Soul), was dedicated to nonviolence, and his vision of restoring the viability of small, self-sufficient villages with their communal lifestyles and labor-intensive, small-scale manufacturing was a form of **social anarchism**. For the next two decades, he devoted himself to the cause of Indian independence. That goal was finally achieved in 1947 after World War II left Britain with insufficient resources to manage much of its colonial empire.

To quell rising tensions between Hindus and Muslims, independence included partitioning the country into Hindu India and Muslim Pakistan, which consisted of East and West Pakistan on opposite sides of India. East Pakistan would later gain separate nationhood as Bangladesh in 1971. The partition caused national chaos as twelve million refugee Hindus, Muslims, and Sikhs left their homes to relocate with their respective religious groupings. Violent riots took the lives of more than half a million people during the first three days of independence.

Gandhi's calls for religious tolerance led to his assassination by a Hindu nationalist in 1948. Indians then elected his political ally, Jawaharlal Nehru, as the nation's first prime minister. Both Gandhi and Nehru advocated democracy, equal rights, and improved status for women as reflected in the abolition of the caste system shortly after independence. Both men distrusted capitalism, equating it with domination by foreign powers, and sought national self-reliance to free India from dependence on other countries.

After, Gandhi's death, the Indian people elected Jawaharlal Nehru (1889–1964) as their first head of state. In contrast to Gandhi's social anarchism, Nehru hoped to lead India toward a modern, industrialized, mixed economy. Private property and markets were prevalent in India, so the country would have elements of capitalism, but Nehru also planned to rely extensively on government control of the economy. To gain national self-sufficiency, the government pursued an ISI policy by erecting trade barriers (e.g., tariffs, quotas, and subsidies) and discouraging

Figure 14.1 Nehru and Gandhi confer with each other. (© Getty Images/UniversalImagesGroup)

foreign investment. Following the Soviet growth model, India emphasized the expansion of heavy industry. Some British companies were nationalized along with the life insurance industry, and the government invested public funds in steel, coal, and electricity, as well as creating several SOEs.

India faced modernization with many daunting challenges. In addition to religious conflicts, colonialism had left 65 percent of the population in poverty, with 85 percent of the nation's wealth in the hands of only 2 percent of the households. Women, more than half of whom remained illiterate, possessed few rights. To accelerate growth, the government created the Indian Planning Commission in 1951 with authority to develop five-year plans to guide economic development. The commission engaged only in **indicative planning**, with no mandatory quotas or targets. In an effort to steer business activity toward manufacturing, the government enacted laws and regulations requiring official permits and licenses to open or expand businesses. Indians cynically joked that the British Raj had been replaced by the "license-permit Raj." The difficulty in gaining these permits led to pervasive corruption as bribing government bureaucrats became an accepted part of doing business.

During the 1950s, economic performance failed to meet expectations; the growth of the economy barely exceeded the rate of population growth. As a result, the annual growth in per capita income was little more than 1 percent. However, India did benefit by remaining nonaligned in the Cold War and therefore being able to solicit aid from both the United States and the Soviet Union.

Nehru died in 1964, and his daughter, Indira Gandhi (1917–1984) was elected prime minister in 1966. She intensified Nehru's focus on developing heavy industry and using government regulations to steer the economy. The government enacted a law limiting the size of firms and another controlling access to foreign exchange by firms needing to import resources. A wave of nationalization of industry included the fourteen largest banks and the coal, textile, wheat farming, paper, chemicals, pharmaceutical, petroleum, electrical equipment, fertilizer, transportation, and communications industries. The iron, steel, and copper industries remained in private hands but were placed under state control. Along with this tilt toward socialism, India became more closely aligned with the Soviet Union during the 1970s. Lingering hostility toward capitalism led the Indians to prefer trading with a socialist nation, and the Soviet Union had a strong interest in maintaining a large client state in Asia after parting ways with China in the late 1950s.

The combination of a growing **public sector** and OPEC's 1973 quadrupling of oil prices created an economic crisis as inflation, food shortages, and a deteriorating balance of trade forced Prime Minister Indira Gandhi to declare a state of emergency in 1975. Voted out of office in 1977, she regained power in 1980. After supporting government actions viewed as offensive by the minority Sikh population, Indira Gandhi was assassinated by her Sikh bodyguard in 1984. Her son, Rajiv Gandhi (1944–1991), succeeded her as prime minister and remained in office until 1991 when he, too, was assassinated. The younger Gandhi loosened many of the restrictions on business, and the economy responded strongly, growing at an average annual rate of 5.5 percent during the remainder of the 1980s. However, this growth was achieved, in part, through massive foreign borrowing and a growing **national debt**.

When the Soviet Union disintegrated in 1991, India lost not only its major trading partner but also its primary source of oil and natural gas. A resulting balance of payments deficit and the near exhaustion of its reserves of foreign currency caused international lenders to lower its credit rating. Faced with bankruptcy, India applied for and received emergency loan assistance from the International Monetary Fund.

An economic crisis can set the stage for a major transformation of the economic system. Newly elected Prime Minister Narasimha Rao (1921–2004) appointed economist Manmohan Singh as Minister of Finance. Singh initiated a broad package of sweeping reforms, including devaluation of the currency (rupee) to make exports more competitive, tax reforms to promote exports and encourage foreign investment, tight monetary and fiscal policies to reduce inflation and the government's budget deficit, lower tariffs on imports, a less complicated application process for acquiring business licenses, and privatization of many SOEs. The results were impressive, as the annual growth rate rose to 7 percent by 1995.

India in the Twenty-First Century

Singh was elected prime minister in 2004, and the growth rate rose to an average of nearly 8 percent from 2004 until 2012. Between 1991 and 2012, the Indian GDP quadrupled. However, growth slowed to 4.4 percent in 2013 as the rupee depreciated and higher import prices caused inflation. When Singh chose not to run for reelection in 2014, the opposition party won a landslide victory and Narendra Modi became prime minister. Modi campaigned on a probusiness, promarket platform and promised to continue Singh's movement toward a more pure form of capitalism. Spurred in part by optimism over Modi's policies, the Indian growth rate rose to 5.6 percent in 2014.

India possesses vast potential for future development. The country offers excellent universities, a healthy democratic political system, and a growing middle class that creates strong demand for consumer products. With much of the 1.2 billion population still living in rural areas, India is likely to experience strong extensive growth as previously untapped human and natural resources enter the national economy. Half the population is younger than age twenty-five, meaning that the labor force will grow rapidly in coming years. India will not face the problems shared by most developed countries of having to support an aging population in the near future. The median age in India is twenty-seven, compared to thirty-seven in China, forty in the United States, and forty-six Germany.

However, several challenges could derail the Indian economy. Most of the recent growth has been in the service sector; India provides call centers and performs financial, legal, and accounting services for Western corporations. Along with a thriving computer software industry, these jobs employ urban, well-educated, English-speaking Indians, but the benefits of growth have not been widely shared throughout the country. The poverty rate in rural areas remains approximately 50 percent, with more than one-third of the population living on less than $1.25 per day. High rates of illiteracy, malnourishment, high birth rates, unsafe drinking water, suppression of women, and lack of infrastructure will continue to hinder development. Despite the official abolition of the Hindu caste system after independence in 1947, discrimination based on religion, ethnicity, gender, and social status remains widespread. In 1992, a riot between Muslims and Hindus in the state of Gujarat resulted in more than 1,000 deaths. In the northern states of Jammu and Kashmir, a majority Muslim population continues to struggle for independence. Religious conflict may continue to flare up because Prime Minister Modi is the leader of the Hindu nationalist Bharatiya Janata Party, which has traditionally been less tolerant of Muslims than the Indian National Congress party established by Mahatma Gandhi. One indication of increasing religious intolerance is the recent criminalization of the sale of beef in several Indian states. Devout Hindus have long revered the cow and will not eat beef, but the new law applies to all citizens within the affected states, including Muslims, and makes the sale of beef punishable by up to five years in prison.

Several other potential problems loom over India's future. Corruption has been reduced but is still widespread, and government operations suffer from lack of transparency. The high degree of inequality could impede development by suppressing consumer demand for domestic goods. In addition, large landowners have used their political power to prevent construction of schools that might enable the children of tenant farmers to leave the land, and money lenders have an incentive to maintain a desperately poor portion of the population in need of loans. The Indian government has attempted to circumvent the power of money lenders by providing small business loans (microloans) to poor citizens, particularly women. Children in poor families often enter the labor force instead of going to school, so nearly 4 percent of the labor force consists of children younger than age fourteen. Finally, like China, India potentially faces a "middle-income trap" as rising wages reduce its advantage in cheap labor and cause businesses to relocate to lower-wage countries such as Indonesia, Myanmar, and Thailand.

The collective memory of British imperialism causes many Indian leaders to treat any criticism of the nation as an attack by foreign powers. Politicians deny or suppress claims that women are treated as second-class citizens, that public sanitation is primitive, that corruption is pervasive, and that infanticide and sex-selective abortions are used to increase the proportion of male to female births. As a result, the problems are not met head on with aggressive public policies. To his credit, Prime Minister Modi has raised many of these issues and proposes that at least one-third of the parliament be composed of women.

IRAN

Iran (also known as Persia) is one of the oldest continuous civilizations in the world. Today Iran is poised for economic growth, but this growth is dependent on the balance of power in its political system. On one side are fundamentalist religious groups who desire strict adherence to Islamic religious doctrine. They are challenged by pragmatic, secular political leaders who want Iran to partici-pate more fully in the global economy.

Early History

The Persian Empire began around 650 BCE and at its peak stretched from Egypt to India. In the seventh century CE, the Prophet Muhammad (570–632 CE) initi-ated a religious movement in Arabia known as Islam that claimed direct lineage to the early Christian prophets, including Jesus. Muhammad's teachings, as re-corded in the Koran (Qur'an) share with early Christianity a defense of the poor and dispossessed against the wealthy and powerful.

After Muhammad's death, disputes over his successor led to a split between Shia and Sunni Muslims. Despite this internal division, Islam spread rapidly throughout the Middle East, and Muslim armies defeated the Persians. For the next ten centuries, a succession of different empires rose and fell, but by 1501, the Safavid dynasty reunified Persia as an independent state and established Shia Islam as the official state religion.

During the Qajar dynasty (1785–1925), the Portuguese, Dutch, British, and Russians all began imperialistic forays into Persia. Persia never became an official colony, but the Russians to the north and the British in India steadily carved off pieces of the country to add to their empires. The Qajar ruler (shah) viewed for-eign trade as a means to enrich the monarchy, and when oil was discovered in 1909, foreign interest in Persia escalated dramatically. The British initiated a joint venture with the Persian government called the Anglo-Persian Oil Company, which would later become British Petroleum. The British paid royalties to the Persian government in exchange for access to the oil, but the royalties were smaller than the taxes on the oil paid to the British government.

As the Russian and British presence in Persia increased, the two countries signed the Anglo-Russian Convention, which effectively ended Persian sovereignty. The British occupied the south while the Russians remained in the north, and they jointly controlled the Persian economy. However, the Russian Revolution in 1917 changed this cooperative agreement as the British expanded their presence to protect oil supplies from the spread of communism. In 1921, the British conspired with the Persian military to stage a coup. The Qajar shah was left on the throne, but a military officer named Reza Kahn (1878–1944) took control of the country with support from the British. Four years later, the shah abdicated and Reza Kahn became Reza Shah Pahlavi, the ruler of Persia.

Modernization in the Twentieth Century

Reza Shah had grand ambitions to turn Persia into a secular, modern nation. He opened schools to women and forbade them to wear traditional clothing (chadors) that covered all of their bodies except hands and eyes. He created a secular judiciary system, established a modern civil service, and initiated land reform by taking land from religious organizations (waqfs) and distributing it to farmers. Impressed by Germany's success with state capitalism prior to World War I, Reza Shah initiated state-led development focused on manufacturing and oil. His admiration for Germany led him to conclude that Adolf Hitler represented the wave of the future, and he emulated Hitler by strengthening the military and centralizing political power. In 1935, he changed the name of Persia to Iran (land of the Aryans) to revive a very early name for Persians that Hitler was also using to create a sense of racial identity among Germans. During World War II, Reza Shah's sympathies for Germany led the Soviets and the British to jointly occupy Iran. They forced the shah to abdicate and installed his son, Mohammad Reza Pahlavi (1919–1980), as the new ruler.

Shah Mohammad Reza shared his father's commitment to modernization, secularization, and industrialization. He used oil revenue to establish SOEs in iron, steel, sugar, cement, and textiles. In addition, the government pursued an ISI strategy by providing low-interest loans and protective trade barriers to promote domestic manufacturing. In 1944, the government established comprehensive indicative planning of the economy. Although the shah was the nominal ruler of the country, his power was limited by a democratically elected legislature that had considerable independence to enact public policy. In 1951, Prime Minister Mohammad Mosaddegh (1882–1967) nationalized the British-controlled oil industry. In response, the British, with the support of the shah and the US Central Intelligence Agency, funded and instigated an overthrow of the democratically elected government. The coup failed, causing the shah to flee the country in fear of public reaction. However, a second coup in 1953, again instigated by British and US intelligence agencies, succeeded. The shah returned to power and placed the oil industry under control of British Petroleum and several American oil companies.

In 1963, the shah initiated the White Revolution (so named because it would be bloodless). He opened the country to foreign investment and privatized many of the SOEs. Like Bismarck in Germany, the shah recognized the need to provide benefits to all sectors of society in order to maintain political stability. He initiated profit-sharing and job security plans for industrial workers and granted women the right to vote and to enter many professions previously closed to them. The government instituted free education through the university level, free healthcare, disability benefits, improved public health facilities, and land reform to end the quasi-feudal conditions in rural areas where sharecroppers had been forced to surrender most of their produce to landlords. More than 90 percent of sharecroppers became land owners as a result of the White Revolution. The economy responded strongly with 10 to 12 percent annual growth through the 1960s and 1970s. Growth was partially attributable to foreign aid from the United States and Britain and to rising oil revenue after the OPEC price increase of 1973. By 1977, money from oil exports accounted for 79 percent of the government's revenue.

The Islamic Revolution

Given the strong performance of the Iranian economy, what factors would subsequently lead to the shah's downfall in an Islamic revolution? First, the shah's corruption was undeniable. He had accumulated vast wealth from oil royalties and land grabs. Second, British and American support for his government rendered the shah suspect in the eyes of most Iranians. Third, the shah maintained an extensive secret police force (SAVAK) that spied on citizens and arrested thousands of political dissidents. Fourth, by using oil revenue to develop only SOEs and a few large corporations, the shah alienated merchants and small business owners. Fifth, because most development occurred in urban areas, farmers failed to share in the benefits of economic growth. Sixth, the shah lost support of the Shia clergy by confiscating land owned by religious groups and by secularizing Iranian society.

With small business owners providing the funding, the Shia clerics organized a successful revolution in 1979, leading to the establishment of the Islamic Republic of Iran. The shah's appeal for political asylum in the United States was denied, but he was accepted by Egypt, where he died a year later. A high-ranking Shia cleric (ayatollah) named Ruhollah Khomeini (1902–1989) had been directing the revolution from exile in Paris and returned to Iran to become the Supreme Leader of the country. Like the shah, Khomeini sought to build a broad base of support by catering to the interests of many different groups. His calls for social justice attracted leftists, workers, and farmers. His promises to end corruption and reduce regulations appealed to business owners. Nationalists found inspiration in his rhetoric about restoring the glory of the Persian Empire and achieving national self-sufficiency. Devout Muslims welcomed the return of an openly religious state in which public policy would be guided by Islamic principles.

Once in power, Khomeini jailed and executed thousands of leftists and former supporters of the shah. A new constitution maintained a democratically elected legislature but gave religious leaders final authority over public policy. The new government gained direct control of 80 percent of the economy; Khomeini ordered confiscation of all properties owned by the shah and his associates as well as the nationalization of all banks, insurance companies, and many other private businesses. The government engaged in central planning of the economy and imposed Sharia law based on the Koran. Like the Bible, the Koran is written in verses whose meanings are open to interpretation. For example, the Koran calls for cutting off the hands of thieves, but that punishment has not been used because Shia theologians cannot agree whether the hand should be severed at the wrist or at the base of the fingers. The Koran's prescribed punishment for unfaithful wives is stoning.

In the realm of economic policy, the Koran approves of private property and markets, but its condemnation of interest (riba) on loans and extremes of poverty and wealth provides grounds for anti-capitalist sentiment. Like early Christians, Muslims view charging interest on loans as a method by which the rich and powerful take advantage of those in need. An entire system of Islamic banking or Sharia-compliant finance has arisen in Iran and throughout the Muslim world as banks find new ways to operate without explicitly charging interest. Underlying all these practices is the belief that lenders must bear part of the risk associated with loans. In contrast, Western banks often seek to transfer all risk to the borrower by demanding collateral equal to the value of the loan.

To circumvent the prohibition against charging interest, Iranian banks have developed several unique practices. In the case of business loans, the lender and borrower may reach an agreement whereby the lender purchases equipment and raw materials and then sells them to the borrower at a higher price. The resulting profit serves as a substitute for interest on the loan. Alternatively, the lender and borrower may form a partnership and share profits until the loan has been repaid. Using another strategy, the lender purchases an asset and then leases it to the borrower who makes monthly payments totaling an amount greater than the value of the asset. Finally, loans may be classified as venture capital so that repayment of the loan is profit rather than interest. In all of these practices, the lender gains money, but the gain is not called "interest." Banks are also prohibited from paying interest on deposits and so offer prizes such as small household appliances to depositors. For long-term savings accounts, banks may establish profit-sharing programs with depositors.

Sharia law also prohibits gambling, prostitution, and consumption of pork and alcohol. Depending on how strictly the ban on gambling is interpreted, risky investments in financial derivatives, futures contracts, and corporate stock could be made illegal. Even the purchase of life insurance has been challenged as a gamble on one's longevity. Iran and other Muslim countries still struggle to reconcile Sharia law with modern financial markets. However, Muslim banks will not make loans for investments in activities explicitly prohibited by Sharia law.

Another application of Sharia law to the economy is the practice of making charitable donations (zakat) to religious organizations that distribute the money to the needy. Some Muslim countries require citizens to make these donations, and although they remain voluntary in Iran, most Muslims donate 10 percent of their income. In addition, a 20 percent income tax goes to Shia religious authorities to be used for social improvements. This redistribution of income is based on the Islamic commitment to social justice and equality. Finally, Muslim business owners are expected to uphold social justice by paying equitable wages, charging fair prices, making no more than a reasonable profit, and sharing some of their profits with employees. Iran is relying on religion to curb self-interest and create a sense of community.

After the revolution of 1979, Saddam Hussein, the ruler of neighboring Iraq, feared that a Shia state in Iran would embolden the long-suppressed Shia majority in his country. The Iraqi army subsequently invaded Iran, leading to an eight-year war in which 300,000 Iranians perished and another 500,000 were wounded before a negotiated ceasefire in 1988. Coinciding with a global recession in the early 1980s, the war devastated the Iranian economy by creating sharp declines in oil revenue, high inflation, and negative growth. By 1990, the combination of revolution and war had caused per capita GDP to decline by half, returning it to the level of the early 1960s.

The Islamic Revolution initially led to dramatic reversals in the role of women in Iranian society. Schools were segregated by gender, women were forbidden to mingle with men in public, some occupations were closed to women, birth control and abortion were forbidden, and strict dress codes were imposed. However, the Iraq-Iran war forced the government to call on women to enter the labor force to replace the absent males. Also, a rising birth rate persuaded the government to provide access to birth control. With each passing decade, restrictions on occupational choice diminish as women now work in government and occupy many professions. However, men are still permitted to wed multiple spouses, and divorce is much easier for men than for women.

Iran's Economy Today

Iran's political system balances tenuously between democracy and religious theocracy. Both the legislative assembly (Majlis) and the president are democratically elected. However, the president remains subordinate to the supreme leader, who is elected by the assembly of experts consisting of approximately eight-five Shia theologians (Mujtahids). Overseeing all these bodies sits the Guardian Council composed of six theologians appointed by the Supreme Leader and six Islamic legal scholars nominated by the judiciary and subject to approval by the legislature. The Guardian Council maintains veto power over all legislation and over all potential candidates for public office. In the years immediately after the revolution, the Guardian Council leaned toward protecting private property and markets by vetoing nationalization of businesses, workers' councils, and land reform. However, in recent years, the Council has more often blocked legislation aimed at moving toward capitalism.

After Ayatollah Ruhollah Khomeini's death in 1989, he was replaced as Supreme Leader by Ali Khamenei, who had previously served as President. The new president, Akbar Hashemi Rafsanjani, advocated free-market reforms for the domestic economy. He privatized some SOEs and sought to open Iran to foreign trade and investment. In 1997, the next president, Mohammad Khatami, had even more success in moving Iran in a market-oriented direction, but change moved slowly due to the power of the Guardian Council and opposition from the judiciary and national police. A more conservative president, Mahmoud Ahmadinejad, was elected in 2005. Although he pushed for privatization of SOEs, Iran remains predominantly a state-centered, command economy.

In 2006, the United States and other nations imposed an embargo on trade with Iran as punishment for the nation's uranium enrichment program. Iran claimed that it was simply preparing to produce nuclear power, but Western nations suspected the development of nuclear weapons. The trade sanctions have seriously damaged Iran's economy as oil exports and foreign investment have declined sharply. The United States subsequently relaxed the embargo enough to permit subsidiaries of US oil companies to invest in Iran's oil industry. Iran's economy grew at an average annual rate of 5.6 percent between 2005 and 2010, but the sanctions eventually took a toll. The growth of GDP slowed to 3 percent, unemployment rose to 12 percent, and inflation reached 16 percent. In 2015, the Iranian government finally agreed to inspections of its nuclear facilities in exchange for a lifting of the embargo.

In 2013, Iranians elected a moderate president, Hassan Rouhani, who continues the trend toward improving foreign relations and placing greater reliance on the market. The future of Iran will be determined by the shifting balance of power between opposing groups. On one hand, more pragmatic, secular forces seek renewed economic growth through involvement in the global economy and expansion of civil rights. Yet for fundamentalist Shia groups, economic growth is less important than adherence to religious doctrine. They view Iran as creating an alternative to both capitalism and communism that will serve as a model for other Islamic nations to follow. The Shia clerics believe that religion can create a national community in which Islamic values such as cooperation, hard work, honesty, social justice, and concern for the welfare of others will create a moral and prosperous economic system.

SOUTH KOREA

South Korea comprises the southern half of the Korean Peninsula in East Asia, sharing a heavily militarized border with North Korea.

Early History of Korea

Koreans descended from a distinct racial and cultural group, the Tungusic tribe, and their early history is characterized by a series of invasions and wars with neighboring peoples from China and Mongolia. In 1392, the Korean Kingdom of Joseon was founded with the establishment of the Yi dynasty, which lasted approximately five centuries. To retain its sovereignty, the dynasty paid "tribute" to its more powerful neighbor China. As the Yi dynasty intentionally avoided all foreign involvement, Korea came to be known as the "hermit kingdom."

The government was administered by a bureaucracy of Confucian scholars who sought to structure Korean society in accordance with the principles of Confucianism. According to Confucius (551–449 BCE), society is not simply a collection of individuals but an organic whole whose natural order is hierarchy. Subordinate individuals have a duty to suppress their personal interests in order to strengthen their community, but rulers and leaders also have a responsibility to be benevolent, wise, and virtuous. When all citizens fulfill their duties, society will be harmonious and stable.

During the Yi dynasty, most of the populace consisted of rural peasants and craftsmen. Any surplus production was confiscated by large landowners and ruling elites either for their own consumption or to pay tribute to China. Merchants were tightly regulated to ensure that they posed no threat to the regime, so virtually the only route to upward social mobility was through the civil service. Ambitious citizens relied on bribery to cultivate personal relations with government officials.

Colonization by Japan

The Yi dynasty had no internal or external threats and therefore little incentive to increase economic productivity. Korea remained underdeveloped until Japan negotiated a trade agreement in 1876. Other nations began trading with Korea in the 1880s, leading to the gradual emergence of a class of merchants and manufacturers. In 1905, Japan and Russia engaged in war to gain control of Korea. Japan won the war, immediately claimed Korea as a protectorate, and subsequently made it a colony in 1910.

Economic growth accelerated under Japanese rule as colonization brought certain benefits such as the abolition of slavery; modern legal, financial, and educational systems; dispersion of large land holdings; building of physical infrastructure; and the introduction of business skills and technical knowledge. However, like all colonial powers, Japan focused primarily on extracting resources and wealth from Korea. Most businesses of any significant size were under Japanese ownership, so Korea became simply a supplier of labor and raw materials for Japanese firms. The Japanese regarded Koreans as inferior and treated them with condescension.

World War II and the Partition of Korea

As World War II began, Korea benefited from an infusion of Japanese investment in the industries producing military equipment. Japan's eventual defeat devastated Korea because its economy was based primarily on production by Japanese-owned firms and trade with Japan. GDP fell by more than 50 percent as US forces dismantled the Japanese factories used to produce armaments. A massive flow of immigrants exacerbated the economic distress. Two million Koreans who had been living either in Japan or China returned to their newly liberated homeland after the war. To make matters worse, Korea quickly became the center of Cold War tensions between the Soviet Union and the United States. With Soviet troops occupying the northern part of the country and US troops in the south, neither of the superpowers would cede the territory it controlled. To prevent military clashes over disputed territory, the United States proposed splitting the country into two parts, using the 38th parallel as the dividing line.

Koreans in the south attempted to form their own government, but the United States insisted on maintaining temporary military control of the country to prevent a communist takeover. To pave the way for self-rule, the US military flew a Korean exile named Syngman Rhee (1875–1965) from the United States back to Korea. Rhee led the efforts to organize a new government, and in 1948, he was elected by the legislature as the first president of the newly established Republic of Korea (South Korea). Koreans in the north also formed a new country, the Democratic People's Republic of Korea (North Korea), under the leadership of Kim Il-sung (1912–1994), who ruled as a communist dictator until his death.

Following the partition of Korea into separate nations, more than two million people moved from the north to the south. In 1950, North Korean troops invaded the south, capturing the capital city of Seoul and subsequently all of the country except the southeastern region. Under the auspices of the United Nations, the US army pushed the North Koreans back nearly to the border between North Korea and China. At that point, however, the Chinese army poured into North Korea, forcing the Americans to retreat. Although war was never officially declared, by the time this "police action" ended in 1953, the border between the two countries was restored at the 38th parallel. Fifty-four thousand American soldiers, more than three million Koreans, and one-half million Chinese lost their lives. Two-thirds of South Korea's productive capacity was destroyed.

The United States considered South Korea to be vital in stopping the spread of communism, so massive aid flowed into the country during the 1950s. However, much of the money ended up in the hands of business owners with close ties to the government because corruption was endemic in South Korea. The Rhee administration sought to build support by granting preferential treatment to those businesses with political connections. These connections were usually created and sustained with bribes in exchange for benefits such as permits to import raw materials, preferential tariffs and quotas, contracts to supply the government with goods and services, preferential interest rates and tax treatment, and near-monopoly control over markets. President Rhee proved to be an authoritarian who declared himself president for life.

With centralized political authority working hand in hand with favored businesses, concentrations of wealth and power quickly emerged. Like the pre–World War II Japanese zaibatsu, South Korean business organizations called chaebol dominated the economy. These large **conglomerates** consisted of as many as thirty different companies owned by a single family and operating in industries as diverse as mining, transportation, construction, and agriculture. Unlike the Japanese zaibatsu, the chaebol did not have their own bank as part of the organization, but the different firms worked together to ensure success for the entire group.

The Park Regime

From the end of the war in 1953 to 1960, the economy grew at annual rate of 3 percent, but because the population increased at a similar rate, standards of living did not improve significantly. Public anger over corruption and lack of democracy led to large student demonstrations in 1960, forcing President Rhee to flee the country aboard a US Central Intelligence Agency jet. A brief period of democracy led to chaos as various groups struggled with one another to gain control of the government. The following year, a military coup installed General Park Chung-hee (1917–1979) as president, and the United States gave its tacit approval by not intervening. Park encouraged rapid industrialization in order to strengthen South Korea against the communist threat from the north, yet South Korea faced formidable obstacles to development. The country lacked significant natural resources, had few domestic sources of financial capital because of a low saving rate, and faced weak domestic demand due to widespread poverty. Given these restraints, the nation had little choice but to turn outward and pursue export-led growth.

In 1962, the government established an Economic Planning Board (EPB) with authority to prepare detailed five-year plans for economic development. Planned targets were not mandatory, but the EPB had authority to force government budgets to conform to the plan. The Park regime was virtually a military dictatorship, and thus bureaucrats and politicians administered the planning process with little input from business or labor. The government planned the economy with the same discipline and precision associated with military operations. Once the EPB established priorities, other government agencies assigned specific projects to firms and assisted in arranging procurement of resources and credit. Firms were given incentives to reach their targets by the promise of future access to government credit and subsidies.

During the first five-year plan, the Park regime nationalized the entire banking system, enabling government to control the allocation of credit. To alleviate the shortage of domestic financial capital, the country welcomed foreign investors, most of whom were Japanese. The government also worked closely with the chaebol, assuring owners that expanding production would be aided through low-interest loans, import licenses for raw materials, technological assistance, tax relief, subsidies, and protection against imports of consumer products. The plan called for gradually reducing the policy of import substitution in favor of export-led growth.

Imitating the Japanese pattern of development, the South Koreans initially focused on light industries in which their cheap labor gave them comparative advantage (e.g., textiles, clothing, shoes, plywood, and wigs). The government devalued the Korean currency (the won) by 50 percent to make exports more competitive in foreign markets. With government providing more than 30 percent of investment funds for private businesses as well as operating SOEs in steel, utilities, communications, and chemicals, the planned targets were easily surpassed, and the South Korean economy grew at an annual rate of nearly 9 percent during the remainder of the 1960s.

However, this growth had a dark side. South Koreans labored twelve hours a day, six days a week. Any protests drew swift and sometimes violent responses from the police and army. The focus on export industries meant that agriculture and the rural parts of the country suffered, so the rapid growth was accompanied by poverty and inequality.

As early as the 1970s, South Korea's comparative advantage in labor-intensive industries was being lost to countries such as Indonesia and the Philippines. Moreover, the quadrupling of world oil prices in 1973 forced the country to reorient its development strategy. To prevent a deterioration of the balance of payments due to higher oil prices, South Korea needed to develop capital-intensive industries to both replace imports and provide increased profitability for exports. Following this strategy, the government focused on stimulating industries such as steel, ship-building, chemicals, electronics, and machinery. The results of this shift were impressive. As the West endured inflation and stagnation during the 1970s, the South Korean economy grew at an annual rate of nearly 10 percent. Between 1962 and 1979, per capita GDP rose from $87 to $1,500.

South Korea did not escape the impact of a second major increase in the price of oil in 1979 caused by the Iranian revolution's disruption of world oil supplies. President Park was assassinated by his own secret service agents in 1979, and by the early 1980s, as the world sank into the worst recession since the Great Depression, South Korea experienced its first postwar recession. Real GDP fell by 5.2 percent in 1980, and inflation rose to 20 percent annually. As the global recession caused exports to collapse, South Korean firms could no longer make payments on their loans from state-owned banks, resulting in a growing mountain of bad debt.

1980s Reforms and the Dominance of Chaebol

Park's successor, General Chun Doo-hwan, scaled back the role of government in the economy. He partially privatized the banking industry, used tight fiscal and monetary policies to control inflation, cut government subsidies and preferential credit, and reduced barriers to international trade and investment. The economy rebounded strongly, with annual growth averaging 9.2 percent between 1982 and 1986 and then rising to 12.5 percent from 1986 to 1988. Measured from 1980 to 1992, South Korea had the highest growth rate of real per capita income in the world.

Despite the strong economy, increasing numbers of South Korean citizens demanded an end to authoritarian government and risked their lives to engage in mass prodemocracy demonstrations. With world attention focused on Seoul leading up to the 1988 Olympic Games, demonstrators hoped that the government would be forced to make concessions. Indeed, President Chun voluntarily stepped down, and South Korea held its first democratic elections since 1960. The new president, Roh Tae-woo, initiated reforms aimed at increasing civil rights and granting greater bargaining power to labor unions. As a result, membership in labor unions doubled between 1986 and 1990. Rising wages enabled South Korea to develop a strong domestic market for consumer goods and therefore reduce its reliance on exports of capital equipment. Unfortunately, the tradition of political corruption did not end; President Roh was subsequently convicted of accepting $650 million in bribes.

Although the economy thrived, the dominance of the chaebol posed potential problems. By the 1980s, the ten largest chaebol, including Samsung, Hyundai, LG, and Daewoo, produced one-third of South Korea's GDP. If one of them failed, the resulting unemployment could destabilize the entire country. Moreover, these conglomerates were so deeply indebted to the government-owned banks that any defaults in payments could trigger a financial crisis. The chaebol had become "too big to fail," forcing government to extend even more credit when any of them experienced financial difficulty.

In 1993, newly elected President Kim Young-sam initiated a sweeping program of reforms. South Koreans remained committed to the idea that economic development and national strength require a strong, active government, but the economy had become too large and complex for centralized planning. Yet South Koreans were unwilling to adopt free markets and free trade. Instead, the Kim administration opted to restructure the chaebol through additional regulations. To discourage bribery, the government prohibited anonymous bank accounts previously used for illegal transfers of money. To reduce the size and power of the chaebol, the government prohibited any company from investing more than 40 percent of its capital in another company within the same chaebol. The power of a single family over a chaebol was limited by prohibiting companies with majority family ownership from expanding. Additional steps to curb the chaebol included requiring them to reduce their debt, prohibiting entry into new industries, and encouraging the trading of subsidiaries so that each chaebol would become more specialized in fewer industries.

South Korea encountered an unexpected challenge in 1997 when a global financial crisis starting in Thailand spread to Indonesia, the Philippines, and eventually South Korea. The country was affected more than others because of its heavy debt burden and dependence on export markets in Asia. The South Korean currency lost 50 percent of its value, which caused payments on foreign debt to double. The stock market plunged, and eleven of the thirty largest chaebol collapsed during the following two years. Of the seven automobile manufacturers before the crisis, only two survived. In 1999, the failure of Daewoo, which had $80 billion in debt, marked the largest corporate bankruptcy in world history. One-fourth of all manufacturing firms lacked sufficient revenue to make payments on their debts. South Korea was suffering from a classic case of **excess capacity** caused by overly optimistic expansion based on debt.

Surprisingly, the economy recovered relatively quickly thanks to the policies of President Kim Dae-jung (1925–2009). President Kim, a prominent dissident in the prodemocracy movement of the 1980s, initiated an anticorruption drive, privatized the banks, and removed restrictions on foreign investment. In addition, he took further steps to limit the power of the chaebol by forcing them to reduce their debt levels, spin off companies, and increase the transparency of their operations through stricter accounting rules. The subsequent president, Roh Moo-hyun (1946–2009), continued to scale back the privileges of the chaebol by reducing low-interest loans and subsidies from the government.

South Korea in the Twenty-First Century

Since recovering from the Asian financial crisis, South Korea has resumed its position as the fastest growing economy in the world. GDP tripled between 1997 and 2014, placing South Korea on the verge of joining the ranks of mature, industrialized nations. The chaebol continue to play a dominant role in the economy as the share of GDP produced by the ten largest companies rose from 53 percent in 2002 to nearly 80 percent in 2014. Samsung alone accounts for 17 percent of the GDP. Policymakers are engaged in ongoing debates about whether the chaebol benefit the economy due to economies of scale or reduce efficiency due to their **market power**.

In 2012, South Koreans elected their first female President, Park Geun-hye, who is the daughter of former dictator Park Chung-hee. Although she claims that her father's dictatorship was necessary to save the country, President Park promises to focus on improving the lives of citizens rather than strengthening the state.

The success of South Korea poses an enigma. With heavy-handed government intervention, extensive corruption, economic planning, concentrated market power, trade restrictions, and a long absence of democracy, orthodox economic theory would predict a failure to thrive. However, economic theory is traditionally blind to political, cultural, and historical aspects of development. South Korean culture, based largely on Confucianism, stresses education and hard work. South Koreans continue to work long hours and are typically dedicated to their companies. The South Korean government devotes more than 22 percent of its budget to education, particularly in math and the sciences. Literacy is nearly universal, so, as South Korean businesses shift toward "high-tech," capital-intensive production, the labor force is well-prepared for new occupations requiring technical knowledge and skills. Like the Chinese, South Koreans share the collective memory of humiliation and exploitation under foreign occupation. The resulting sense of shame and grievance (hahn) motivates South Koreans to excel not only to achieve personal success but to reclaim the honor of their nation.

REFERENCE

Robinson, Joan. 1962. *Economic Philosophy*. Piscataway, NJ: Aldine.

ADDITIONAL READING

Brazil

Casanova, Lourdes. *The Political Economy of an Emerging Global Power: In Search of the Brazil Dream*. New York: Palgrave Macmillan, 2014.

Fishlow, Albert. *Starting Over: Brazil Since 1985*. Washington, DC: Brookings Institution Press, 2011.

Luna, Francisco Vidal, and Herbert S. Klein. *The Economic and Social History of Brazil Since 1889*. New York: Cambridge University Press, 2014.

Montero, Alfred P. *Brazil: Reversal of Fortune*. Malden, MA: Polity, 2014.

Reid, Michael. *Brazil: The Troubled Rise of a Global Power*. New Haven, CT: Yale University Press, 2014.

Rohter, Larry. *Brazil on the Rise: The Story of a Country Transformed*. New York: Palgrave Macmillan, 2012.

Skidmore, Thomas. *Brazil: Five Centuries of Change*, 2nd ed. New York: Oxford University Press, 2009.

India

Acharya, Shankar, and Rakesh Mohan. *India's Economy: Performances and Challenges*. New York: Oxford University Press, 2010.

Corbridge, Stuart, John Harriss, and Craig Jeffries. *India Today: Economy, Politics and Society*. Malden, MA: Polity, 2012.

Dreza, Jean, and Amartya Sen. *An Uncertain Glory: India and Its Contradictions*. Princeton, NJ: Princeton University Press, 2013.

Harriss, John. *Power Matters: Essays on Institutions, Politics and Society in India*. Delhi: Oxford University Press, 2006.

Panagariya, Arvind. *India: The Emerging Giant*. New York: Oxford University Press, 2010.

Ruparelia, Sanjay, Sanjay Reddy, John Harriss, and Stuart Corbridge. *Understanding India's New Political Economy: A Great Transformation?* London: Routledge, 2011.

Tomlinson, B. R. *The Economy of Modern India: From 860 to the Twenty-First Century*. New York: Cambridge University Press, 2013.

Iran

Abrahamian, Ervand. *A History of Modern Iran*. New York: Cambridge University Press, 2000.

Amuzegar, Jahangir. *Iran: Economy, Society and Politics*. New York: Oxford University Press, 2009.

Axworthy, Michael. *Revolutionary Iran: A History of the Islamic Republic*. New York: Oxford University Press, 2013.

Gheissari, Ali. *Contemporary Iran: Economy, Society and Politics*. New York: Oxford University Press, 2009.

Hooglund, Eric, and Leif Steinberg. *Navigating Contemporary Iran: Challenging Economic, Social and Political Perceptions*. London: Routledge, 2012.

Keddi, Nikki R. *Modern Iran: Roots and Results of Revolution*. New Haven, CT: Yale University Press, 2006.

South Korea

Chung, Young-lob. *South Korea in the Fast Lane: Economic Development and Capital Formation*. New York: Oxford University Press, 2007.

Heo, Uk, and Terence Roehrig. *South Korea's Rise: Economic Development, Power, and Foreign Relations*. New York: Cambridge University Press, 2014.

Kim, Myung Oak and Sam Jaffe. *The New Korea: An Inside Look at South Korea's Economic Rise*. New York: AMOCOM, 2010.

Mo, Jongryn, and Barry P. Weingast. *Korean Political and Economic Development: Crisis, Security, and Institutional Rebalancing*. Cambridge, MA: Harvard University Asia Center, 2013.

Park, Kyung-Ae, and Scott Snyder. *North Korea in Transition: Politics, Economy, and Society*. Lanham, MD: Rowman & Littlefield. 2010.

Pirie, Iain. *The Korean Developmental State: From Dirigisme to Neo-liberalism*. London: Routledge, 2007.

Seth, Michael J. *A History of Korea: From Antiquity to the Present*. Lanham, MD: Rowman & Littlefield, 2010.

Chapter 15

GLOBALIZATION AND ECONOMIC SYSTEMS

"We must ensure that the global market is embedded in broadly shared values and practices that reflect global social needs, and that all the world's people share the benefits of globalization."

KOFI ANNAN,
former Secretary-General of the United Nations

Globalization is the increasing integration and interdependence of national economic systems. The underlying cause of globalization is **economic behavior** as merchants, manufacturers, consumers, and investors seek access to lower-cost resources, exotic goods, markets for domestic goods, and new investment opportunities. Over time, the powerful incentive of profit has led to reductions in economic, political, and cultural barriers to the movement of **financial capital**, natural resources, labor, technology, products, information, knowledge, and cultural practices across national borders. In a global market, businesses compare costs and benefits around the world to determine the most profitable methods and locations for production and distribution. Consumers purchase goods containing components from many distant countries. Understanding the potential consequences of globalization is essential to securing successful national economic systems.

THE HISTORY OF GLOBALIZATION

Globalization can be traced back to the emergence of long-distance trading as exemplified by the Italian merchant Marco Polo's (1254–1324) excursions into central Asia in the thirteenth century. An argument can be made that a global economic system existed as early as the fourteenth century, with China at its center and Europe little more than a primitive outpost (Frank 1998). Global economic integration continued until the early twentieth century, but the combination of two world wars and the Great Depression temporarily reversed the trend as armed conflict and protective trade barriers disrupted commerce. The percentage of global output traded between nations did not return to its pre–World War I level until the 1970s.

As World War II was ending, representatives from the noncommunist nations met at Bretton Woods, New Hampshire, to form a new international financial system. The resulting agreement led to fixed exchange rates between currencies and the designation of the US dollar as the official currency with which nations would settle debts among themselves. To maintain confidence in the dollar, the United States pledged to redeem any dollars held by foreign central banks with gold. The Bretton Woods agreement also created the International Monetary Fund (IMF) and the World Bank, both headquartered in Washington, DC. The IMF provides loans for countries in financial distress, and the World Bank assists low-income nations by financing development projects.

The Bretton Woods system served admirably for twenty-five years until political turmoil, social unrest, and inflation in the United States caused foreign central banks to lose confidence in the dollar. As they attempted to exchange billions of dollars for gold, the United States effectively ended the Bretton Woods system in 1971 by refusing any further redemption of dollars for gold. Subsequently, most nations adopted flexible exchange rates between currencies, removed **capital controls** on the movement of financial capital across national borders, and opened their stock markets to global investors. The result was a unified global financial market in which capital could flow freely toward its highest risk-adjusted rate of return.

In 1947, the non-communist nations sought to promote a global market for goods and services by establishing the General Agreement on Tariffs and Trade (GATT). This organization provided a forum in which member nations could negotiate multilateral agreements to reduce trade barriers and establish rules governing trade. GATT developed the principles of reciprocity, nondiscrimination, and transparency to guarantee that nations would treat their trading partners equally and publicize full information about trade policy. In 1995, GATT was incorporated into the newly created World Trade Organization (WTO) headquartered in Geneva, Switzerland. With 144 member nations, the WTO adjudicates trade disputes between nations and has authority to overrule national policies that violate WTO standards.

The pace of globalization accelerated in the 1980s and 1990s due to technological progress, the end of communism, and deregulation. We shall examine each of these separately.

Technological Progress

A major barrier to the flow of goods and resources around the world has always been the costs of both transportation and coordinating production and distribution over vast distances. Those costs have been substantially reduced by technological developments in transportation, information systems, and telecommunications. Cargo ships twenty stories tall and one quarter of a mile long now carry hundreds of thousands of tons of freight in containers that are unloaded by cranes directly onto trains or trucks for delivery to their final destination. Computer programs and Internet accessibility permit firms to coordinate the operation of multiple facilities in a global supply chain. A computerized global financial market allows the movement of financial capital from one nation to another with the touch of a keyboard. Cell phones and teleconferencing enable individuals and firms around the world to seamlessly consult, negotiate, and transact with one another. In short, technological change has rendered geographical distance relatively inconsequential as a barrier to commerce.

The End of Communism

China's gradual abandonment of communism beginning in 1979 and Russia's abrupt transition in 1991 brought a substantial portion of the world's resources and production into the global market. The downfall of communism also affected other countries that were politically or ideologically aligned with the Soviet Union or China. These countries were typically resistant to free trade, but with communism discredited and the IMF and World Bank pushing the "Washington consensus" that economic success requires full integration into the global economy, they removed most of their barriers to trade and investment. The free flow of resources and goods led to an increasingly unified global market.

Deregulation

Deregulation accelerated globalization by reducing obstacles to trade and investment such as taxes, **tariffs**, quotas, and capital controls. Deregulation unleashed economic behavior from some previous institutional constraints so that profit-seeking could expand and intensify. In addition to being a factor contributing to globalization, deregulation is also a consequence of globalization. In a unified global market, competition creates pressures on all nations to minimize costs of production. Neoliberalism became increasingly influential in the later part of the twentieth century due in large part to a growing realization that national prosperity is potentially threatened by the added production costs associated with taxation and regulations. As financial capital became increasingly mobile, governments adopted policies to reduce production costs to attract and keep businesses within their jurisdiction. These policies included cutting taxes, weakening labor unions, reducing welfare benefits, increasing access to natural resources, and abolishing or easing many government regulations, including antitrust laws. Without the competitive market forces created by globalization, many politicians would have remained reluctant to enact these sometimes unpopular measures.

Deregulation has been pursued not only at the national level but also through various agreements among nations to reduce trade barriers. In 1989, twenty-one nations bordering the Pacific Ocean, including the United States, Canada, Japan, Russia, and China formed the Asia Pacific Economic Cooperation Association. Two years later, six Latin American countries formed the Southern Common Market. The Maastrict Treaty in 1992 created the European Union (EU) to establish common policies and free trade among twelve European nations. That number has since grown to include twenty-eight nations. The United States, Canada, and Mexico responded in 1994 with the formation of the North American Free Trade

Agreement. Several additional proposals for creating regional trading blocs have yet to be ratified. The Free Trade Area of the Americas would include thirty-four nations in the Western Hemisphere. Latin American countries are considering their own organization called the Community of Latin American and Caribbean States. The United States is proposing The Trans-Pacific Partnership consisting of twelve countries, including the United States, Japan, and Australia—but not China. In response, China is advocating a Free-Trade Area of the Asia Pacific that would not include the United States.

The primary obstacle to reaching agreement on these proposals lies in the differing interests of nations. Less developed countries seek the elimination of agricultural subsidies in the industrialized nations, whereas industrialized nations insist on stricter enforcement of intellectual property rights and patents to widen markets for their products. Another divisive issue is safeguards for protecting the environment and human rights. Industrialized nations seek uniform standards that would prevent the developing nations from gaining **competitive advantage** by polluting the environment or exploiting labor.

POTENTIAL STRENGTHS OF GLOBALIZATION

Globalization remains controversial because it leads to institutional changes that benefit some groups and harm others. Plausible arguments can be made in defense of globalization with regard to each of the eight criteria for assessing economic systems enumerated in Chapter Two.

Prosperity

Globalization promotes economic, political, and social/cultural changes contributing to rising material standards of living.

Economic Changes

Globalization widens markets and thereby creates opportunities for nations to specialize in the production of those goods in which they possess **comparative advantage**. Specialization raises productivity as each nation uses its resources to the greatest advantage and, in so doing, gains **economies of scale** and increased expertise through **learning by doing**. Businesses gain access to lower-priced resources and increased opportunities to export, consumers gain a wider variety of available goods, and international competition keeps prices low. Global capital markets direct financial capital toward its most profitable use. Joint ventures and partnerships between firms in different nations facilitate the transfer of technology across borders, allowing more countries to reap the benefits of technological innovation. Global competition places greater pressure on firms in all nations to increase efficiency and innovate. As rising productivity leads to a larger economic surplus, additional financial capital can fund both private investment in **physical capital** and public investment in **infrastructure**. Ideally, globalization sets in motion a positive cycle in which a growing economic surplus leads to more investment in physical capital and infrastructure, which raises productivity and standards of living.

Political Changes

As nations become increasingly integrated in a global market, they experience pressure from their own citizens and from international investors to secure property rights and adhere to the rule of law, both of which are essential to economic growth. **Predatory states** may suffer an exodus of both financial and human capital as investors shift their money abroad and citizens relocate to less oppressive nations. Globalization may also reduce **rent seeking** as trade agreements with other nations limit the ability of governments to grant subsidies and protective tariffs.

Social and Cultural Changes

Economic integration creates pressure on individuals and nations to adopt more productive social relations and cultural practices. Personal traits such as punctuality and a strong work ethic are reinforced through monetary rewards. Education becomes more highly valued when jobs require higher skills and knowledge. Destructive passions such as religious and ethnic hatreds gradually fade as citizens increasingly base their decisions on rational assessments of the costs and benefits of their actions.

Freedom

Globalization expands freedom in both its negative and positive senses. **Negative freedom**, the absence of coercion or restraint, increases with the spread of institutions such as the rule of law, well-defined property rights, and civil rights, including freedom of religion, freedom of speech, and freedom from discrimination. Globalization undermines the power of repressive governments and cultures to constrain individual choice.

Positive freedom expands as the prosperity generated by globalization creates greater opportunities and a wider range of effective choices. Businesses face increased opportunities for trade and investment. Individuals can choose from a variety of religions, political views, and lifestyles. Talented persons may even migrate to other countries to fulfill their ambitions. With increased prosperity, governments can expand freedom by providing improved educational opportunities and access to healthcare.

Justice

As economic integration brings different cultures into contact, **justice** usually triumphs over oppression as property, civil, and human right are increasingly recognized and upheld. For example, women in some developing countries have traditionally been denied access to education, the right to vote, the right to inherit property, and freedom to choose a mate. These practices are gradually receding as women gain economic opportunities and all citizens are exposed to modern notions of fairness and equality under the law. This exposure comes through media, tourism, cultural exchanges, and publicity from other governments and nongovernmental organizations (NGOs).

Justice is also improved as a unified market allows resources to flow toward their most highly valued use. In a perfectly competitive global market, equally productive resources should be equally rewarded regardless of nationality, race, ethnicity, or religion. One reason for existing wage differentials between countries is differences in the quantity and quality of capital. However, a global market may direct financial capital toward low-wage countries, thereby raising labor productivity and pulling wages upward.

Stability

Globalization potentially mitigates some of the factors leading to instability in domestic economies. Domestic **underconsumption** that might cause insufficient **aggregate demand** may be offset by increased exports. Problems associated with domestic **overinvestment** and **excess capacity** may be resolved as profitable business opportunities abroad serve to maintain optimism among investors and absorb excess financial capital. International competition erodes the **market power** of domestic firms, thereby keeping inflation in check. To the extent that instability results from errors in macro policy, a global economy disciplines domestic policymakers by amplifying the negative consequences of any mistakes. For example, if excessive government spending or excessive money creation causes inflation, the economy will also suffer from declining exports and a growing deficit in its **balance of trade**.

Peace

As national economic systems become more integrated, citizens from different nations become more familiar with one another's values and culture. This increased understanding and respect for cultural differences reduces the likelihood of conflict. Also, when nations benefit economically from trade, foreign investment, the spread of technology, and tourism, they face strong incentives to avoid any conflict that would disrupt commerce. In the past, nations have often engaged in wars to gain access to resources, but in a global economy, foreign resources can be obtained more easily through trade than through war. When nations are engaged in extensive trade with one another, they have rarely gone to war. Finally, to the extent that globalization generates prosperity and modernization, conflicts based on ethnic identity or religious beliefs are reduced because all groups have greater opportunities for social mobility through productive employment.

Sustainability

Globalization may promote sustainability by creating sufficient prosperity to foster both the ability and the desire to protect the natural environment. Prosperity enables nations to fund research leading to the development of "green" technologies and to afford the costly measures required to reduce pollution.

Prosperity also contributes to popular support for environmentalism. Individuals living at a subsistence level may be so concerned with immediate survival that preserving the environment remains a low priority. However, as incomes rise and basic needs are met, citizens increasingly focus on quality-of-life issues such as safe neighborhoods, social justice, quality education, and a clean environment. A popular movement to protect the environment did not emerge in the United States until the 1960s, when a broad middle class with sufficient economic security finally turned its attention toward sustaining the natural world.

Human Development

The connection between globalization and human development rests on the expansion of prosperity, freedom, and cross-cultural awareness. Growing prosperity provides the financial means to nurture talents and abilities. Individuals face an expanded range of possibilities in choosing their lifestyles, values, and work. The exposure to different cultures awakens ambitions that might otherwise have lain dormant. The spread of communications technology empowers formerly isolated and marginalized populations to gain a sense of collective identity and self-determination. Those nations most integrated into the global economy are typically more tolerant and respectful of cultural differences, giving their citizens greater freedom to develop unique abilities and pursue alternative lifestyles.

Democracy

The "Arab Spring" refers to the recent wave of popular uprisings against authoritarian governments in the Middle East and North Africa. These revolts were almost certainly fostered by globalization as exposure to industrialized cultures created demands for human rights and representative democracy. More generally, as globalization has expanded prosperity around the world, a flood of rising expectations challenges corruption, censorship, and repression. Citizens increasingly demand transparency and accountability in their governments. Political dissidents willingly risk imprisonment and even death in order to speak out against tyranny and injustice. Democracy is ascendant; the number of electoral democracies in the world has grown from 69 in 1990 to 117 in 2014.

Globalization fosters increased awareness among citizens of all nations that their commonalities are greater than their differences. This global consciousness is essential to the formation of shared values and democratic political institutions required to collectively resolve global problems that spill across national borders such as terrorism, pandemics, illegal immigration, drug trafficking, human trafficking, organized crime, poverty, pollution of the oceans, and climate change.

POTENTIAL WEAKNESSES OF GLOBALIZATION

For nearly every argument in favor of globalization, a plausible rebuttal exists. Assessing global integration entails weighing the pros and cons, and, as is true for national economic systems, no single objective criterion exists for measuring the performance of the global economy. The following aspects of globalization raise concerns about its viability and desirability.

Reduced Prosperity

Globalization offers the potential for substantial economic benefits, but the distribution of those benefits is highly uneven. Nations may lose or gain comparative advantage, resulting in plant closings and job loss in some industries while others flourish. In theory, the workers losing their jobs in declining industries would be reemployed in expanding industries, but unemployed steel workers are not readily employable by computer software companies. The United States has lost a substantial portion of its manufacturing sector to foreign firms, with less than 12 percent of the labor force currently engaged in manufacturing. As US firms either relocate or outsource production to other countries, jobs disappear or are replaced by part-time and temporary positions with lower wages and reduced benefits. Although high unemployment rates in industrialized nations cannot be attributed solely or even primarily to international trade, competitive pressures created by globalization exert downward pressure on wages and undermine job security.

As workers around the world increasingly compete for jobs in a global labor market, any income based on the market power of labor unions is subject to erosion by competitive forces. Furthermore, as unions lose power, they become less appealing to potential members. Union membership in the United States has declined to less than 7 percent of private sector workers.

Another factor posing potential limitations on prosperity is the mobility of financial capital. A nation's economic surplus provides the resources for **capital accumulation** and growth. If that surplus, in the form of financial capital, is invested in more profitable opportunities abroad, then a nation suffers reduced means to increase its physical capital and to improve its infrastructure.

Finally, globalization may undermine prosperity by eroding property rights. No global government exists to provide uniform protection of property rights; therefore, foreign firms can sometimes violate these rights with impunity. Examples include industrial espionage, infringements of patents and copyrights, and counterfeiting.

Limited Freedom

The market exerts a powerful discipline by penalizing choices that are inconsistent with profit maximization and capital accumulation. For example, employers who choose to provide workers with generous fringe benefits may lose competitive advantage and ultimately fail. Factory owners opting to dispose of their waste in an ecologically sound manner may lose competitive advantage due to higher costs. The market motivates individual choices with a single goal—higher profits leading to more rapid capital accumulation. Although individuals may ignore the dictates of the market, they do so at the risk of poverty, lost jobs, and failed businesses. By intensifying competition and undermining many of the

institutional constraints on profit-maximization in the developed nations, globalization narrows the range of feasible choices facing individuals and business.

Globalization also limits freedom by recreating **collective action problems**
that may have been previously solved at the national level. For example, the institution of the forty-hour workweek ended the competitive pressure on employers
in industrialized nations to extract more labor by lengthening the workweek.
However, as firms in developing countries enter the global market without such
restrictions, they may gain a competitive advantage by requiring longer work-
weeks. Similarly, the environmental regulations that limit pollution in the industrialized nations may be nonexistent or loosely enforced in developing nations.
Laws protecting worker rights in more developed nations are routinely violated
in developing countries as indentured servitude and conditions approaching
slavery exist. To summarize, globalization creates increased opportunities to
defect from institutions designed to solve collective action problems and therefore weakens those institutions in every nation.

Confronting collective action problems requires trust, cooperation, and a
strong developmental state. By creating winners and losers, globalization undermines solidarity and unity within nations and among nations. For example, the
1997 Kyoto Protocol for reducing carbon emissions failed because nations could
not reach a consensus on who should bear the burden. Lower-income nations
argued that developed nations could more easily afford to control emissions, but
the US Congress refused to ratify the bill, claiming that it would restrict the nation's economic growth. Not until 2014 did the United States and China agree to
jointly take the lead in the battle against global climate change.

Injustice

Globalization may create injustice by exacerbating inequality, undermining rights,
and shifting the pattern of burdens and benefits in society in favor of owners of
capital.

Increasing Inequality

Although progress in countries such as China and India may be reducing inequality between average national income levels, the gap between rich and poor
within nations is increasing virtually everywhere in the world. Globalization
bears a substantial responsibility for this phenomenon; owners of more scarce
and mobile resources such as financial capital and some types of human capital
(e.g., scientific knowledge, financial acumen, and entrepreneurial ability) gain
significantly higher incomes while owners of plentiful and immobile resources
(e.g., manual labor skills) experience declining standards of living. Inequality
does not necessarily violate justice unless it becomes so extreme that equality of
opportunity and social mobility are restricted. Those conditions, in turn, depend
on how the wealthy utilize the economic surplus that accrues to them in the form
of profit, rent, and interest. If the surplus is invested in physical capital and innovation contributing to economic growth and increased opportunities for all

citizens, then inequality is likely to be regarded as fair and just. However, if the wealthy squander the surplus on luxurious lifestyles, investment in speculative assets, or investment abroad, the perception of injustice grows along with public resentment and anger.

Increasing inequality also threatens justice by enhancing the power of some groups over others. For example, concentrated wealth provides the financial means to fund mergers and acquisitions that reduce competition and increase the market power of large corporations. Concentrated wealth also enables a minority of the population to exert disproportionate influence over the political process. As the wealthy gain power, they restructure and manipulate the market for their own benefit, thereby breaking the link between income and productivity that forms the basis for justice in the market.

Erosion of Rights

Rights in any society are defined through the political process and by cultural traditions. Industrialized nations have, over time, developed a wide array of property rights, civil rights, and human rights. The protection of rights can entail costs such as providing legal counsel for alleged criminals, ensuring that citizens have access to the basic necessities for survival, funding public education, and, in some countries, providing healthcare. As developing countries in which these rights have not been established enter the global market, competition to reduce costs places the rights of citizens in all nations at risk. To gain a competitive advantage, business owners may reduce employee healthcare benefits, seek to weaken labor unions, and pressure government to reduce regulations and social benefits.

Shifting Burdens and Benefits

As global competition creates pressures on firms to reduce costs, who bears the burden? In real-world markets, where power as well as productivity determines income, relative power determines the sacrifices made by different groups. As a general rule, owners of capital are more powerful than workers not only because of their wealth, but because the mobility of capital gives them the upper hand in any negotiations. Capitalists can always threaten to take their resources elsewhere unless their demands are met. By increasing the array of investment opportunities around the world, globalization has increased the power of capitalists not only in negotiations with labor unions, but also in exerting influence over government. As a result, the brunt of the burden of reducing costs in the global economy falls on the least powerful groups in society. Wages remain stagnant, job security fades, fringe benefits decline, and income taxes become less progressive as governments cut tax rates on income from capital and rely increasingly on regressive value-added or sales taxes.

In the United States, business lobbying groups pressure government to eliminate the corporate income tax, to replace employer-provided health insurance with personal medical savings accounts to pay for healthcare expenses, and to replace the social security system with private retirement accounts. The increased power of capitalists also results in attacks on government programs offering social benefits. Not only do these programs necessitate higher taxes, but benefits such as unemployment compensation, disability insurance, food stamps, and rent subsidies enable some potential workers to remain out of the labor force and therefore reduce downward pressure on wages. If all citizens had no alternative but to work, increased competition for jobs would reduce production costs by driving wages lower. The welfare state expanded during the Great Depression when capitalists feared the growing power of labor unions and the threat of socialism. Now that labor unions have been weakened by global competition and socialism is discredited, capitalists feel little need for the welfare state and urge their governments to reduce social benefits.

Instability

The developed nations have established a variety of institutions and policies to maintain economic stability within their borders. Globalization undermines the effectiveness of those national institutions, thereby creating the potential for instability on a global scale.

Underconsumption

Following the Great Depression and the development of Keynesian economics in the 1930s, both business leaders and government officials recognized the futility of wage cuts as a strategy for gaining competitive advantage. Reducing wages may lower the costs of a single firm, but if all firms follow suit, the resulting reduction in purchasing power leads to underconsumption and declining business profitability. Many nations solved this collective action problem by strengthening labor unions, enacting minimum wage laws, and creating social benefits to prevent surplus labor from driving down wages.

Globalization has revived the problem of underconsumption by undermining the national institutions designed to keep wages from falling. Unions have lost power, the real minimum wage has declined, and social benefits are being reduced throughout the industrialized world. Surplus labor results in high unemployment, making wage cuts an attractive strategy for employers, who justify reduced wages as the sacrifice required to remain competitive in international markets. In a global economy, underconsumption in any single nation caused by wage cuts may be offset by increased exports due to lower wage costs. However, export-led growth poses a global collective action problem. If one nation increases exports by keeping wages low, its economy may flourish. But if all countries pursue the same strategy, the result is underconsumption and stagnation on a global scale. For one country to base its growth on low wages and exports, another country must have sufficiently high wages to purchase those exports.

Another potential cause of underconsumption is a high saving rate caused by increasing inequality. Saving poses another collective action problem. In what economists call "the paradox of thrift," saving by an individual is prudent and wise, but if everyone saves, the level of spending may be insufficient to maintain economic growth. Japan is currently experiencing the downside of excessive saving, and to the extent that globalization fosters growing inequality, a "savings glut" may keep the global economy in a perpetual state of stagnation (Rajan 2010).

Overinvestment

Businesses may expand too rapidly, either because of excessive optimism about future sales or as part of a strategy to gain dominance over an industry by being the first firm to gain economies of scale. Overinvestment is the result of a collective action problem. While expansion may benefit a single firm, if all firms in an industry expand simultaneously, they are likely to create excess capacity and declining profitability. In the past, nations have attempted to alleviate overinvestment either through economic planning or through the formation of industry associations to coordinate investment. Globalization has not only weakened those national institutions but has also created competition between national industries to gain dominance in global production. With no global institutions to coordinate investment decisions, overinvestment fueled by excessive optimism and aggressive efforts to increase market share inevitably lead to periods of excess global capacity and a resulting disruption of economic activity.

Loss of Comparative Advantage

As globalization leads nations to specialize in producing goods in which they have a comparative advantage, their economies lose diversity and become more vulnerable to changes in consumer tastes, technology, or resource availability. For example, the Russian economy depends heavily on exports of oil and natural gas. If those resources are exhausted, if world oil prices decline, or if concerns about global climate change lead to the development of alternative energy sources, the entire Russian economy would suffer.

Capital Mobility

In the global economy, financial capital flows around the world, seeking the highest risk-adjusted rate of return. Immense sums of money can be transferred from one nation to another in milliseconds. This hypermobility of capital may destabilize national economies by causing rapid fluctuations in currency exchange rates and by creating fear and panic. In 1997, international investors lost confidence in Thailand's economy and began withdrawing financial capital. Like a contagious disease, the loss of confidence spread throughout Southeast Asia, then to Russia, Brazil, and eventually the United States. Only coordinated action by the US government and several large financial institutions eventually restored confidence and averted a more serious global financial crisis.

Rapid inflows of financial capital can also destabilize national economies. An abundance of capital increases the likelihood of overinvestment and eventual excess capacity or speculative investments in real estate and risky financial assets. In 2006, two years before the financial crisis of 2008, Federal Reserve chairman

Ben Bernanke warned of a "global savings glut." Money from all over the world was pouring into US financial markets, creating a speculative bubble in real estate and causing money managers to invent risky new financial assets to absorb the excess financial capital. The result was the worst recession since the Great Depression.

Less Effective Macro Policy

Globalization undermines the effectiveness of domestic stabilization policies. An expansionary monetary policy designed to stimulate growth by lowering interest rates may fail if investors divert financial capital abroad in search of higher interest rates. The effects of an expansionary fiscal policy may be offset if rising prices and wages cause imports to increase and exports to decrease.

Social Conflict

Although global markets may create wealth, opportunities, and cultural homogenization, they can simultaneously undermine any institution failing to promote profitability and capital accumulation. The problem posed by relying on profitability as the measure of an institution's worth is that some highly valued social and cultural practices have evolved not because of their profitability but because they provide meaning and purpose essential to forming stable human identities and relationships. Neither religious and spiritual rituals nor celebrations of cultural heritage and national pride are directly profitable for most practitioners. The spread of a more secular, cosmopolitan, Westernized culture around the world has led to a backlash as individuals and communities feel threatened by the erosion of their national, ethnic, and religious identities. In what has been called "reactive retribalization," some individuals respond to globalization by organizing to defend their communities against the perceived threats of cultural dissolution, immigration, and loss of security. Ironically, globalization's pressures for cultural conformity have spawned an opposing wave of strident nationalism, ethnic chauvinism, and religious fundamentalism. Entire nations are disintegrating along ethnic or religious lines.

By subjecting nations and cultures to the demands of profitability, global markets create winners and losers. When the losers are single individuals or businesses, their frustration is unlikely to create social conflict and may, in fact, spur them to improve productivity. But when entire communities or nations sense that their way of life is being undermined by forces over which they have no control, their collective rage creates the potential for terrorism and war.

Finally, because globalization entails the elevation of market forces at the expense of governmental authority, global order is no longer maintained by one or two hegemonic nations whose overwhelming power prevents other nations from disrupting the status quo. During the post–World War II era, the Soviet Union maintained order in much of the Eastern Hemisphere, whereas the United States did the same in the Western Hemisphere. This bipolar political order has disintegrated as neither nation remains capable of policing the world.

Lack of Sustainability

To the extent that globalization succeeds in promoting economic growth, the environment and its natural resources will be subject to increasing depletion and stress. Currently, the 12 percent of the global population living in the United States and Western Europe accounts for 60 percent of global consumption. If other nations even approach Western levels of energy usage, resource depletion, and pollution, the natural environment may be irreversibly damaged.

The competitive pressures created by globalization have renewed the collective action problem associated with environmental pollution. In the past, industrialized nations have reduced pollution through regulations and "cap-and-trade" policies, but no global government exists to impose uniform environmental regulations. As a result, each national government has an incentive to ease regulations to reduce business costs and give its industries an advantage in global competition.

If globalization is successful in spreading industrialization to the poorest nations, rates of population growth will inevitably increase due to improved sanitation, disease control, and nutrition. Not only will each person consume more, but a growing population will lead to more consumers and increasing stress on the environment. If these countries eventually achieve comfortable standards of living, the birth rate is likely to decline, but by then, environmental destruction may have passed a critical point of no return.

Restricted Human Development

Globalization may interfere with human development by creating imbalances within communities, by diminishing opportunities for meaningful work, and by limiting leisure.

Unbalanced Communities

An essential role of communities is to provide an arena in which members gain a sense of personal identity. Without identity, humans struggle to define core values and to find meaning and purpose in their lives. Two different aspects of human existence are essential to enable individuals to form personal identities—individuation and belonging. In the process of individuation, people distinguish themselves from others through outstanding achievements and corresponding rewards. On the other hand, a sense of belonging comes from membership in a cohesive group based on shared values and commitments. Ideally, communities should balance the needs for individuation and belonging by supporting achievement while continuing to value all members. However, globalization potentially disrupts this balance. The penetration of competitive market forces and economic behavior into communities jeopardizes the trust, sympathy, and respect essential to a sense of belonging. At the same time, globalization has generated a backlash against individual autonomy that pushes other communities to suppress individual achievement in order to maintain the emotional comfort of belonging to a stable, traditional culture. In either case, these unbalanced communities fail to provide their members with the conditions for full human development.

Lack of Meaningful Work

Global markets dictate efficiency, and efficiency often requires extreme specialization of labor. As a result, many jobs become increasingly routine and repetitive. Although this is less true in developed nations, where routine work is increasingly automated or outsourced, the degradation of work is clearly evident in developing countries, which often rely on sweatshops, long hours, unsafe working conditions, and low wages to attract foreign capital.

Lack of Leisure

The English economist John Maynard Keynes (1883–1946) predicted that within a hundred years, the average work day in the industrialized countries would be three hours (Keynes [1930] 1963). He reasoned that because capital accumulation increases over time and improves labor productivity, three hours of work per day would be sufficient to secure a comfortable standard of living. However, Keynes failed to consider two factors. First, our expectations about what constitutes a satisfactory standard of living have risen along with productivity, and this process has been fueled in part by capitalism's reliance on advertising and a culture of consumerism. Second, Keynes neglected the pressure created by global competition to minimize production costs. No matter how productive labor becomes, competition compels employers to extract as much labor as is legally permissible from their employees. In theory, any employer failing to maximize hours of labor per worker will experience higher per-unit production costs and loss of competitive advantage. As a result, despite rising productivity, citizens around the world find themselves with less leisure time for recreation or other interests.

Erosion of Democracy

Democracy entails political decisions based on "the will of the people" as determined through elections in which each citizen has an equal vote. Majority rule is constrained only by constitutional provisions and by individual rights established either by a constitution or through the democratic political process. Globalization poses challenges to democracy by weakening the sovereignty of national governments and by shifting the balance of power within nations.

Diminished National Sovereignty

A sovereign government is subject to no higher authority. National sovereignty is currently being undermined by the global market's power to override the intentions of governments and voters (Strange 1996). Without sovereignty, the ability of governments to regulate or supplement the market's shortcomings is weakened. Instead, governments increasingly become the handmaidens of the global market by revising institutions in response to market pressures. International competition and global financial markets often punish nations whose governments enact higher taxes, more stringent environmental regulations, or protections for labor unions and human rights. When governments lose sovereignty, they can no longer effectively resolve collective action problems because globalization provides individuals and corporations with opportunities to defect from national institutions such as taxation and environmental regulations by relocating to more "business-friendly" nations. For example, transnational corporations engage in **transfer pricing** to make their profits artificially appear in nations with lower corporate income tax rates. Through **corporate inversions**, transnational corporations merge with a foreign competitor, move their headquarters to another country, and pay that country's lower tax rate. In the United States, corporations avoid taxes on their foreign profits by leaving the money abroad.

Shifting Balance of Power

The mobility of capital essentially forces governments to pursue policies favored by owners of capital. This disproportionate power violates the basic democratic principle of "one person, one vote." Instead, a relatively small minority of the electorate wields power far beyond its numbers, and democracy degenerates into a plutocracy or predatory state.

CONCLUSION

During the twentieth century, the major political battles within industrialized nations centered around efforts to place institutional constraints and supports on the operation of markets. Those institutions, which performed admirably during the three decades following World War II, were gradually rendered obsolete by globalization and by the evolving structure of national markets. The global mobility of resources has, to a significant extent, unleashed the market from its former institutional framework and left governments with inadequate revenue to compensate for the market's shortcomings.

Competitive capitalism was long ago rendered obsolete by market failures, including instability, externalities, and economies of scale. In the past forty years, the other varieties of capitalism examined in this book have all been compromised by globalization. The planned capitalism of Japan and France floundered as the best intentions of planners were stymied by global competitive forces over which they had no control. Germany's organized capitalism, based on high wages and **patient capital**, could not withstand widespread defections from political and social institutions as investors, banks, and corporations took advantage of more profitable investment opportunities abroad. The high taxes required to fund welfare capitalism in Sweden and France caused both domestic and international investors to shun those countries. Regulated capitalism in the United States led to rising production costs and subsequent loss of competitive advantage in global markets for much of the manufacturing sector. The neoliberal capitalism adopted by Britain and the United States in response to globalization nearly destroyed the global economy as depressed wages and soaring profits led to a worldwide "savings glut" that swamped financial markets and created unsustainable asset bubbles.

Russia's state capitalism is mired in corruption and lacks the necessary efficiency and innovation to compete in global markets. The current success of China's version of state capitalism is partially explained by the timing of its development. China is experiencing the rapid growth that typically accompanies the transition from an agricultural to industrial economy and may encounter many of the same problems afflicting Western nations once that transition is completed. Given the dysfunction of current economic systems around the globe, what institutional reforms might lead to a new system capable of securing the potential benefits of globalization while minimizing its potential weaknesses? A preliminary sketch might include the following efforts to revitalize communities, strengthen nations, and regulate the global economy. These proposals are not intended to provide an endpoint toward which economic systems might evolve but merely to suggest several institutional reforms that might improve economic performance in the near future.

Revitalizing Communities

Communities are essential in creating **social and cultural capital** in the form of trust, shared values, social cohesion, civic virtue, and a variety of organizations and associations. Communities reduce **transaction costs**, solve collective action problems at the local level, and provide members with meaning and purpose to motivate productive and creative activity. Yet, communities have been subject to institutional **crowding out** by both states and markets. States have assumed responsibility for many of the functions previously performed by communities, thereby weakening members' attachment and participation. At the same time, the expanding influence of markets promotes **economic behavior**, causing individuals to rationally assess the costs and benefits of community membership. As communities become less functional, members perceive fewer benefits and declining participation is reinforced. Given the strong political and economic forces aligned against communities, their revitalization will require concerted efforts at all levels of government.

Chapter Five presented a variety of strategies to rebuild communities, but those solutions require adequate funding. Communities are a **public good** in the sense that the **free-rider problem** discourages individuals from contributing either money or time to community revitalization. To overcome this collective action problem, British economist and Nobel laureate James Meade (1907–1995) advocated the creation of a citizens' trust fund relying on money from a more progressive estate tax and a tax on wealth. The fund would be used to ensure equal education for all citizens, widespread home ownership, and the establishment of "labor-capital partnerships" in the form of enterprises in which both workers and owners of capital hold shares of stock and receive dividends (Meade 1993).

Similar proposals rely on the earnings of sovereign wealth funds. In recent years, more than sixty governments have established pools of financial capital derived from ownership or taxation of natural resources such as oil and natural gas. These sovereign wealth funds currently hold more than six trillion dollars, and earnings from the funds are used either to reduce taxation or provide social benefits. For example, Alaskans pay no state income tax because the government is financed by the Alaska Permanent Fund, which receives money from oil exploration and drilling. Rather than eliminating the state income tax, earnings from the fund could be devoted to the development of Alaskan communities.

Another approach to revitalizing communities, called asset-based community development, attempts to identify and mobilize a community's human capital and financial assets. However, many communities possess few assets, so some economists have proposed "asset-based redistribution" (Gates 1998; Bowles and Gintis 1999; Alperovitz et al. 2010). Whereas redistribution of income may have adverse effects on incentives for productive activity and typically serves merely to temporarily reduce human misery, providing low-income individuals and communities with access to productive assets would potentially enable them to become self-sufficient and thrive. Specific proposals include promoting home ownership with low-interest mortgages, increasing funding for college scholarships, providing incentives for low-income households to accumulate wealth by creating savings accounts with higher rates of interest, and providing credit to encourage the formation of non-profit enterprises and employee stock-ownership programs (ESOPs). Money for asset-based redistribution could come from taxes on wealth or from income tax deductions for private donations to nonprofit charitable organizations. These organizations would compete for funding based on their effectiveness in revitalizing communities.

In developing countries, some governments and NGOs are promoting community development through small business loans to low-income citizens who lack sufficient collateral or credit history to obtain access to financial capital through traditional financial institutions. The provision of "microcredit," pioneered by Bangladeshi economist Muhammad Yunus, has been so successful that Yunus was awarded the Nobel Peace Prize in 2006. Microcredit mobilizes entrepreneurial energy, particularly among women, that might otherwise have remained dormant (Yunus 2010).

Strengthening Nations

In responding to the challenges posed by globalization, nations can choose between two broad paths of institutional reform. The first will be followed by default if citizens, corporations, and governments take no collective action and simply follow their short-term self-interest in responding to changing market conditions. This path, sometimes referred to as the "low road" or the "race to the bottom," would allow the market to dictate the nature of society's institutions. In compliance with market pressures for cost minimization, national governments would reduce taxes and regulations, weaken labor unions, cut social benefits, reduce environmental regulations, and relax the enforcement of antitrust laws. As a consequence of tax cuts, government programs such as education, health-care, social security, highway construction, and enforcement of any remaining regulations would be either privatized or diminished due to lack of funding.

The low road represents a contest to gain competitive advantage in the global economy by minimizing production costs. It may be a viable strategy for one firm or even one nation, but the low road encounters a host of collective action prob-lems. If all nations follow this route, most will not only fail to gain competitive advantage but will suffer environmental degradation, underfinanced physical and social infrastructure, low wages, stagnation due to underconsumption, a de-teriorating social safety net, concentrated economic and political power, and the social conflict that accompanies growing extremes of wealth and poverty. The low road is particularly ineffective for industrialized nations because they cannot possibly compete with developing countries on the basis of low wages, low taxes, and lack of regulations.

A second path to institutional reform requires collective action by citizens and their governments. This "high road" or "race to the top" seeks to gain competitive advantage by improving productivity rather than by directly reducing production costs. Higher wages need not threaten competitive advantage as long as productiv-ity remains correspondingly high. Pursuing the high road is desirable not only to avoid environmental degradation, increasing inequality, and loss of public goods, but because changes in technology have made skilled labor and high-quality infra-structure the most important determinants of comparative advantage. Natural resources, technology, and capital are all available to any nation through global markets, but the nations with highly productive labor forces, technological inno-vation, and advanced infrastructure will prosper in the global economy.

Unfortunately, the high road to a successful economic system is partially blocked. Many of the institutions contributing to high productivity are public goods and therefore require government provision. Productivity is enhanced with improved physical and social infrastructure such as transportation and communication systems, education, healthcare, vocational training, scientific research and development, a healthy and sustainable natural environment, po-litical stability, and social order. Global competition blocks the high road not only by reducing tax revenue to fund public goods but also by increasing the in-centives for opportunism and defection that undermine existing public goods. For example, when corporations can relocate to countries with less stringent en-vironmental regulations, nations attempting to protect the environment are pressured to ease their regulations in order to retain businesses.

Regulating the Global Economy
The high road will become fully accessible only when collective action problems can be solved on a global scale. During the decades following the Great Depres-sion and World War II, governments in the industrialized nations created thriv-ing economic systems by establishing political institutions to restrain and support

the market. Now, however, the market has escaped those institutional constraints by becoming a global system without a uniform institutional framework including environmental regulations, antitrust laws, human rights, tax policy, and financial regulations. The global market has grown more powerful than any single national government, forcing governments to engage in a contest to attract financial capital by reducing taxes and regulations. Just as strong national governments were essential to solve national collective action problems, global governance is necessary to solve global collective action problems.

The idea of global cooperation is not new (Mazower 2013). In 1795, the German philosopher Immanuel Kant proposed an agreement among nations to maintain peace. The Geneva Conventions of 1864 and the Hague Conventions of 1899 established laws to settle international disputes. In the aftermath of World War I, fifty-eight nations (excluding the United States) formed the League of Nations to secure peace. The failure to prevent World War II doomed the League of Nations, but it was replaced in 1946 by the United Nations. Today, thousands of international governmental organizations exist, including the United Nations, the WTO, the World Bank, the IMF, the Organization for Economic Co-operation and Development, and the International Court of Justice.

The authority of these organizations is limited by political opposition within nations to any loss of sovereignty. Yet, to effectively solve global collective action problems, global governance must include the power to impose sanctions or penalties on certain categories of opportunism. Solving global collective action problems by penalizing free riders can be accomplished in several ways. To minimize any loss of national sovereignty, the sanctions could simply take the form of publicizing socially irresponsible corporate behavior so that consumers can "punish" the violators by redirecting their spending. In 1978, West Germany created a Blue Angel symbol, which was placed on products manufactured in an ecologically-sound manner so that consumers valuing environmental protection could vote with their dollars to express that preference. Similarly, a "fair trade coffee" label enabled consumers to identify coffee produced by growers paying fair wages and using environmentally sustainable methods of production. In addition, many NGOs such as Greenpeace, Oxfam, and Amnesty International publicize environmental degradation and violations of human rights. As a result of this publicity, corporations concerned about their reputations now experience financial incentives to behave in a socially-responsible manner.

The effectiveness of these social efforts to solve collective action problems is limited by two factors. First, given the complexity of production processes in the global economy, consumers and even governments and NGOs may lack information about where or how goods are produced. Corporations may continue opportunistic behavior, believing their operations to be hidden from public scrutiny. Second, consumers, knowing that their individual choices of which products to buy will not have a perceptible effect on the environment or working conditions, may choose to be free riders by purchasing less expensive products manufactured without environmental safeguards or protections of human rights.

A second approach to solving global collective action problems would require cooperation between national governments. Rather than relying on NGOs or the media to expose opportunistic corporate behavior, governments would establish agreements mandating the release of full information on all production practices as well as monitoring to ensure the accuracy of the information. This increased transparency would make corporate activity fully visible to the public, thereby increasing the incentives for social responsibility. However, this strategy suffers from an absence of standards specifying which corporate practices are considered irresponsible as well as a lack of formal sanctions to deter opportunism.

The major obstacle to global governance is the trade-off between national sovereignty and enforcement of agreements aimed at solving collective action problems. Effective global governance would require nations to cede a degree of sovereignty to an international governing body with power to impose sanctions on violations of global regulations. Global governance could establish production standards related to environmental sustainability and protection of worker rights. These standards would be formed through multilateral negotiations between countries and would not necessarily be uniform due to differences in national circumstances and priorities. For example, a uniform global minimum wage would not be realistic given differences between nations in cost of living and job opportunities. Once production standards were established, a global regulatory agency could impose sanctions on violators in the form of tariffs. For example, nations refusing to limit emission of greenhouse gases might be subject to a "carbon tariff" on their exports to eliminate the competitive advantage gained by avoiding the cost of emission controls or use of alternative sources of energy.

*   *   *

The viability of these proposed reforms at the local, national, and global levels is enhanced by their potential for mutual support and reinforcement. Strong communities foster the trust and civic virtue essential to cooperative problem-solving by national and global governments. Strong states pursuing the "high road" provide the high-quality infrastructure and funding needed to revitalize communities and strengthen national economies. By creating a degree of uniformity in regulation, taxation, and protection of human rights, global governance enables nations to take the "high road" without defections from cooperative agreements and loss of tax revenue. Competition among corporations would no longer consist of locating the lowest taxes, most lax environmental regulations, or least-protected labor, but would instead focus on technological innovation, product development, and customer service. States and local governments would no longer compete to attract businesses by granting tax concessions that drain public resources, but would instead compete by offering excellent schools, health-care facilities, and recreational opportunities.

Despite the potential benefits of global governance, any efforts to establish global institutions will confront an inevitable trade-off between accessibility and autonomy. On one hand, an international government would need to be relatively autonomous in order to resist rent seeking. At the same time, if global governance is to be democratic, it must be responsive to the public and accountable for its actions. The key to bridging these seemingly opposing goals is transparency in the form of publicizing the deliberations and rationales underlying global policies. The shortcomings of markets are sufficiently well-known to enable policymakers and the public to distinguish between blatant rent seeking and legitimate efforts to solve collective action problems.

The market serves an admirable role in allocating resources efficiently while preserving a wide scope of freedom for individuals and businesses. The proposals made here are not intended to destroy markets but to preserve them by correcting their shortcomings. Since the inception of capitalism two centuries ago, the eras in which markets were most endangered by government authority occurred when market failures were left unchecked. The central problem facing nations today is that global markets have eroded the institutions established by national governments to secure thriving economic systems. Unless the challenge posed by globalization is met, the unregulated market is likely to reproduce on a global scale the same maladies that afflicted national economies during the nineteenth and twentieth centuries. Issues such as environmental degradation, poverty, racial and ethnic conflict, instability, concentrated wealth and power, imperialism, and violations of human rights may be joined by threats of terrorism, biological weapons, mass migrations, and pandemics. If the global market remains unregulated until disaster is imminent, future generations may react as many Germans did during the 1930s and accept the virtual elimination of markets. Preserving the legitimacy of markets requires acknowledgment of their limitations and appropriate political and social institutions to address their failures. Markets function best when securely embedded in developmental states and vibrant communities.

REFERENCES

Alperovitz, Gar, Steve Dubb, and Ted Howard. 2010. *Rebuilding America's Communities: A Comprehensive Community Wealth Building Federal Policy Proposal*. College Park, MD: The Democracy Collaborative.

Bowles, Samuel, and Herbert Gintis. 1999. *Recasting Egalitarianism: New Rules for Communities, States, and Markets*. London: Verso.

Frank, Andre Gunder. 1998. *ReOrient: Global Economy in the Asian Age*. Berkeley, CA: University of California Press.

Gates, Jeff. 1998. *The Ownership Solution: Toward a Shared Capitalism for the 21st Century*. Reading, MA: Addison-Wesley.

Mazower, Mark. 2013. *Governing the World: The History of an Idea, 1815 to the Present*. New York: Penguin Books.

Meade, J. E. 1993. *Liberty, Equality, and Efficiency*. New York: New York University Press.

Keynes, John Maynard. (1930) 1963. *Essays in Persuasion*. New York: W. W. Norton.

Rajan, Raghuram G. 2010. *Fault Lines: How Hidden Fractures Still Threaten the World Economy*. Princeton, NJ: Princeton University Press.

Strange, Susan. 1996. *The Retreat of the State: The Diffusion of Power in the World Economy*. Cambridge, UK: Cambridge University Press.

Yunus, Muhammad. 2010. *Building Social Business: The New Kind of Capitalism that Serves Humanity's Most Pressing Needs*. New York: Public Affairs.

ADDITIONAL READING

Bhagwati, Jagdish. *In Defense of Globalization*. New York: Oxford University Press, 2004.

Campbell, John L. *Institutional Change and Globalization*. Princeton, NJ: Princeton University Press, 2004.

Chirico, JoAnn. *Globalization: Prospects and Problems*. Thousand Oaks, CA: Sage, 2014.

Held, David. *Global Covenant: The Social Democratic Alternative to the Washington Consensus*. Cambridge: Polity Press, 2004.

Ravenhill, John, ed. *Global Political Economy*, 4th ed. New York: Oxford University Press, 2014.

Rodrik, Dani. *The Globalization Paradox: Democracy and the Future of the World Economy*. New York: W. W. Norton, 2011.

Sachs, Jeffrey D. *Common Wealth: Economics for a Crowded Planet*. New York: Penguin Books, 2009.

Schwartz, Herman. *States versus Markets: The Emergence of a Global Economy*. New York: Palgrave MacMillan, 2010.

Sparke, Matthew. *Introducing Globalization: Ties, Tensions, and Uneven Integration*. Malden, MA: Wiley-Blackwell, 2013.

Steger, Manfred. *Globalization: A Very Short Introduction*, 3rd ed. New York: Oxford University Press, 2013.

Stiglitz, Joseph. *Making Globalization Work*. New York: W. W. Norton, 2007.

Westra, Richard. *Exit from Globalization*. New York: Routledge, 2014.

Glossary

Adverse selection either buyers or sellers engage in transactions they would not have chosen if they had full information about the product or characteristics of the other party.

Aggregate demand total effective demand for all final goods and services. Aggregate demand is the sum of consumption spending, investment spending, government spending, and spending on exports minus spending on imports.

Allocation the process by which economic resources are directed toward the production of final goods and services going to individuals and businesses. Allocation determines what will be produced, how it will be produced, and who will receive the final goods.

Antitrust laws laws designed to maintain effective competition among firms by preventing concentrations of economic power.

Appreciation an increase in the value of an asset. A currency appreciates when a decrease in supply or an increase in demand within currency markets causes it to gain value in terms of another currency.

Backward linkage a stimulus to one industry benefits the suppliers of that industry by increasing demand for their products.

Balance of payments a measure of all economic and financial transactions between one nation and the rest of the world during a specific time period.

Balance of trade a measure of exports from and imports into a nation during a specific period of time. The balance of trade has a deficit when imports exceed exports and a surplus when exports exceed imports.

Barrier to entry anything that inhibits new firms from entering a market. Barriers to entry may be caused by economies of scale, by strategies of existing firms to discourage additional competition, or by government laws and regulations such as patents and required licenses.

Bundled legislation the grouping together of many diverse bills for a single vote by a legislature.

Capital man-made means of production. See also Physical capital, Financial capital, Human capital, Social capital, and Cultural capital.

Capital accumulation the process by which capital increases over time through investment in productive assets (e.g., physical capital, human capital, social capital, and cultural capital) or in assets whose value increases over time (e.g., stocks, bonds, land, and gold).

Capital controls legal restrictions on the movement of financial capital across national borders.

Capitalism an economic system in which the means of production are privately owned, resources are allocated through markets, and wage labor is the dominant form of work.

Cartel a group of firms in the same industry engaged in explicit collusion to increase market power and profitability.

Civil society the realm of human affairs not directly associated with either the market or the state.

Classical liberalism an ideology developed in the late eighteenth century to defend private property, free markets, and minimal government intervention.

Collective action problem a situation in which the pursuit of self-interest leads to a worse result than could be achieved through cooperation and adherence to rules.

Collusion cooperation between businesses to raise profitability by restricting competition. Collusion may be either explicit or tacit.

Communism an economic system in which the means of production are owned by the state and resources are allocated through government planning. Alternatively, Marx envisioned communism as an economic system arising after socialism in which the means of production are owned and controlled by "the associated producers," the state "withers away," and people work according to their abilities and are rewarded according to their needs. Marx's vision of communism is similar to social anarchism.

Comparative advantage the ability of a person, region, or nation to produce a good relatively more efficiently than other persons, regions, or nations.

Competitive advantage the ability of a firm to produce goods that cost less, are unique, or are accompanied by better customer service than similar goods produced by other firms.

Complete markets markets are complete when all mutually beneficial transactions occur.

Concentration ratio the percentage of an industry's output controlled by the largest four firms in the industry.

Conglomerate merger the joining together of two firms operating in unrelated industries.

Conservatism an ideology based on preserving past institutions, particularly hierarchical authority and traditional communities. See also Social conservatism and Economic conservatism.

Consumption spending spending by households to purchase consumer goods and services.

Corporate inversion the relocation of a corporation's headquarters to another country with lower taxes.

Countercyclical policy the use of expansionary fiscal and monetary policies during recessions and contractionary fiscal and monetary policies during expansions to maintain stability.

Craft union a labor union composed exclusively of workers with the same skill or occupation.

Crowding out a possibility that increased government borrowing causes less private investment due to rising interest rates.

Cultural capital rules, norms, and traditions that improve economic performance.

Culture a term popularly used to refer to a society's artistic expressions, including literature, theater, music, paintings, dance, and film. However, social scientists use the term culture more broadly to encompass the values, traditions, religion, language, social norms, ideologies, and behavioral patterns of a particular society.

Defection a self-interested violation of a formal or informal set of rules.

Deficit an excess of expenditures over income during a specified period of time.

Deficit spending government spending in excess of tax revenue.

Deflation a drop in the average level of prices.

Demerit goods goods deemed so harmful that they should be banned.

Demosclerosis dysfunction of the political system caused by a proliferation of interest groups.

Dependency theory the claim that international trade impedes the growth of developing nations.

Depreciation a decline in the value of an asset. A currency depreciates when an increase in supply or a reduction in demand within currency markets causes it to lose value in terms of another currency.

Depression a severe recession. There is no clear demarcation between a recession and a depression.

Devaluation an official and deliberate reduction in the value of a nation's currency in terms of other currencies.

Developmental state a government that actively promotes economic development to improve the lives of all citizens.

Dual economy an economy with two distinct segments—a primary sector consisting of large corporations and labor unions, and a secondary sector consisting of nonunionized workers, small businesses, and farmers.

Dynamic efficiency increasing output over time from a given amount of resources.

Economic behavior seeking to maximize gain and/or minimize sacrifice.

Economic conservatism an ideology defending private property, free markets, and minimal government intervention. See also Classical liberalism and Neoliberalism.

Economic efficiency a situation in which no reallocation of resources can improve the well-being of one person without reducing the well-being of someone else. See also Pareto optimality and Static efficiency.

Economic system the framework of economic, political, social, and cultural institutions affecting the allocation of resources.

Economies of scale increasing the scale of operations of a firm causes the average cost of producing a unit of output to decline.

Economy the institutions directly involved in the allocation of economic resources for production, distribution, and consumption of goods and services.

Embargo a government-imposed ban on trade with another country.

Entrepreneurship the combination of innovation, risk-taking, and management undertaken by individuals to start and expand businesses.

Equity fairness. See also Justice.

Excess capacity a firm has excess capacity when its most efficient level of output is greater than its profit-maximizing level. An industry has excess capacity when all firms together are able to produce more output than can profitably be sold to consumers.

Extensive growth increases in output attributable to increased availability of resources.

Externality the actions of one individual or business create costs or benefits for others that are not reflected in market prices.

Fascism an economic system in which the means of production are privately owned and resources are allocated through government planning. Fascism also typically entails a single-party state, suspension of civil liberties, and persecution of minorities and political dissidents.

Feudalism an economic system in which the manor is the basic unit of production and resources are allocated according to custom and tradition.

Financial capital money to be used for starting, operating, or expanding a business.

Fiscal policy changes in government spending or taxation for the purpose of changing aggregate demand.

Foreign exchange the currencies of other nations.

Forward linkage a stimulus to one industry benefits other industries by reducing the costs of their inputs.

Free-rider problem individuals have no incentive to voluntarily pay for a public good because they cannot be excluded from enjoying its benefits.

Free trade the absence of legal barriers to the exchange of goods.

Freedom See Negative freedom and Positive freedom.

Goods the products (including services) of businesses and government. Consumer goods are produced for households, capital goods are produced for businesses, and public goods are produced for society as a whole.

Governance structure a set of interrelated institutions whose purpose is to coordinate human activity. The three primary governance structures are market, state, and community.

Gross domestic product (GDP) the value of all final goods and services produced within the borders of a country during a given year.

Hegemony leadership or domination by one country over others.

Homo economicus a Latin term meaning economic man. Homo economicus seeks to maximize gain and/or minimize sacrifice.

Horizontal integration the merging of firms operating at the same stage in the production of the same product.

Human capital knowledge and skills that increase the productivity of labor.

Hyperinflation an extremely high rate of inflation.

Identity politics efforts by ethnically homogeneous communities to gain self-determination and recognition through the political process.

Imperialism the exploitation of one nation by another nation.

Incomes policy government efforts to control the rate of increase in wages and other forms of income through guidelines and consultation with interest groups.

Indicative planning government efforts to develop a broad vision of the future direction of the economy. Indicative planning may establish output targets, but the targets are not mandatory.

Industrial policy government efforts to improve the performance of the economy by changing the structure of markets and the incentives guiding the behavior of firms.

Industrial union a labor union in which all members work in the same industry while performing different jobs within that industry.

Infant industry an industry that is just beginning in a particular nation.

Inflation a rise in the average level of prices.

Inflationary psychology the belief that inflation will continue into the future.

Infrastructure the supportive institutional framework facilitating economic activity. Physical infrastructure includes transportation and communication systems, dams, levees, and water treatment and sewage facilities. Social infrastructure includes the educational system, healthcare, job training programs, and police and fire protection.

Insolvency the inability to meet one's financial obligations. An insolvent firm's liabilities exceed its assets so that its net worth is negative.

Institution a cluster of rules coordinating a particular type of human interaction by reducing conflict and creating stable expectations about appropriate forms of behavior.

Institutional coherence the compatibility or complementarity of different institutions.

Intensive growth increases in output attributable to improved technology.

Interest rate the price of borrowing money or the reward for saving money in the form of an interest-bearing asset.

Interlocking directorate the same individuals are appointed to boards of directors of competing firms.

Intermediate institutions organizations standing between the state and the individual (e.g., churches, teams, clubs, and neighborhoods).

Investment the purchase of new capital.

Justice rewards and punishments are in accordance with individual rights, merit, or deservingness.

Labor force participation rate the percentage of the adult population currently working or actively seeking work.

Laissez-faire a French term that translates as "let it be" or "leave it alone." In economics, laissez-faire means minimal government intervention in the economy.

Learning by doing the process of gaining skills and knowledge while performing a task or operating a business.

Leverage the use of borrowed money to purchase assets.

Liberalism See Classical liberalism and Modern liberalism.

Libertarianism an ideology that defends private property, free markets, and minimal government intervention. Libertarianism is similar to classical liberalism but with even more stringent restrictions on the scope of government activity.

Logrolling the legislative practice by which politicians agree to support each other's favored policies.

Manpower policies efforts by government to improve the performance of labor markets.

Market the interaction of buyers and sellers exchanging assets.

Market failure any inability of the market to achieve economic efficiency.

Market power the ability of sellers to control the price of their resource or product due to imperfect competition.

Market socialism an economic system in which the means of production are socially owned and markets are the primary institution for allocating resources.

Mediation in labor relations, mediation refers to the process of reaching agreement between a union and an employer with the help of an independent third party.

Mercantilism an economic system based on the use of state power to enrich a nation by limiting domestic competition and promoting a balance of trade surplus.

Merger the joining together of two firms.

Merit goods goods deemed sufficiently essential that every person should have them regardless of ability to pay.

Modern liberalism the ideology that developed in the late nineteenth century defending private property and an active role for government in regulating markets.

Monetarism an economic theory claiming that instability is caused by too little or too much money in the economy.

Monetary policy changes in the money supply intended to raise or lower aggregate demand by causing interest rates to change.

Monopoly an industry with only one seller of a good.

Moral hazard individuals do not bear all the consequences of their actions and therefore act in ways that are detrimental to others.

National debt the amount of money owed by a government to holders of government bonds. The national debt is the accumulation of all past budget deficits minus any budget surpluses.

Natural monopoly a situation in which economies of scale are so substantial that a single firm can most efficiently produce a good.

Natural rate of unemployment the rate of unemployment caused by imperfect competition in labor markets.

Negative freedom individuals are subject to no external restraint by others or by government.

Neoliberalism an ideology based on a revival of the classical liberal defense of private property, free markets, and minimal government intervention.

Oligopoly an industry with only a few sellers.

Opportunism the pursuit of self-interest in ways that violate formal or informal rules and therefore harm the interests of others.

Overinvestment investment leading to greater productive capacity than is needed to meet demand for a good.

Pareto optimality a situation in which no person can be made better off without making someone else worse off. See also Economic efficiency and Static efficiency.

Parity the price of a good rises at the same rate as the cost of producing that good.

Path dependence future possibilities depend on what happened in the past.

Patient capital financial capital controlled by individuals or organizations willing to forego short-term profitability in expectation of long-term profitability.

Per capita GDP GDP divided by the size of a country's population.

Perfect competition a market with many small buyers and sellers, a homogeneous product, costless entry and exit, and full information for all participants.

Physical capital buildings, machinery, tools and equipment, and inventories.

Political business cycle fluctuations in the economy caused by government stimulation prior to a presidential election and an intentional slowdown after the election.

Political entrepreneur a politician who favors legislation for the purpose of maximizing votes and income to ensure reelection.

Polity the realm of social affairs governed by authoritative laws enacted by the state.

Poll tax a tax that takes an equal amount from each taxpayer regardless of income.

Positive freedom the ability to effectively make choices leading to a fulfilling life.

Predatory pricing a business strategy of temporarily reducing the price of a good to drive competitors out of business.

Predatory state a government seeking to increase the power and wealth of select groups rather than promoting the well-being of all citizens.

Price discrimination charging different prices to different groups of customers.

Price leadership one firm in an industry sets the price and all other firms match that price.

Price war firms react to predatory pricing by cutting their own prices.

Private sector the nongovernmental portion of the economy.

Privatization transferring activities performed by government to the private sector.

Productivity a measure of the quantity of output derived from a unit of input.

Profit the difference between revenue from the sale of goods and the cost of producing those goods.

Property rights rules determining ownership of resources and goods. Property rights include the right to exclude others from use of the good; the right to sell, give away, or rent the good; and the right to bequeath the good.

Prosperity a rising level of income and wealth.

Public good a good that is (1) nonexclusive, meaning that there is no practical way to exclude individuals from enjoying its benefits, and (2) nonrival, meaning that one person's enjoyment of the good does not reduce its availability for others.

Public sector the governmental portion of the economy.

Quota in international trade, a quota is an upper limit on the amount or value of a good that can be imported.

Rate of return the annual gain in the value of an asset divided by the original value.

Rational expectations expectations about the future based on what has happened in the past.

Rational ignorance citizens decide that the costs of voting and becoming well-informed about public issues outweigh the benefit of their vote and therefore choose to remain uninformed about public affairs.

Rational myopia politicians favor programs with immediate benefits to ensure reelection.

Real GDP GDP adjusted to remove the effect of inflation.

Real interest rate the quoted interest rate minus the rate of inflation.

Real wages wages adjusted to remove the effect of inflation.

Recession two consecutive quarters of declining economic output.

Reciprocity responding to other people's behavior in a similar manner.

Regulatory capture businesses or other interest groups gain control of government agencies through lobbying, campaign contributions, and promises of future jobs for government employees.

Rent seeking efforts to gain additional income either by suppressing competition in the market or by influencing government policy.

Resources the inputs used to produce goods and services. The four categories of resources are land, labor, capital, and entrepreneurship. Economic resources are also called factors of production.

Revaluation an official and deliberate increase in the value of a nation's currency in terms of other currencies.

Revenue money earned from the sale of goods or, in the case of government, money received from taxes and other fees.

Right-to-work laws state laws that ban requirements of union membership as a condition for employment.

Saving income not spent for consumption or paid in taxes.

Scarcity pricing the rise in the price of a resource as it becomes depleted.

Social anarchism an economic system in which resources are collectively owned and allocated through decisions made by members of a community.

Social capital institutions and organizations that improve economic performance by generating trust, shared information, and cooperation.

Social conservatism an ideology that defends private property but calls on government to restrict the market by enforcing moral standards and by protecting citizens from the more disruptive aspects of market competition.

Socialism Marx envisioned socialism as a transitional stage between capitalism and communism in which property would be owned by the government and resources would be allocated through government planning. In modern usage, the term socialism refers to a hybrid of capitalism and communism in which both private and public ownership of property are present, both markets and planning are used to allocate resources, and the state is democratic.

Society a broad term for the totality of human affairs within a specified geographic area.

Sovereignty supreme and independent political authority over a geographic area.

Stagflation a combination of high unemployment and high inflation.

State a political entity possessing authority to establish laws governing a specified territory and to exercise coercion in enforcing those laws.

Static efficiency a situation in which no reallocation of resources can make one person better off without making someone else worse off. See also Economic efficiency and Pareto optimality.

Stop-go cycles periodic recessions intentionally created to reduce imports and relieve downward pressure on a nation's currency.

Subsidy a payment by government to encourage a particular business or activity.

Sustainability the ability of a system to perform well over an indefinite period of time. The term may be used to refer to the ecosystem, economic systems, or institutions.

Tariff a tax on imported goods.

Tax expenditure tax loopholes, deductions, and credits that reduce government revenue and enlarge the budget deficit.

Technical efficiency maximum output from a given amount of resources.

Technology method of production.

Tiebout effect an economic theory suggesting that people move to areas where local government spending patterns most closely align with their interests.

Trade deficit an excess of imports over exports.

Trade policy efforts by government to change the level of imports and exports.

Trade surplus an excess of exports over imports.

Transaction costs costs of making exchanges in the market that are not directly related to the production of the good or service. Examples include time and resources devoted to searching for trading partners, gathering information, negotiating deals, preparing contracts, and monitoring and enforcing compliance with contracts.

Transfer pricing an accounting strategy used by transnational corporations to shift profits to nations with lower taxes.

Tying contract a contract obliging the buyer of one specific good to purchase a different good as well.

Underconsumption a failure of consumption spending to keep pace with increasing output.

Underground economy economic transactions not reported to the government either to avoid taxes or because they are illegal. The underground economy is also called the black market.

Value-added tax a tax on the value-added at each stage in the production of a good. The retail price of the good includes the value-added tax.

Vertical integration the merging of firms operating at different stages in the production of the same product.

Wage-price spiral rising wages cause businesses to raise prices, and higher prices cause workers to demand wage increases.

Index